Library of
Davidson College

THE RISE OF
THE EGALITARIAN FAMILY
Aristocratic Kinship and Domestic Relations
in Eighteenth-Century England

Portrait of Mrs. Delany by J. Opie. "She was the highest bred woman in the world and the woman of fashion of all ages [Edmund Burke]," and as such, she was England's most accomplished kin-keeper. Copyright photograph from the National Portrait Gallery, London. Reproduced by permission.

THE RISE OF THE EGALITARIAN FAMILY

Aristocratic Kinship and Domestic Relations in Eighteenth-Century England

RANDOLPH TRUMBACH
Baruch College
City University of New York

ACADEMIC PRESS
New York   San Francisco   London
A Subsidiary of Harcourt Brace Jovanovich, Publishers

This is a volume in

STUDIES IN SOCIAL DISCONTINUITY

A complete list of titles in this series appears at the end of this volume.

Copyright © 1978, by Academic Press, Inc.
ALL RIGHTS RESERVED.
NO PART OF THIS PUBLICATION MAY BE REPRODUCED OR
TRANSMITTED IN ANY FORM OR BY ANY MEANS, ELECTRONIC
OR MECHANICAL, INCLUDING PHOTOCOPY, RECORDING, OR ANY
INFORMATION STORAGE AND RETRIEVAL SYSTEM, WITHOUT
PERMISSION IN WRITING FROM THE PUBLISHER.

ACADEMIC PRESS, INC.
111 Fifth Avenue, New York, New York 10003

United Kingdom Edition published by
ACADEMIC PRESS, INC. (LONDON) LTD.
24/28 Oval Road, London NW1 7DX

Library of Congress Cataloging in Publication Data

Trumbach, Randolph.
  The rise of the egalitarian family.

  (Studies in social discontinuity series)
  Based on the author's thesis, Johns Hopkins
University, 1972.
    Bibliography: p.
    1. Family--England--History--18th century.
2. Aristocracy--History. 3. Kinship--History.
I. Title. II. Series: Studies in social dis-
continuity.
HQ615.T78   301.42'1'0942   77-82421
ISBN 0-12-701250-8

PRINTED IN THE UNITED STATES OF AMERICA

*For Blanche and Alvan Trumbach
who have waited patiently*

Contents

List of Illustrations	ix
List of Tables	xi
Acknowledgments	xiii
List of Abbreviations	xvii

Introduction		1
I	Kindred and Patrilineage	13
	Prohibited Degrees of Marriage	18
	The Rules of Mourning	33
	The Rules of Inheritance	41
	Remarriage	50
	Friendship, Patronage, and Connection	61

II	Settlement and Marriage	69
	Settlement, Patrilineage, and Domesticity	72
	The Eldest Son and His Wife	77
	The Younger Son	87
	Daughters: Settlement, Mésalliance, and Romantic Marriage	97
	Marriage Ceremonies	113
III	Patriarchy and Domesticity	119
	Household Size and Composition	124
	The Great Family versus the Little Family	129
	Household Hierarchy and Discipline	134
	Patriarchy and Servants	141
	Property in Wives and Children	150
IV	Childbearing	165
	Conception	166
	Contraception	170
	Pregnancy	176
	Childbirth	180
V	Mothers and Infants	187
	Infant Mortality	188
	Children and Disease: Cold Bathing and Inoculation	191
	Mother's Milk, Wet Nurses, and Artificial Foods	197
	Two Case Studies: The Lennoxes and the Spencers	208
	Attachment, Innovation, and Maternal Supervision	224
	Childhood Experience and Adult Life	230
VI	Fathers and Children	237
	The Male Role and Childrearing	239
	Nursery Life and Gender Identity	243
	Parental Roles and School Reform	252
	Domesticity in the School: Parental Surrogates	265
	Male Sexual Behavior and the Limits of Domesticity	281
	Conclusion	287
	Appendix A Kinship Terminology	293
	Appendix B Sources for the History of Settlement	297
	Bibliography	299
	Index	315

List of Illustrations

Frontispiece Portrait of Mrs. Delany.	
Sketch of Horace Walpole.	xx
Portrait of the duke of Newcastle and the earl of Lincoln.	12
Incestuous and licit spouses for an Englishman.	24
Pedigree of the dukes of Newcastle.	48
Pedigree of the dukes of Ancaster.	59
Portrait of Lord Chancellor Hardwicke.	68
Portrait of the marquess of Halifax.	118
Portrait of the countess of Sunderland.	164
Portrait of Lady Mary Wortley Montagu and her son.	186
Portrait of Samuel Parr.	236

List of Tables

1.1	Prohibited Degrees of Marriage	22
1.2	Degrees of Mourning	35
A.1	Individual Kinship Terms in the Eighteenth Century	295
A.2	Collective or General Kinship Terms	296
B.1	Histories of Settlement and Sources of Information for 57 Aristocratic Families	297

Acknowledgments

I began work on this book 11 years ago and finished it in the spring of 1977. Most of the information on which it is based was gathered in 1967 and 1968. I wrote the first version of Chapters 4 and 5 in the spring of 1969. These I revised and presented, along with the first three chapters, as my dissertation to the Johns Hopkins University in 1972. In the spring of 1975 I recast the material in the first three chapters and wrote Chapter 6. In the spring of 1977 I at long last wrote the final version of the general introduction. The material on schools in Chapter 6 was the last composed but the first gathered, for like everyone else I began under the influence of Ariès and took for granted that when one studied the family, one started with the history of education. But by the time I wrote my dissertation, I had turned to the history of infancy under the influence of John Bowlby's psychological theory. One of my examiners, however, pointed out that my presentation of the material on kinship was anthropologically naive, and it was to remedy this that I recast the manuscript in 1975. Finding my publisher and the production of the book have taken the remainder of the time. It has sometimes seemed to my friends that I was an unconscionably long time in bringing this project to an end. But I hope that the final product will to some degree reward their kindness and patience. The pauses and the fallow periods (in 1969–1971 and 1973–1975) have certainly been useful to me. In them I learned to teach, discarded a great deal of commonplace intellectual baggage and took on what I hope is better, and saw the purpose of my studies change from pure curiosity to a desire to contribute to the movements of my time.

I discovered my material in a number of libraries and record offices. I wish to thank the staffs of the Eisenhower and Welsh libraries at Johns Hopkins, the Pratt and the Peabody libraries in Baltimore, the British Museum, the Newberry Library, the University of Chicago Libraries, the Baruch College Library, and the New York Public Library. I prepared to tour the county record offices in England by using the catalogs in the National Register of Archives. The county archivists and their staffs were almost uniformly helpful. I must mention especially those of Kent and Lincolnshire and those of the University Library in Nottingham and the Sheffield Central Library. The Librarian at Chatsworth was also very kind. But my fondest memory must be of the Essex office where a neophyte was helped through his first manuscripts with tact and patience.

I wish to thank Lord Fitzwilliam and his trustees for permission to use the manuscripts at Sheffield. Mr. W. S. Lewis sent me a copy of a letter. Professor R. F. Bond lent me a transcript. Lady Monson deposited some papers for my use. Dr. T. H. Hollingsworth allowed me to have copies made of his materials. Dr. D. N. Thomas allowed me to microfilm his thesis. I wish to thank them all, and also the owners of all the collections so conveniently deposited in the record offices. Only two noblemen thought fit to deny me access to their papers on the ground of privacy. But then some gave permissions that I was in the end unable to use.

During these 11 years I have received support from a number of sources that I must thank: fellowships from the Woodrow Wilson Foundation; an internship from the University of Chicago; and grants from the Newberry Library and the Research Foundation of the City University of New York.

To two men I am indebted in ways that cannot be easily repaid. Trygve Tholfsen taught me as an undergraduate and made me want to be a historian; he has remained my friend and patron. David Spring has formed my mind. He led me to the topic of this book and then gave me

Acknowledgments

full freedom and every encouragement to do it as I saw fit. He was patient when I took 6 years to do my thesis. He carefully criticized the different stages of the manuscript. But, above all, he took me seriously as a scholar (as he does all his students) from the day I entered Hopkins. None of us has ever heard from him that wicked doctrine that a dissertation was an exercise. We were always at work on our first book.

A number of colleagues have read my manuscript and offered criticism and encouragement: Ervand Abrahamian, Carol Berkin, Myrna Engelmeyer, Margaret Jacob, Clara Lovett, and Edward Pessen. Others have also read the manuscript in whole or in part and offered useful comment: Roy Bartolomei, Lloyd deMause, Neville Dyson-Hudson, May Ebihara, M. W. Flinn, Mary Beth Norton, Orest Ranum, Dean Rapp, Joan Scott, Eileen Spring, Sanford Thatcher, Richard Vann, and Peter Whelley. Antonia Nofi, my former student, served as a research assistant. And all my students have patiently endured and encouraged my interest in the family, whether I was teaching ancient Greece or Israel, the Renaissance in Florence, or eighteenth-century Europe.

My brothers have managed to keep up their interest in my book. To my grandmother, Mildred Avery, and the other women of my family, I owe a special debt for giving a fascinated child a taste for taking pleasure in the anecdotes and ceremonies of kinship. My obligations to my parents I have tried to express on another page. And to my best friend, who has for years endured my conversation on these and other subjects, I hope some day to offer another work.

List of Abbreviations

Add. MSS	Additional Manuscripts
Bristol Diary	S.H.A. Hervey, ed., *Letterbooks of John Hervey, First Earl of Bristol* (Wells: Suffolk Green Books, No. 2, 1894).
Bristol Letterbook	S.H.A. Hervey, ed., *Letterbooks of John Hervey, First Earl of Bristol* (Wells: Suffolk Green Books, No. 1, 1894), 3 vol.
B.L.	British Library
Coke	J. A. Home, ed., *The Letters and Journals of Lady Mary Coke* (Edinburgh: David Dougles, 1889–1896), 4 vol.
Delany	Lady Llanover, ed., *Autobiography and Correspondence of Mary Granville, Mrs. Delany* (London, 1861), 3 vol. (1862), 3 vol.
EcHR	*Economic History Review*

H.M.C.	Historical Manuscripts Commission Reports
Hardwicke	P. C. Yorke, *The Life of Hardwicke* (Cambridge: University Press, 1913), 3 vol.
Hertford	H. S. Hughes, *The Gentle Hertford* (New York: Macmillan, 1940).
Hollingsworth	T. H. Hollingsworth, "The Demography of the British Peerage," Supplement to *Population Studies*, **XVIII**, 1964.
Lady Mary	Robert Halsband, ed., *The Complete Letters of Lady Mary Wortley Montagu* (Oxford: Clarendon Press, 1965–1967), 3 vol.
Laws	*The Laws Respecting Women* (London, 1777).
Leinster	Brian Fitzgerald, ed., *Correspondence of Emily, Duchess of Leinster* (Dublin: Irish Manuscripts Commission, 1949–1957), 3 vol.
Locke	John Locke, *Educational Writings*, edited by J. L. Axtell (Cambridge: University Press, 1968).
N.U.L.	Nottingham University Library
Orrery Papers	Cork and Lady Orrery, eds., *The Orrery Papers* (London: Duckworth, 1903), 2 vol.
R.O.	Record (or Archives) Office
S.C.L.	Sheffield Central Library
Walpole	W. S. Lewis *et al.*, eds., *Horace Walpole's Correspondence* (New Haven: Yale Univ. Press, 1937–).

Note: Spelling and punctuation in quotations have frequently been modified. The relevant dates are Old Style, but with the year beginning in January. When an individual bore more than one title in his life, I have usually kept him to a single one within a particular example.

Sketch of Horace Walpole by T. Lawrence. Walpole may well have been England's most accomplished gossip. Copyright photograph from the National Portrait Gallery, London. Reproduced by permission.

Introduction

This work began as a study of the aristocratic family in eighteenth-century England. But now it will also serve to illustrate the two major changes that the European family has undergone in the thousand years of its history. The first of these changes occurred when the various European aristocracies adopted a patrilineal ideology around the year 1000. The various barbarian peoples had previously organized their relations into systems of cognatic kindred. Each individual had stood at the center of a unique circle of kinsmen connected to him through both mother and father and through his spouse. Inheritances were equally divided among all the children; the position of women with regard to property and divorce was relatively high; and friendship was a stronger bond than kinship. In such a society it must have been difficult for any single aristocratic family to maintain its social position from one generation to another. But with the introduction of feudal institutions, it became the ideal to maintain the continuity of the aristocratic family. Brothers and their male cousins began to hold property in common. Sometimes special rights were given to the eldest son, and at other times only one son was allowed to marry. Women lost most of their property rights, and their status was further lowered by the introduction of practices like the use of wet nurses, which implied that they were more wives than mothers. Aristocratic men came to rely more on their paternal relations than on their friends. This patrilineal ideology sometimes penetrated peasant society when one son was favored over the others or when patrilineal family names were adopted. But all levels of society continued to give some allegiance to the principle of cognatic (or ambilateral) descent in matters like the forbidden degrees of marriage. The alternation between kindred and patrilineal principles therefore became an important part of the social dynamics of traditional European society.

This was certainly the case in eighteenth-century England, as the first two chapters of this book undertake to show. English aristocrats felt forbidden to marry the same relations on both a father's and a mother's side, and many on a wife's as well. They mourned equally for all three kinds of relations. But in the succession to the title that gave a seat in Parliament, and in the inheritance of the estates that supported this dignity, their usual practice was patrilineal and primogenitural. This, however, was never absolutely so. There were a few titles to which women might succeed, and by intestacy or deliberate will women sometimes inherited estates. But in the normal course, the family settlement mediated between the claims of kindred and patrilineage by guaranteeing provisions for widows, daughters, and younger sons. The conflicts between the two principles were less amicably resolved when the death of a spouse made remarriage possible. A woman, her children, or her property might be claimed as the permanent possession of her husband's lineage, and a widower's relations-in-law might be anxious to prevent the children of a second wife from displacing those of the first. But though the continuity and power of an individual family might be maintained through patrilineal and primogenitural practices, aristocrats nonetheless found that in their political alliances, friendship was far more important than kinship. The parliamentary connection might have a core of patrilineal cousins or brothers-in-law; but an individual's relations were as likely to belong to someone else's connection as not; and the bulk of any man's following was composed of his neighbors, his friends, and his clients. Outside of the dynamics of individual families, the shape of English society was determined by the fluidity and the egalitarian relations characteristic of kindred structures.

When the European aristocracies adopted a patrilineal ideology to protect themselves against the consequences of kindred principles, it is likely that they acted as did other aristocracies in similar circumstances. Aristocracies as widely different in time and place as those of ancient Greece and medieval Japan offer parallels. But the second major change that the European family experienced in the late seventeenth and the eighteenth centuries was probably unique. There occurred a shift from a patriarchal to an egalitarian or domestic system of household relationships. In Western societies the patriarchal household was of ancient provenance. It was enshrined in the *Odyssey* and in the law codes of Exodus and Deuteronomy. Its basic presumption was that at the head of each household stood a man who in his roles as master, father, and husband owned his wife, his children, his slaves, his animals, and his land. The authority of a master over his household was the model for all dependent relationships, including that of king and subject. Many men were the property of other men; and all women and children, of some man. This pattern of subjection was first questioned in the seventeenth century by Western men. By the end of the eighteenth century this questioning had led to the assertion that all men were created equal. For the first time all forms of slavery were discredited in men's minds. The equality of men and women was declared. And children received some recognition of their independent existence. The causes of this egalitarian movement are obscure. The rise of a market economy, limited monarchy, Christianity, and kindred structures may all together have produced this great change, but certainly none of them alone was responsible. The course of the movement is far from complete even today in the Western world, where neither the equality of all men nor of women with men (let alone of children with adults) is yet secured. But the egalitarian idea has moved beyond the bounds of Western society, and throughout the world it supplies what there is of a common modern morality.

In eighteenth-century England the egalitarian idea profoundly affected the domestic lives of aristocrats. The equality of men and women raised the possibility of true and equal friendship between husband and wife. Romantic rather than arranged marriages became the ideal and the practice, and after marriage husband and wife expected to be each other's constant companion. The property rights of married women increased. Pregnancy and childbirth came to be viewed as natural processes (rather than as diseases) in which men might take a legitimate interest. And divorce, which had begun as a way to rid a man of an adulterous wife, became for some women the means to escape a loveless marriage. Aristocratic women came to see themselves more as mothers than as wives. They gave up wet nurses and either nursed themselves or experimented with artificial foods. They stopped swaddling. They introduced inoculation, cold bathing, and a new system of toilet training. But, above all, they spent more time with their children and attached them more firmly to themselves, with the probable consequence that the death rate for aristocratic children was dramatically decreased to a level that the general population did not achieve for another century. Aristocratic men shared, to some degree, this new interest in children. They concerned themselves about the health of their babies, and when they sent their sons away to school, they tried to provide them with surrogate parents. But, in the end, the traditional means by which the adult male's identity was formed placed serious restrictions on the extent to which a man could treat a woman as an equal or a father take seriously the independence of his child. The independence of a servant was much easier to accept. In fact, the new ideal of domesticity encouraged the separation of the private lives of parents and children from the world of servants. Men were prepared to deny that they stood as fathers to their servants. They gave up some of the traditional means of controlling their religious and sexual behavior. They sometimes allowed servants to have families of their own. And they were content to be tied to them by a wage contract.

Both the pattern of European kinship and the organization of its households have become frequent concerns of historians, but the two have usually been treated in isolation from each other, and the distinctions between kindred and patrilineage or the patriarchal and the domestic (or nuclear) households have not been made consistently or clearly. It has been the medievalists who have usually studied kinship patterns. Lancaster studied the kindred in Anglo-Saxon society. Herlihy and Duby have shown how the elites of Italy and France adopted a patrilineal ideology. Kent has revealingly examined the operation of patrilineal ties in Renaissance Florence. But these studies have failed to note the continuing presence of kindred ties among the aristocracy and in the wider society. The work of Diane Hughes has indeed shown the marked differences in kinship behavior between aristocrats and artisans in Genoa; and while she does not say so, these differences can be most elegantly accounted for by the presence of two opposing systems of kinship—patrilineage for the great and kindred for the poor.[1]

[1]Lorraine Lancaster, "Kinship in Anglo-Saxon Society," *British Journal of Sociology*, IX, 1958, 230-250, 359-377; David Herlihy, "Family Solidarity in Medieval Italian History," in *Explorations in Economic History*, VII, 1969-1970, 173-184; Georges Duby, "Lineage, Nobility and Chivalry in the region of the Mâcon during the Twelfth Century," in Forster & Ranum, eds., *Family and Society* (Johns Hopkins University Press, Baltimore: 1976); F. W. Kent, *Household and Lineage in Renaissance Florence* (Princeton: Princeton University Press, 1977); D. O. Hughes, "Urban Growth and Family

Introduction

Historians who study the modern period have usually been mesmerized by the nuclear family of the sociologists, and have tended to see the history of the family as equivalent to the composition and relations of the household. This is true of Ariès' great pioneering work on the history of childhood. He argued that the idea of childhood as a distinct phase of life emerged in the seventeenth century when children were no longer socialized by apprenticeship to a household but by attendance at school. Previously, children had simply been seen as little adults. It would have been more accurate, however, to say that they had been classified as dependents along with women and servants, and to see that the changes in status of children cannot be fully understood unless those experienced by the women and servants of the patriarchal household are also investigated. Some of the historians of seventeenth-century England like Macpherson and Hill have looked at the consequences of the patriarchal idea in politics, but they have considered only the difficulties and changes of status of adult male servants. Peter Laslett began, of course, with such concerns, but he and his battalions have increasingly deployed their resources on the limited question of the number of persons to be found living in a household, and whether they were related by blood or marriage. To their satisfaction they have proven that most households were what they call nuclear. But Berkner has retorted that they have only shown that families were nuclear at a certain stage of the domestic cycle. There is the further difficulty that the term nuclear family has traditionally been used to describe not simply a household composed of parents and their children but also to indicate a certain quality of affective relations among them. This Lawrence Stone and Edward Shorter have recognized when claiming, in one case, that the nuclear family arose among the English elites in the late seventeenth century and, in the other, that domesticity raised its head among the European working classes in the middle of the nineteenth century.[2] Stone and I have independently

---

Structure in Medieval Genoa," *Past & Present*, No. 66, 1975, and "Domestic Ideals and Social Behavior: Evidence from Medieval Genoa," in Rosenberg, ed., *The Family in History* (Philadelphia: University of Pennsylvania Press, 1975).

[2] Philippe Ariès, *Centuries of Childhood* (New York: Vintage Books, 1962); C. B. Macpherson, *The Political Theory of Possessive Individualism* (Oxford: Clarendon Press, 1962); Christopher Hill, *Society and Puritanism in Pre-Revolutionary England* (London: Secker & Warburg, 1964); and *The World Turned Upside Down* (New York: Viking Press, 1972); Peter Laslett, *The World We Have Lost* (New York: Scribner's, 1965); Peter Laslett and Richard Wall, eds., *Household and Family in Past Time* (Cambridge: University Press, 1972); L. K. Berkner, "The Stem Family and the Developmental Cycle of the Peasant Household: An Eighteenth-Century Austrian Example," *American Historical Review* LXXVII, 1972, 398–418; Lawrence Stone, "The Rise of the Nuclear Family in Early Modern England," in Rosenberg, ed., *The Family in History* (Philadelphia: University of Pennsylvania Press, 1975), and *The Crisis of the Aristocracy 1558–1641* (Oxford: Clarendon Press, 1965); Edward Shorter, *The Making of the Modern Family* (New York: Basic Books, 1975).

come to very similar conclusions on certain points. But he does not make what he calls the nuclear family and what I call domesticity (it existed very well in a household with 40 servants) part of a larger egalitarian movement. And his treatment of kinship, both in his essay and in his great book, is either perfunctory or incomplete.[3] He simply declares that kinship was once patrilineal and then became nuclear. In saying this he makes two errors, of course. He confuses domestic relations with the kinship network. And he does not see that the aristocracy alone was firmly committed to patrilineal principles, mainly in regard to inheritance; that in other matters they, like the rest of society in nearly all things, operated on kindred principles; and that therefore English society received much of its basic shape from the relative fluidity and egalitarian relations of kindred structures.

In this study of the aristocratic family in eighteenth-century England, I take the eighteenth century to mean the three generations between 1690 and 1780. It is a period that had a distinct economic, political, and intellectual unity. In 1688 a system of government was established by which a limited monarchy and a landed aristocracy joined together to rule through Parliament. It went unchallenged until the 1780's. The 1690's saw the establishment of the organs of public credit that allowed England to finance more successfully than any other European nation the various wars which by 1763 had made it the largest of commercial empires. The economic dominance of the landed and commercial elites that was founded on this system was not challened until after 1780 when industrialization began to produce a new kind of wealth. Intellectually the period is dominated by neoclassical modes, with Swift at its beginning and Johnson at its end, and the appearance after 1780 of romantic ideas. Within this 90-year period, it is possible to justify generational differences every 30 years or so. In politics they may be marked by mentioning the Glorious Revolution, the ascendancy of Walpole, and the accession of George III. But I also intend to argue that in the history of the aristocratic family, each of these generations had its own ethos.

I have taken the aristocracy to mean the approximately 160 families whose eldest male possessed the hereditary right to sit in the House of Lords, and from whom nearly all the members of eighteenth-century governments were drawn. The documentation for such a class is exceptionally good, and it is for this reason that I have chosen to study them. I have looked at the family papers of 30 families, and from these papers I have put together full financial histories over three gen-

[3]This was written before the appearance of Lawrence Stone, *The Family, Sex and Marriage in England 1500–1800* (New York: Harper & Row, 1977), but the criticisms still stand.

erations. These settlements, wills, deeds, acts of Parliament, and Chancery proceedings have often allowed the skeleton of a family's emotional history to be constructed; but, unfortunately, for some families all that was available were these dry bones. For 20 of them, however, there was enough correspondence to add flesh, coloring, and the words of life. I have also managed to find adequate correspondence over three generations for 10 families whose settlements I have not seen. There is full literary documentation for another 10 families still, but usually only for a single generation. And there is information on the history of settlement for one and sometimes two generations in another 27 families. I have been able, therefore, to know with some degree of thoroughness the history of at least 40 of the 160 families who are the subject of this study.

For the group as a whole it has also been possible to gather certain statistics. T. H. Hollingsworth has arrived at their death, fertility, and nuptial rates. D. N. Thomas has calculated the social class of wives. And I have collected bits and pieces: first-cousin marriages, second marriages, schooling. Some kinds of statistics I would, I hope, have given what I have to know: precisely how many children were inoculated, which mothers nursed, how many married for love. But in such cases, I have been obliged to argue from the impression of the literary evidence or from knowledgeable contemporary estimates. One thing the eighteenth century did systematically on its own. It reconstructed its families and preserved the results in *Collins's Peerage*.

I have drawn on information from four other sources—moralists, law reports and legal treatises, physicians, and imaginative writers in poetry and prose. This material was directed to all of literate society, but much of it was aimed very specifically at the sophisticated gentry who came up each year to London and, within this group, very often at the aristocracy itself. I have always tried to take from these writers those items in which they claimed or seemed to be describing actual practice. And when I have had to be content with an ideal recommendation, I have tried to track down at least a single example from the correspondence. All this was simple with the law reports, which are actual cases and almost always aristocratic. The physicians who wrote were usually those who had aristocratic London practices, and often enough they state explicitly that their recommendations are based on experience gained from such a practice. With the moralists I have preferred (when I could find them) aristocrats or their chaplains; but I have been careful to discount bourgeois prejudice, since the criticism of aristocratic family life by professional men was among the earliest forms of class consciousness. This prejudice was especially rank among the novelists and has misled a number of my predecessors.

From the imaginative writers, therefore, I have tried to take only three things: the language of social description, the occasional sociological comment, and the presentation of archtypal situations. I hope I have never tried to transform the particular situations of imaginative characters into presentations of actuality.

Of my evidence only two kinds are really systematic—the statistics and the financial documentation. The literary evidence I have used in a variety of ways, and in some instances, no doubt, it is less convincing than others. In a few instances I have related an anecdote not as a proof but simply to illustrate a trend otherwise established. Sometimes two examples from different generations have been juxtaposed, and when they have seemed different, I have suggested that the matter under discussion had changed in the course of time. But, of course, it may well be that the variation always existed. When, however, the second example is accompanied by a contemporary statement that matters had changed, I have taken the case more nearly proven. By contrast, when two quite different persons at different times make a similar statement and hang it on the same crucial word, I feel quite certain of my ground. For if two eldest sons declare they are the "slaves" of their families, and two women say that the religious education of children is the "most material" thing, one knows that one has hit upon a stock phrase and a common attitude. But the greatest conviction is given by literary evidence when an extended case study can be constructed in which every phrase reverberates with the trends one has been led to expect by other sources—then I am as convinced as by any parade of numbers. And when I can construct not one but two or three or four such studies I no longer feel the need (let alone the inclination) to apologize for my evidence. If in all this I have seemed to say the obvious, I think it is nonetheless worthwhile, for the traditional literary historian must begin to state more explicitly the way in which he has learned to arrive at his probabilities, even if it was only from the attentive reading of his masters and not from a course in statistical technique.

But I have found my masters not only among the historians. The anthropologists have provided me with the distinction between kindred and lineage. It is clearly a technical distinction that I think historians would do well to accept. I came to it by first reading Robin Fox's general book and then moving on to Befu on the Japanese, Murdock on southeast Asia, Hoben on Ethiopia, and finally back to Japan with Nakane.[4] I hope that in return anthropologists will find our histor-

---

[4] Robin Fox, *Kinship and Marriage* (Harmondsworth: Penguin, 1967); Harumi Befu, "Patrilineal Descent and Personal Kindred in Japan," *American Anthropologist*, LXV, 1963, 1328–1341; G. P.

Introduction   9

ical studies of elites useful, for their studies are usually limited to peasants for the same reason that historians deal mainly with aristocrats—namely the accessibility of information.

The distinction between patriarchy and domesticity I have made on the basis of my reading of historians—Finley on the ancient *oikos*[5] and Macpherson, Hill, and Laslett on the seventeenth-century household. I hope that this distinction will serve to free us from the thralls of the nuclear family of the sociologist.

I must also state that whenever in the last two chapters I have felt the need of a psychological theory, I have consciously ignored Freudian and psychoanalytic models. There has recently been an effort to found an entire historical field on the basis of the application of these theories. It has produced some useful information on the history of infancy,[6] but I think it is on the whole a misguided attempt to hitch our wagon to a falling star. I have found Freudian theory especially inappropriate in studying the effects of egalitarian feelings on childrearing since it is so profoundly condescending in its attitude toward children. (A similar condescension toward women has already been noted by some feminists.) "In general," Freud wrote, "so far as we can tell from our observations of town children belonging to the white races and living according to fairly high cultural standards, the neuroses of childhood are in the nature of regular episodes in a child's development, although too little attention is still being paid to them." Childhood, in other words, is by its nature a disease. And Erik Erikson, so beloved by some historians, does not do much better: "Long childhood

---

Murdock, ed., *Social Structure in Southeast Asia* (Chicago: Quadrangle Books, 1960); Allan Hoben, *Land Tenure among the Amhara of Ethiopia* (Chicago: University of Chicago Press, 1973); Chie Nakane, *Kinship and Economic Organization in Rural Japan* (London: Athlone Press, 1967). I also found use for Nur Yalman, *Under the Bo Tree* (Berkeley: University of California Press, 1971); and Edmund Leach, "Complementary Filiation and Bilateral Kinship," in Jack Goody, ed., *The Character of Kinship* (London: Cambridge University Press, 1973).

[5]M. I. Finley, *The World of Odysseus* (New York: Viking Press, 1965), and *The Ancient Economy* (London: Chatto & Windus, 1973).

[6]David Hunt, *Parents and Children in History* (New York: Basic Books, 1970); Lloyd deMause, ed., *The History of Childhood* (New York: The Psychohistory Press, 1974). The introduction to the latter is a fantasy with the Freudian drives autonomously changing the course of history. It is perceived correctly that there was a major change in the eighteenth century in childrearing, but there is no attempt to relate this to the history of the family. The purpose of the exercise seems to be, on the one hand, to wallow in the melancholy melodrama of the Freudian world and, on the other, to rejoice that our age (and the editor) has finally achieved true adult maturity. The history of the world must repeat the history of the individual according to the Freudian model, and therefore the history of the ancient world is butchered to make a Freudian holiday. Hunt's book is more moderate, but its usefulness doubtful, especially in the light of E. W. Marvick, "The Character of Louis XIII: The Role of His Physician," *The Journal of Interdisciplinary History*, IV 1974, 347-374. It should be said that a number of the case studies in deMause are useful.

makes a technical and mental virtuoso out of man, but it leaves a lifelong residue of emotional immaturity in him."[7]

I have preferred to use instead John Bowlby's theory of attachment, with its presumption that a child seeks from the very beginning to establish relations with other human beings and that those relations do not arise (as they do for the Freudians) as a secondary consequence of the satisfaction of oral, anal, and sexual drives. In addition, Bowlby never presumes that a disordered adult state is a reflection of a previous one which in a child was healthy or to be expected. His theory is therefore egalitarian; and it seems to me that when a modern egalitarian comes to study in the eighteenth century the effects on children of the breakdown of patriarchy and the appearance of equality, he does best to use a modern theory that is as untainted by patriarchy as our own imperfect liberation from contempt for children will allow. But Bowlby's theory also has certain technical advantages for the historian and the type of evidence available to him. Freud was interested in instinctive drives that are internal and unobservable. Bowlby observes external behavior, which is what the historian will find described in his sources. For Freud physiology was primary, for Bowlby it is social behavior; and the historian is a sociologist and not a biologist. For Freud the primary explanation for individual action was the unconscious, for Bowlby it is actual experience; and here again the historian's concerns and sources should dispose him to choose the latter. The humanity, theoretical elegance, and practicality for the historian of Bowlby's theory have therefore convinced me to use it in the last two chapters. Since Bowlby has no theory of sexual development (as for him sexuality is an instinct activated at puberty), I have turned to Simon and Gagnon, who offer a theory of sexual development that sees sexuality as an instinct channeled from puberty onward by social experience.[8]

The anthropologists, historians, and psychologists have, in effect, all provided me with analogies from societies other than eighteenth-century England. They have thereby helped me to form the fragmentary narratives constructed from literary and statistical evidence into larger probabilities, of each of which there is evidence that some eighteenth-century individual was aware, though I have not had the luck (as one

---

[7]Sigmund Freud, *Inhibitions, Symptoms and Anxiety* (1926), in J. Strachey, trans., *Complete Works* (London: Hogarth Press, 1959), **XX**, 147–148; E. H. Erikson, *Childhood and Society* (New York: Norton, 1963), 16.

[8]John Bowlby, *Attachment and Loss* (London: Hogarth Press, 1969–1973), 2 vol; J. H. Gagnon and W. S. Simon, *Sexual Conduct* (Chicago: Aldine Press, 1973).

anthropologist has)[9] to come upon a single source that repeated back at me the entire system of kindred and lineage, patriarchy and domesticity that I have proposed. But I think it is time that modern historians no longer delude themselves into thinking that the thickness of their sources allows them to arrive at truth and to admit, as the more venturesome historians of the ancient world have done when faced with exiguous evidence, that we construct probabilities on the bases of series (statistical or archaeological), literary evidence, and analogy.

The general aims of the chapters that follow are threefold. First, they intend to show the principal reasons for which a historian might study the family: that it is the basic unit of class consciousness and standing; that it is society's chief socializing agent; that within it sexual roles are broadly acted out; and that it largely regulates demographic patterns. Second, these chapters put flesh on the claim that the most useful analysis of the European family sees it as having two competing forms of kinship organization since the eleventh century—the kindred and the partilineage—and, since the seventeenth century as having two forms of household organization—the patriarchal and the domestic. The third general intention is to argue that European society was held together by friendship, patronage, and neighborhood and not by kinship. This, I maintain followed from the nature of kindred; but there was also abroad in eighteenth-century Europe a conscious ideological egalitarianism that would transform most political structures at the end of the century. By mid-century it had already decidedly modified the patterns of authority and relationship within the families of the English aristocracy. My specific aim is to suggest that if in the eighteenth-century English aristocratic families maintained individual position through patrilineal means, and the power of their group through friendship and patronage, it is likely that their continuing success in a revolutionary age was due in large part to their internalizing in their domestic relations at the earliest possible moment the morality of the revolutions of the modern age.

---

[9]E. A. Hammel, *Alternative Social Structures and Ritual Relations in the Balkans* (Englewood Cliffs, N.J.: Prentice-Hall, 1968), 4.

Figure 1.1 *Portrait of the duke of Newcastle and the earl of Lincoln by G. Kneller. The relationship between the two men expresses the importance of patrilineal continuity. Newcastle, who had no son, adopted Lincoln's. Lincoln was the husband of Newcastle's sister, but his family had inherited a title without an estate from a distant cousin. Copyright photograph from the National Portrait Gallery, London. Reproduced by permission.*

I

Kindred and Patrilineage

English (and most of European) kinship was cognatic since individuals traced their descent from both father and mother. Each individual belonged by birth to two overlapping groups of kinsmen and joined a third when he adopted most of the kinsmen of his spouse. The result was that no individual shared with another exactly the same universe of relations. Anthropologists call these individually unique groups kindreds to distinguish them from lineages in which individuals share with many others descent from a single ancestor, whether through men (patrilineage) or women (matrilineage). English kinship could then be described as a system of cognatic kindreds.[1] It is a type of organization that has appeared in many parts of the world and that has

[1]For general discussions of this concept, see Robin Fox, *Kinship and Marriage* (Harmondsworth: Penguin, 1967); G. P. Murdock, ed., *Social Structure in Southeast Asia* (Chicago: Quadrangle Books, 1960); J. D. Freeman, "On the Concept of the Kindred," *Journal of the Royal Anthropological Institute*, XCI, 1961, 192–220.

been studied especially in Japan, Ethiopia, and southeast Asia. All these cognatic systems share certain characteristics with regard to the rights and obligations of kinship and the types of social structures founded on them. It is likely in such systems that all children inherit equally, regardless of sex or the order of birth. The rights of women are greater than in patrilineal systems. Ties between brothers and sisters and between husbands and wives are among the strongest since these individuals come closest to having identical kindreds. Ties to relations beyond the circle of parent, spouse, and sibling are largely ceremonial. Marriage to any relation, whether by blood or marriage, is often forbidden. An individual must therefore call on friends, patrons, and neighbors as well as kinsmen if he is to successfully promote his interests. Friendship, conceived as an instrumental rather than an emotional relationship, is the strongest of all ties. In such a society it is very likely that no child will succeed to the position held by his father or mother. Such a degree of social mobility is, of course, inimical to family continuity and is often seen as especially threatening to aristocrats, and sometimes to peasants as well. An attempt, therefore, is often made to impose a patrilineal and primogenitural ideology (sometimes in the interest of a government organized on feudal lines) but the continuing right of younger children to be provided for and the possibility of direct or indirect inheritance by women show the abiding influence of cognatic and kindred structures.

It is useful to contrast the European kindred with that of Japan or Ethiopia as a means of clarifying the position in England. For England stood midway between the relatively egalitarian society of traditional Ethiopia and the less flexible system of Japan. In Ethiopia an individual was equally descended from both parents, and this was reflected in kinship terminology. The property of both parents was equally divided among all children regardless of age or birth order. But each individual had potential claims to the property descended from all of his great-grandparents. These claims were limited in one of three ways: by the closeness of descent compared to other claimants and one's knowledge of it; by geographical proximity to an estate; and by the cachet that political power might give one in prosecuting a claim. The rights of women were considerable. A woman's conduct might be subject to correction by her guardian or her husband; but she had equal rights in inheritance, her property remained her own after marriage, and she had an equal right to divorce. There was no sense of lineage. There were no family names. Bastards suffered no disabilities. Remarriage was frequent. The closest relation that could be married was a sixth cousin. And there was no principal heir. Each man in his own lifetime made a personal collection of land and offices by various means. The land was divided equally at his death, and in less than 50% of the cases did a son succeed to his father's office. In this extremely mobile society each man made his own way calling on the ties of kinship and friendship, patronage and neighborhood.[2]

Japanese kinship was at base also cognatic, and this was reflected in its kinship terminology, which remained stable over several centuries. But in the Middle Ages, under pressure from feudal institutions, a strong patrilineal ideology penetrated all levels of society with the result that primogeniture was introduced and the status of women lowered.[3] Japanese kinship henceforth operated by two different principles. At weddings and deaths an individual's personal kindred offered support on cognatic principles: Relations by both parents and affinal as well as consanguineal kinsmen made their appearance. But inheritance was patrilineal. Only one son, inherited, and while there was a strong perference for the eldest, a younger son or a son-in-law might be substituted. Fictive lineages were set up, composed of a main household and its branches, in which the latter were not necessarily consanguineal relations. A high proportion of all marriages were to consanguineal or affinal relations. The mother was the least important figure in the household. The sons of concubines and of wives had the same rights. "The womb," it was said, "is a thing to be borrowed." But lineage principles did not apply equally to all groups: Peasants were forbidden to take family names. And the ties of patronage and neighborhood remained important. Patrilineal ties had nonetheless deeply affected this originally cognatic society. There was not to be found in it anything like Ethiopia's egalitarian social structure; and when Ruth Benedict came to contrast Japanese with Western society in the twentieth century, it was precisely the absence of egalitarian social structures that she singled out as Japan's most salient characteristic.[4]

---

[2]Allan Hoben, *Land Tenure among the Amhara of Ethiopia* (Chicago: University of Chicago Press, 1973).

[3]R. J. Smith, "Stability in Japanese Kinship Terminology: The Historical Evidence," in Smith & Beardsley, eds., *Japanese Culture* (New York: Wenner–Gren Foundation, 1962); W. H. McCullough, "Japanese Marriage Institutions in the Heian Period," *Harvard Journal of East Asiatic Studies*, XXVII, 1967, 103–167; G. B. Sansom, *Japan: A Short Cultural History* (New York: Appleton-Century-Crofts, 1962), 362–365.

[4]Chie Nakane, *Kinship and Economic Organization in Rural Japan* (London: Athlone Press, 1967), is the fundamental authority in the light of which the account of the eighteenth century by Thomas C. Smith, *The Agrarian Origins of Modern Japan* (Stanford: Stanford Univ. Press, 1959), should be read; Ruth Benedict, *The Chrysanthemum and the Sword* (New York: Houghton Mifflin, 1946). On Japanese kinship, it is also worth seeing, Harumi Befu, "Patrilineal Descent and Personal Kindred in Japan," *American Anthropologist*, LXV, 1963, 1328–1341; J. C. Pelzel, "Japanese Kinship: A Comparison," in Freedman, ed., *Family and Kinship in Chinese Society* (Stanford: Stanford Univ. Press, 1970); and Harumi Befu, Takashi Koyama, Y. Scott Matsumoto, E. W. Johnson, all in *Japanese Culture*. Nakane has brilliantly used her kinship studies as a means of analyzing contemporary Japanese society in her book *Japanese Society* (Berkeley: Univ. of California Press, 1970).

In Europe, feudal organization also introduced patrilineal principles into a society previously structured around cognatic kindreds. But patrilineages began as aristocratic institutions and remained so. They were never adopted by the European peasantry. There was, therefore, a constant tension between patrilineage and kindred from the tenth century on when family names, primogeniture, and the depreciation of the rights of women began to appear.[5] The class differences in kinship organization can hardly be better seen than in medieval Genoa. Aristocrats were known by their fathers' names; artisans by the name of their trade or by either a father's or a mother's name. For the aristocrat the strongest tie was to his male relations; for the artisan, to his wife. Aristocrats lived in joint households, artisans in nuclear. Aristocrats married early, artisans late. Aristocratic women had few property rights, were likely to remain widows, and depended on their kinsmen for advice. Artisan women had strong property rights, frequently remarried, and were advised by their neighbors. An aristocrat buried his ancestors in the family chapel; the artisan might leave his estate to the parish church. But even the aristocrat had his ties to his personal kindred, and under the right influence, he might ignore patrilineal principles and prefer in his will the children of a second wife, rather than treat all his sons as equally his descendants. It is likely that this dual kinship system, one for the peasant and another for the aristocrat, will be found everywhere in traditional European society after the twelfth century. An analysis of kinship in modern Argentina suggests that it has persisted into the twentieth century.[6] Although the aristocracies of Europe learned to shield themselves from the egalitarian consequences of kindred structures, patrilineal organizations never became the norm among peasants. Consequently there was a structural base on which the ideological egalitarianism of the seventeenth and

---

[5]Lorraine Lancaster, "Kinship in Anglo-Saxon Society," *British Journal of Sociology*, IX 1958, 230–250, 359–377; D. A. Bullough, "Early Medieval Social Groupings: The Terminology of Kinship," *Past & Present*, No. 45, 1969; David Herlihy, "Family Solidarity in Medieval Italian History," *Explorations in Economic History*, VII, 1969–1970, 173–184; George Duby, "Lineage, Nobility and Chivalry in the Region of the Mâcon during the Twelfth Century," in Forster, ed., *Family and Society* (Baltimore: Johns Hopkins Univ. Press, 1976); Sidney Painter, "The Family and the Feudal System in Twelfth Century England," *Speculum*, XXXV, 1960, 1–16.

[6]D. O. Hughes, "Urban Growth and Family Structure in Medieval Genoa," *Past & Present*, No. 66, (1975), and "Domestic Ideals and Social Behavior: Evidence from Medieval Genoa," in Rosenberg, ed., *The Family in History* (Philadelphia: Univ. of Pennsylvania Press, 1975); Arnold Strickon, "Class and Kinship in Argentina," *Ethnology*, I, 1962, 500–515. F. W. Kent, *Household and Lineage in Renaissance Florence* (Princeton: Princeton Univ. Press, 1977), has studied three lineages, but without adequately considering kindred ties. J. C. Davis, *A Venetian Family and Its Fortune 1500–1900* (Philadelphia: American Philosophical Society, 1975), Chap. 1, distinguishes, in effect, between lineage and kindred, but makes no analytical use of the distinction.

eighteenth centuries could be built. Traditional Japan lacked the base, and Ethiopia, the ideology.

It is unlikely, however, that any European aristocracy ever managed to construct complete patrilineages. It is certain that the eighteenth-century English aristocracy did not, and it is the aim of this chapter to demonstrate why this was so. The chapter is divided into five parts. The first two consider the prohibited degrees of marriage and the rules of mourning. They show that in regard to sexual taboo and the ceremonial acknowledgment of kinship, aristocrats operated on the presumption of cognatic kindreds like the rest of society. But unlike other Englishmen they legitimated cousin marriage, treating marriage as an act of incorporation that preserved status rather than as an alliance that might advance it. They also concentrated their attention on the inner circle of parent, spouse, and sibling, and they made the bonds between brothers and sisters and between husbands and wives among the more important. Patrilineal ties were reserved for the inheritance of land and succession to titles. But the third section of the chapter shows that although aristocrats might try to bypass female inheritance and tie their estates to their titles as a means of maintaining family continuity, they might nonetheless be forced by demographic failure to adopt a sister's son or a son-in-law; through intestacy, an estate might also be separated from a title and divided equally among female heirs; and a man, if he were free, might choose to do this from affection for his wife or daughters, or from pique at his brother or cousin. Patrilineal and kindred principles, in short, contended with each other in the rules of inheritance. The battle was most clearly drawn (as the next section explains) over the issue of second marriages. Widows were discouraged from remarrying because of the rights her husband's relations felt themselves to have in her person, her fortune, and her children. The remarriage of men was also opposed, though less strongly, and on kindred rather than patrilineal grounds, since a man's second marriage was likely to bring into existence two competing sibling groups; this might tempt him to treat all his children as equal members of his own patrilineage, sharing between two groups of children what by right belonged only to the first. But the ties of kinship, even among siblings or with patrilineal relations, were not sufficient in this society to accomplish anything beyond the bounds of family concerns. The aristocrat who wanted to organize a political or a religious connection to make governments or to save souls did not rely on kinsmen alone but turned to neighbors, dependents, and friends. Friendship (as the final section suggests) was the dominant relationship in this fundamentally kindred society, and relations were friends, though the best of them.

Prohibited Degrees of Marriage

The forbidden degrees of marriage were based on those in the eighteenth chapter of Leviticus, as these had been expanded by the medieval canon lawyers. They were given the force of English law by a series of Henrician statutes (25 Hen. VIII, c. 22; 28 Hen. VIII, c. 7). They were usually enforced by the ecclesiastical courts, which could excommunicate offending individuals (a punishment of no real consequence) and declare the children of incestuous unions illegitimate, thereby preventing them from inheriting property. The ecclesiastical courts were inclined to take the position that all of the medieval canon law was in force unless it had been specifically repealed by parliamentary statute. Individuals were able to appeal, however, to the secular courts for a prohibition against the interpretations of the spiritual courts. By this means the common-law judges at the Restoration interpreted the Henrician statutes to mean that a marriage that had previously been held illicit was no longer so: They declared that Englishmen were free to marry their first cousins. But the secular courts refused to overturn another prohibition against which there was a similar agitation—they upheld the rule (that was thought to be implied by Leviticus) that a man was not free to marry his deceased wife's sister.

These ascendancies of the common-law courts over the spiritual courts were victories for patrilineal over kindred principles. For the spiritual courts usually sided with equality rather than male dominance. They treated adultery in men and women as equal crimes; they held the bastard to be bound by the rules of incest as much as the legitimate child; they allowed children to contract valid marriages without parental consent; they divided inheritances equally between older and younger children and between sons and daughters; and until 1660 they prevented the excessive accumulation of property that first-cousin marriage would have facilitated in some families. The legitimation of cousin marriage therefore represented a partial invasion by patrilineal ideals of the realm of kindred equality and cooperation.

This was the system the eighteenth century inherited. It favored marriages with close consanguineal relations but forbade them with close affines. There is some evidence that this represented a conflict between classes, for the aristocracy and certain parts of educated opinion supported cousin marriage while some other social groups thought of marriage as an alliance that could be maintained when one sister had died and there was still another unmarried. It was the difference between seeing marriage as an act of incorporation that *maintained a* family's standing, since cousin marriage (in which a daughter married the son of her father's brother) prevented the loss of a family's name or land, and seeing it as an alliance that could *improve* a family's social standing. This preference for incorporation was probably also connected to the sibling solidarity that is often a feature of systems of cognatic kindred. For popular horror at incest centered on two figures—the brother's widow and the wife's sister. Both of these individuals had been brought by marriage into the solidarity of a man's siblings, which lay at the heart of kindred. They therefore had to be treated like consanguineal sisters. They could not be married, and it was wicked but exciting to think of sleeping with them.

Cousin marriages were usually conceived of as marriages made by women. At the Restoration it had been, as Jeremy Taylor put it, "a great question amongst all men, whether brothers' and sisters' children, or cousin germans may lawfully marry." It was a marriage that the spiritual courts were inclined to prosecute on the ground that the canon law forbade it. But in 1669 Chief Justice Vaughan declared that "marriages between cousin-germans, and all marriages between collateral cousins, which were prohibited very far before the Council of Lateran and since it, those to the fourth degree" had in fact been made legal by the Henrician statute and that a prohibition could be used against spiritual courts to prevent them from prosecuting such marriages. Taylor himself had felt that there was no clear prohibition against such a marriage in the Old Testament and that if there were, it was not certain that it bound Christians. As for the law of nature, it had "nothing to do with the marriage of cousin germans, save only that she hath left them to their liberty"; the only marriage it forbade was between parent and child; there was unlikely to be any genetic reason against cousin marriage; and there were positive goods that could arise. The typical cousin marriage was conceived as one in which a woman married her father's brother's son (or paternal parallel cousin). This, as Samuel Dugard said, kept her estate in her father's family. Nearly half of all cousin marriages were of this kind. But Taylor also noted that a mother who arranged for her daughter to marry her brother's son (the bride's maternal cross cousin) thereby preserved "her father's name in her own issue, which she had lost in her own person and marriage."[7] It was an argument that must have had some appeal since such marriages

---

[7]Jeremy Taylor, *Ductor Dubitantium* (London, 1660), 286, 292–318; Edward Vaughn, ed., *The Reports and Arguments of . . . Sir John Vaughan* (London, 1706), 211, 218; Samual Dugard, *The Marriages of Cousin Germans Vindicated* (Oxford, 1673), 113.

were almost a quarter of the total. (The remainder were almost all to the son of a woman's father's sister—there was only one to the son of her mother's sister.) But the question was not easily put to rest. Four years after Vaughan's decision, Dugard felt it worthwhile to bring out a book in which he vindicated such marriages. It was hardly wasted effort, for two years later Rochester was still having Artemisia write to Chloe in the country that

> ... with careful prospect to maintain
> This character, lest crossing of the strain
> Should mend the booby breed, his friends provide
> A cousin of his own to be his bride.[8]

In the eighteenth century statute law and the law of Moses allowed first cousins to marry, but the feeling against such marriage did not entirely die out. It is likely that its persistence can be explained on grounds of differences in regional and class perceptions of kinship. John Cleland had the hero of his Memoirs of a Coxcomb (1751) explain that upon hearing of the impending visit of his cousin Mrs. Rivers, he, from "the narrow notions I had imbibed by a country education, assorted me no more prospect of an affair of gallantry, than if I had been told my grandmother was coming." His aunt eventually warned him of "the impropriety of my entertaining any serious thoughts of an engagement with my cousin, as she called her" but the impropriety his aunt perceived lay principally in the inequality of their fortunes. He soon found that the relationship was "distant enough to annihilate any scruple about our nearer approaches" and happily bedded Mrs. Rivers. Cleland's reference to his country education reflects the commonplace contrast between London and provincial society; the latter view held that "tis not modish to know relations in town," and could make a character like Sir Wishful declare "here's your cousin Tony, belike, I mayn't call him brother for fear of offence."[9] But it is difficult to know how seriously to take this sort of thing, and it is unlikely to have affected aristocrats, who were all followers of town fashion.

---

[8] Earl of Rochester, Complete Poems, ed. by D. M. Veith (New Haven: Yale Univ. Press, 1968), 111. In the debates over Lord Roos's divorce in 1670, it was taken for granted that only the Roman Catholic peers would find a marriage between first cousins objectionable, see F. R. Harris, The Life of ... Earl of Sandwich (London: John Murray, 1912), 2 vol., II, 320, 328.

[9] Baron and Femme (London, 1719), 38; James Johnstoun, A Juridical Dissertation Concerning the Scripture Doctrine of Marrage Contracts and the Marriages of Cousin-Germans (London, 1734); John Cleland, Memoirs of a Coxcomb (London, 1926 reprint), 54–55, 59; William Congreve, The Way of the World, in Davis ed., Complete Plays (Chicago: Univ. of Chicago Press, 1967), 439–441.

The class differences are certainly clearer than the regional ones and were noted. Lady Mary Wortley Montagu complained of Richardson that he had "no idea of the manners of high life" and that he miscalculated the degree to which convention interdicted sexual feeling between first cousins. She told her daughter that "such liberties as pass between Mr. Lovelace and his cousins are not to be excused by the relation. I should have been much astonished if Lord Denbigh should have offered to kiss me, and I dare swear Lord Trentham never attempted such an impertinence to you."This kiss would have been impertinent because cousin marriage was a possibility, and an approved one. When Andrew Foley married his first cousin, Mrs. Delany—that great arbiter of propriety—declared that her cousin Mr. Foley had had "a very happy marriage in his family."[10] But writers for middle-class audiences continued to take for granted that there was no possibility of sexual feeling even between second cousins. They might admit the legality of cousin marriage and still discourage it on the grounds of discretion and "deference to so common an opinion" that cousins "never live happily and prosperously together."[11]

Nevertheless, even among aristocrats the number of such marriages was quite small, for they normally used the family settlement to guarantee family continuity and the integrity of the estates. It was only when a man allowed female inheritance (a kindred rather than a patrilineal practice) that there was any necessity for cousin marriage. In our first generation (1690–1720) there seems to have been only one such marriage. In the next 30 years .8% of all marriages were between first cousins, or only a fraction more than the cases in which two brothers married two sisters (.7%). But in the next generation it went up slightly to 1% (and marriages between pairs of siblings fell to .5%). Aristocrats, therefore, only very gradually took advantage of the liberty the law allowed them, and the highest percentage of such marriages was about equal to what it is at present for English society as a whole.[12]

[10]*Lady Mary*, III, 97; *Delany*, I, 1862, 492.
[11]Richard Steele, in Bond, ed., *The Spectator*, No. 496, 1712 (Oxford: Clarendon Press, 1965), IV, 260; *The British Apollo*, 23–28 April, 20–25 August, 8–10 September, 22–27 October, 1708 (this writer accepted the prohibitions against marrying a wife's sister or a brother's widow, 10–15 September 1708, 4–9 February 1708–1709). See also *The Gentleman's Magazine*, XVI, 1746, 362, 658–659, XX, 1750 9–14, 69, 447–449, for discussions of marriage to first and second cousins, and Richard Steele, *The Tender Husband* (London: 1778 ed.), 25–26.
[12]Fox, *Kinship*, p. 223. A nineteenth-century calculation placed such marriages at about 4%: G. H. Darwin, "Marriages between First Cousins in England and their Effects," *Journal of the Statistical Society*, XXXVIII, 1875, Pt. 2, 153–179. He was anxious to show that such marriages did not lead to insanity.

An aristocratic woman felt free to marry her first cousin. Two brothers might marry two sisters and thereby increase the solidarity of sibling groups. But it was illegal for an aristocratic man to marry his deceased wife's sister. To understand this, we must begin by setting out the complete table of prohibited degrees. Thomas Salmon[13] drew up one as follows:

Table 1.1
Prohibited Degrees of Marriage

Consanguinity	Affinity
Of the man's part a man may not marry his	
1. Mother	1. Father's wife
2. Father's sister	2. Uncle's wife
3. Mother's sister	3. Father's wife's daughter
4. Sister	4. Brother's wife
5. Daughter	5. Wife's sister
6. Son's daughter or daughter's daughter	6. Son's wife or wife's daughter
	7. Daughter of his wife's son or daughter
Of the woman's part a woman may not marry	
1. Father	1. Mother's husband
2. Father's brother	2. Aunt's husband
3. Mother's brother	3. Sister's husband
4. Brother	4. Husband's brother
5. Son	5. Daughter's husband
6. Son of her son or daughter	6. Son of her husband's son or daughter

Source: Thomas Salmon, *A Critical Essay Concerning Marriage* (1724), p. 164.

I have converted this table into a chart (Figure 1.2) showing not only the forbidden but also the licit degrees of marriage within a man's kindred. It is given from a man's point of view because the crucial prohibition is against marriage to a deceased wife's sister. The chart shows, first, that the kindred was cognatic since a man was equally

---

[13]Thomas Salmon, *A Critical Essay Concerning Marriage* (London, 1724), 164; a similar table is in *Baron and Femme*, 36–37; but the most elaborate tables, along with a copious quotation of the statutes and the canons (though, significantly, nothing on cousins), are in Edmund Gibson, *Codex Juris Eccleciastici Anglicani* (London, 1713), 2 vol., I, 499ff.

forbidden to marry the sisters of his father and of his mother. Second, marriages were incorporative in that affinal relations were treated equally with the consanguineal, for a man could marry neither his wife's sister nor the widows of his uncles, his brothers, or his sons. But there was generational limit to this equality of the consanguineal and the affinal, for a man could marry the widow of his consanguineal great-uncle; and there was also a limit to the incorporation of siblings by marriage, for a man could marry the sister of his brother's wife and the daughter of his wife's sister.[14] (But the mother of the latter was his deceased wife's sister, whom he could not marry.) Third, the kindreds had at their core a group of siblings and siblings-in-law: a man, his wife and her siblings, his own siblings and their spouses. And, finally, generational authority between groups of siblings was guaranteed by forbidding the marriage of nephew and aunt and of father and daughter.

Everyone agreed that marriages in the parental line were forbidden, as Lord Bolingbroke asserted, in order to prevent the reverence that children felt for their parents from being converted into a sexual feeling that would have dissolved "the order of those little commonwealths and introduce a licentiousness of manners" that children would "carry with them and diffuse in the greater" commonwealth of the state. Nearly everyone would also have agreed that this was the one prohibition certainly written into the law of nature. But the prohibition of the marriage of uncle and niece was seen to be merely conventional, though operating to the same end. Some, indeed, found the marriage of uncle and niece more acceptable than that of aunt and nephew, for in the latter case the aunt lowered her authority, whereas an uncle would have the authority of a husband.[15] Even so, without a ready knowledge of Leviticus, religious persons were likely to think like Lady Sarah Cowper: "a son of Colonel Harrington has married his Aunt, the widow of his mother's brother, reputed a great fortune as they call it. I was ready to excuse it, there being no consanguinity in the case, till I read (Levit. 18:14), thou shalt not uncover the nakedness of thy Father's brother, thou shalt not approach to his wife, she is thine aunt." Consanguinity, therefore, was a stronger bond than affinity, and the parental bond stronger than the avuncular. But the most pressing business was to secure patriarchal authority.[16]

---

[14]*Vaughan Reports*, pp. 206–250; Thomas Leach, *Modern Reports* (London: 1793 ed.), I, 25.

[15]*The Works of Lord Bolingbroke* (London, 1884), 4 vol., IV, 227–229; Taylor, *Ductor*, p. 299; John Alleyne, *The Legal Degrees of Marriage* (London, 1775), 11; John Fry, *The Case of Marriages between Near Kindred* (London, 1756), xvi; Dugard, *Marriages*, 82–85.

[16]Herts. R. O., D/EP 51, April 9, 1706. See also A. O. Aldridge, "The Meaning of Incest from Hutcheson to Gibbon," *Ethics*, LXI, 1951, 309–313.

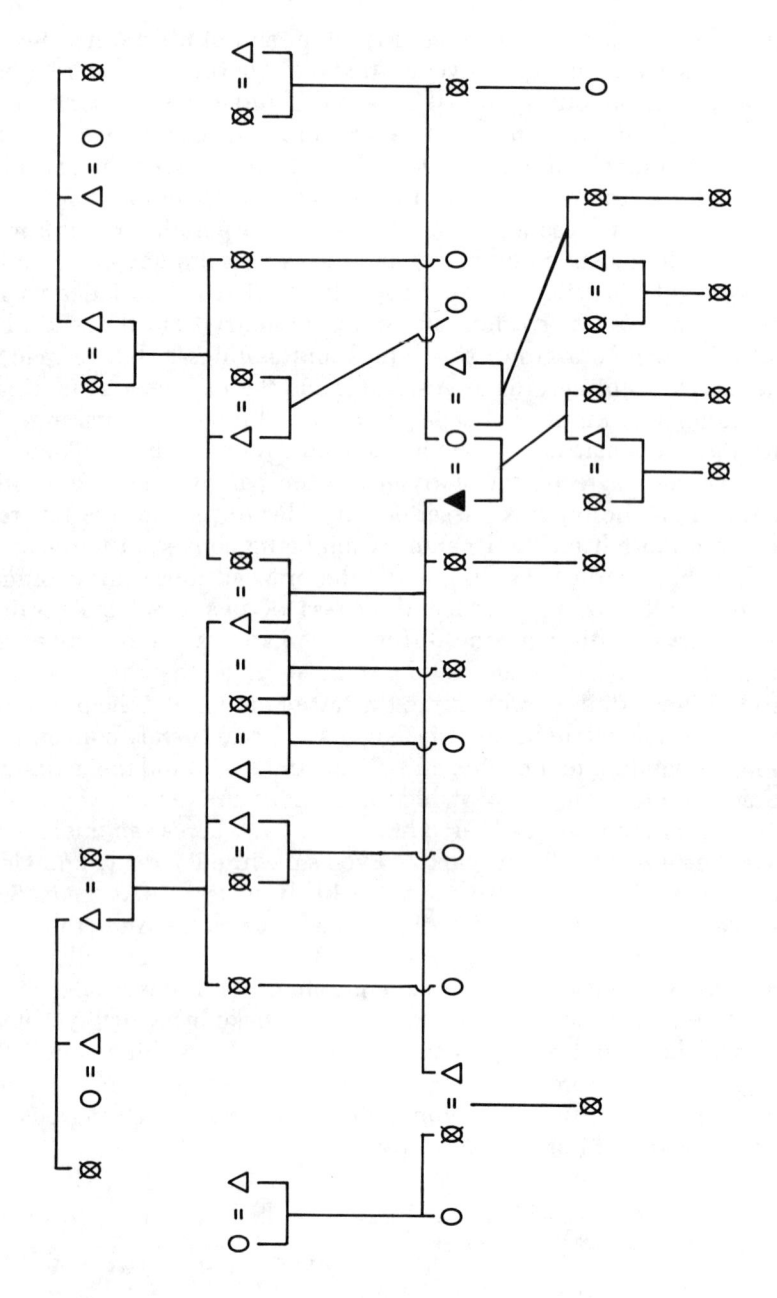

Figure 1.2 Incestuous and licit spouses for an Englishman.

Affinity became a difficulty, however, when parental status was extended to the parents of one's spouse. It was usual to refer to parents-in-law simply as "my mother" or "my father," with sometimes the addition of a title or surname. The ideal that the relationship was supposed to match can be seen in Mrs. Boscawen's claim that her daughter very much wanted Lady Gower's "favour and friendship, and will cultivate it with greatest attention. The word *daughter* in her vocabulary means so much real affection, duty, and tender attachment that Lady Gower has acquired a *child* rather than lost one by her son's marriage."[17] But the actuality seems to have been more difficult. The Duchess of Marlborough, recalling her mother-in-law, remarked that "from the beginning of the world there has not been two women that were good mothers-in-law." (The bad odor of a mother-in-law was increased by stepmothers also being called mothers-in-law.) Mothers-in-law were, in fact, avoided. Lady Rockingham once told her husband that he had undone her by not calling on his mother-in-law:

> For I can see she is hurt at it: how would you take it if I was to go into any country where your mother happened to live, and not to give her so much as a call? Upon my word, my dear, it is very unpardonable in you, for though there can't be affection in those cases yet there is a decency, and a decency that is really requisite: and I must entreat you to make it up by giving a call at Bryam, or writing a note to my mother giving very good reasons why you could not.[18]

This prohibition could be interpreted not simply as against marriage, but also as against sex with both mother and daughter. Lady Cowper wrote in her diary:

> The Duke of Buckinghamshire matches with Lady Angle as would be thought natural daughter to King James by the Countess of Dorchester, who wonders she will marry, and says it is better to call for drink only, when she feels dry. I heard the Bishop of Sarum say, "It was matter of horror to think a man should lie with both mother and daughter; for tis said he first enjoyed that Lady [Dorchester], who, when she found herself with child, desired he would marry her; but he ingeniously replied: "Madam, I can die for you but not marry you." [Die = sexual climax.]

But this was again a case in which the clergy carried about with them more of a knowledge of Leviticus than the laity had use for in their daily lives.[19]

---

[17]*Delany*, 1862, I, 565.
[18]David Green, *Sarah Duchess of Marlborough* (London: Collins, 1967), 39; S. C. L., WWM. R. 168-187.
[19]Herts. R. O., D/EP 51: April 9, 1706.

The prohibition against the marriage of brothers and sisters was taken as a good way of "preventing of uncleanness ... as families are now generally circumstantiated, male and female children being usually brought up together," and also of forestalling unseemly competition "since many brothers might have the same kindness to one sister, or might have but one amongst them all [and then] the mischief would be horrible and infinite." But with the Genesis narratives in mind, it was impossible to root the prohibition in the law of nature, since the children of Adam and Eve must necessarily have married each other.[20] The real difficulty in sibling solidarity, however, arose from the probability of remarriage and whether on such an occasion brothers and sisters-in-law were forbidden to think of each other as possible partners.

The incidence of remarriage was relatively high. It has been calculated that between 50 to 60% of the children of peers married. Of these between 14 and 17% remarried once, and of those married twice, about 11% married yet a third time. Men remarried almost three times as often as women. This is not surprising, since it is probable that the death of a wife in childbirth was one of the more frequent causes of second marriages. And the women who died in childbed were likely also to have been the most fertile and to have left to their husbands a large family of young children.[21] In such a situation a man cast longing eyes on his wife's sister as the woman who could most easily rear his children and manage his household. Part of the curiosity of the prohibition against these marriages was that it was based on an analogy since it was not specifically mentioned in the eighteenth chapter of Leviticus. It was necessary to argue that as one was not allowed to marry a brother's widow, one could not marry a wife's sister, for *ubi eadem ratio, ibi idem jus*; or it was said that a wife's sister stood "in the same degree of proximity as the nephew's marrying his father's brother's wife." But not all analogies that could be drawn out of Leviticus were acceptable. Chief Justice Vaughan declared that a man could marry his great-uncle's wife and that he could marry the daughter of his wife's sister; but marriage to the wife's sister herself he accepted as forbidden.[22] Neither Leviticus nor arguments from analogy were therefore crucial to the prohibition. It was rather dependent on either some principle of sibling solidarity or some function of marriage.

---

[20]Fry, *Marriages*, 103; Taylor, *Ductor*, 296–298; Caleb Fleming, *The Oeconomy of the Sexes* (London, 1751), 4.
[21]Hollingsworth, 21–22, 42; D. N. Thomas, "Marriage Patterns in the British Peerage in the Eighteenth and Nineteenth Centuries," M. Phil. Thesis, University of London, 1969, 188.
[22]Edmund Gibson, *Codex Juris Eccleciastici Anglicani* (London, 1713), I, 498–499; *The Miscellaneous Works of Charles Blount* (London, 1695), 138–139; *Vaughan Reports*, 206–250, 302–329.

Those who argued in favor of such marriages were likely to make an emotional appeal to the values of domesticity. John Alleyne put the case most forcefully:

> The particular instance of a marriage between a man and his deceased wife's sister, can never be presumed to be unnatural or bad. What duty can be confounded? What violence offered to human happiness? Many conveniences may result from it. Experience teaches us that the aunt, however kind as such, becomes the most affectionate mother-in-law; the severe loss of the husband is in some degree mitigated; and the hope of her children being tenderly bred, comforts, in the moment of departure, the expiring mother.

To so powerful a plea, the answer was that "the conjugal union produces family compacts, the extending of which forms a chief link in the great chain of society" and that if this prohibition was enforced, men would "constitute new compacts, new relations and friendships." In rebuttal to this, Alleyne could only say that if a man in his lifetime made one connection with a strange family, that was surely all that society could expect.[23]

In the more imaginative ambience of a novel, the same sort of appeal was made. In 1728 *The Illegal Lovers* set up the archtypal situation. It is a story told by a friend. After Bellario has lost his beloved wife, her sister, Lindamira, takes the wife's children into her home. Bellario then contracts a passion for his sister-in-law, and while she nurses him through an illness, the tongues of the gossips begin to wag. A male friend undertakes to tell her of the sinfulness of incest and denounces the spiritual courts. Bellario, having realized the hopelessness of his passion, kills himself. Lindamira is driven to distraction for a time, but having reflected that she has not actually sinned, she recovers, marries, and continues her care of Bellario's children.[24] This is the tone in which Alleyne approached the question, and it is the tone in which contemporary gossip treated these cases.

The history of two generations of the Leveson Gower family shows that Alleyne had his point. A man needed a woman to care for very young children and to take grown-up daughters out into the world. But the history of the Leveson Gowers also shows that marriage was an arrangement of property as well as a source of domesticity, and that second marriages were capable of causing great difficulties over inheritance. Therefore remarriage in general, and not just to a deceased wife's sister, was opposed. The first Earl Gower married Lady Evelyn

---

[23]Alleyne, *Degrees*, 11–12, 55–56.
[24]R. A. Day, *Told in Letters* (Ann Arbor: Univ. of Michigan Press, 1966), 174–175.

Pierrepoint in March 1712. Before the year was out she had borne her first son, and when after 14 years of marriage she died, she had had 11 children. At her death Gower was left with 9 children, the eldest of whom was 11 and the youngest, not quite a year old. Gower did not marry again for 7 years; and when he did, he chose a young widow who within 10 months had a daughter and died. Both these wives, like his own mother, had probably died from the effects of childbearing. Gower now had on his hands 3 sons and 7 daughters; 2 of his daughters were old enough to be out in society and his eldest son was within 3 years of his majority; but the remaining children were all under 14 and one was an infant. He married this time within less than 2 years and within a month of the first marriage among his daughters. He again chose a widow who had borne her first husband no children. For 13 years she had been a widow with a jointure of £2000, and there were those who wondered at the match: "Everybody thinks him a lucky man to get a woman of her understanding and fortune," said Mrs. Delany, and then went on to remark that she could not "but call her sense in question to engage with a man so encumbered with children, but love removes great obstacles."[25] The third Lady Gower was indeed made of strong stuff; she bore her new husband 3 sons and a daughter, and she outlived several of her stepchildren and very nearly all of her own.

Gower's third son lived to succeed to his father's titles and was himself made Marquess of Stafford. Stafford, like his father, married three times. His first marriage lasted less than a year and a half, for his wife died in childbed, 5 days after her infant son. Two years later Stafford married Lady Louisa Egerton, and by her he had a son and three daughters. Lady Stafford died after 13 years of marriage and a fortnight after the birth of her third daughter: She had always been "at death's door after her lyings-in," Lady Rockingham said, and she supposed that "this time she has been so much weaker as to occasion her death; 'tis a terrible loss to her young family . . .: she was a real good woman; a *good wife* without dispute she was, and perhaps now she is gone, her husband may be so sensible of it to make him miserable."[26] Whether he was miserable or not, Stafford, like his father, was left with a young family to care for; but he found that he had a substantial advantage over his father, whose remarrying had saddled his children with a 37-year lawsuit over the family property. Stafford's own mother had been the third of 3 sisters, and at her death her older sisters were both married and had families of their own. His wife, however, had

[25] Sir Egerton Brydges, ed., *Collins' Peerage* (London, 1812), II, 441–453; *Delany*, I, 1861, 557.
[26] S. C. L., WWM. R 168–179.

been the eldest of 3 sisters, and while at her death her youngest sister had been married for some 8 years, her second sister Lady Caroline was unmarried and 37-years old. Lady Caroline moved into her brother-in-law's house and undertook the care of his children. Seven years later Stafford decided, like his father, to marry a third time, and he probably did so because he wanted a wife to take his daughters into society. He decided to make this marriage, unlike his previous one, a love match. He declared he would flirt with no one but his wife and accompanied her everywhere. His wife agreed to ask Lady Caroline to stay on with her nieces and nephews. One of Stafford's grown daughters was at first shy of her stepmother, but within 2 years of her marriage, Lady Stafford was actively courting the young duke of Devonshire for the sake of the same young woman.[27]

Both father and son had evidently decided to make their third marriage for love and for the sake of their children. But both their marriages produced property disputes. Stafford's sister had certainly opposed his marriage, and she had perhaps done so from her knowledge of the family quarrels that her father's third marriage had occasioned. For Gower's third wife had been masterful. When he was on the point of resigning office in 1742, he was "fool enough to give the true reason for his being dissatisfied, 'Oh! my wife, it is my wife.'"[28] At his death she went to law to secure her surviving son's rights under the will his father had made at the time of the third marriage. For 37 years the family lawsuit dragged on till it was finally compromised with Stafford in 1783, 14 months before Lady Gower's own death. At Stafford's death, similar but less acrimonious difficulties arose, for the son of his third wife wrote that he saw "difficulties without end before my [half-] brother and myself and his trustees can come to a final settlement of the exchange of land mentioned in the will."[29]

The Leveson Gower family shows something of the reason why men remarried; it shows that any second marriage was a financial alliance and not simply a means of providing a new wife or a mother, as the sentimental advocates of marriage to a deceased wife's sister would have had it. In addition it reveals a common situation: When men remarried, there was often no sister-in-law available, and when there was she might turn out to be an unmarriageable spinster. Actual cases in which the taboo was broken and such a marriage made are hard to find. John Quick said that he wrote because he had been told there were four

[27]Coke, II, 271, 223, 276, 389, III, 268.
[28]Staffordshire R. O., D.593/C/21/3. 7, C/22/2.
[29]Lady Granville, *Lord Granville Leveson Gower* (New York: Dutton, 1916), 2 vol., I, 440.

men in London who had contracted such marriages. The second daughter of Lord Teynham, to her family's dismay, eloped with her dead sister's husband. And it was rumored, incorrectly, that Lord Trevor stayed away from the House of Lords because he had married his wife's sister.[30] The taboo was therefore effective. Gossip consequently had to concentrate on those situations that most nearly approached the taboo.

The case of Lord Grey of Werke was notorious. He had been tried in 1683 for abducting his living wife's sister, and in the 1690's his story was taken as the material for a novel—*Love Letters between a Nobleman and his Sister.* (The title makes the most of the ambiguity in kinship terminology by which a sister-in-law could simply be called a sister.) The story still had enough interest in 1701 for Lady Cowper to note in her diary: "The Lord Grey who debauched his wife's sister, when her parents sought by the help of public justice to retrieve her out of his clutches, he made her say she ran away from them to escape the lewd solicitations of her own father, which I verily believe (from divers circumstances) was an indecent lie." Grey, apparently had realized that incest between father and daughter was the only offense powerful enough to balance or overshadow his own crime.[31]

Two other stories of incest titillated the London drawing rooms later in the century. They were both stories of men desiring a brother's wife—which for the eighteenth century was the relationship parallel to marrying a wife's sister. Lord Euston was violent and vicious. Before his marriage he sat next to his future wife at dinner, stared at her until she was nervous, and finally remarked, "Lady Dorothy, how greedily you eat! It is no wonder you are so fat." After the marriage he brutally forbade his mother-in-law his house, nearly fought a duel with his father-in-law, and was seen (within a fortnight of his marriage) lusting after his brother's widow. Within a year his wife was dead, and it was said that he and his sister-in-law were about to marry, and that he was inquiring what he would need to do to keep out of the spiritual courts. "What a monster he will show himself to be," exclaimed Mrs. Delany, "and his co-partner in wickedness no less so!" But Euston evidently decided the costs were too great and remained a widower to his death.[32]

From Ireland came a similar but more spectacular tale. It was the story of "a little incest, heightened by pretty strong circumstances of

---

[30]John Quick, *A Serious Inquiry...Whether a Man May Lawfully Marry His Deceased Wife's Sister* (London, 1703); Kent R. O., Roper MSS calendar; H. M. C., Portland MSS, V, 573.

[31]Cecil Price, *Cold Caleb* (London: Andrew Melrose, 1956); Herts. R. O., D/EP 49:15 May 1701.

[32]*Correspondence between Frances Countess of Hertford... and Henrietta Louisa, Countess of Pomfret* (London, 1805), 3 vol., II, 163; Walpole XVII, 174–175, XVIII, 255; Delany, II, 1861, 205.

Iricism," as Walpole put it. Lord Bellfield had married a daughter of Lord Molesworth for love; she was handsome but poor. Lady Bellfield fell in love with her brother-in-law, and they conducted a correspondence under the names of Silva and Philander.[33] When her husband discovered the affair and confronted her with it, she admitted all and said that her last child was her lover's and that "she had no pleasure with any man like she had with him." Bellfield locked her in a garret and went after his brother with a pistol, but the young man escaped to England. Bellfield then approached his father-in-law and asked his advice. But Lord Molesworth replied that he "might do what he pleased; that having committed such a crime as incest and confessed it, he should have no concern about [her], and the rather because she was only his bastard by his wife before he married her."[34]

The brother's wife and the wife's sister—around these two figures incestuous fantasy and the rules of exogamy centered. To contract a marriage to either fell, first of all, under the general disapproval of second marriages, but a better reason can be found for such strong feelings of revulsion: the sibling solidarity found in other systems of cognatic kinship.[35] Still more of an explanation is required, however; for although there was agitation to allow the marrying of a wife's sister, there was never any heartburning over a brother's widow. The two sisters-in-law were not equal. There was no direct alliance with the family of the brother's widow, but there was with the wife's sister; and any number of societies have used the sororate as a means of maintaining an existing alliance. When the prohibition against the wife's sister is put alongside the legitimation of cousin marriage, two opposing systems of marriage emerge, one favoring ties with close affines, the other with consanguines. The probability of this is increased by an analogous situation in the United States. Bernard Farber has found there precisely two such opposing systems distributed by class and region.[36] It is therefore possible to say that there was in force in England from the Restoration to the early twentieth century, a system of marriage that approved cousin marriage and discouraged mar-

---

[33] Walpole, XVIII, 220.

[34] H. M. C., Egmont Diary, III, 271–272. For two other cases, see The Annual Register, 2, 1759, 98, 8, 1765, 219, 232.

[35] R. N. Pehrson, "Bilateral Kin Groupings," 290–292, E. Friedl, "Dowry, Inheritance and Land-Tenure," 134–135, in Jack Goody, ed., Kinship (Harmondsworth: Penguin, 1971); R. N. Pehrson, "The Bilateral Network of Social Relations in Könkämä Lapp District" International Journal of American Linguistics, 23, 1957, Pt 2, 46; n. 17.; Elaine Cumming and D. M. Schneider, "Sibling Solidarity: A Property of American Kinship," American Anthropologist, LXIII, 1961.

[36] Bernard Farber, Comparative Kinship Systems (New York: John Wiley, 1969), Kinship and Class (New York: Basic Books, 1971), and Guardians of Virtue (New York: Basic Books, 1972).

riage to affines, and that throughout the eighteenth and the nineteenth centuries there was an agitation to change this.[37] The enforced system conceived of marriage as an act of incorporation;[38] the other saw it as an alliance that could be maintained by remarriage. Incorporation maintained social status; it kept the family name from being lost and the family property from being distributed. But alliance could be used to improve social standing. The law upheld the first system as long as the aristocracy was supreme; the other was substituted (1907) when, finally,[39] the middle classes came into their own. It is ironic, but indicative of the power of domesticity, that both sides used domesticity to justify their position. The aristocracy (as the next chapter shows) gave up, in the name of love, using marriage as a means of making a man's fortune and thereby helped to destroy marriage as an alliance. The middle classes advocated marriage to the deceased wife's sister because it was the best means to comfort the dying wife, the widowed husband, and the motherless children. But the changes and continuities in the laws of incest show as well as do any indicators how much English society was dominated by its aristocracy. Aristocrats changed the law on cousin marriage so that the integrity of their patrilineages could be protected from the consequences of female inheritance. But the strongest tie an aristocrat had was to his siblings by birth and to those he acquired by his own marriage and the marriages of his siblings. The greatest threat to their solidarity lay in the likelihood that the death of a man's wife would allow him to remarry; this would weaken his ties to his wife's kindred. But if these ties might be protected by remarriage to her sister, such a marriage would deny entirely the existence of any sibling relationship between a brother and a sister-in-law. Given a choice between maintaining an alliance with his wife's family and protecting the solidarity of his sibling group, the aristocratic chose the latter. This meant that when he looked for the support of his relations, he turned first to the solidarity of his sibling group and then to his patrilineal cousins.

The English aristocracy's pattern of endogamy, by which it allowed—but did not especially practice—cousin marriage while totally forbidding marriage with near affines, placed it along with the rest of European society halfway between a highly mobile cognatic society like Ethiopia and a relatively closed one like Japan. In Ethiopia mar-

[37]There is a frivolous essay on the nineteenth-century agitation, C. F. Behrman, "The Annual Blister," *Victorian Studies*, XI, 1968, 483–502.

[38]The distinction between incorporation and alliance I take from E. R. Leach, *Rethinking Anthropology* (London: Athlone Press, 1971), 20–21.

[39]See the suggestive ninth chapter of Peter Laslett, *The World We Have Lost* (New York: Scribner's, 1965).

riages with relatives through the seventh degree were forbidden, as they had been in Europe until the Fourth Lateran Council (1215). In a traditional Japanese village, by contrast, marriages between cousins could account for nearly a quarter of the whole; uncle and niece married as well; and it was common for a widow to marry her husband's brother and a widower his wife's sister.

The English aristocracy's pattern can also be contrasted usefully with those of other social groups in its own country, with other elites, and with isolated communities in Western society. In Catholic countries the dispensing power of the papacy allowed the elite to marry their cousins, their nieces, and their sisters-in-law, and it also made possible a similar pattern for isolated peasant communities. But even Protestant elites could have a higher rate of endogamy than the English aristocracy—as, for instance, among the planters of the American colonies, where in one Maryland county in the generation after 1760, one-fifth of all marriages were between cousins. But though the English aristocracy might appear relatively open in comparison with a Latin or an American elite, they might well have seemed otherwise at home. For unlike the greater part of English society which disapproved of cousin marriage (at least since the later Middle Ages), the aristocracy had freed itself to consolidate familial property through such means.[40] And the aristocracy also remained steadfastly opposed to that section of English society that hoped to treat marriage as an alliance for the sake of social mobility; for the law would not allow men to marry their wives' sisters or women their husbands' brothers. Indeed, it is likely that the aristocracy's relaxation of the first taboo further enforced the other, since cousin marriage denied that equivalence of siblings and cousins which is sometimes taken as evidence that marriage is being treated as an alliance.

The Rules of Mourning

The rules of incest did not in the usual course of life affect the majority of aristocrats. They were, furthermore, legal rules to which

---

[40]Hoben, Land Tenure, 151; James V. Neel et al., "The Incidence of Consanguineous Matings in Japan," American Journal of Human Genetics, I, 1949, 156–178; Nakane, Kinship, 159, 164–166; J. F. Embree, Suye Mura (Chicago: Univ. Of Chicago Press, 1939), 88–89; Verena Martinez-Alier, Marriage, Class and Colour in Nineteenth-Century Cuba (London: Cambridge Univ. Press,1974), 87–91, 170–173; S. T. Freeman, Neighbors (Chicago: Univ. of Chicago Press, 1970), 126; J. R. Fox, "Kinship and Land Tenure on Tory Island," Ulster Folklife, XII, 1966, 1–17; H. G. Gutman, The Black Family in Slavery and Freedom, 1750–1925 (New York: Pantheon, 1976), 89, 561–562; R. H. Helmholz, Marriage Litigation in Medieval England (London: Cambridge Univ. Press, 1974), 77–87; Pehrson, International Journal of American Linguistics, XXIII, Pt. 2, 1957, 520.

legal penalties were attached. In this they were unlike the ceremonies marking the events of the life cycle that are more typical of kindred ties in other societies.[41] Although aristocratic ceremony was enforced by moral disapproval rather than by legal penalty, it was, nevertheless, the means by which most aristocrats regularly affirmed their ties of kindred. There were ceremonies attached to birth and marriage, but the most important occurred at death. Visiting a newly delivered woman, tipping her child's wetnurse, or standing godparent at the christening all took notice of child's birth, but the conventions and their expense were minimal; they were not extensively discussed, and one had usually to be physically present to observe them. As for marriage ceremonies, they were being deliberately simplified. By the end of our period, men were marrying in private houses, at night, and in the presence of a few witnesses. They stopped sending marriage favors to their friends and relations, and they sometimes even neglected to inform them of the marriage.[42] It was quite otherwise, however, with mourning the dead.

The essence of mourning was to wear somber clothes for various periods of time according to the closeness of the relationship to the dead and the public knowledge of that relationship. The ritual had three different audiences: It indicated to outsiders that one properly valued the relationship; it kept peace with living relations for whom such public ceremony was important; and it allowed one to cope with one's own grief. There was, in each family, an older woman who kept track of the death of relations and announced to the rest of the family the appropriate degree of mourning. Mourning was expensive, fashionable, and public; and it could last from a week to a year. It can be used as another proof that individuals organized their relations around them into cognatic kindreds. The rules of mourning reveal that spouses, parents, and siblings formed the central core of one's kindred; that husbands and wives were incorporated into each other's kindred by marriage; that the parental tie was stronger than the avuncular, the consanguineal stronger than the affinal, and the marital tie, the strongest of all. It shows that it was becoming difficult to distinguish degrees of cousinhood and that cousins had moved to the outer limits of one's kindred; that remarriage took an individual out of one's circle of relations; and that servants were excluded from the family. Table 1.2 indicates the period of mourning required for each relative. Only the

---

[41]G. P. Murdock in G. P. Murdock, ed., *Social Structure in Southeast Asia* (Chicago: Quadrangle Books, 1960), 5.
[42]For birth ceremonies, see Chap. 4, and for marriage, see Chap. 2.

Kindred and Patrilineage 35

Table 1.2
Degrees of Mourning

12 months	Husband or wife
6 months	Parents or parents-in-law
3 months	Sister or brother
	Uncle or aunt
6 weeks	Sister-in-law
	Uncle or aunt
3 weeks	Uncle or aunt
	Aunt who remarried
	First cousin
2 weeks	First cousin
1 week	First and second cousin
	Husband of stepmother's sister

periods of mourning for spouses and parents remained constant throughout the century.

It was highly indecent to mourn less than a year for a husband or wife, and anyone who broke the rule had to face considerable disapproval from his relations. Lady Rockingham feelingly objected when her brother-in-law remarried a few weeks before his mourning was up. And when the duchess of Leinster married her children's tutor, her younger sister told her that the remainder of their family "think it will hurt you vastly in the world to have married within even a year after your mourning; and they are vastly hurt at its being before the mourning was out." Some women mourned for 2 years: Mrs. Delany laid it down that "my mama must not wear black handkerchiefs with her second year's mourning." It was also possible to go into a perpetual mourning, but one ran the risk of being mocked, as Horace Walpole mocked the duke of Montagu, for making "a vow of ever wearing weepers for his vixen turtle."[43]

Children mourned half a year for their parents, and as with all the longer periods, the time was divided in two: 3 months of first mourning and 3 of second. The somberness of clothing was slowly decreased. Three months after her father's death, Mrs. Delany, who Burke described as "the highest bred woman in the world and the woman of fashion of *all* ages,"[44] told her sister from the midst of metropolitan fashion that "you should if you keep strictly to the rules of mourning, wear your shammy gloves two months longer, but in the country if it is

---

[43]Kent R. O., U471.c.6; *Leinster*, **II**, 129; *Delany*, **I**, 1861, 101; *Walpole*, **XXXII**, 315–316.
[44]Simon Dewes, *Mrs. Delany* (London: Rich & Cowan, n.d.), xi.

more convenient to you, you may wear black silk; you might have worn black earrings and necklace these two months." And within a month of their mother's death, Mrs. Delany explained that she thought "black bombazeen will do very well in a sack. I have one in a manteau and petticoat which I wear when in full dress, at home, and a dark grey poplin; and abroad, undrest, a dark grey unwatered tabby: I shall make no more dark things;—after three months black silk is worn with love hood, and black glazed gloves, for three months more." Mourning was clearly a ceremony for the public eye, but not as much was demanded at home or in the country as in London or in company. There was an equality, once again according to Mrs. Delany, in the mourning for one's parents and for those of a husband or wife.[45] And this is one of the better indicators that married persons incorporated each other's parents into their own kindred.

Husbands and wives, indeed, mourned equally for all of each other's relations, though not necessarily with good grace. Lady Royston was a Campbell with many cousins; she had a relation who was stricter in these matters than Mrs. Delany; and therefore her husband, who was not fond of black, had been forced a number of times into mourning for relations of his wife about whom he knew nothing. On the death of Royston's uncle (the husband of his father's sister), Lady Royston could consequently write with unconcealed glee to send him from his mother

> her orders to condole with you upon the death of Mr. Billingsley, as she knows it is with true and unfeigned sorrow that you will hear the news of 1-2-3-4-5-6 weeks of mourning for your good uncle. For my part, as I have not such a natural antipathy as some of my friends show to black coat or gown, I am very easy upon the matter. I only rejoice that the six weeks mourning is not to be laid at my door, that it is de votre chef, and that in the future balance of our accounts, I may lump a great number of *cousins* against the article of this Mr. Billingsley. (Poor man! I never saw him in my life.) Well but now, can't you make some use of this misfortune if it must happen? I fear you will wish a great mortality among my hundredth cousins for the succeeding six weeks....

She proposed that "if we can't contrive to get half a dozen of them dispatched out of our way in time" (with a week for each cousin out of the 6 for the uncle), that perhaps he could "endeavour to persuade Lady Harriet to antedate at least their obit, or to be contented with the payment of a black coat to be shown to the town for such a space of time, and by fixing the name of any family she choose to each successive week, give you a discharge in full for any further claims they can have upon you."[46] Family loyalty and family incorporation, it is clear, forced

---

[45]*Delany*, II, 1861, 96, 478–479.
[46]B. L., Add. MSS, 35, 376, ff 40–41.

men and women into public ceremonies for which they had no taste. And to satisfy the demands of the living for family reputation and respect, they mourned the death of individuals whom they may never have seen and for whom they certainly had no feeling or affection.

To mourn a cousin or uncle, whether by blood or affinity, was a source of difficulty, and the difficulty was reflected in the change and uncertainty that surrounded the degrees of mourning for these relations. The conventions of mourning seemed to have remained fixed throughout the century for the circle of parent, spouse, or sibling, but relations beyond that circle were held in uncertain regard. In the early eighteenth century, when her uncle Hatton died, "upwards of eighty-five years old," Lady Nottingham had told one of her younger sons that "this would be three months mourning for you here." But Mrs. Delany told her sister at mid-century that they were to mourn 3 weeks for the wife of their mother's brother (their mother was to mourn her sister-in-law twice as long) but that as she was "not known in Staffordshire, I think it of no consequence to put it on there." And in 1780 Lady Pembroke informed her son, on the death of her sister's husband, that it was "six weeks mourning for you, a month black buckles and sword, and a fortnight coloured sword and buckles" and that "you must mourn for him though abroad, as an Uncle is very near, and in France it will be well known."[47] The length of mourning clearly changed; there remained its purpose of publicly acknowledging a relationship to those who knew of it; but there was great uncertainty about the assigned length of time.

Mourning for cousins went through similar changes. "I see poor Lady Hotham (my cousin) is dead at Bristol," Lady Rockingham wrote to her husband, "which is a fortnight mourning, if not three weeks for us, for I don't know whether there is any difference in the mourning for a first or a second cousin." Even Mrs. Delany was unsteady in this matter. She prescribed a fortnight's mourning on the death of her cousin, Lord Weymouth, in 1751, but 3 years later only a week's mourning for Lord Gower, yet both men seem to have been equally related to her; Sir Bevil Granville had been Mrs. Delany's great-grandfather and the great-great-grandfather of Weymouth's wife and of Gower himself. In addition Mrs. Delany had worn only a week's mourning for the husband of Gower's aunt who was her first cousin. Mrs. Delany had then mourned a week for both a first and second cousin, but she had mourned twice as long for a man who had married one of her

---

[47]Pearl Finch, *History of Burley-on-the-Hill* (London: Bale & Danielsson, 1901), 2 vols., **I**, 258; *Delany*, **II**, 1861, 276; Lord Herbert, ed., *Henry, Elizabeth and George (1734–80)* (London: Jonathan Cape, 1959), 429.

Carteret cousins of whom she was especially fond. Mourning of 1, 2, 3 weeks were all possibilities, but by 1769 "the present fashion," as Mrs. Delany told her niece, dictated a week for cousins of all varieties.[48] It is clear that the difference between first and second cousins, between cousins one could marry and those one could not, had been obliterated, and that all cousins were being placed on the furthest periphery of one's relations. Aunts and uncles, whom some saw no difficulty in marrying, were moving slowly to join them there. For a relation one could marry could not be part of the core of an individual's kindred.

If some of the bonds created by marriage could be stronger than those by blood, remarriage loosened ties; and the practice of household patriarchy in mourning disappeared altogether. Lady Pembroke had her son mourn her brother's wife for 3 weeks whereas he had mourned her sister's husband twice as long, for his aunt had remarried after the death of her husband. And Lady Cowper once acknowledged the tenuousness of uncleship by remarriage when she mourned a week for the husband of her stepmother's sister. Patriarchy, in the earlier eighteenth century, had usually been recognized at death by putting the liveried servants into mourning. Even then there were limitations; the mourning of an uncle did not require it; and Lady Harcourt had wondered on the death of her grandson "whether it is necessary to put our livery servants in mourning, he being but a child." By the middle of the century it had become very old-fashioned to do this, even for the closest adult relations. "I suppose my brother will mourn the old mourning," Mrs. Delany wrote at her mother's death; "*I shall* as I am at such a distance; I have put my maid and the housekeeper into mourning, and D[octor] D[elany] has put his own servant out of livery into mourning, though it is not now a general fashion, but as it is a mark of respect D.D. thought it right to do so, and we are now of a time of life to indulge the *dictates of the heart* more than the reigning *fashion*."[49]

To mourn was to perform a public act, and to do it correctly was part of high fashion. As part of that fashion one mourned, however, not only for one's relations but for the king and all his relations—one of the last remnants of royal patriarchy. Deaths in the royal family therefore occasioned high society, and those who aspired to it, to go into mourning. It was done with some enthusiasm, for it was a marvelous opportunity for conspicuous consumption: "About mourning: bombazeens quite plain, broad-hemmed muslin; or *white crape*, that looks like old

[48]S.C.L., WWM. R. 168–188; Delany, III, 1861, 11, 261–262, I, 1862, 247.
[49]Lord Herbert, ed., Pembroke Papers 1780–1794 (London: Jonathan Cape, 1950), 35; *Delany*, I, 1862, 92; Finch, Burley-on-the-Hill, I, 258; E. W. Harcourt, ed., The Harcourt Papers, (Oxford, 1876–1905), 12 vol., II, 145; Delany, II, 1861, 476.

flannel, seven shillings a yard, and won't wash; Turkey gauze is also worn, which is thick and white, but extravagant as it does not wash, dirties in two days, and costs five shillings a yard; the mourning will be worn six months, three in crape and bombazeen." On the other hand, visits to court were taken as opportunities to lessen the mourning in one's own family. Lady Grantham, in her first season as a young bride, was in a quandary whether to go to court in the mourning she was wearing for her husband's relative. She compromised and wore white and gold, with black ornaments and a black ribbon in her cap. But the case of the duke of Montagu was more severe; "and it required a jury of matrons and divines to persuade him he would not go to the devil and his wife, if he appeared in scarlet and gold on the Prince's birthday—but he is returned to close mourning like Hamlet, and every Rosencrans and Gildenstern is edified both ways."[50]

Aristocrats, however, mourned or refused to mourn, not only as a means of publicly acknowledging kindred. They also used these ceremonies either to express hostility toward the dead or to cope with private grief. But the public nature seems to have fitted these ceremonies more for the former than for the latter. Not to mourn at all, or to do so with bare propriety, were effective means of venting one's hostility. When Lady Cowper died, her sister "Mrs. Liddell made her appearance soon after her death without the least regard to common decency of dress," and those who observed this were driven to speculate whether it was out of her anger that Lady Cowper had left her no legacy with which to buy her mourning clothes. Mrs. Delany had been forced by her own relations to marry into a family that treated her badly, and consequently when the sister of her first husband was widowed, she told her own sister that "I am informed my sister Levington is a widow, Mrs. Woodfield is now making her weeds. I shall make it as slight as I can without offence." The second duchess of Marlborough effectively tormented her parents by mourning the bastard children of her father's sister, for, as her mother put it, "if the Duchess of Cleveland and the Duchess of St. Albans don't mourn for such sort of relations, they have very few to mourn for." But the duchess mourned her son Blandford "in nothing but her manteau," for she said "that his behaviour towards her must justify her being at least indifferent to his death."[51]

[50]*Delany*, III, 1861, 475; cf. 32–33, 35, 474, 537–538, 584, 607; Joyce Godber, *The Marchioness Grey of Wrest Park*, (Bedfordshire Historical Records Society, 1968), 108; *Walpole*, XXXII, 315–316.
[51]H. T. Dickinson, ed., *The Correspondence of Sir James Clavering* (Surtees Society, 1967), 153; *Delany*, I, 1861, 171; Green, *Sarah*, 236; Earl of Ilchester, ed., *Lord Hervey and his Friends, 1726–38* (London: John Murray, 1950), 81, 83; Cf. Maud Wyndham, *Chronicles of the Eighteenth Century*, (London: Hodder & Stoughton, 1924), 2 vol., II, 310.

In contrast, the use of the public form to express private grief was likely to be frowned on as romantic or farcical. When Walpole's niece put on mourning for the duke of Ancaster, to whom she claimed she was to have been married, he exclaimed that she had acted on precedent and had "behaved in the most reasonable manner, shown very proper concern, but nothing romantic or extravagant." But to the eyes of others it seemed quite otherwise. Lady Mary Coke related that the girl's mother had written to Ancaster's mother that "Lady Horatia had given the Duke of Ancaster a lock of her hair, which she desired might be returned to her, and also she desired the Duchess of Ancaster would order a lock of the Duke's hair to be cut off and sent to her daughter as she intended to mourn for him." At this Lady Mary could only exclaim, "Did you ever hear of such nonsense, or such folly? But as the message comes from the House of Folly, it is less surprising." And the dowager Lady Gower was even more severe, declaring that "to write such stuff to the Duchess of Ancaster at a time when she must be under the deepest affliction, I look upon as the height of cruelty, the motive vanity, for it can answer no other purpose."[52]

To some it seemed that women were especially prone to excessive mourning. When Jonathan Swift visited the mother and sister of Lady Ashburham, he found them both in tears at her death. For this he chided them, and later wrote: "There is something of farce in all these mournings, let them be ever so serious. People will pretend to grieve more than they really do, and that takes off from their true grief." He himself preferred another course, and approved of the duchess of Hamilton, who on her husband's death "never grieved, but raged, and stormed, and railed." Swift had probably noticed the difference between a mourning pattern that was satisfying to dependent women and the rage that was more usual in men, and he had, of course, preferred the latter. Others had another explanation for female mourning. "This dismal and troublesome vanity" wrote Abel Boyer, "is most prevailing with ambitious women; for their sex rendering them unable to advance themselves by eminent virtues, they strive to signalize their reputation by the pageantry of an inconsolable sorrow."[53] But some men also acted in this way, and there is therefore another possible explanation. The forms of public grief were reserved for the acknowledgment of kindred. They could not be easily used to relieve grief for those for whom one had deep feelings—a husband, a child, or a sister. If one tried to do so, one was likely to be driven to excess and to be scorned. For it was not

---

[52]Walpole, XXXIII, 114; Delany, II, 1862, 451-452.
[53]Frederick Ryland, ed., Swift's Journal to Stella (London: George Bell, 1897), 415, 413; Abel Boyer, The English Theophrastus (London, 1702), 65.

possible to transform the obsequies of mere convention into the true heart's cry.

The Rules of Inheritance

In aristocratic society one mourned for one's relatives, and married them or not, on the presumption that they were organized into a cognatic kindred around oneself. When it came to the inheritance of land or money, one was part of a group descended from the same two common ancestors. There was however, a strong tendency to resist the logic of cognatic descent, with its demand for an equal division among all children and between both sexes, and to substitute instead a patrilineal and primogenitural ideology. In the succession to family names and titles this ideology was most pronounced, since a woman at marriage took her husband's name and could almost never inherit a title of nobility from the male ancestor to whom it had been granted. Titles went instead to the oldest surviving male descendant. But the land that was needed to give social consequence to the political power that came with the title's automatic seat in Parliament was not inherited by the same rule, and here was the rub. Most noblemen arranged for land and title to be inherited together on patrilineal and primogenitural principles. But they were also free to leave the land to their daughters and to allow a naked title to be inherited by their closest male relation. If they died intestate, the result was the same.

There were actually in operation different rules of inheritance for titles, for land, and for money, and the ideal in all three cases could be set aside by special circumstances. A title, when there was no son, might be inherited by a brother, an uncle, or a cousin; or when the original patent did not allow this (and sometimes when it did), a new title might be created for a daughter's husband or a sister's son. And there was the highly exceptional patent that allowed a daughter to inherit her father's title. Land normally went to the eldest son and then to the oldest male patrilineal relative; but by intestacy, and by individual affection or perversity, it could be equally divided among daughters. Intestate estates in property other than land (22 & 23 Charles II, c. 9) were equally divided among all children, male and female, but by will or settlement a man might leave his money to buy more land for the successor to his title, and younger children were usually given money inheritances when the land went to their eldest brother.

An aristocratic family could best guarantee its continuing consequence by attempting to construct a patrilineage in which title and land were inherited together by the eldest male; but when it attempted to do this, it acted against the strong customary current in peasant society that favored equal inheritance.[54] And even the principles of the common law of intestacy in land made the construction of a true patrilineage difficult since they insisted that descent was from the same pair of ancestors (and not just the male), and since they also allowed men to inherit through women and permitted women to inherit directly in some cases. Blackstone gave the classic exposition of this common law of intestacy. A man's descendants were either lineal or collateral; that is, they were either descended filially from himself and his wife or descended "not only from the same ancestor but from the same couple of ancestors." Among one's lineal descendants, sons inherited before daughters, and the eldest before the younger sons. But if there were only daughters they inherited jointly. If there were no lineal descendants, the eldest males descended from one's paternal grandparents inherited, and then the females jointly and so one continued back, always preferring eldest males descended through paternal lines. After all such heirs were exhausted, the land went to the eldest male produced by one's maternal grandparents, and then to the females jointly, and after that to the eldest males descended through paternal great-grandparents and so back infinitely. The eldest male in a paternal line always had the preference, but women and maternal lines could eventually inherit, and women always inherited jointly. There was a strong patrilineal tendency but at the very beginning of this complicated process cognatic principles decided the basic direction. For if an aristocrat had married twice and had had sons by both wives, it was not his sons by the second wife who inherited his land when all the children by the first had died; instead, it went to his own brother, who was the nearest cognatic heir of the children by his first wife.[55]

There were several aspects of this system that left men unhappy. There was, first, the exclusion of halfsiblings, which, as Blackstone said, carried a hardship with it. For though a man's half siblings were part of his kindred and he could neither marry them nor their children, yet they were emphatically not part of his lineage and could not directly inherit his property.[56] This situation could be changed by a man's including his children by all his wives in the settlement of his estates, but such a decision could lead to bitter resentment, as we shall see that it did in the family of the duke of Ancaster.

[54]Joan Thirsk, ed., *The Agrarian History of England and Wales, 1500-1640* (Cambridge: University Press, 1967), index s. v. inheritance customs; Jack Goody, Joan Thirsk, E. P. Thompson, eds., *Family and Inheritance* (London: Cambridge Univ. Press, 1976), Chaps. 5, 6; Margaret Spufford, *Contrasting Communities* (London: Cambridge Univ. Press, 1974).
[55]William Blackstone, *Commentaries on the Laws of England* (Oxford, 1768), 4 vol., II, 202-234.
[56]Ibid., II, 202-210.

The second point of contention was that land always descended lineally but never ascended; that is, fathers never inherited from sons, or grandfathers from grandsons. To the patriarchal mind this seemed a great difficulty. John Locke protested that were it not for the "right of being nourished and maintained by their parents, which God and nature has given to children and obliged parents to as a duty, it would be reasonable that the father should inherit the estate of the son and be preferred in the estate before his grandchild."[57] And it seemed to him especially arbitrary that even when there were no grandchildren, a man was still unable to inherit from his son. There were actually two cases, one in 1708 and one in 1754, that attempted to overthrow the principle, but it was upheld; and in the latter case Lord Hardwicke gave two reasons for doing so. There was, first, the right of children to be provided for and educated, but there was also, in effect, the logic of sibling solidarity. For when Sir John Evelyn attempted to claim his grandson's estate in preference to the boy's surviving brother, his lawyers had argued that according to the civil law both Evelyn and the surviving brother were related to the dead boy in the second degree. But Hardwicke, with precedent behind him, held that English law viewed brotherhood (when both parents were the same) as an absolute condition of which there were no degrees, while grandfathers in terms of both civil law and common law were two degrees distant from their grandsons.[58] The sibling solidarity, which was part of kindred, was more powerful than patriarchy in questions of inheritance, but in inheritance both kindred and patriarchy were ultimately subordinated to lineage.

The point of greatest tension, however, was located at the gap between lineal and collateral inheritance where the decision was whether to allow a daughter to inherit the land and take it with her to another patrilineage. Men who decided to do so were likely to face great opposition in their lifetime and to have their memory reviled after death. When the daughter of Sir Arthur Kaye married Lord Dartmouth's son, Kaye settled £1727 of the yearly worth of his estate on his daughter and her husband. The remaining £273 he kept at his disposal in order, as he said, "to preserve respect." But he promised that it would be eventually settled on Dartmouth's family and asked that this promise be considered "as the strongest part of his settlement because his honor was engaged for it." Kaye's honor, however, could not withstand

---

[57] John Locke, in Laslett, ed., *Two Treatises of Government* (Cambridge: University Press, 1970), 225–226.

[58] J. T. Atkyns, *Reports of Cases... in ... Chancery in the Time of Lord Chancellor Hardwicke* (London, 1794), 3 vol., III, 762–765.

family pressure. He gave one part of the unsettled land to his wife, who sold it after his death, and the other part went to his brother's son. His sister had indeed urged him strongly and repeatedly to settle all his land on their nephew, telling him "to consider what in honor, conscience and justice he owed to his *Family*." But Kaye replied that he "took his daughter not his nephew to be his family," and he complained that his sister was being especially unkind since she had asked him, before she had had a son, how to cut "the entail of all her husband's estate, to get it settled on her own daughters." To Dartmouth, Kaye could only say that what he had given his nephew was only a "heap of stones" with which "he thought it was proper he should have some land about." As a consequence of these contentions, Kaye's daughter had no regard for her father's family and was careful at her death to exclude them from the guardianship of her children.[59]

Kaye had been free to prefer his lineal to his collateral heirs and to leave his land to his daughter rather than to his nephew; but he had perhaps been influenced not only by affection for his daughter but also by the prestige of the Dartmouth connection. When the ninth earl of Derby disinherited his brother in favor of his daughters it was more clearly a preference for one's children over regard to the family title and name; but Derby was perhaps influenced as much by hatred of his brother as Kaye had been by Dartmouth's prestige. Derby's only son died while on the grand tour. In this event his marriage settlement called for Derby's two daughters to share £12,000 and for his younger brother to inherit the estates along with the title. But Derby was a cantankerous man: He had quarreled with his mother and his brothers over money, and he tried to prevent his brother's election to Parliament. When he died in 1702 his will gave £10,000 to each daughter and certain lands to his brother. In the following year, however, the daughters brought a suit to prove their title to a part of the family estates; for their father had purchased some lands and had managed to break the entail on others, and as these had not been settled on their uncle, they were the co-heirs. The tenth earl protested and accused his nieces of withholding crucial papers. Two attempts were made at having a settlement arbitrated, but it took a series of lawsuits stretching over 7 years (in which it was found that the entail had been broken) and

---

[59]Staffordshire R.O., D. 1778, **I**, ii, 580–581. Sir William Grimstron, by contrast, would not leave his estates to his only daughter who married the heir of the Marquess of Halifax; instead, he left them to his great-nephew William Luckyn on the condition that he change his name to Grimston. Christopher Clay, "Marriage, Inheritance and the Rise of Large Estates in England, 1660–1815," *EcHR*, **XXI**, 1969, 504–505.

another arbitration, to arrive at a division of the family estates satisfactory to both uncle and nieces.[60]

It was not only the disposal of a man's land to which a collateral heir could object, for if a personal estate were large enough, its disposal could lead to equal discontent. The fourth lord Middleton was a younger son who succeeded in fee (or absolute ownership) to all his family's estates. Since Middleton had no sons, at his death his first cousin succeeded to the title and to estates of £9000 a year. Middleton, however, had left his wife not only her jointure but all of his personal estate as well, and when she remarried, therefore, she had an income of £25,000 a year. At her death she left £10,000 to her sister, £5000 to her brother, £2000 to each of her second husband's children, £1000 to each of the children of the fifth Lord Middleton's younger brothers, and £500 each to Middleton's daughters. Lady Middleton had committed all the great sins. She had enriched a second husband's children and her own siblings at the expense of her husband's cousins. The fifth Lord was aggrieved, and a few months after her death he wrote up "a few anecdotes for the use of my posterity that family errors may not be repeated." He explained that the previous four lords (his cousins, uncle, and grandfather) had been destroyed by drink and gout and that the late dowager Lady Middleton had "brought very little if any fortune at her marriage into this family and I think it very ill became her to plunder this family of such a great sum of money." From Middleton's point of view the personal estate should have been used to buy more land to settle on the bearer of the family's title. At his own death the Middleton estates were worth £8000 more a year than when he had received them; and of the total £17,000 a year, he settled £10,000 on the holder of the title and only £7000 on his son. In addition, his family piety moved him to leave annuities of £200 each to the nephew and great-nephew who eventually succeeded to the titles. His daughter-in-law made a careful note of all these matters at her husband's death and pointed out that the son (the sixth lord) had taken his father's admonition to heart. For he arranged that the seventh lord Middleton should inherit an income of £30,000. The fifth and the sixth lords had more than tripled the worth of the estates attached to their family's title and for nearly a hundred years had held before the family's eyes the wicked example of the drunken, gouty, and impious line from which their collateral branch had rescued the title.[61]

[60]Lancashire R.O., DDK/14/4; 15/5, 22; 1617/7, 21,31; 15/26; 1617/42; 1618/14; 17/9; 1620/10.
[61] N.U.L., NeD 410–411; MiF12; MiF8; Mil M 36.

If men allowed women to inherit land or other significant property, it was because they had no regard for a family identity that extended over several generations; for only through the patrilineal inheritance of titles and their supporting estates could such an identity normally be maintained. For the majority of men it therefore seemed "incumbent on the ancestor to leave some provision for the maintenance of the honor," and a man could be accused of "want of gratitude to the Crown" if he left his titles naked of their estates.[62] A careful man like Lord Stanhope provided, as he told his younger brother, that "nothing shall be agreed that can prejudice you or any person to whom the title of Lord Stanhope may happen to descend in the succession to the real estate which was my father's and designed by him to go along with the title, for I would have no peer reduced to a necessary dependence where I could help it." Stanhope explained that by this he did not intend that the estate should never be sold, but only that the proceeds of any sale should be resettled on the title and not be included in his personal estate, through which it could pass out of the family.[63]

A man was likely to prefer to succeed to a lineal rather than a collateral title, and thus when the second lord Nottingham inherited from his cousins the older title of Winchilsea, he told his son: "[I know] very well that I cannot refuse the title of Winchilsea and all you say of it is very right, but I am not debarred from using the addition of Nottingham in all deeds and papers I shall sign, nor even in the House of Lords in my subscribing the oaths and tests and any protestations, for this I will certainly do to distinguish my branch of the family from the former." Nottingham was determined to mark the excellence of his junior line, and it was a determination which was strengthened by the last two earls of Winchilsea's having been his pensioners.[64]

A man's family identity resided not only in his title but also in his estates, and an aristocrat unfortunate enough to have no son or brother to inherit his title could, on the strength of his estate, commandeer his daughter's husband or his sister's son into changing his name and continuing the line. Few men were in the political position of the duke of Marlborough, who was able to have his titles made inheritable through his daughters when it became apparent that no son would survive him. And even when titles were inheritable through women, the relations of a woman's husband were likely to find the situation

---

[62]The English Reports, XXIV, 689–690: cf. Charles Ambler, Reports of Cases... in Chancery (London, 1829), 163.
[63]Aubrey Newman, The Stanhopes of Chevening (London: Macmillan, 1969), 106.
[64]J. H. Plumb, ed., Studies in Social History (London: Longmans, Green, 1955), 174.

distasteful. When earl Gower's eldest son married the countess of Sutherland, the wife of his half-brother concluded that "the children must be called by her name" but fancied that "this is arbitrary." But Gower's other relations thought otherwise, and at their urging he asked for and received the title of marquess of Stafford in order to take precedence, for "they were very earnest in their wishes and expressions as they did not like that Lord Gower's descendants should derive their name and title from their mother."[65] (This battle, however, the Sutherland fortune eventually won when 50 years later the family were made dukes of Sutherland.) It was therefore wiser to provide a daughter with a husband with fewer pretensions. When the heiress of the Percys, earls of Northumberland, married the sixth duke of Somerset, her husband agreed to change his name to Percy, but after the marriage he persuaded her to release him from the obligation. It was only two generations later that the identity of the Percy estates reemerged. For when Somerset's son was survived by a daughter, the dukedom passed to his cousins, but the Percy estates were inherited by the daughter. When she married Sir Hugh Smithson, he was happy to take the Percy name, the earldom was revived, and the Northumberlands, ignoring two generations of oblivion, took up Percy traditions with a vigor that struck Horace Walpole as ludicrous.[66]

The dukes of Newcastle provide the best example of a set of estates and its attached title managing to perpetuate itself through the recruitment of sons-in-law and nephews (see Figure 1.3). When the second duke of Newcastle died in 1691, he was survived by three daughters and his wife. He left his estate to his wife and then to his daughter Margaret, Lady Clare. His unmarried daughter Arabella was given £20,000, but to his daughter Lady Thanet he left nothing. Yet Lady Thanet was the only daughter to have borne a son. She and her husband therefore tried to have her father's will overturned on the ground of insanity. The challenge did not succeed, and 3 years later Lord Clare was made duke of Newcastle in consideration of his father-in-law's estates. When 17 years later this duke died, his marriage had produced only a daughter. Newcastle in his will had tried to divide his estates between his daughter and his sister's sons. His principal heir, Thomas Pelham, offered to marry his cousin as a means of keeping the estates together. She rejected the offer and married Lord Oxford. As Lady Oxford, she contested the will and eventually received all the estates of

---

[65]Cecil Aspinall-Oglander, *Admiral's Widow* (London: Hogarth Press, 1943), 116–117; Lady Granville, *Lord Granville Leveson Gower* II, 6.

[66]*Collins's Peerage*, II, 361–362; *Walpole*, IX, 264–265.

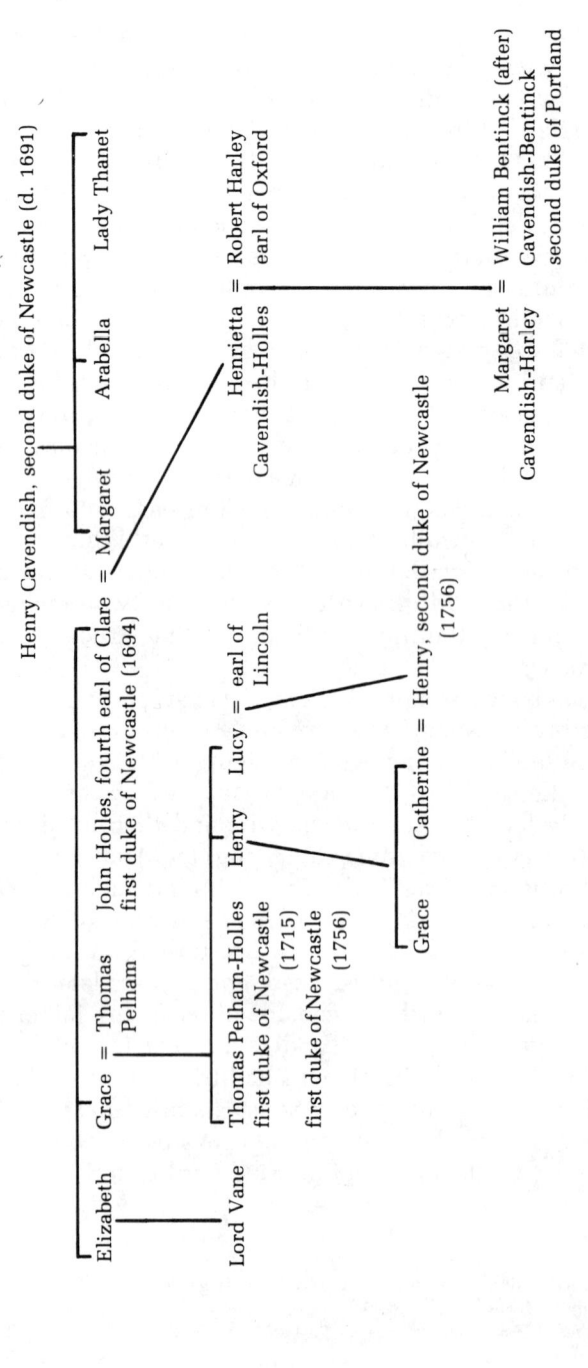

Figure 1.3 Pedigree of the dukes of Newcastle.

her mother's family as well as those purchased by her father after he had made his will. Her cousin, Thomas Pelham, got the remainder of the estates; he added his uncle's surname to his own and was created duke of Newcastle in consideration of his uncle's estates. (When Lady Oxford died without a son, she left her estates to her daughter and son-in-law on the condition that they take the name and arms of the first of these three dukes of Newcastle.) Duke Thomas had no children; his brother had only daughters. The duke therefore decided to settle his estate, his title, and his affection on his sister's son, the ninth earl of Lincoln.[67]

The earls of Lincoln were willing to be adopted, for they were a collateral branch who had inherited a title without the estate. The fifth earl had died unmarried and intestate. His title was inherited by his seventh cousin, but the estates went to his sister's children. For though he had made a will leaving the estates to his cousins in the event of their succeeding to the title, the will had been broken by the preparations he had made for his marriage. The sixth earl was therefore obliged to get by on his father's estate of £600. After his death, his widow and his minor son went to court against the nephews and nieces of the fifth earl; but they lost and were obliged to beg the king for a pension of £200. The seventh earl on reaching his majority could hope to improve his situation by marriage or by office. But as he had a penchant for independence, he refused to vote for the Peace of Utrecht and lost his chance of office. He was, nonetheless, rewarded, for Lord Torrington admired this stance and left him estates of £3400 a year. In the next reign he managed to get enough from office to buy land worth another £600 a year as well, but his estates were encumbered with three generations' worth of provisions for younger children, to the amount of £26,696. His marriage saved his house. His wife was Newcastle's sister. Her portion of £12,000 was settled on their younger children, and Newcastle was willing to settle his £24,000 a year on their eldest son. Financial solvency was achieved, but the independent identity of the earls of Lincoln was extinguished.[68]

Before the duke of Newcastle (of the third creation) could achieve his heart's desire, however, he was obliged to deal with the claims, under his own uncle's will, of his cousin and his brother. Lord Vane, his cousin, agreed to be cut out of the entail in exchange for £40,000;

---

[67]Nottinghamshire R.O., DD. 4P/43/3, 35/36, 60, 73, 62, 107, 155; DD.4P/35/50; N.U.L., Ne D 132; R. A. Kelch, *Newcastle*, (Berkeley: Univ. of California Press, 1974), 44.
[68]H.M.C., *House of Lords MSS, 1695–1697*, 260–262; W. A. Shaw, ed., *Calendar of Treasury Books*, **XXI**, Pt. 1, ccxxv, **XVII**, Pt. 1, 69; N.U.L., NeC 4386, 4271, 4386.

and while the negotiations were under way, Newcastle remarked that "if this thing can be done just and honourably, it will make me easy for my own life, and give me the satisfaction of settling my estate upon the only representatives of my own family and who must be in every respect the dearest to me." But his brother Henry Pelham held out for his daughters' rights, and the only way to get Lincoln in was to marry him to the eldest of them (his first cousin). Pelham evidently had felt no compulsion to favor a nephew over his daughters. Newcastle was furious and threatened to "break off all correspondence with my brother and his family," but he was obliged to agree. The marriage took place; Lincoln was loaded with enough sinecures to increase his income fivefold; and in 1756 Newcastle had a new patent issued that allowed Lincoln in 1768 to succeed as the second duke of Newcastle of the fourth creation.[69] Between 1690 and 1780 there were four dukes of Newcastle none of whom were father and son and each of whom held his title by a different patent of creation; yet all four were a single line joined by a continuity of connection to a set of landed estates. Because of the consequence of the Newcastle wealth, a son-in-law and two nephews had been recruited out of their own patrilineages into that of Newcastle and had had their family names changed or expanded. The earls of Clare, the Lords Pelham, and the earls of Lincoln had been devoured by the estates of the dukes of Newcastle. Names, titles, and estates—around these three entities the English aristocracy tried to construct the patrilineages that principally set apart their patterns of kinship from those of the majority of Englishmen.

Remarriage

It was difficult to act on patrilineal principles in a society so deeply cognatic in its structures. Where questions of property were not directly involved, aristocrats themselves entirely accepted cognatic principles. But the two sets of principles were always in potential conflict, and never more so than on the occasion of remarriage. (It is a pattern that appears in at least one other society, where conflicts over the care of the children of a first marriage were also the result of the difficulties in reconciling patrilineal and cognatic principles.)[70] In England the

---

[69]*Hardwicke*, I, 253, 362; N.U.L., NeD 132, NeC 4386.
[70]R. M. Keesing, "Kwaio Fosterage," *American Anthropologist*, LXXII, 1970, 755–775. In colonial America the conflicts between kindred and patrilineal inheritance activated by a second marriage could lead to accusations of witchcraft. Paul Boyer and Stephen Nissenbaum, *Salem Possessed* (Cambridge, Mass.: Harvard Univ. Press, 1974), Chap. 6.

opposition to second marriages often centered on the care of the children of the first marriage, but even when there had been no children, it was still present. Remarriage by a woman seemed to disregard patrilineal concepts of both real and symbolic property, and it could lead a man to disregard cognatic presuppositions. A woman who remarried raised the question of the extent to which she, her children, or her land and money had become the property of her husband's patrilineage. A man who remarried seemed to disregard the kindred of his wife into which he had been incorporated; he was likely to produce two competing sets of children rather than a unified sibling group; and he was also likely to try to reconcile these tensions by treating all his children simply as part of his lineage, as the product solely of his loins rather than as the joint effort of a pair of ancestors. In the end the only way out of the dilemma was not to remarry. For a man this was difficult because the patriarchal conceptions of the male role required him to have a woman as housekeeper or nurse if not as wife and mother. For both men and women the new ideal of domesticity made such forbearance more difficult since some people remarried because, as Mrs. Delany said, "they liked matrimony." But ultimately it is likely that domesticity with its stress on the romantic attachment of husband and wife, and on warmth between parent and child, strengthened the resolve of some individuals not to remarry. The improvements in the death rate may have meant, in any case, that fewer individuals were widowed. It is certain that from the sixteenth to the nineteenth century there was a continuous decline in the numbers that remarried. In the sixteenth century, a third of those who married once did so a second time; in the seventeenth century, the figure fell to 22%; and in the eighteenth century, it was down to 16%. It was a trend that continued into the nineteenth century when the percentage fell to 12 and it was only reversed when twentieth-century divorce brought the number of remarriages back up again to seventeenth-century levels.[71]

Women were certainly under heavy pressure not to remarry. But as widows they were, in fact, legally free to dispose of themselves and even of their property if they had had no sons or had made the right settlement. Such freedom in a woman was distasteful to the presumptions of patriarchy. An attempt was therefore made to use shame where the law was of no avail, and so it was said that a widow who remarried was foolish or unchaste: "The disconsolate widow Stafford," wrote that acid spinster Lady Isabella Finch, "has some intimates who say she looks pretty well by candlelight not so by daylight . . . ; however, as she

[71]Delany, I, 1861, 478; Hollingsworth, 22.

has a good jointure, I don't doubt but some gentleman that wants a maintenance will make her the compliment of saying she's a good night-piece, and the widows are such fools, I should not be surprised if she believes him." The unchasteness of the act could strike some quite hard. John Hill said that he had always looked upon such marriages "as a strange breach of female modesty, and have considered it as little more than a limited and authorised prostitution." Even those aristocrats who did not go so far as this still thought it "a spot" on a woman's chastity, though a small one, as the duchess of Leinster was told when she remarried.[72] But the foolishness of the act was the chief deterrent. There was an entire repertoire of tired stories about widows in heat whose property had been latched on to by a pair of fine young calves; they may be found sprinkled through the ballads of the day and the correspondence of Horace Walpole.[73] But it is likely that the aristocratic woman was spared the public demonstration against such marriages that the village boys of England (and France) were likely to impose on neighbors who had made such marriages.[74]

A woman who had children by a first husband and then remarried raised questions as to who possessed authority over those children. Was it the new husband who was her master, or was it the head of her first husband's patrilineage? There actually was in Parliament in 1697 a bill to deprive a mother of the guardianship of her children if she remarried, and only the prorogation of Parliament prevented its passage. But what Parliament could not encompass, husbands (to whom the law gave the ownership of children) did with no difficulty in their wills. The first duke of Ancaster appointed his wife joint guardian with his trustees of their children but only so long as she remained a widow, and his son did the same.[75] Even when there was no legal necessity, there could be family pressure to symbolically acknowledge where the ownership of the children lay. When the duchess of Leinster remarried, her brothers and sisters claimed to oppose it not on the ground that it was a mésalliance with a clergyman but that it would vex her eldest son, who had inherited his father's rights. She therefore felt obliged to

---

[72]S.C.L., WWM.M. 8(22); [John Hill], *On the Management and Education of Children ... by the Honourable Juliana-Susannah Seymour* (London, 1754), 16; *Leinster*, **III**, 115.

[73]*The Widow's Catechism* (London, 1709); Walpole, **IX**, 260, 401, **XVIII**, 481, **XXII**, 210-211.

[74]E. P. Thompson, "'Rough Music': le Charivari Anglais," *Annales: E.S.C.*, **XXVII**, 1972; N. Z. Davis, "The Reasons of Misrule: Youth Groups and Charivaris in Sixteenth-Century France," *Past & Present*, No. 50, 1971.

[75]H.M.C., *House of Lords MSS, 1695-1697*, 547-548, (cf. S.C. Cox, ed., *Reports of Cases ... in ... Chancery ... Collected by William Peere Williams* (London, 1826, 6th ed.), 3 vol., I, 702-706; Darcy v. Lord Holderness); Lincs. R.O., 5 Anc. 2/A/3, 2/A/36.

offer to give up the care of her younger children. Her brother, the duke of Richmond, said that "he would do it if he was *you*, and refuse it if he was your son; for that you ought to be delicate about putting them under the care of a father-in-law, and that William ought to be sure that they could be nowhere so well as with you."[76]

A dead husband's father could feel it necessary to step in and place a proprietary claim on his son's children. Lady Lewisham, the daughter-in-law of Lord Dartmouth, had been left the guardianship of her three children by her husband. When she made a second marriage to Lord North and took her children to live with her, she wrote a paper recommending that in the event of her death her children's affairs should be jointly managed by Dartmouth and North (who already had two children by his first wife). She then died from childbirth. At her death, Heneage Legge, Lewisham's brother, wrote to Dartmouth that the "young people desire to be left all together in the house for the present." North told Dartmouth that he had "never made any distinction between your Lordship's grandchildren, and my own children, and so I never mean to do it. I hope they will always look upon my house as their home, and me as a father. . . . There is such a fondness among our children that a separation would almost break their hearts." Legge explained to North that Dartmouth did not disapprove of Lady North's having joined him with North in the guardianship of his grandchildren; but North was evidently uneasy for he felt obliged to say that he was "sure her only motive for doing it was to give me opportunities of essentially showing the sincere affection and regard which she knew me to have for them." Dartmouth was actually jealous, and to him Legge had to say that he believed Lady North's "reason for naming your Lordship if you look back to the date of the paper, was for fear any of her own relations should interfere; though at the same time she thought and believed, they would of course belong to your Lordship, as undoubtedly they do; and she added Lord North to take as much trouble off your Lordship's hands as she could."[77]

Lady North had evidently distrusted her family, the Kayes, knowing the difficulty they had caused her father over her inheritance. But she was also concerned that Dartmouth's age would make it difficult for him to do much, and she had therefore provided that Legge should be the other guardian if the old man died. Chancery evidently agreed with her and appointed North and Legge as guardians. But there was no doubt that these children belonged to the patrilineage into which they

[76]*Leinster*, II, 128–129.
[77]Staffordshire R.O., D.1778, I, ii, 753, 761–762, 765.

had been born and that their mother's placing herself under a new husband's authority did nothing to change this.

A woman faced opposition to her remarriage even when she had had no children, for her dead husband's family could still feel that it had some rights either to her person or to her fortune. Presumably it was on the first ground that the Marlborough family opposed the remarriage of Lady Blandford, for she had certainly brought no fortune into the family. Mrs. Delany reported that Lady Blandford's father-in-law "Lord Godolphin and some of that family pretend to find fault with her, which they had *no right to do*, for they never used her well." They had indeed treated her miserably, and clearly Mrs. Delany thought that, therefore, they had no moral right (there was no question of a legal one) to keep her.[78]

A widow's remarriage raised other questions. Would she give to her new husband or to her new children property that belonged by right to her first set of children? Or, when there were no children, would she give to her husband property that should have been incorporated into her first husband's patrilineage? A widow was therefore encouraged to give up herself but not her property if she remarried. Bishop Hough calmed Lady Kaye's scruples by telling her, when she had thoughts of marrying the duke of Kent, that he saw "no reason why your Ladyship should not make him happy in yourself, provided it be upon terms in no way prejudicial to the children you are blessed with. Let him be contented to share your annual income, and no way to concern himself with your fortune." Another bishop, however, had once granted that it was difficult for a woman to make such a distinction and had allowed that in the case of mothers who hastened to make second marriages, "the necessity of going to law with them is more frequent and more urgent than with fathers, . . . because they seem to have translated their interest and affection to another family." To deal with such conflicts, the courts eventually established two rules: Any settlement that a widow made on her children before she began the negotiations for her second marriage could not be overturned by her new husband, whether or not he had had knowledge of it before the marriage. But any secret settlement that was made once the marriage negotiations had begun were held to deprive a husband of his just expectations and were therefore void.[79]

---

[78]*Delany*, I, 1861, 478; Green, *Sarah*, 279-282.

[79]Staffordshire R.O., D1778, I, ii, 614; William Fleetwood, *The Relative Duties of Parents and Children* (London, 1705), 71-73; Cox, *Peere Williams*, I, 358-361; *A General Abridgement of Cases in Equity* (London, 1793, 5th ed.), 2 vol., I, 58-59.

Even when there were no children in a first marriage, a woman's remarriage raised difficult questions of property, especially if her first marriage had been made for the purpose of continuing her own patrilineage. Lady Rockingham's first marriage had been to her first cousin. She was a great heiress worth £5500 a year, but as she bore Rockingham no children, full power over her fortune reverted to her.[80] She then married Lord Guilford as his third wife, and again she bore no children. But she willed him all her property, and when on her deathbed she told him what she had done, "he said he was sorry for it, but begged she would tell him who she wished he should give the estate to when he died, but she refused giving him an answer." Now Guilford knew that his wife's sister, who was long since dead, had had three children and that his wife had raised them, and he also knew that there were her Rockingham cousins to be remembered. But where Guilford might be embarrassed or in doubt, others were certain. Lady Mary Coke thought Lady Guilford had acted cruelly in leaving nothing to the son of Rockingham's sister, and she declared that her silence "conveys to me, whatever it does to his Lordship, that she meant he should return it to her family, but would not lay him under the obligation by telling her sentiments."[81] For Lady Mary felt that cousins (or perhaps nephews) should have taken precedence over a second husband. By contrast, Lady Exeter, who did not marry her cousin and only married once, solved the conflict between loyalty to her husband and to her patrilineage by leaving her fortune to her husband only for his life and then to her father's nephew.[82]

A widow's in-laws could make personal claims on her; the widower's in-laws had no such privileges, for in marriage a man kept full possession of himself. Nonetheless, his wife's relatives did object to his remarriage on the grounds that it showed a lack of feeling for his dead wife, that it exposed his children to the unkindness of a stepmother, and that it required his wife's servants to give their loyalty to a new mistress. Such objections had to be dealt with, but in the end the conceptualization of sexual roles that made it impossible for a man to care for children or manage a household overrode them all.

Of those men who remarried, at least half—those who already had a male heir—did so because they wanted a woman's company or needed a wife to care for their household and children. It was a decision that was quickly made in most cases, for a quarter of such men

---

[80]South Carlton, Monson MSS, G (100)/156; Kent R.O., U471.c.11.
[81]*Coke*, I, 105, 108.
[82]*Walpole*, IX, 184.

married at the end of their year's mourning, and by the end of the third year after a wife's death, more than half of those who remarried had already done so. (The rate of remarriage was slightly faster among those who remarried because they had not had an heir born to the first marriage.) Some men waited until their daughters had grown up and either needed a woman to take them into society or could move out on their own to avoid conflicts with a stepmother. If a man had not married within a decade of his wife's death, it was most unlikely that he ever would. "My wife has been dead eleven years," Lord Athenry wrote, "and seeing the mischief occasioned by second marriages in other families, I determined to live single."[83]

Some men, however, could not wait out even their year's mourning. Lord St. John's wife bore four children and died. Within less than a year St. John had decided to marry again, but he found himself facing the disapproval of Lady Rockingham, his wealthy and childless sister-in-law. "I do not wantonly marry," he tried to persuade her, "I want a companion if not a nurse, one at least that will submit to a crazy constitution." Lady Rockingham, however, wanted to be certain of several things: that the inheritance of the children and their mother's jewels were secure from the new wife, that St. John would honor his wife's memory by mourning her a full year, and that her maid was discharged. For Lady St. John on her deathbed had asked that if St. John "should marry again, which she was certain you would, that poor Dorrell might not stay to be used ill by the Lady or her servants." St. John, in fact, found Dorrell useful, and though she was "desirous and willing to stay," Lady Rockingham was adamant. With regard to the year's mourning, St. John said he hoped she would not think he acted with "either hurry without reason, or want of due regard to that person for whose memory I do solemnly declare I have and always shall have the highest esteem, love and veneration for, but sure since I do marry again, a fortnight can be of no sort of consequence to the dead, or in the least shock the living, since custom authorizes it frequently." But Lady Rockingham was shocked; she told him to "do what you like about it"; and in wishing him joy, she hoped he would "not be disappointed in Miss Clarke as you are determined to marry, but find every qualification in her that you can desire in woman, but there is no knowing a person's temper till one has lived some time with them."[84]

The adjustments in a household that a new wife made necessary were often dreaded. When Lord Carteret remarried he invited his

[83]H.M.C., *Dartmouth MSS*, III, 156.
[84]Kent R.O., U471.c.6.

Kindred and Patrilineage 57

mother to the ceremony, but she did not go; his four daughters, according to Mrs. Delany, "my Lord would not invite, for fear it would affect them too much, and has indeed acted with a tenderness towards them I did not imagine had been in his nature." But it was the behavior of the housekeeper that really scandalized Mrs. Delany. For when the new couple, accompanied by the bride's mother and sister, went home at night, they found that whereas his mother and his eldest daughter had gone to bed, the housekeeper was still up "to do honors and help to undress the bride. Have you a notion of that?" Mrs. Delany asked her sister. "I really thought Faver had loved poor Lady Carteret, but if she had, was it possible for her to go through such a scene."[85] To prevent such scenes and to deal with the "great disquiet" that could arise "when mothers-in-law and daughters are nearly of an age,"[86] it was sometimes judged best to arrange a new household for the young women. Lord Lindsey gave his daughters an increased allowance if they should choose to live elsewhere after they had lived for 5 years with a stepmother and were about to come of age. And the duke of Kent arranged at his second marriage that his two granddaughters should live with a housekeeper at Chelsea.[87]

Families found it difficult to believe that a man could manage such multiple ties, but Lord Sunderland was standing proof to the contrary. He fell passionately in love with each of his three wives. But as the second of these wives was a Churchill, it proved especially difficult to get the third. The duke of Marlborough had been relectant to give his daughter Lady Ann to Sunderland on the ground that Sunderland was disconsolate for the death of his first wife; but Sunderland solved the difficulty by falling passionately in love with Ann once he had seen her.[88] When it came her turn to die, she worried about her successor and asked him not to be "as careless of the dear children as when you relied upon me to take care of them. But let them be your care, though you should marry, for your wife may wrong them when you don't mind it."[89]

Sunderland did marry a third time, and justified it to his mother-in-law on the ground that it gave him "a companion and one to manage the concerns of his family in order to lessen his expenses." The wife, however, was only 15, and the duchess snorted that this "was marrying

[85]*Delany*, II, 1861, 294.
[86]*Hardwicke*, II, 582-583.
[87]Lincs. R.O., 5 Anc. 2/A/3/16; Godber, *Marchioness Grey*, 12.
[88]J. P. Kenyon, *Robert Spencer, Earl of Sunderland, 1641-1702* (London: Longmans, 1958), 267, 308, 313.
[89]Green, *Sarah*, 199-200.

a kitten; and really I do think it odd for a wise man at forty-five to come out of his library to play with puss." But the duchess's most pressing fear was over property. Her grandchildren, she thought, would yet "come to London behind coaches, as the Duke of Bolton's children did, to get shoes and stockings from their aunts," for another marriage meant "another brood of children—beggars with the titles of lords and ladies—that can have nothing but what he almost robs his former children of."[90]

That the first set of children would be beggared by the second was the great fear of a man's kindred by his first wife. A new wife, as Lord Hardwicke said, would be "contending for the interests of her own children, she will strive to gain more influence as old age and its concomitants may grow upon you; and everything which they acquire, your children will think themselves wronged and defrauded of." It was better, Lord Chesterfield told his relation in such a situation, if a man still felt the cravings of the flesh, to "follow the sacred example of the ancient Patriarchs, and take a handmaid." The other protection was to write provisions for a second marriage into the settlement of the first.[91]

This is what the Berties and most families did. But even with such safeguards, the situation could become acrimonious. In three of the four generations before 1750 the head of the Bertie family married more than once. In two generations a second marriage was necessary because the first had either produced no children or only a daughter. Two of the remarriages seemed to have been made for companionship rather than out of family necessity (see Figure 1.4). It was one of these that produced a large crop of younger sons whose interests created difficulties. The family settlements could not deal with them, and the matter had to be settled by an act of Parliament.[92]

It had become customary in the Bertie family to have the family settlements provide that the father and son making the agreement should each have the power to grant jointures not only to their present but also to their future wives. Powers to raise mortgages were also granted to father and son. While no specific use for this money was declared, it is clear that it was intended as provision for the children of a second marriage, for the sums were usually raised at the individual's death and added to his personal estate, and that estate was then divided among his younger children.

[90]Ibid., 208–209.
[91]Hardwicke, **II**, 582–583; Bonamy Dobrée, ed., *Letters of Chesterfield* (London: Eyre & Spottiswoode, 1932), 6 vol., **VI**, 2672, cf. 2575, 2668–2669.
[92]B.L., *The Case of His Grace Peregrine Duke of Ancaster*; Lincs. R.O., 5 Anc. 2/A/1/2, 2/A/2, 2/A/3/17, 2/A/3, 2/A/7, 2/A/6, 2/A/36; B. L., Private Act, 25 Geo II, c.3.

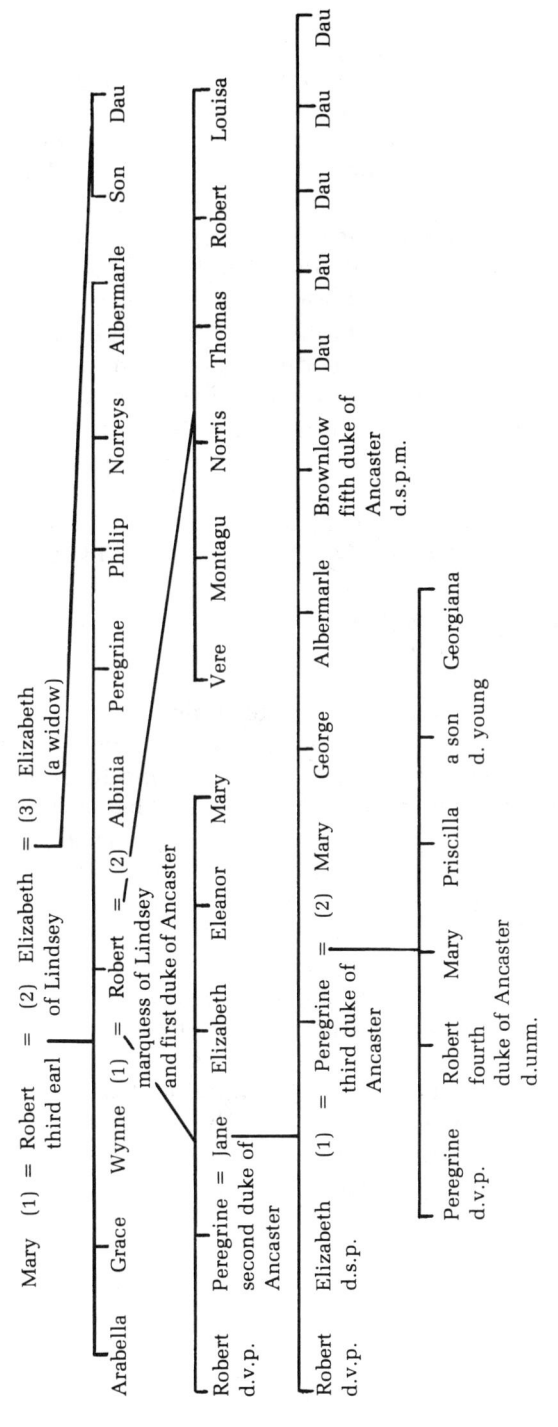

```
Mary (1) = Robert    = (2) Elizabeth    = (3) Elizabeth
              third earl       of Lindsey            (a widow)
                                  |
      ┌────────┬──────┬───────────┴──┬────────────────────────┬─────────┬─────────┬──────────┐
   Arabella  Grace  Wynne (1) = Robert = (2) Albinia  Peregrine  Philip  Norreys  Albermarle  Son  Dau
                              marquess of Lindsey
                              and first duke of Ancaster
                                  |
      ┌────────────┬──────────────┼──────────────┬─────────┐       ┌──────┬────────┬──────────┬──────┬──────┐
   Robert      Peregrine = Jane  Elizabeth    Eleanor    Mary    Vere  Montagu  Albermarle  Norris  Thomas  Robert  Louisa
   d.v.p.      second duke of
               Ancaster
                                  |
      ┌──────────────┬────────────┴──────────┐                                              ┌────┬────┬────┬────┬────┐
   Robert       Elizabeth (1) = Peregrine = (2) Mary   George   Albermarle              Brownlow  Dau  Dau  Dau  Dau  Dau
   d.v.p.       d.s.p.         third duke of                                            fifth duke of
                               Ancaster                                                 Ancaster
                                  |                                                     d.s.p.m.
      ┌──────────────┬──────────────┬──────────────┐
   Peregrine    Robert      Mary      Priscilla   a son   Georgiana
   d.v.p.       fourth                            d. young
                duke of Ancaster
                d.unm.
```

Figure 1.4 Pedigree of the dukes of Ancaster.

In this way the third earl of Lindsey in 1682 was allowed to give his wife a £500 jointure if he married a fourth time, and his son could give £1000 to a second wife. The father could raise £3000 by mortgage and the son £4000. In 1711 the next generation provided that the father could give a third wife £1500 and the son could give £2000 to a second, and that each could raise £15,000 by mortgage. But in 1735 the settlement between the second and third dukes was at once more detailed and more inefficient in these matters. It provided for jointures on remarriage in the usual way, but it innovated as regards the children of a second marriage. The second duke was given the power to raise £10,000 in the usual way. But the third duke's sons by a second wife were each to have £300 a year if there had been only two sons by the first wife, and £400 if there had been none. Unfortunately, there was nothing said about the daughters of a second wife. Therefore, when the duke was obliged to remarry to get an heir, he had to apply for an act of Parliament to rectify the omission since, as he said in his pointed argument "it would be almost in vain to attempt to enter into any treaty for a second marriage with a lady of suitable rank and quality, where no kind of provision could be made for the daughters of that marriage."

The act was necessary because the duke was only the life tenant of his estate, and the interests in the estate of his unborn son, his brothers, and his half uncles had to be protected. His son he proposed to compensate with £ 800 a year at his majority. His brothers, he clearly felt, had already been favored too much in his father's will, but he was willing to give them the power to appoint jointures and portions if they succeeded to the estates. To his half uncles, however, he proposed to give nothing, and they petitioned against the bill. The duke excluded them since he thought that as the children of a second marriage they had already gained too much. They had been willed annuities out of the personal estate of the duke's grandfather, and that personal estate had partly been raised by exploiting the marriage of the duke's father. But the greatest crime was that they had been included in the entail of the estates that had been brought into the family by the duke's grandmother and not by their own mother—this, as the duke's case said, was "still more extraordinary" for these men were "not at all of the blood of the said Dame Grace Wynne." The duke's grandfather had allowed his desire to treat all his sons as a single patrilineage descended from himself alone to get the better of the principles of cognatic inheritance. The judges appointed to consider the bill upheld the duke's claim. They ignored both the uncles and the brothers, agreed on his son's claims, and allowed him to provide for his daughters. Clearly, settlements could be used in an attempt to persuade a man's heir to ignore the logic of cognatic inheritance and by a father's authority establish that all his children, though by different wives, were equally related. But in this case it did not work, and it is doubtful that it would have in any. Nothing had been accomplished except the destruction of both generational cooperation and sibling solidarity.

Friendship, Patronage, and Connection

Through sibling solidarity and patrilineal ties an aristocrat expected to receive the effective support of his kinsmen. Matrilineal ties were less important. Indeed, one clergyman, put it that by the marriage of our parents "we are entitled to a double set of relations, whereas without it a child might very probably never be able to know any other than its mother, and that relation many times is capable of being but little service as to the affairs of the world."[93] The weakness of matrilineal ties was due not so much to the position of women as to the fact that when a woman was incorporated into her husband's patrilineage, she was regarded as lost to her own. For this reason Lord Warrington warned his heir not to give a daughter more than her fair share of the inheritance "out of a prospect of advantage that may thereby accrue to your family; yet if it be not certain, but only in probability, it is not advisable to do it: for your daughter may forget the stock from whence she sprang and keep all to herself."[94] Men, in addition, were disinclined to think that they could receive favors at a woman's hands. Edward Finch could ill endure to be told by his sister that "the women of the family had been the credit and indeed the support of it ... by the figure they had made in the world and the service they had done the brothers by having married people of fortune and interest who had brought them into Parliament." In protest he was led to say unavailingly that "he had not his seat from any brother-in-law." [95]

Finch's aid had come, however, not through his mother's relations but through his sister's husband. And brothers-in-law and brothers indeed formed the core of any man's kindred. For it was to the members of his kindred and to his patrilineal relations that an aristocrat turned when he wanted aid from his relations in the formation of a political connection in Parliament. In Queen Anne's time, Lord Orford was sup-

---

[93] John Ford, *Two Discourses Concerning the Necessity and Dignity of the Institution of Marriage* (London, 1735), 8-9.

[94] Henry, Lord Warrington, *Works* (ed. by J. Delaheuze) (London, 1694), 335.

[95] Romney Sedgwick, *The House of Commons 1715-1754* (New York: Oxford Univ. Press, 1970), 2 vol., II, 31.

ported by the sons of his father's brother and by their nephews and the husbands of their nieces.[96] Lord Nottingham (Edward Finch's father) called upon his brother and his patrilineal cousins, but his relationships through female lines were weaker. His mother's family gave him no support, and only a minority of the relations of his two wives and of his brother's wife were of any aid. Two of his daughters married men who were already his political supporters, and his niece's husband remained outside of his political circle.[97] Two Harley brothers married two Foley sisters, and together three Foleys and three Harleys, with their in-laws and their cousins, sat in Parliament.[98] In George III's day, the Duke of Newcastle wrote that "the Duke of Devonshire thought he owed it to himself and his family to require those immediately belonging to him, his brother and his brother-in-law, to resign their employments, which they both most readily did."[99] Lord North was supported by eight of his relatives. One of them was a matrilineal cousin, but the others were connections made either through his own marriage or the second and third marriages of his father.[100] Although it would be difficult to prove, there is perhaps enough of a direction in these examples to suggest that over the course of the century sibling ties were growing more important than patrilineal.

But though an aristocrat might call his political group his connection and thereby use for it the same collective word that he applied to his kinsmen as a whole, kinship was in truth never the chief organizing factor in eighteenth-century politics. For patrilineal relatives did not necessarily agree: Seven Berties were Tories and three were Whigs.[101] And brothers-in-law could survive political differences: Lord Weymouth, who belonged to the Bedford connection, married the sister of the duke of Portland, who was a pillar of the Rockingham group; and the one told the other that "I can assure you that the most mortifying circumstance in my life, has been the differences of opinion which has been between your Grace and me in politics, but at the same time I cannot despair that time and circumstances will at length bring us together."[102] It has been estimated for Queen Anne's reign that for

---

[96]Geoffrey Holmes, British Politics in the Age of Anne (London: Macmillan, 1967), 239, 494 n. 77.
[97]Henry Horwitz, Revolution Politics (Cambridge: University Press, 1968), 258–274; id., "Parties, Connections and Parliamentary Politics, 1689–1714; Review and Revision," Journal of British Studies, VI, 1966.
[98]Holmes, British Politics, 259; Robert Walcott, English Politics in the Early Eighteenth Century (Oxford: Clarendon Press, 1956), 67–68.
[99]Walpole, XXII, 97, n. 20.
[100]Ian R. Christie, The End of North's Ministry 1780–1782 (London: Macmillan, 1958), 200–201.
[101]Holmes, British Politics, 330.
[102]N.U.L., PwF 8751.

every family relationship between members of Parliament that involved a political association, there were three or four that did not.[103] But even when parties declined and the connection came into its own, it was almost never simply a family group. There might be a core of relatives, but the bulk of any major politician's followers consisted of those who had been brought into Parliament by his electoral interest or who followed him because they were his neighbors, or his friends, or were loyal to him because he had been the means of making their way in their professions. Patronage and friendship were more solid bonds than were blood or marriage. The English aristocracy in its function as a ruling elite did not to any great extent depend upon ties of kinship. When they did, they tended— in keeping with the dual organization of those ties into cognatic kindreds and patrilineages—to prefer either their brothers and their brothers-in-law or the brothers and nephews of their fathers to their maternal relations.

Most aristocratic men, from whatever cause, were part of some political connection. Aristocratic women had less occasion to organize themselves, but the countess of Huntingdon, in her attempt to convert the aristocracy to enthusiastic religion, gathered around herself a religious connection whose vital links were between women (although it had its male adherents).[104] Lady Huntingdon was herself converted by one of her husband's two pious sisters, but the other women who appeared most often in her circle were bound to her by friendship. Her friends, however, often came in groups of sisters and sisters-in-law. Her most intimate friends were Lady Luxborough, Lady St. John, and Lady Rockingham. The first two were sisters-in-law, the last two were sisters; and the three women often appeared with Lady St. John's husband and his brother Lord Bolingbroke. Lady Huntingdon recommended to one daughter of Lord Scarborough that she go to Whitefield's sermons, and the new convert soon brought her two sisters along. Lady Glenorchy persuaded her sister-in-law Lady Grey to take her husband and her daughters to Lady Huntingdon's chapel. Other parents brought their children: At one prayer meeting, the Duchess of Montagu came with Lady Cardigan, and Lady Hinchinbrooke brought her son. Lord Dartmouth, the most pious aristocratic man of his day, was introduced into the Huntingdon circle by his stepfather's third wife, Lady Rock-

---

[103] Holmes, British Politics, 328.

[104] [A.C.H. Seymour], The Life and Times of Selina Countess of Huntingdon (London, 1839), 2 vol., I, 14, 90, 97, 98, 20, II, 68, I, 108–109, II, 32–33, I, 17–18, 458–459, 30. There were also groups of clergymen attached to this connection (I,379), but given their lower social standing, their ties to the Countess were those of patronage. But, of course, what everyone shared in the group was a theological orientation.

ingham, whom we have already met with her sister and her brother-in-law in Lady Huntingdon's most intimate circle of friends. Dartmouth quarreled with his father's brother over religion; Lady Huntingdon effected a reconciliation through his aunt; and Dartmouth then brought aunt, uncle, and a slew of other relations to Lady Huntingdon's prayer meetings. The relationships between sisters and sisters-in-law were certainly important in building up the smaller units of this connection. The ties between husband and wife, or mother and child, were also important, though less so; it is likely that some husbands like Lord Chesterfield came only for entertainment; and Lady Huntingdon could convert neither her own husband nor her son. Occasionally a nephew brought an uncle, and Lord Lisburne met the countess through his cousin. But friendship was the primary tie between Lady Huntingdon and most of her converts.

Friendship and kinship were not, however, easily distinguished in the eighteenth century. The most protean word in an individual's vocabulary was "friend." It could mean one's close or distant relation, a patron or a client, an individual to whom one was tied by mutual sponsorship, or someone attached by warm affection. The phrase "friends and relations" might be used to distinguish affinal from consanguineal relations; it did not imply that a friend was not a relation. Friend was the most commonly used kinship term; a husband's best friend was his wife, and a child's, his parent. But "friend" was also the most frequently used term of individual social classification.[105] This linguistic usage was an old one in Europe. The Latin documents of the eighth century refer to the members of an individual's kindred as his *amici*, and a fifteenth-century young woman testified that she would not marry unless her *amici* consented. In Icelandic (and Scandinavian) usage *fraendi* were relations but also as many other people in society as possible.[106] But it is more to the point to notice a similar usage in Ethiopian society where *firra* for one group and *zamad* for another include relatives of all kinds as well as anyone whom one helps or is helped by. In short, it is likely that in traditional societies with cognatic kindreds, friendship, as understood in its instrumental rather than expressive sense, is the most important social tie. It has been suggested that in such societies it is especially easy to form personal friendships

---

[105] Harold Perkin, *The Origins of Modern English Society, 1780–1880* (London: Routledge & Kegan Paul, 1969), 45–48; Alan Macfarlane, *The Family Life of Ralph Josselin* (Cambridge: University Press, 1970), 43. See Appendix A for a general account of kinship terminology.

[106] D. A. Bullough, "Early Medieval Social Groupings: The Terminology of Kinship," *Past & Present*, No. 45, 1969, 12; Helmholz, *Marriage Litigation*, 50; G. W. Rich, "Changing Icelandic Kinship," *Ethnology*, XV, 1976, 10–11.

since they are not impeded by loyalty to organized lineages. But, of course, it is also the case that where kinship ties are so weak, one cannot rely on them alone and must reinforce them by those of neighborhood, friendship, and patronage—whether one is a twentieth-century peasant in Sicily or Ethiopia or an eighteenth-century English lord.[107] The difficulty in distinguishing friendship from kinship in eighteenth-century society ought not, therefore, to be taken as an indication of the importance of kinship ties but rather the contrary: The truly significant institution was friendship. It probably follows from this that our contemporary distinction between friend and relative has arisen from the discrediting of certain forms of overt patronage, and that kinship has therefore, in a sense, changed its nature and grown in importance as it has come to be distinguished from patronage and friendship.

The phrase "friends and relations" sometimes served to make a distinction (common in kindred societies) between an inner core and an outer fringe of relations. "Such as are parents, wife, children, I call and understand by the name of relations in this place," wrote William Ramesey. "All other kindred as brethren, uncles, cousins, etc. come either under the notion of superiors, equals, inferiors or friends." Ramesey's distinction was certainly accurate for the aristocracy in putting cousins and uncles at some distance from the center of an individual's concern. We have seen just such a tendency in the rules of incest and mourning. But he was inaccurate in regard to "brethren." Mrs. Delany stated the norm more clearly when she told her niece that she was "happy beyond expression to find the natural friendship subsisting among you and your brothers; no friends can be so truly depended upon as relations (if they are worthy and sincere)." A woman like Lady Sarah Bunbury, who had "reaped such surprising advantage" from "the pleasure, comfort and satifaction arising from the affection of brothers and sisters," looked upon "it as almost our first duty to cultivate so natural an affection." But Lady Sarah was writing this to a woman who had quarreled with her brother. A mother like Lady Spencer, writing to a married daughter, gave a less biased and more comprehensive statement of kindred obligations when she said that to "relations and connexions" more distant than husband, parents, and

---

[107]H. S. Lewis, "Neighbors, Friends and Kinsmen: Principles of Social Organization among the Cushitic-Speaking Peoples of Ethiopia," *Ethnology*, XIII, 1974, 156 n.6; D. N. Levine, *Wax and Gold* (Chicago: Univ. of Chicago Press, 1965), 76–77; E. R. Wolf, "Kinship, Friendship and Patron-Client Relations in Complex Societies," in Banton, ed., *The Social Anthropology of Complex Societies* (London: Tavistock, 1966); J. D. Freeman, "On the Concept of Kindred," *Journal of the Royal Anthropological Institute*, XCI, 1961, 212; Jeremy Boissevain, "Patronage in Sicily," *Man*, I, 1966, 18–33.

siblings, "nothing is required but what the goodness of your heart will naturally dictate—civility and attention to all."[108]

Mrs. Delany's statement confirms the point that friendship was the larger institution under which kinship was subsumed. Lady Spencer neatly reproduced the table of mourning degrees in her summary of obligation. But all three women by their fondness for describing these relations as "natural," remind us that what they are describing are the norms of kindred and not of patrilineal behavior. The point is reinforced by noting that natural or illegitimate children (as we shall see) were bound by the rules of incest but had no rights of inheritance. Out of natural kinship came the mutual assistance of friendship, the ceremonious observation of relationship, and the numinous boundaries of sexual taboo. Kindred structures, in other words, were so fundamental to this society that they were taken to be part of the natural order which men had given to them. By contrast, the world of the common law with its heavy patrilineal bias was contrived and man-made. But the looseness of obligations, the ease of social mobility, and the freedom of individual choice that can be seen to grow out of this natural world were unsatisfactory to aristocrats intent on maintaining the social and political place of their families. For them the legitimation of cousin marriage and the attempt to secure patrilineal rules of inheritance were preferable to sibling solidarity and the equality of the sexes. But their success was always partial. The conflicts that arose over remarriage and the difficulties in tying an estate to a title show this. In the end a compromise had to be made between kindred and patrilineal principles. Its result was enshrined in the family settlement of property, which is to be the subject of the next chapter. Through these documents a woman's kindred protected her property from her husband's demands, and everyone set out to balance the claims of younger children against their eldest brother. But in keeping with the bias of a kindred society, a man was ultimately free to decide what provision, if any, he would make for his children from the property that he had bought for himself or had inherited free of obligations.

Traditional English kinship was, by the eighteenth century, engaged, therefore, in a perpetual attempt to balance the conflicting claims of two systems. It was always to some degree an unequal struggle since patrilineal principles tended to operate much more within the narrow sphere of strictly familial concerns than did kindred principles. And it

---

[108]Murdock, Southeast Asia, passim; (William Ramesey), The Gentleman's Companion (London, 1672), 90; Delany, I, 1862, 83; Lady Ilchester and Lord Stavordale, The Life and Letters of Lady Sarah Lennox 1754–1826 (London: John Murray, 1902), 225; Chatsworth MSS, V, 62: 14 April 1775.

is a point worth reiterating that this was so even among the aristocracy; for though individual families within it might maintain their position through patrilineal means, the group as a whole in its activity as a political elite acted on principles of social organization that flowed far more from kindred structures. On the other hand, it is likely that until the eighteenth century, the patriarchal organization of domestic relations with its gerontocratic and masculine emphases had helped to weight the scales in favor of patrilineage. But, of course, from the eighteenth century onward it was the case that the increasingly egalitarian relations between men and women and parents and children (that the second half of this volume will describe) made the position of a patrilineal ideology more and more difficult to maintain.

An English lord, holding as the eldest son of his line a hereditary seat in Parliament and enjoying the produce of his great estate, might seem to have been the very embodiment of patrilineal power. But this is largely an illusion. This English lord inherited his title and his estate only because he was his mother's son as well as his father's. He felt himself as equally bound to the parents and the siblings of his mother and his wife as to those of his father. He mourned his mother as fully as he did his father, and he mourned longest of all for his wife. The women among his contemporaries whom he felt least free to marry were those to whom he had given the standing of sisters. The men on whom he most depended were his brothers by blood and marriage. But for all of them, whether brother or sister, father, mother or wife, he had no greater accolade than to call them his best friends. For whenever he tried to effect anything with his power among them, or among his other acquaintance, it was always to the bond of friendship that he first appealed.

Figure 2.1 Portrait of Lord Chancellor Hardwicke by T. Hudson. As chancellor he limited the rights of younger children to marry as they pleased, but as a politician he used his connections to provide for the children of the aristocratic family he founded. Copyright photograph from the National Portrait Gallery, London. Reproduced by permission.

II

Settlement and Marriage

Parents in the eighteenth century would have said that their duties to their children were completed once they had settled them. It was a linguistic usage that went back to the early sixteenth century, and it could mean either securing a marriage for a child or arranging for a son's steady employment.[1] For aristocrats it usually meant the former. A man like Chesterfield thought the usage inelegant and sneered at fathers who were "impatient till their boobies come home to be married, and, as they call it, settled." But others used it with no self-consciousness. When the duke of Portland and his sister set about canvassing matrimonial prospects for a friend, she remarked that "you seem anxious to have him settled"; and when her own marriage was being discussed, she wrote that "my Father ... I dare say, would

---

[1]*Oxford English Dictionary*, s.v.settle, V, 3,5,6, et s.v. settlement, **I**, 1, b,c, **II**, 2, a.

have no objection to my being settled."[2] But aristocrats could not be settled without a settlement—a word that had come into vogue at the Restoration to describe the legal disposition of family property. (At the same time it also came to mean the right of the poor to be supported by the parish when they had no family property.) When such a settlement was finally made, it took a child as much from under its parents' wings as did marriage, and made him independent—"what I design to settle on the children," Lord St. John wrote, "will make them quite independent of me." St. John was speaking of his younger son and daughter, and one of his difficulties was to judge what was their proper share of the family property. For it was also his "opinion and ever will be, that where the bulk of the estates and the honors descend, there all helps should be given; I am for putting the head of a family as clear and independent as possible."[3] The settlement's most important business was therefore to balance the claims of family continuity and greatness embodied in the position of the eldest son against a satisfactory provision for younger children and for wives; to mediate between the conflicting claims of kindred and patrilineage.

The family settlement was, more often than not, a marriage settlement made for the eldest son. The negotiations that produced it were conducted among the members of the inner core of the heir's kindred, that is, among his father and his father-in-law, himself, and his wife. The eldest son received most of the estates, but he could not sell them, and his power to mortgage was severely limited. His unborn younger sons were given fixed inheritances in money which were freed from the whim of either himself or their eldest brother. These inheritances could later be augmented from unsettled family property, and a second son was often given an estate of his own by his father or his maternal grandfather, or by an uncle. Daughters in the eighteenth century were also given fixed inheritances rather than the negotiable dowries that had prevailed in the seventeenth. But daughters were not normally allowed to inherit land. Instead, when there were no sons they were given larger inheritances in money, and the land went to an uncle or a male cousin. In these ways the tendency in kindred systems to expect equal inheritance among all children was balanced against the patrilineal concern for corporate identity across the generations. But the patrilineage was usually a minor concern of the settlement, for the

---

[2]Bonamy Dobrée, ed., *Letters of Chesterfield* (London: Eyre & Spottiswoode, 1932), 6 vol., V, 1884; N.U.L., PwF 4531, 4499b.
[3]Kent R.O., U471, c.6.

settlement had to be renewed in each generation; instead, the greatest effort was put into the division of property within the sibling group. The settlement was drawn up by a man's kindred, and its principal aim was to secure sibling solidarity and to avoid generational conflict.

The family settlement in the eighteenth century did not, however, simply make stronger the claims of kindred over those of patrilineage. It also made greater allowance for romantic rather than arranged marriages, for domesticity over patriarchy. For the easiest means by which patriarchy could control a child's marriage was to have his inheritance depend on a settlement made at his marriage rather than at the marriage of his father. The typical family settlement, which guaranteed a child his inheritance no matter what his behavior, allowed for greater freedom of marriage. But the battle over romance was waged over the marriage of daughters rather than of sons, for a woman had more to lose since she took her husband's social standing. The financial independence of a daughter will not, however, explain the willingness of her parents that she should marry for love. It is rather the other way round. Aristocrats in the eighteenth century were viewing marriage as a means to maintain social status (incorporation) rather than to improve it (alliance) as we have already seen with cousin marriage. Provided a daughter married within her social class, her choice of a husband could be left to her. Divorce, as we shall see, similarly became possible because marriage was no longer so much a question of property. And in 1753, at the beginning of the generation in which most aristocratic marriages were made for love, there was finally passed an act that gave parents control over the marriages of their minor children. The act was opposed on the ground that it increased patriarchal power and served the interests of aristocratic patrilineages, but in truth it passed for quite different reasons. There had been attempts at such an act for at least two generations. They had always passed in the Lords but failed in the Commons. And they seem to have failed there primarily because younger sons were jealous of their right to run off with an heiress and by this means repair the disabilities that primogeniture had inflicted on them. By 1753 this argument had lost its appeal. The position of younger sons had improved; but, even more, it had become distasteful, even to them, to use marriage for financial gain. Marriage had become, instead, the cornerstone of domesticity. In marriage and the family settlement, one will therefore find the best evidence of the equilibrium that was struck between kindred and patrilineage, domesticity and patriarchy; but one will also find that in the years between 1690 and 1780, generation by generation, domesticity was winning out over patriarchy in the making of a marriage and that since the marriage settlement was negotiated by a man's kindred, so was kindred gaining ascendancy over patrilineage.

Settlement, Patrilineage, and Domesticity

The family (or strict) settlement was the means by which aristocratic families undertook to bypass the claims on their land that the rules of intestate inheritance gave to their more distant relations; but it also relaxed the prohibition of English law against perpetual entails;[4] and at the same time it limited the powers of mortgage and alienation that the eldest son possessed. It made for a degree of economic flexibility, which a more conservative mobility like the Prussian one did not have;[5] and at the same time it made it unlikely that a family with a hereditary role in the government would suddenly be impoverished because of an extravagant heir. It was a system devised by three or four generations of conveyancers whose precedents were written into the law by a series of cases in Chancery which run from the duke of Norfolk's in 1681 to the duke of Marlborough's in 1763. These cases were usually settled by an appeal to the House of Lords, for the Lord Chancellors were anxious that the aristocracy themselves ratify all far-reaching decisions about land ownership.[6] The upshot was that the common law rules of inheritance had by the eighteenth century become "a matter of curiosity than of any real use" since it was possible for an individual to contravene them in his will and for a family to do the same by its settlements.[7]

Under strict settlement it was possible for a man to settle his estates on himself for life, then on his living heir and on any other living

---

[4]The relevant literature is: H. J. Habakkuk, "Marriage Settlements in the Eighteenth Century," *Transactions of the Royal Historical Society*, **XXXII**, 1950; G. E. Mingay, *English Landed Society in the Eighteenth Century* (London: Routledge & Kegan Paul, 1963); Eileen Spring, "The Settlement of Land in Nineteenth-Century England," *American Journal of Legal History*, **VII**, 1964; Christopher Clay, "Marriage, Inheritance, and the Rise of Large Estates in England, 1660–1815," *EcHR*, **XXI**, 1968. For the sources on which I depend for my account of family settlements, see Appendix B.

[5]Frederick the Great tried to get his nobility to adopt a system under which the head a family could administer and mortgage the family estates free from the control of his relations. See Albert Goodwin, ed., *The European Nobility in the Eighteenth Century* (New York: Harper & Row, 1967), 95–98.

[6]A. W. B. Simpson, *An Introduction to the History of the Land Law* (London: Oxford Univ. Press, 1961), 93–98, 195–224; D. E. C. Yale, ed., *Lord Nottingham's Chancery Cases* (Selden Society,1951–1961), 2 vol., **I**, lxxxii–xc, **II**, 904–914; R. H. Eden, ed., *Reports of Cases in ... Chancery from 1757 to 1766* (London, 1827), 2 vol., **I**, 403–424.

[7][Robert Robinson], *A Discourse Concerning the Laws of Inheritance in Fee* (London, 1736), vi–vii.

persons, and finally for a period of 21 years beyond the death of his heir or of the last living person (a remainder man) named in the settlement. This meant that he had limited what could be done with his land for his lifetime and for that of his heir, and until his unborn grandson came of age. The system prevented a man who had been granted a life interest in an estate from making that interest absolute. It did this by granting to trustees the right to maintain the interests of a man's unborn sons. When a son was eventually born, he acquired a vested interest in the estate and could bar the entail, but he was unable to draw any income (save by exorbitant mortgage) from that estate until he came into it at his father's death. A father therefore had the power to induce his son to consent to the son's being made, in turn, a life tenant of the estate in exchange for a present income. This, however, is to make it sound unduly like a contest of wills, for fathers and sons were usually quite ready to resettle the estates when the son reached his majority or married. It is, indeed, one of the most decisive indicators of family solidarity that can be produced, though it would be incorrect to think that there was not sometimes hard bargaining, or that a son did not on occasion later feel that his father had taken undue advantage of his youth and inexperience.

The settlement could be made, then, at either a son's majority or at his marriage. In the families I have studied it was more often done at marriage than not, and in some cases a settlement made at majority was so done as to require a new one at marriage. (If an heir married before his majority, it was necessary to apply for an act of Parliament enabling him to make a settlement.) A settlement made at a majority provided a son with an income during his father's lifetime; it made provision for actual or probable younger children; it appointed jointures for probable widows, and pin money for wives; and it gave powers to receive rents and to raise mortgages within agreed limits. A settlement made at marriage would do all these things; but it would sometimes indicate as well the uses to which a wife's fortune was to be put; it might also do nothing more than activate powers created in a previous settlement; and it was always certain that the bride's father would expect to be a party to these negotiations.

A settlement could be made by a man's will as well. In a will, lands that had been inherited in fee or lands that had been bought since the last settlement could be settled, and in this case the settlement was sometimes on a younger son. A man often took this opportunity to increase a faithful wife's jointure. He might apportion among his younger children the lump sum appointed for them by a previous settlement, and he could also choose to increase their portions out of his personal estate. And, finally, out of that personal estate (and often fatally for the peace of his family) he provided for the children of his second marriage when he decided that their mother's fortune was not a sufficient provision for them.

An heir, then, enjoyed the chief part of his family's revenue, but he could not sell the sources of that revenue and take all for himself. He could grant leases for a number of lives or for 21 years, but he was seldom allowed to take fines.[8] For a fine was a lump sum paid by a tenant upon taking out his lease that proportionately decreased his rent; and it was felt that such a fine constituted part of an estate's capital and that one heir ought not to be allowed to waste capital at his successor's expense. This heir was in aristocratic families almost invariably the eldest son, who inherited the family title and the right to sit in the Lords; for in the 30 families I have studied closely there is only a single instance of an eldest son's being disinherited.

But the family settlement was not simply an arrangement between father and son; it was also the result of a long and intense negotiation between a man and his father-in-law. Lord Rockingham reminded his heir that "your settlements if you continue in the same mind must be settled by ourselves and then proposed to the Lady—you may see by Lord Granby's affair, this is a work of time, his has taken up more than a whole year."[9] For a woman's father was anxious not only that she should be protected but also that her children should inherit her husband's land; so that the settlement family was a three-generational unit composed of parents and parents-in-law, husband and wife, and the heir and his siblings.

The insistent presence of a father-in-law could be resented on two grounds. First, he could seem to be attempting to expropriate another man's patrilineage by arranging the inheritance of his land; and, second, his insistence on a guaranteed inheritance for his grandchildren could be taken as an interference with a father's power to reward or punish the virtue or disobedience of his children. The head of a great house could be obsessed with the idea of making an eldest son and quite oblivious that others did not share his obsession. Lord Hertford helped to prolong to 8 months the negotiation of his younger son's marriage when he tried to insist that a small estate of £250 a year be

---

[8]The only two estates on which I have found fines levied were those of Lord Arundell of Wardour (Private Act: 30 Geo II, c. 23) and those that Lady Lymington inherited from her father John Conduit (22 Geo II, c. 43).

[9]S.C.L., WWM. M8-76. Lady Weymouth frequently complained to her brother about the length of time lawyers took to draw up settlements (N.U.L., PwF 8747 et passim).

settled on an eldest son, although all the rest of the young couple's fortune, since it was in stocks and cash, was settled equally on all the children.[10]

The best example of these difficulties is the negotiation between Lord Dorchester and Edward Wortley for the hand of Lady Mary Wortley Montagu. Lord Dorchester began from the position that he had "no inclination to see his grandchildren beggars," and therefore expected that Wortley would settle his estate on his daughter's son. Wortley objected that if he were required to settle land that was worth much more than the portion in money that his wife brought, "nothing like a proportion between the land and the money" would be observed and the reversion of the estate would be hers and not his. Besides, "where two live well together 'tis a thousand to one that her heirs will have the greatest of what he has." But Dorchester required a certainty that his grandson should have all; whereas Wortley told Lady Mary that "if I marry I must have more liberty over my estate than your father seemed willing I should." In any event, after several months of this, Wortley and Lady Mary cooled toward each other. Dorchester arranged another marriage, but Lady Mary refused on the ground that she could not love the man. Wortley renewed his suit, was told that it was now hopeless to approach her father, ran away with her, and married her without a settlement. At his death, Wortley was free of restrictions and did just what Dorchester had feared: Disapproving of his heir, he left the bulk of his estate to his daughter and her second son.[11]

In his complaints about her father, Wortley had a less than eager audience in Lady Mary. She explained that she had no hand in making settlements: "People in my way are sold like slaves, and I cannot tell what price my master will put on me." Wortley was incredulous and asked, "was you ever free in any other family where discourses of that kind did not make up a great part of the conversation?" But Lady Mary was adamant, and romantic, and declaimed that "'tis indifferent to me whether I have £10,000 or £50,000, and shall never quarrel with my family by pretending to direct them in the matter." And when she did say that she agreed with his arguments, she cautioned him that "my thinking you in the right will not persuade others that you are so."[12]

---

[10]Warwickshire R.O., CR 114/III/7/viii. The lawyer charged £ 50.6.2 to draw up the settlement. It was quite common when younger children married each other to settle their fortunes in money equally on all children. See, e.g., Herts R.O., Panshanger MSS, 8379; Staffs. R.O., D. 539/D/1/2.

[11]*Lady Mary*, I, 51, 78–79, 125, 135, *et passim*; Robert Halsband, *The Life of Lady Mary Wortley Montagu* (New York: Oxford Univ. Press, 1960), 275–276.

[12]*Lady Mary*, I, 64, 67, 69, 80.

As an outlet for his feelings Wortley wrote out a number of his objections to Dorchester's demands. He lent the notes to his friend Steele, who used them in two numbers of *The Tatler* (18 July and 10 September 1710).[13] In his notes he set down more clearly than in his letters to Lady Mary his objections to her father's proposals.[14] His strongest was that settlements catered to the aristocratic desire of founding a great family that would last, and that it did so at the expense of those presently alive. For settlements did more than "settle a competency on each child"; they were "intended to preserve a family [and] to keep up a race," and this despite the irony that "the father makes himself miserable for fear his son should not be a great man, whereas the first of a great family has commonly the most worth." A woman's father by this means could find an alternative way of getting an estate for his family, and a citizen who married his daughter to a great family could achieve his desire "to continue his estate to her heir and keep up his family." Wortley conceded that it was perhaps useful to have settled estates with the nobility "where a part of the government is placed" but that "in all other cases it is ridiculous to think of keeping up a family, or for a man to value himself for being of any race, unless there are particular privileges assigned it." Primogeniture he thought similarly vain, for it prevented a father from expressing his affection for his younger children or from rewarding a faithful wife. This hope of continuing a family through settlement and primogeniture turned marriage into a "sale of the women" in which each "makes a kind of auction of herself." If there were no bargaining the "only question would be whether the two parties liked each other" and "all would marry for liking." Love between husband and wife, and equality among children, were better than founding a family; kindred and domesticity should win out over patrilineage. It is an attractive picture, but the central fact that remains is the patriarchal power. Wortley wanted to be free to reward and punish his wife and children. The economic independence that pin money gave a wife in marriage was disapproved of on the ground that it "put matrimony out of countenance"; and settlement he said, treated a man like a child for it acted as though he were "fit to be under guardianship" and unfit "to be at his own disposal."[15] Settlement did indeed cater to patrilineal pride but it also put down patriarchy; and it may be that even as romantic love loosened the knees

[13]R. P. Bond, "Mr. Bickerstaff and Mr. Wortley," in Henderson, ed., *Classical, Medieval and Renaissance Studies* (Rome: Edizioni di Storia e Letteratura, 1966), 2 vol., II.
[14]Sandon Hall, Wortley MSS, VII, 130–134, 258–261.
[15]Sir John Guise, probably under *The Tatler's* influence, had similar ideas a little later. See G. Davies, ed., *Memoirs of the Family of Guise* (Camden Society, 1917), 140–141, 152–153.

of aristocracy, it tightened the hold of patriarchy on the wives and children, the love of whom it sang.

The Eldest Son and His Wife

An eldest son was the head of his family and as such was expected to marry and provide an heir, to administer the family settlements under normal circumstances, and to secure the interests and cooperation of his younger siblings. He was, as one admiring uncle said, "the stallion of our family,"[16] and if he were an only son he was "indispensably obliged to propagate his name."[17] But if he had younger brothers he could attempt to delegate this duty. Lord Shaftesbury declared that he did not care to make himself "a slave to a great house and family"; he professed to be willing to treat his brother as if he had "been my elder son." Finally, however, when his brother would not marry "to honour and support his family," he did so himself, produced an heir, and died.[18] The duke of Bedford, who under his mother's influence came a virgin to his marriage, decided "to let his estate go to his brother, rather than go through the filthy drudgery of getting an heir to it."[19] In addition, if an eldest son could produce only daughters, his younger brother might come to the rescue. "Mr. Yorke has no son," wrote a third son to the second. "If he is ten years between every child, with the chance of girls, our hopes are in you."[20]

An eldest son knew that once his heir was produced, his most pressing duty was to defend his patrimony, which meant defending his settlement. "My armor is made of parchment," Lord Orrery wrote, "my head-piece and breast-plate are my mother's marriage settlement."[21] And he was obliged not only to defend it from strangers but to administer it for the sake of his siblings. This could lead to contentiousness. Lord Winchilsea gave up the thought of an "active life" because, as he told his father, "I always look upon myself as being the eldest, to be the slave of the family." As he managed to produce only daughters for whom portions had to be found, he frequently, after his father's death, fought with his brothers and sisters over the payment of their annuities and legacies. His brother Henry threatened to go to law against him and

---

[16]W. D. Cooper, ed., *Savile Correspondence* (Camden Society, 1858), 133.
[17]*Orrery Papers*, I, 63.
[18]Benjamin Rand, *Life . . . of Shaftesbury* (London: Swan Sonnenschein, 1900), 317, 405–407, 410, 428.
[19]*Lady Mary*, II, 55.
[20]*Hardwicke*, II, 182–185.
[21]*Orrery Papers*, I, 113.

his sister Isabella finally took away her portion from him and bought an annuity from her brother-in-law, Lord Rockingham. Rockingham, as a trustee of the settlement, was frequently called on to make peace.[22] For trustees, in general, were crucial to family peace. It was an office that Gibbon considered as "an essential duty of social life"; and it was one usually discharged without fees; for the law looked upon trusts "as honorary, and a burden upon the honour and conscience of the person intrusted, and not undertaken upon mercenary views."[23]

When neither family solidarity nor the mediation of trustees were of any avail and resort was made to the courts, an eldest son was prevented from using his privilege as a peer to obstruct his siblings from receiving their legacies or portions.[24] His siblings found, however, that though they had ultimately a legal protection against their eldest brother, he had an automatic claim upon their respect, while they were obliged to work at keeping his good will. "For an elder brother of a family," Lady Sarah Lennox explained, "is *commonly* reckoned to be looked upon with respect merely because he is the head of the young part of the family; and though he may treat his brothers and sisters with unkindness and deserve great blame, yet he seldom is looked upon as 'obliged in decency' to take any notice of any of his family more than common civility, if he don't like them."[25] It was not a doctrine that won automatic assent, but that its truth ultimately had to be accepted shows how much patrilineage could conquer sibling solidarity. But the provision guaranteed by a settlement ensured that younger siblings were not usually subject to the merest whim of an eldest brother. Settlement always mediated between the claims of kindred and patrilineage.

An eldest brother might seem capricious and indecent to his younger siblings, but he could regard himself as the slave of his family's interests. For he was, after all, only the tenant for life of the estates, and the power they gave to him to live like a lord was quite circumscribed. He certainly could not sell a settled estate without an act of Parliament, and after 1706 all such acts were carefully scrutinised by two judges to insure that they did not destroy the rights of a man's

---

[22]Pearl Finch, *History of Burley-on-the-Hill* (London: Bale & Danielsson, 1901), 2 vol., I, 177; S.C.L., WWM. M8(45) et *passim*.

[23]J. E. Norton, ed., *The Letters of Edward Gibbon* (London: Cassell, 1956), 3 vol., II, 31–32; J. T. Atkyns, ed., *Reports of Cases . . . in . . . Chancery in the Time of Lord Chancellor Hardwicke* (London, 1794), 3 vol., II, 60.

[24]H.M.C., *House of Lords MSS, 1692–1693*, 6, *1697–1699*, 420.

[25]Lady Ilchester and Lord Stavordale, *The Life and Letters of Lady Sarah Lennox 1745–1826* (London: John Murray, 1902), 240.

family.²⁶ A life tenant could mortgage an estate only for the sums his family had agreed upon at his marriage, or for the sums he allowed himself at his son's marriage. These powers of mortgaging were negotiated between father and son, and a son did not always feel that the arrangement had been equitable. The third duke of Ancaster complained that at his marriage his father was given the power to charge the estates with £10,000 in addition to the £10,000 his own father had allowed him; that in exchange the third duke was given £1002 a year for his maintenance, or that in effect he had bought from his father an annuity at 10 years' purchase, but that his father had in turn not allowed him "to charge the estate with a single sixpence." The duke sought the only relief available to him and persuaded Parliament to pass a private act in his favor.²⁷

There was always the possibility, however, of borrowing on the life interest in an estate. This the third duke of St. Albans did, but he eventually found himself in over his head. He applied to Parliament to be allowed to break his family settlements, to place the bulk of his income in the hands of trustees while he lived abroad on an annuity, and to sell some estates. He had no sons of his own, but his uncles and cousins (who eventually inherited the title) had to be satisfied. They evidently consented to the arrangements when some of the estates were retained in settlement. And 9 years later, these arrangements were changed in the duke's favor when the trustees had paid off all the extraordinary debts and there remained only the mortgages authorized by the settlements of the duke and his father, since on these he was only obliged to keep down the interest.²⁸

The knowledge that an estate was entailed often made it quite difficult to receive credit even from tradesmen. When, because of an incompetent steward, Lord Cowper found that he was living £ 1000 beyond his annual income, his old tutor wrote to him that he was "ashamed to tell you what I have heard, since I saw you, that some of your tradesmen threaten. You may easily believe them dissatisfied and impatient to be paid: they know your estate to be entailed and that in case of death they must trust to my Lady's honour."²⁹ Lord Torrington explained to his friend and debtor the duke of Portland that his debts to tradesmen were "not very great as my credit amongst them is not very high."³⁰

²⁶H.M.C., *House of Lords, 1704–1706*, xxxix.
²⁷B.L., *The Case of his Grace Peregrine Duke of Ancaster*.
²⁸B.L., Private Act, 7 Geo III, c.6, 16 Geo III, c. 110.
²⁹Hertfordshire R.O., Panshanger MSS, Bx 19, St. 226: 13, 23 September 1733.
³⁰N.U.L., PwF 2379.

A dutiful son, though not legally obliged to do so, undertook to pay his father's debts. Lord Cardigan was at great pains to see that his nephew the duke of Richmond paid the debts of his father, telling him that "it would redound to your honour to see your father's debts paid" and that "the sooner it is done, the more happy you will be in all respects, for no man of honour can be easy when he sees families ruined for want of their just due."[31] There were, of course, sons capable of being deaf to such pleas. Lord Jersey drove his mother to distraction when he refused to pay her husband's debts; she told her friend and trustee Lord Dartmouth that she believed "my son has a mind to expose his father's memory." She tried repeatedly to get the lord treasurer to persuade the queen to pay her husband's debts, and she eventually went to court against her son, as she told her trustee, "to help the creditors which he would cheat."[32]

A father, however, did not necessarily leave all of the family estates settled; he might trust instead the discretion of his heir. Lord Huntingtower had one-quarter and the duke of Montagu one-half of their estates unsettled.[33] The greater part of the estates of the dukes of Beaufort remained unsettled for 50 years, since the fourth duke left his son £14,350 a year in settled estates but £20,000 a year unsettled.[34] Sometimes, as with Lord Monson, almost the whole was settled but £1000 a year was left free for some special purpose.[35] At other times, a father, like the duke of Ancaster or Lord Gower, arranged that once his heir came of age, the two of them should have the power, as long as both were alive, to make and break the settlements as they jointly chose.[36] But a father with full power over his estate could punish as well as reward. Lord Willoughby, as a younger son, unexpectedly succeeded to title and estate; he broke the entail on the estate, and when his eldest son displeased him, he took the estate away from the title and settled it on his younger son.[37]

But it was not only his father's property over which an heir had limited control. The property his wife brought was also usually settled. If it was not settled, there were two rules that applied, one for her land and another for her fortune in money. A husband was entitled to the rents and profits of his wife's real property as long as the marriage

---

[31]Earl of March, *A Duke and his Friends* (London: Hutchinson, 1911), 2 vol., I, 80, 137–137.
[32]Staffs. R.O., D 1778/ I, ii, 328, 3–8; see also, *Walpole*, XXXII, 287.
[33]*Walpole*, XXI, 439, IX, 94.
[34]Staffs. R.O., D.593/C/22/4.
[35]Lincs. R.O., Monson MSS, 3/XXV, 489.
[36]Staffs. R.O., D. 593/C/22/4, C/723/1, C/23/2.
[37]Shakespeare's Birthplace Trust: Willoughby de Broke MSS.

lasted. At his death she or her heirs regained entire possession, but at her death, he was entitled to the land for the remainder of his life if they had children. A wife's personal property, on the other hand, came at marriage into her husband's absolute possession. But the terms of most family settlements modified these rules in one way or another.[38]

Most women who married peers brought fortunes in money (£25,000 on the average) rather than in land. In a sample of 65 such marriages, only 14 women had portions mainly or entirely in land, though some of them did inherit land after their marriages. A wife's estate was usually settled on her husband's family, but there could be special provisions that brought the arrangements closer to the common-law rules. When Lady Rockingham married, she brought her cousin £5500 a year in land, and it was provided that if they had no sons the land came back to her; if they had daughters both of their estates would be charged for their portions.[39] But the duchess of St. Albans was allowed, if she had no children, to leave only some of her estates as she pleased, and the duchess of Bolton was allowed to settle £1000 a year of her estates as she wished.[40] When Jane Brownlow married the duke of Ancaster she brought £10,000 and nearly £800 a year in land. The land was settled first on her sons and then on her daughters, but if she outlived them all, she could have back her land by paying her husband's family another £10,000.[41] As far as land went, the common law was more generous to a woman than was settlement practice. For aristocratic families were determined that once a family estate had been increased by marriage the vagaries of demography should not take it all away.

They were more generous with money. The law gave a woman's money entirely to her husband, but family settlements and Chancery often arranged it otherwise. If a wife's relatives or her trustees made difficulties in paying her portion and her husband took them to Chancery, he would find that it was the practice of that court, as the lord chancellor put it, "to enforce the husband, before he recovers by the aid of equity his wife's portion, to make a settlement; ... although it seems to break in upon the legal title, which the husband has to his wife's personal estate."[42] The settlement made at a man's marriage sometimes declared the uses to which a portion was to be put. These could be that

---

[38]*Laws*, 149.
[39]Kent R.O., U 471. E4; South Carlton, Monson MSS, G (100)/156; Kent R.O., U 55.T651.
[40]B.L., Private Act, 7 Geo III, c. 116; B.L., Private Act, 11 Geo I, c. 15.
[41]Lincs. R.O., 5 Anc 2/A/3/17, 5 Anc 2/A/3, 3 Anc 2/5/15.
[42]S. C. Cox, ed., *Reports of Cases ... in ... Chancery ... Collected by William Peere Williams* (London, 1826), 3 vol., III, 204.

the money should be invested in land to swell the consequence of a husband's family, or that it should be given to trustees to invest as a means of providing the portions of younger children, or that it should be used to pay off a family's debts which had been incurred more often than not in providing for the younger children of a previous generation. It was sometimes simply stated that all or part of a portion was to go to a woman's father-in-law, in recompense, no doubt, for the annuity he gave the young couple. The portion was sometimes shared between father and son. But more often than not, no explicit use was declared, in which case it must have gone to a woman's husband.[43]

If we cannot positively say to what use portions were put, there is, nevertheless, no doubt that fathers always demanded that their daughters be provided for after a husband's death. This provision was called her jointure, and its amount was negotiated on the basis of the portion the daughter brought at her marriage. The usual proportion between jointure and portion was £100 for every £1000 of a portion, but sometimes more or less was given.[44] It was also usually arranged that a woman should receive £400 or £500 a year during her husband's lifetime for her own use. This was a provision that had begun to be made in the second quarter of the seventeenth century. By the 1690s it was called pin money and had become quite usual.[45] There were those who continued to object to it on the ground that it intimated "to the young people, that they are very soon to be in a state of war with each other" and that "separate purses between man and wife, are ... as unnatural as separate beds."[46] And whereas a woman could claim from her husband's successor all arrears of her jointure, she was not legally

---

[43]In the settlements I have read there were only 38 instances in which uses were declared. In only five cases was it directed that the portion was to be laid out in land: Two of these were in the cases of younger sons who had otherwise but miniscule estates and two others were in a family recently raised to the peerage. This must lend support to Clay's contention (EcHR, XXI, 1969, 507–509) that, contrary to J. H. Habakkuk, portions were only seldom used as a means of extending the possessions of the landed class as a whole and that portions were far more often used simply to finance other portions.

[44]The second Lord Monson, having made an improvident marriage with a woman who had only £1500, by his will allowed his heir to give only £80 for every £1000 (Lincolnshire R.O., 7 Nott. 3). Lord Bristol allowed the same proportion by his will (Bristol Diary, 243). Lord Dorset by his will allowed his heirs to jointure £100 for every £1000 (Kent R.O., U269. T70/11). A man like the third Earl Cowper, who had inherited a great deal, gave his wife £500 though she brought only £4000 (Hertfordshire R.O., Panshanger MSS, C. 1238). When the Marquis of Rockingham's daughter married Lord Fitzwilliam, his lawyer told him that "the Lady's fortune is proposed to be £15,000. To follow the usual method of making jointures, it would be proposed to settle for that fortune 1500 a year in lands" (S.C.L., WWM. M 8/55). I have collected 64 instances of the jointure/portion ratio for peers.

[45]Based on 53 instances of pin money of peeresses; Lawrence Stone, The Crisis of the Aristocracy, 1558–1641 (Oxford: Clarendon Press, 1965), 635.

[46]D. F. Bond, ed., The Spectator (Oxford: Clarendon Press, 1965), 5 vol., III, 52; Richard Steele, The Tatler, No. 199.

entitled to more than a year's arrears of her pin money at her husband's death.[47]

Property that a woman inherited during her marriage was at law her husband's. But the relations from whom she inherited often gave the land or money to trustees as a means of insuring that a woman enjoyed it free of her husband's control. Chancery even declared in 1725 that if a will gave property to a woman for her own use without naming trustees, it was to be considered that her husband was her trustee and that he could not touch the bequest. In 1746 this doctrine was expanded to mean that any bequest from an individual who might be considered a stranger to a woman and her husband was to be taken as a gift for her separate use, with her husband as trustee. A married woman, however, could make a will during her marriage only with her husband's consent, and after her death he was free to decide not to act upon it; if a woman made a will before her marriage, her marriage revoked it. But on the whole, women were increasingly being given the possibility of financial independence.[48] Some men feared this, and some women reveled in it. Pin money was denounced as "the foundation of wives' rebellion and husbands' cuckoldom."[49] And when the duke of Portland tried to persuade his mother to allow part of the trusts of his marriage to be placed on land she held in her own right, she replied that "as by mother's will I am independent, I am determined to keep myself so, and must beg you will never mention it to me again."[50]

The property that a woman brought into a marriage was always an important factor in an heir's choice of his wife; but after 1720 it is very likely that whether they loved each other was increasingly important. Nevertheless, an eldest son might still find that his sense of family obligation won out over his personal inclinations. Lord Bristol, who learned to love both of his wives, was anxious in 1720 to persuade his eldest son to marry a landed heiress as a means to "recruit again those necessary dimunitions of my estate which suitable provision for eleven younger children must occasion"; the marriage would in addition, he said, assure to his family "a perpetual plenteous independancy."[51] In the next generation Lord Lincoln fell very much in love with Lady Sophia Fermor, but at the insistence of his uncle the duke of Newcastle, he gave her up because of "the many incumbrances upon my estate."

---

[47]*General Abridgement of Cases in Equity* (London, 1793), 2 vol., I, 65–66.

[48]Cox, *Peere Williams*, II, 316–319, cf. I, 125–126, for the earlier state of the law; Atkyns, *Reports*, III, 393, 399; *Abridgement of Cases*, (1768 ed.), II, 157.

[49]Richard Steele, *The Tender Husband*, 1705 (London, 1778 ed.), 22.

[50]N.U.L., PwF 787.

[51]*Bristol Letterbook*, II, 121–122.

He married, instead, his first cousin, for she brought with her the Newcastle estates. But he did so with a heavy heart, declaring that "never did I want to be rich before nor ever did I despise riches in comparison of real merit so much as I do at present."[52] In the same decade, however, Lord Malpas stood up against the pressure of his relations, although "his father's profusion called for his restoring the estate." He married the woman he loved, though she was neither wealthy nor beautiful, and the two of them managed to live so happily together that at his death his relations were forced to admit that they had been in the wrong.[53] Their admission was eased by the temper of the times, for by 1780 when Lord Althorp married, the decision could be based entirely on affection. When Althorp fell in love with Lord Lucan's daughter, who had no fortune, his only concern was that he should not allow his feelings to show before his parents had consented. His elder sister was obliged to reassure him that she was "sure he would meet with all the indulgence and everything he could wish for" from their parents. But there is no doubt that the path of true love was smoothed by Lord and Lady Spencer's being "perfectly satisfied though she has no fortune; indeed in that family it was not wanted."[54]

Even where a family did need a fortune, there were class restrictions as to where it might be gotten. For one-quarter of the wives of aristocratic men were the daughters of lords, and at least another half were drawn from gentry families. Aristocratic men, for instance, did not notably make it a practice to marry the daughters of wealthy merchants; a mere 3% of them did.[55] It was quite exceptional when three Lords St. John in a row married such women; they probably did so from the same cause that had forced Lord Lincoln to disregard the trend toward romantic marriage; they were the descendants of a younger son who had inherited a title without a great estate.[56] An aristocratic father was likely to disapprove of such a match, even when, by 1780, it came accompanied by romantic love: "Lord Deerhurst was going to be married to a brandy merchant's daughter in the city," wrote the duchess of Devonshire; she "had a very good fortune and was really attached to him but that Lord Coventry is very angry."[57] Even marriages to the daughters of professional men (who were not also from landed society)

---

[52]*Walpole*, **XXX**, 6–7, n. 31, 23, n. 14, **XVIII**, 245.
[53]*Ibid.*, **XXII**, 210, **XIX**, 340 and n. 3.
[54]Chatsworth MSS, **V**, 278; *Walpole*, **XXIII**, 249, n.4.
[55]*Hollingsworth*, 8–10; D. N. Thomas, "Marriage Patterns in the British Peerage in the Eighteenth and Nineteenth Centuries," (M. Phil. Thesis, University of London, 1969), 149, 165.
[56]Dean Rapp, "Social Mobility in the Eighteenth Century: The Whitbreads of Bedfordshire, 1780–1815," *EcHR*, **XXVII**, 1974, 388.
[57]Chatsworth MSS, **V**, 475.

were likely to meet with disapproval: "I hear Lord Sussex is going to be married to a clergyman's daughter in Northamptonshire by name Miss Drury," the duchess of Portland said; she clearly had not heard of the Drurys and so she added, "I hope it is not true."[58]

The duchess had good reason to be sensitive in these matters, for in two generations in her husband's family, a younger son made a compromising marriage. Her husband's uncle married his mistress but found that his brother and sister-in-law would never recognize his wife: His "grief on this account contributed as much, if not more, to his death than the gout."[59] And when her husband's brother married an author's daughter, the duchess of Devonshire wrote that on the day after the wedding Lord Edward came to see her: "They stay three weeks in town at Mr. Muster's and then go into the country forever. The Duke of Portland came in while Lord Edward was here and talked very good naturedly to him, but when he was gone, upon my saying something about it, he looked very grave and did not answer me."[60] A mésalliance, if one were a younger son, could therefore result in social ostracism. An eldest son had greater freedom, and like the duke of Ancaster could to some degree get by with marrying the daughter of a rich jockey.[61] But if he did so in his father's lifetime, and his father were an irascible man, he stood the chance, before 1720 at least, of being disinherited.

Richard, Lord Willoughby, married a seamstress and was extravagant. His father strongly disapproved and in 1720 settled the family estates on his younger son, John Verney. (This he was apparently free to do since he inherited as a younger son and had not been fully bound by the family settlements.) Richard was given an annuity of £300, and had £500 of his debts paid and £2000 settled on any children he might have. He was to receive the annuity from a banker, and certain conditions were attached to it. If he asked for any part of it before it was due, or if he disposed of it to anyone else, the annuity was to stop entirely. If he or his wife came to the family home, or indeed to any place in Warwickshire—unless asked to by his father or merely traveling through on the road—£200 of the annuity was to be taken away. His father died in 1728, and Richard succeeded to the title. His mother died a year later, and he immediately tried to take over the estate that had been settled on her for her jointure. But all his claims failed, including

[58]N.U.L., PwF 10,687: 31 May 1777.
[59]Sir Lewis Namier and John Brooke, The House of Commons, 1754-1790 (London: Her Majesty's Stationery Office, 1964), 3 vol., II, 83.
[60]Chatsworth MSS, V, 475 (the Duchess of Portland and the Duchess of Devonshire were sisters-in-law).
[61]Walpole, XXIV, 499-500.

his attempt to prove that his father had been mad. His younger brother John came into all the family estates.[62]

The condition of a Lord with £300 a year was not a happy one. He was soon in deep financial distress. He leased a house and some land near Lichfield at £60 a year, but by 1732 he was 2 years in arrears of his rent, and he owed his landlord more than £50 for corn and hay. The landlord, John Wightwich, after receiving a great many empty promises, ordered his attorney to take out a distress on Willoughby's goods, which fell largely on the stock of the undertenants. Willoughby assigned his annuity to his landlord, and then immediately wrote to his banker and to his brother forbidding them to pay anything to Wightwich. Wightwich complained to John Verney that this was such "unworthy behaviour that I am amazed that a man of his rank can be guilty of it." But Willoughby told John that "the annuity is what I now most rely on, and things are cheap here, so I find I can live genteely on it," that "without keeping this annuity I should not be able to keep touch with any here." He added that he was determined to look for another house "so that I shall get rid of this brute, and hope then to have my Lady's company, which is the [one?] enjoyment I can have, for she is determined not to come here, but lives now at Horthale."[63]

All this had taken place in July. By September Willoughby was in trouble again. He asked his brother for an advance on the annuity since he was without clothes or money. One of his creditors had actually seized his clothes and his peerage robes. Willoughby threatened that when Parliament sat he would use his privilege to call the man to account. But in the meantime he was going to the Stafford quartersessions, evidently to prosecute the case. His brother had opened himself to such appeals by giving Willoughby permission to visit the family seat. Willoughby now assured him that he might "depend on my ever living in friendship with you." And he volunteered that he would "live entirely in Staffordshire, only once a month pay a visit to Lady Willoughby, for she does not care for Staffordshire."[64]

Here was a lord obliged to go to court for small debts; a lord reduced to having the robes of his dignity taken away by his debtors and to threatening them with his parliamentary protection. And here was an eldest son so dependent on his younger brother's good will that he was obliged to ask his permission to visit the family seat. And his woes were not over. His wife had refused to live with him, and in 1734 he

[62]Shakespeare's Birthplace Trust, Willoughby de Broke MSS, 1322[a], 1438, 1440, 1327, 1326, 1326[a], 1329[a], 1444, 1672, 1658.
[63]Ibid., 1448, 1649.
[64]Ibid., 1649.

was obliged to assign her a third of his annuity when they separated. He could manage to reap the harvest neither of primogeniture nor of patriarchy; and he had been brought to such a pass because his father, freed from the restraints of settlement, had claimed an absolute right to control the marriages of his children and had been able, when he found his will flouted, to invert the primogenitural order. Willoughby was obliged to seek solace in another man's property and ran off with the wife of a stocking weaver named Stiff.[65]

The Younger Son

Primogeniture, strict settlement, and the position of women, therefore, secured the independence of a family's head. But primogeniture also meant that younger sons and daughters had to be provided for by means other than their inheritance of the family estates. The courts sometimes held that parents were legally obliged to make such a provision. Lord Macclesfield said in 1723 that equity placed younger children "on a level with creditors, taking it to be a debt by nature from a father to provide for all his children, as well the youngest as the eldest." In 1736 a master in Chancery modified this doctrine by claiming that provisions for children were "not merely voluntary, for parents are obliged to make a reasonable provision for them at their death, as well as in their lifetime, and if they did not, the law did it for them" since "children have an equity, as creditors and purchasers have, though not in an equal degree, they being a middle species between those and volunteers." But Lord Hardwicke, interposed his authority as chancellor and took away all force of the doctrine by maintaining "that the parent is judge of the *quantum* of the provision, the terms on which he will give it, and by the law of *England* may, if he thinks fit, absolutely disinherit a child."[66] Kindred might put in a claim for equality among children, but in this society individual freedom had the greatest claim of all.

Parents were, then, legally at liberty to make whatever provision for their children they wished. Aristocratic parents were, however, determined that as many of their children as possible should enjoy independence. But since independence was not in the normal course of events the state to which a woman would aspire, and since primogeni-

[65]H.M.C., *Egmont Diary*, II, 218.
[66]*The English Reports*, XXIV, 689–690; M. J. West, ed., *Reports of Cases... in Chancery* (London, 1827), 258–435.

ture did as much as was possible to establish the independence of a family's head, it was on the position of their younger sons that parents expended their greatest efforts. So much was this so that the provision made for younger sons is where we see the network of aristocratic kinship enacting its most instrumental role.[67] Parents began by limiting the number of their younger children in the first two generations of our period; in the third, their economic position had so improved that this was no longer necessary.[68] In their family settlements parents were therefore able to portion their sons, especially after 1720, on at least an equality with their daughters. And ultimately younger sons did better than their sisters, for their provisioning did not stop with annuities or portions. For their relations sought to advance them in the world by procuring for them advantageous marriages, lucrative professions, and sinecures. In addition, when it could be arranged, a second son was endowed with an estate, for however small it might have been, there was no independence like that which came from owning land.

We should begin with portions. Full information for the history of settlement has been assembled for 30 families between 1690 and 1780. Among these families there were before 1720 11 instances in which younger sons were provided for by annuities, but there were 15 instances in which they were provided for by portions or lump sums of money. (Annuities are usually said to have been capitalized at two-or three-fifths the cost of a portion.) Of a further 11 settlements drawn from other families in this period, 2 provided annuities and 9 portions. When younger sons were given portions, they were always given as much as their sisters, and it was usual throughout the century to arrange that when there were two younger children that they should, on the average, equally share about £16,000, no matter what their sex. Among the 30 families after 1720, there were only 3 instances in which sons were given annuities; and in all 3 families, sons were given por-

---

[67]This is a view of the younger son's place that goes against the current orthodoxy that Habakkuk's authority has established. See Habakkuk, "Marriage Settlements"; id., "Daniel Finch, 2nd Earl of Nottingham: His House and Estate," in Plumb, ed., *Studies in Social History* (London: Longmans, Green, 1955), 156–159. Habakkuk is followed on this point by Mingay (*Landed Society*, 28–36), though it is interesting that the one actual provision for younger children that Mingay cites (35) makes no distinction between daughters and younger sons. Clay, who is critical of Habakkuk, seems to accept his authority at this point ("Marriage, Inheritance," 507). David Spring, "English Landownership in the Nineteenth Century: A Critical Note," *EcHR*, IX, 1957, 474–476, points out that in this period younger sons did as well as their sisters and sometimes better: His generalizations, I would claim, may be extended back to the beginning of the eighteenth century.

[68]*Hollingsworth*, 31, 43–45, 51. It is unlikely then, as Habakkuk supposed, that aristocratic estates by 1750 were staggering under a load of debt occasioned by portions for younger children. See H. J. Habakkuk, "Landowners and the Civil War," *EcHR*, XVII, 1965, 130–151, and Habakkuk, "Marriage Settlements," 29–30.

tions in the next generation. But after 1720 there were 36 instances among the 30 families in which sons received portions, and in a miscellany of 26 settlements from nearly as many families, the same thing was done. In the first of our generations, then, it was nearly as usual to give a son an annuity as to give him a portion; in the second, annuities had become somewhat rare; and in the third, they had practically disappeared. But in all settlements, except five, there was a clear provision made for younger children, both male and female, after 1690. This was a great change from the seventeenth century, when family settlements had guaranteed the inheritance of younger children only in the case of a marriage that produced daughters but no sons.[69] Daughters after 1690 were being given inheritances rather than dowries, and their younger brothers were no longer obliged to be content "with that which the cat left on the malt heap."[70]

The case of the dukes of Devonshire shows in full the generational developments in the history of settlement, and it also shows what could be done for a younger son over and above the provisions of his father's marriage settlement. At the marriage of the second duke in 1688, it was provided that in the event there were no sons, one daughter was to receive £20,000; and if there were more daughters £30,000 was to be divided among them. This settlement, however, made no provision at all for younger children in the event that there was an eldest son. To rectify this, the duke in 1711 made a new settlement which provided £6000 for each daughter and £500 a year for each of his three younger sons. In the same year he actually appointed £6000 to each of his 5 daughters, but in 1717 he revoked the £500 a year to his sons, one of whom had died, and by an act of Parliament gave Lord James land in Yorkshire and Lord Charles land in Nottinghamshire as well as an annuity of £500. Two years later, on the marriage of his eldest son, there was settled on the future duke's prospective younger children £10,000 for one, £20,000 for two or three, and £6000 each for four or more, with no regard to sex. The second duke's wife, by her will in 1723, divided among her children a legacy of £40,000 that her brother had given her: £4000 to one daughter, £3000 to another, £9200 for two

---

[69] Stone, Crisis, 635–645. The five exceptions after 1690 fall into this category. In casual reading I found six settlements of this kind before 1690.

[70] Thomas Wilson, quoted in Joan Thirsk, "Younger Sons in the Seventeenth Century," History, LIV, 1969, 360. So assured did the rights of younger sons become that in 1779 when Lord Spencer and his only grown son approached their lawyer to change some detail of their settlements, he told them to their amusement that "it would be so wrong to injure the younger brothers and it would ruin his reputation. . . .my father pacified him by assuring him you [Lady Spencer] would not be brought to bed in a week" (Chatsworth MSS, V, 259).

younger sons, and nearly £24,000 worth of jewelry for her eldest son and her three remaining daughters. In 1725 the duke (under a settlement of 1678) gave £300 a year or more to Lord Charles, but 3 years later, at Charles' marriage, he revoked all previous settlements on him and gave him instead slightly more than £1000 a year in land and an annuity of £500, over and above £12,000 in stock that Charles had picked up somewhere. The second duke died a year later.

The third duke in 1745 settled £500 a year on his three younger sons. Two years later his eldest son's marriage provided an opportunity to resettle family affairs. He gave the £6000 to his youngest daughter and to each of his younger sons that was theirs under his own marriage settlement, but he also received a power to grant to his younger sons, in fee or entailed, land worth up to £2000 a year. His eldest son, in turn, was given £10,000 for one younger child, £15,000 for two, and £6000 each for three or more; he also could give £2000 in annuities to his younger sons; and he could appoint to them, in fee or entailed, land of £2000 a year. It was becoming customary for the Cavendishes to give their younger sons portions, annuities, and land all together.

The third duke, between 1751 and 1753, settled £600 a year in land on his sons Lords Frederick and George, and by his will in 1753 gave to Lord John, his fourth son, £14,000, which by a codicil a year later he increased to £16,000, this being closer to the value of land of £600 a year. A decade later Sir William Lowther of Holber Hall left to Lord George his estates (George's sister had married Thomas Lowther), and Lord George, who was a second son, settled those estates on himself and then on his brother Frederick, a third son.

Their brother the fourth duke was able to provide for his younger sons with even greater magnificence. His mother-in-law Lady Burlington left him all her property for his life, which he was to divide among his children as he pleased. Consequently the duke died in possession of a personal estate of nearly £7600 a year. He had two younger sons and a daughter, and by his will he divided this fortune among them, giving two shares to each son and one to his daughter. Lady Dorothy got £30,000 instead of the £6000 due her under her father's settlement and married the duke of Portland. Each younger son got an annuity of £1000, £1400 a year of Devonshire estates (which was to revert at their death to the title holder), and a £6000 portion due them under their father's settlement. But they also received £1000 a year each of the Burlington estates, and they shared the residue of the duke's personal estate. "The loss of such a man to his children is terrible," said Lady Dalkeith at the Duke's death; "he has left them great fortunes, made them independent indeed"; and Lady Dalkeith was not perfectly informed quite how much he had left to his younger sons. All in all, they had each come into an inheritance of £5000 a year.[71]

Lady Burlingtons, however, came in short supply, and for a younger son marriage was always the easiest way to independence. "I have thought of an honourable match for Col. J[ohn] to give him his desired independence," Mrs. Boscawen wrote to her husband about his younger brother. "Tis an ancient virgin; vastly preferable to a battered harridan."[72] Marriage could have the advantage of an assured independence that the laborious uncertainties of a profession did not, and while a man could depend on his relations to make a match for him, it was also possible to make a marriage very much on his own.

Charles Townshend is an excellent example of a younger son who found marriage the easiest way to indulge himself in the independent pleasures that an eldest son might take in public business. Lord Townshend intended that Charles should make his way in the world as a lawyer; he therefore consented to his entering Parliament with great reluctance, for he feared that the Commons would divert Charles from the pursuit of his profession; and he was in fact eventually obliged to seek office for Charles when the latter used his ill health as a bludgeon against the law. But to pursue the career in politics that he desired, Charles needed more than Lord Townshend would give, and he found his solution in a marriage to a wealthy widow who was 8 years his senior. At the time of his marriage he coerced out of his father 8 of the £20,000 that Lord Townshend had for his younger children; he got more than his father thought to be his fair share; but he nonetheless declared that the haggle had made him "resolve to withdraw from every family transaction as a sort of business in which I never act unhurt." But Charles was now free to indulge his love of public business, to provide for his own children, and to astound the world. "He wanted nothing but independence to let him loose," said Horace Walpole, "I propose great entertainment from him; and now, perhaps, the times will admit it."[73]

But a younger son with no land often found it difficult to make the sort of marriage he desired. The case of Lord Bristol's sons is instructive.[74] Bristol was attempting to make his family "great and indepen-

[71]Chatsworth MSS, L/19/16, 20, 27, 30, 33-35, 38-39, 48, 53, 58, L/13/9, L/14/5, L/68/12; Duke of Argyll, *Intimate Society Letters of the Eighteenth Century* (London: Stanley Paul, 1910), 2 vol., I, 302: Lady Dalkieth thought the younger sons had only got £ 2000 a year, which is a good example how far off the estimates of such matters in contemporary gossip could be.

[72]Cecil Aspinall-Oglander, *Admiral's Wife* (London: Longmans, 1940), 230.

[73]Sir Lewis Namier and John Brooke, *Charles Townshend* (London: Macmillan, 1964), 21-23, 30, 34-36, 98, 152.

[74]*Bristol Letterbook*, II, 123, 121-122, III, 244, 54-60, II, 126-127, III, 62, III, 209.

dent for many generations," but his family was large and the task difficult. Consequently he proposed to Carr, his eldest son, various marriages to heiresses as a means to "recruit again those necessary diminutions of my estate which suitable provision for eleven younger children must occasion." Carr died unmarried and was succeeded by John, who while still a younger son had married a woman without a fortune, a thing that his father many years later told him "even the weakest of moderns you see have more wit than to do" and that had been especially foolish "with all those advantages of person, wit and beauty which you possessed." But none of Bristol's sons seemed to have been overly adept at trading on the beauty that they inherited from their mother.

William seems initially to have done best. He made his addresses to the only daughter of Thomas Ridge. Ridge at first refused to give his daughter "such a portion," as Bristol put it, "as would make her and you with what I can possibly spare at present, more easy together than you are asunder." What Bristol could spare was £3000 on which 4% was to be paid until his death. Bristol contended with Ridge over the disposal of his son's £3000. Ridge wanted it to go to his daughter if she survived her husband; Bristol proposed that if there were only daughters by the marriage, Miss Ridge's £8000 should be enough and that unless there was a son, the £3000 ought to be left "to support the Earldom." Ridge insulted Bristol, but the latter had to be patient as his son was in love, and eventually the interest on the £3000 was settled on Miss Ridge. She died a year after marriage, having borne a daughter.

Another of Bristol's younger sons, Thomas, had previously been disappointed in a marriage he desired, since his prospective wife's relations insisted "on a settlement in land [which] it will not now be in my power to comply with, and therefore I hope and trust God's good providence will provide some other way for his happiness." Yet another son, Henry, married Catherine Aston. Her brother's estate was entailed on her if he had no children, but otherwise her portion of £4000 was, by her father's settlement and will, dependent on her marrying with her mother's consent. Lady Aston rejected Henry and his £300 a year, because, as she said, he "had no property by which he could make any provision for his wife or family." The young people married nonetheless, and Bristol, while he said that it was foolish, would not forbid it for fear the entail should some day vest and "furnish the world and your own heart with a handle to reproach me with having hindered you from making your fortune." Henry eventually went to law against his mother-in-law to get his wife's portion, despite his father's advice;

but Lady Aston won the day when the lord chancellor decreed that all her daughter had to be paid was her maintenance of £70 a year.[75] Death came to Henry's aid, however; his brother-in-law Sir Thomas died, the entail vested, and Henry took orders and changed his name to Aston. He would "not even put the arms of his own family upon his coach" but chose instead a "motto which is *Alias et Idem*, for he says he was Harry Hervey a poor officer and a wicked rake, whereas he is Harry Aston, a rich clergyman, and he hopes a worthy one."[76] For many parents, beauty and charm in a son-in-law were hardly enough to balance landlessness.

Younger sons in some families did manage to do better out of marriage than the Herveys. Six sons of the first duke of St. Albans sat in Parliament, and five of them married heiresses. One of them, Lord Sidney Beauclerk, had an unsavory reputation as a determined fortune hunter.[77] Still, that family's exploitation of marriage ought not to be overdone, for another of them married for love the impecunious daughter of Lord Lovelace. Lady Hertford commented that she had seen the couple and that "they appear very happy; and I hope, for both their sakes, they will continue to be satisfied with the very moderate share of fortune they have chosen by this alliance. For people of their rank, this will require some prudence, as well as a great deal of passion; for, to live in a cottage on love, has a much better effect in a stanza of a ballad, than in real life."[78]

Romantic love, then, could reduce for a younger son the number of ways available to him for improving his situation. Indeed, younger sons may have been especially vulnerable to such a feeling, for, as Vanbrugh put it, "younger brothers have nothing to settle but their hearts." But aristocratic society as a whole was finding it difficult to accept anything other than romantic marriage. For, as Spencer Cowper told his eldest brother, though there was "another way indeed of mending oneself, that is by marriage," yet "how can anyone expect to be happy, where their choice is directed by gain? It was so small a motive with you in your choice that you can recommend it to no one, your choice was directed by affection, and you have succeeded accordingly." It is therefore no great surprise to find that whereas in the seventeenth century every third aristocratic male married a woman

---

[75] West, *Reports of Cases*, 350–437.
[76] *Hertford*, 314.
[77] Romney Sedgwick, *The House of Commons 1715–1754* (New York: Oxford Univ. Press, 1970), 2 vol., I, 448–450.
[78] *Hertford–Pomfret Corresp.* I, 140–141.

with a great fortune, in the eighteenth such marriages fell to one in four.[79]

If marriage was being closed off (and it had never been available to all), the alternatives were a sinecure or a profession. It was unlikely, however, that the first was ever secured without a seat in Parliament, and for a man like Cowper, therefore, the only way of adding to his fortune was to enter a profession. Cowper chose the least prestigious— the church. It was the profession Lord Chesterfield recommended to "a good, dull and decent boy"; for a "boy of a warm constitution, strong animal spirits, and a cold genius" he chose the army or the navy; but for "one of quick, lively and distinguishing parts," the law. (Medicine and trade were for aristocrats not real options.) The law was certainly the best: Chesterfield called it "the truly independent profession." But, in truth, no aristocratic boy was ever really willing to drudge at a profession, even at the law. Charles Townsend deserted it as quickly as he could for marriage and office. Therefore, when marriage was not used to make one's fortune, the real alternative, if temperament allowed and one's family could encompass it, was to get into Parliament and look for a place. Peregrine Bertie certainly told his son that he hoped his inheritance would let him find his "circumstances too good to push and struggle for the beginnings of business" in a profession where "a man must have good friends and strong elbows to make his way." He proposed instead Parliament or a place, either of which was "honourable and may be profitable if a man get them upon good terms." It is probably no coincidence, therefore, that the generation after 1750 should be the first in which romantic marriage was clearly the rule and also the one in which eighteenth-century politics was notoriously reduced to place hunting.[80]

Whether younger sons had a profession or no profession, or had failed in attempting a profession, the House of Commons was the best lottery, as one Bertie put it, "to push their fortunes in." When Henry Finch from laziness failed as an academic, his family decided that "a

---

[79]Sir John Vanbrugh, *The Provoked Wife*, 1697, ed. by C. A. Zimansky (Lincoln, Nebraska: Univ. of Nebraska Press, 1966), 111; Edward Hughes, ed., *Letters of Spencer Cowper* (Surtees Society, 1956), 6, 13; Thomas, "Marriage Patterns," 184–178.

[80]Dobrée, *Letters of Chesterfield*, V, 2193–2194 (cf. Rand, *Shaftesbury*, 281–283); Namier and Brooke, *Townshend* 21–23; Peregrine Bertie, *A Memoir of Peregrine Bertie* (London, 1838), 102–103; Sir Lewis Namier, *The Structure of Politics at the Accession of George III* (London: Macmillan, 1961). F. M. L. Thompson shares my scepticism about the commitment of younger sons to their professions and suggests that they flocked into the class of 20,000 "gentlemen and ladies living on incomes" that Colquhoun identified in 1801 (in E. L. Jones and S. J. Woolf, eds., *Agrarian Change and Economic Development* (London: Methuen, 1969), 58–59).

provision out of Parliament" was "most agreeable to his circumstances," and he eventually got from a sinecure the £1000 a year that gave independence.[81] Fathers like Lord Hertford and Lord Hardwicke actually bred their sons to be courtiers rather than politicians so that they might always be in office enjoying the necessary supplement to their portions that either marriage or a profession had not fully achieved.

Lord Hertford had seven sons, and save for the youngest, who took orders, all sat in the Commons. Two of these married heiresses, and three had professions from which they quickly retired. In their management of their parliamentary affairs, the father came to be described as having "a constant appetite for all preferments for himself and his family, with the quickest digestion and the shortest memory," and his eldest son was said to be "ambitious of establishing a great power in his family, both by income and parliamentary interest."[82]

Lord Hardwicke had five sons: Four had active professions, one was a clergyman. Four sat in the Commons, and two married heiresses. The third son, Joseph, having once rejected an heiress with £40,000 whom his family had found for him, thought of marrying for love a woman with £5000; but he was full of trepidations that he would lose the "protection of my family and friends"; and he held back. When, upon the fall of a government, his father came under pressure to have his sons resign their offices, Joseph remarked that he was anxious to stay on as he was 40, and "in the situation of a younger brother" he feared "being thrown out of life or obliged to begin again." Hardwicke was not anxious to force any of his sons to resign, for, as he said, "two of them have families"; and he could not easily ask them to give up "what it will probably never be in my power, at my time of life, to assist them to retrieve." When two of them did resign, he left the poorer of them a compensatory annuity in his will.[83] After the death of the second son, Charles, who was one of those "who have no regard for the party they are bound to, but as it is the ladder to their own ambition and interest," the rest of the family went over to the court.[84] For the Yorkes were in Parliament as a means of establishing the greatness and independence of their family. Political independence and family independence were achieved in different ways.

[81]H.M.C., *Ancaster MSS*, 249–250; Namier, *Structure*, 19–20.
[82]Namier and Brooke, *House of Commons*, III, 424–426.
[83]*Hardwicke*, II, 154, 178–185, 433, 475, 486; Namier and Brooke, *House of Commons*, III, 680.
[84]John Brooke, *The Chatham Administration* (London: Macmillan, 1956), 289–290; cf. Ian R. Christie, *The End of North's Ministry, 1780–1782* (London: Macmillan, 1958), 74–75, 126–127, 334–335.

But if sinecures were better than professions, a landed estate was best of all. In *Mansfield Park*, Miss Crawford was surprised that Edmund Bertram was designed for a profession, and, more, that he should choose the church, which was for the youngest; for, as she explained, "you know there is generally an uncle or a grandfather to leave a fortune to the second son."[85] She was right, except for the fact that it only occurred in one case in three and that the estate was as likely to come from a father as from a maternal grandfather or an uncle. In the 30 families I have studied closely, 10 were able to give estates of varying size to younger sons, usually to the second, and 6 did so for several generations. In 10 instances it was the father who gave the estate, though it is likely that in some cases the land had originally come from his wife's or his mother's family. In 8 instances it came from a maternal grandfather, who having no sons of his own, in effect adopted his daughter's second son; for it was often a condition of the inheritance that the son take his grandfather's name. Six paternal and 3 maternal uncles gave estates, which occasionally they had come by in the same manner. If this sample of 10 families out of 30 is joined to the fact that 35% of the marriages of eldest sons were to heiresses who would have brought estates with them, it then becomes highly likely that the estimate that every second son in three was given an estate will stand.[86] But it was certainly not invariable that a maternal estate went to a second son. When Lady Oxford died it was widely expected that she would leave her great estate to her daughter's second son; "many people," said Mrs. Delany, "have taken that fancy into their heads." But Lord Edward only got £1000 a year and £30,000: "no despicable fortune for a younger son, even of a duke." The estates went to his eldest brother with the requirement of taking the arms and name of Lady Oxford's family.[87]

In some families, like the Cavendishes, the Willoughbys, the Watsons, or the Howards, younger sons received their estates as part of an agreed family practice. In other cases, however, such action either aroused hostility or grew out of it. The ninth earl of Derby quarreled bitterly with his mother, and therefore when she died, she left her estate to a younger son.[88] The second Lord Leigh left his younger son an estate that had come for that purpose from Leigh's uncle, but he also

---

[85] Jane Austen, *Mansfield Park*, 1816, Bk. 1, Chap. 9, ed. by R. W. Chapman (London: Oxford Univ. Press, 1966), 91–92.

[86] The ten families were Devonshire, Norfolk, Leigh, Middleton, Rockingham, Ancaster, Derby, Newcastle, Hardwicke, and Dorset; see Thomas, "Marriage Patterns," 184.

[87] *Delany*, III, 1861, 385, 395; Notts. R.O., DD. 4P/33/50.

[88] Lancs. R.O., DDK. 15/14, 20/19.

gave him half of £24,500 worth of unsettled land, and this caused a fracas with his eldest son, the third lord. This lord in turn quarreled with his eldest son and left to a younger the land he had bought and the land his wife had inherited.[89] In short, there was no certainty that even a second son would be able to avoid the drudgery of a profession or the necessity of place hunting, but there was a great possibility that the rigors of primogeniture would be softened for at least one of a lord's younger sons—that a second son would enter into the promised land and declare his independence as the representative of his maternal grandfather's patrilineage.

Daughters: Settlement, Mésalliance, and Romantic Marriage

A younger son was settled by his portion and his marriage, his profession and his sinecure; and the aim of it all, was to make him independent. A daughter was really settled only by her marriage, and as a woman, her independence was never fully established. But since a woman took her husband's social standing, her marriage was of greater moment to her than a man's to him. It is therefore appropriate to take the marriage of aristocratic women as the focus of the question of parental control of marriage, romantic love, and mésalliance. Between 1690 and 1750, parents sought and won the right to control the marriages of their minor children; but this authority came to be severely limited. For beginning in the generation after 1720, arranged marriages so gave way to romantic marriages that by 1780 it could be estimated that three marriages in four were made for love.[90] But it was still expected, even in the generation after 1750, that aristocrats would marry within their own social class. Aristocrats throughout the century married for one of five reasons, alone or in combination: because the spouse was rich, or powerfully connected, or beautiful, or virtuous, or for these or other reasons, beloved. Throughout the century aristocratic women moved freely in society before their marriage; this sometimes made arranged marriages difficult but facilitated romantic ones. But whereas women who entered into arranged marriages were, like French or Italian women, free to move in mixed company without their husbands, romantic marriage imposed a different pattern, for it expected that a

---

[89] Shakespeare's Birthplace Trust: Leigh of Stoneleigh MSS: S&W II, 5/10, 5/16, 3/4, 3/7, Series D; Stoneleigh Bn 9a, Series B; Leighton Buzzard, Bx 2 Bn. 2.
[90] J. Marchand, ed., *A Frenchman in England 1784* (Cambridge: University Press, 1933), 50.

woman always went into mixed company with her husband and that in his absence she was either with other women or with her children.[91] It is no wonder, then, that the English were slow to realize that an Italian lady's cicisbeo was not her husband's cuckold.[92]

Even at the height of romantic love, however, it was not acceptable for an aristocratic woman to marry outside landed society, even though her husband might be an officer or a lawyer, a clergyman or a physician. When Lady Pembroke married a captain of no birth or fortune, one pious lady scandalized another by saying that "as Lady Pembroke could not be easy to live without him, she had acted more prudently if she had taken him on any other terms"; and the king exclaimed, "I can't bear when a woman of quality marry one don't know whom!"[93] Lady Jane Evelyn's relations refused to rejoice with her when she married a physician, for though they knew his character to be excellent and thought that he was perhaps a "gentleman by birth and certainly by education and manners," they still could not "but think it an unequal match."[94] Both these women were widows and free to choose. When an unmarried girl did the same, the cries were even more desperate. It was "a melancholy affair" when one of them married an actor, and the Duchess of Argyll went into harangues when another eloped with a country clergyman. In this regard matters had not changed at all since 1691, when William Walsh wailed that heiresses who ran away and widows who ruined themselves by second marriages, as well as wives who cuckolded their husbands, never did so with "a man of sense" but with "chaplains, dancing masters, butlers and footmen."[95]

In the generation after 1690 when fathers proposed that their children marry for love, they were more likely to do so in the case of sons than of daughters; for daughters were the traditional means of making alliances, and the idea of marriage as an alliance between families was still strong. Men formed in the uncertain age of Restoration politics were likely to think very much in this way. Lord Halifax once rejected a French noblewoman for his son because "the alliance, though very honorable, is of no manner of use or support to an English family" and because "considering our sky looketh very changeable . . . the argument

[91]Ibid., 19, 48–50; Lord Chesterfield, The World (London, 1755), No. 151, 20 November 1755: "a sober, formal sort of married women . . . who live domestic lives. . . . Like turtles, they are true and tender to their lawful mates, and breed like rabbits to beggar and perpetuate their families."

[92]Lady Mary, I, 270–272, 429–430; H. L. Piozzi, Observations and Reflections, 1789, ed. by H. Barrows (Ann Arbor: Univ. of Michigan Press, 1967), 52, 425.

[93]Hertford, 400; Walpole, XX, 281.

[94]Delany, I, 1862, 463.

[95]Walpole, XXII, 218–219, IX, 154 [William Walsh], A Dialogue Concerning Women (London, 1691), 14–15.

of alliance may grow much stronger, and... your nephew may by a wise and reasonable choice... do a great deal towards the preservation of his family." Similarly Lord Warrington spoke of a daughter's marriage as done "out of a prospect of advantage that may thereby accrue to your family." But Warrington added that "in the matching of any of your sons, but especially your eldest, neither force nor too much flatter him into the liking of any to whom his own inclination don't in some measure prompt him."[96] Lord Nottingham similarly wrote that "in the marriage of my daughters, their particular happiness is chiefly to be aimed at; in that of my son I wish you could carry that prospect a little further." But for a man of Nottingham's generation, such sentiments did not mean that he left his children free to marry at their will. One daughter was married to the duke of Somerset sight unseen, and Nottingham told Somerset that he was "well pleased with the honor of his alliance." And when his eldest son made his addresses to Lord Denbigh's sister, Nottingham's consent was reluctant, which caused Bishop Hough to write that "where there is great plenty one would expect that common discretion should give preference to those virtues and good qualities" without which, as Nottingham himself had said, "marriage is a yoke like that of tying the dead to the living."[97]

It is therefore with regard to daughters that one hears in this generation of enforced marriages. Lord Lansdowne commanded his niece to make a marriage which secured "to his interest by such an alliance one of some consequence in his country." No one asked her what her heart felt, and everyone urged her that it was her duty to submit, "to be settled in the world and ease my friends of an expense and care."[98] If a young woman managed to say that she could not love the man proposed, her relations were likely to say to her, as they did to Lady Mary, that "they found no necessity of loving; if I lived well with him, that was all that was required of me, and that if I considered this town, I should find very few women in love with their husbands and yet a many happy."[99] But by 1720, opinion was changing. Lord Tankerville rejected a number of good offers for his daughter, then chose a man she hated, and threatened to kill her if she did not marry him. When she ran off and married someone else, it was Tankerville whom opinion blamed: "One can't wonder at children's disobedience," Lady Bristol

---

[96]Cooper, ed., *Savile Correspondence*, 145; Henry, Lord Warrington, *Works* ed. by J. Delaheuze (London, 1694), 33–34.
[97]Finch, *Burley-on-the-Hill*, I, 204, 240–246; Staffs. R.O., D 1778, I, ii, 613 (Bishop Hough).
[98]*Delany*, I, 1861, 24–28.
[99]*Lady Mary*, I, 134.

told her husband, "when they have such parents"; but, of course, she excepted "such a father as you."[100]

The reputation of romantic love, however, was never great with this generation. A singular woman like Mrs. Manley might write that "parents think their children can never be unhappy, if they but take care of their interest, which is the true reason that we so seldom see people of condition fortunate in their marriages." But to even an ardent feminist like Mary Astell, when a woman married for love it usually meant that she had made a mésalliance. She could not see that there was any "real kindness between those who can agree to make each other miserable." A man of lower station could never imagine without inordinate vanity that "his person and good qualities should make compensation for all the advantages she quits on his account." And a woman was wrong to degrade herself from her rank and "thrust herself down to a meaner drudgery... a caring not only to please, but to maintain a husband." The reasonable consensus was, as Bishop Fleetwood put it, that while children were not to marry without their parents' consent, parents were to remember, first, that it is "so much more in people's power to keep themselves free from engaging their affections than it is to settle them where other people please," and that they ought not in choosing a child's partner "to let the consideration of fortune and estate so preponderate and overweigh all other considerations of form and favor, birth and education, virtues and good qualities, as to neglect them." Choose for a child someone rich enough, and yet sufficiently beautiful, well-bred, and kind, as to be capable of being loved.[101]

Romantic love might be received doubtfully by this generation, but mercenary marriages were being discountenanced. One of the best signs of this is the decline of the professional matchmaker, whom aristocratic society, with the aid of the courts, had outlawed by 1720. The courts used the most effectual means at their command by declaring that bonds made to pay the matchmaker were not enforceable at law, and they consistently upset such bonds from the late seventeenth century onwards. In a case before the House of Lords in 1695 it was decided that a bond of £1000 to pay £500 that Thomas Thynne had taken out to have his marriage to Lady Ogle arranged was to be set aside on the ground "that marriages ought to be procured and promoted by the

---

[100]Bristol Letterbook, II, 132–133, 137.

[101]Mary de la Riviere Manley, Secret Memoirs... from the New Atalantis (London, 1709), 115; Mary Astell, Reflections upon Marriage (London, 1706), 12, 38; William Fleetwood, The Relative Duties of Parents and Children (London, 1705), 40, 44, 50, 55.

mediation of friends and relations and not of hirelings." In another case in 1701 Lord Warrington asked two of his relations to promote his marriage to one of the heiresses of a London merchant as a means of extricating his estate from its encumbrances. They, in turn, went to a pair of brokers, and Warrington took out a bond to pay the brokers a thousand guineas. The match occurred. But one of Warrington's relations kept the money for himself; Warrington therefore went to law to recover the money, was successful, and in the process got out of paying the brokers when the bond was squashed.[102] But mercenary marriage did not die easily; the duchess of Marlborough employed a broker in 1716 to arrange her daughter's marriage to the duke of Newcastle after she quarreled with Vanbrugh, who had initially undertaken it at the duchess's request and as a service to her family. Nevertheless, die it did; and Vanbrugh, with the character of Coupler in his play, had helped to kill it.[103]

The courts had another reason for setting aside marriage brocage bonds besides their distaste for a marriage market. It was that such bonds could be used not only by a guardian to sell his ward or a mother her daughter, but they were a standing temptation to outsiders as well, and "tend to the betraying and oftentimes to the ruin of persons of quality and fortune." For before 1753 it was possible in England for a minor to contract a legal marriage without the consent of his father or guardian. Lord Tankerville as a young man was tricked into marrying a woman of the town and had to be carried off to the country by his relations "to see how he is to be bought off." Lord Wharton found that the lord chief justice's warrant was of little use when his son was married without his consent; it allowed him to enquire "who were aiding and assisting to the stealing of his son"; but the marriage was legal and stood.[104] Stealing a son, however, was not the great crime. It was, rather, the theft of a daughter that was the real nightmare. For a woman's property became her husband's, and she took his social standing. And a woman, being an irrational creature, was likelier to yield to the blandishments of love. To steal an heiress was therefore the quickest way to make a man's fortune—this was the common doctrine of the

---

[102]R. L. Loveland, ed., *Shower's Cases in Parliament* (London: Stevens & Haynes, 1876), 98–100; H.M.C., *H of L MSS 1712–1714*, 270–271; other cases may be found in *The English Reports*, XXIII, 553, 852, 983, **XXVII**, 1169–1172, **XXVIII**, 503–504.

[103]David Green, *Sarah Duchess of Marlborough* (London: Collins, 1967), 205; Sir John Vanbrugh, *The Relapse*, 1696, ed. by C. A. Zimansky (Lincoln, Nebraska: Univ. of Nebraska Press, 1970), 25–29, 111–114, 123–128. A similar character appears in Steele, *Tender Husband*, 20.

[104]Loveland, ed., *Shower's Cases*, 98–100; H. Manners Sutton, ed., *The Lexington Papers* (London, 1851), 76–77; Lady Verney, ed., *Verney Letters of the Eighteenth Century* (London: Ernest Benn, 1930), 2 vol., II, 23.

stage before 1710—and it had a special appeal to younger sons. Consequently when the act that made all this impossible was finally passed in 1753, Charles Townshend indignantly asked whether new shackles were "to be forged to keep young men of abilities from mounting to a level with their elder brothers."[105]

Several times before 1753 attempts were made to pass bills against such marriages. Bills were brought forward in 1677, 1685, 1689, 1691, 1695, 1711, and 1735. They usually passed in the Lords and failed in the Commons. And it is likely that they failed there because the Commons were filled with younger sons. The bill of 1691 was brought in after Mary Wharton, a 16-year-old heiress, was dragged from her coach and married to the younger brother of the Duke of Argyll, but it was rejected because it "might hinder many younger brothers from making their fortunes." At least three of the bills were specifically aimed at preventing servants from marrying their masters' children either to themselves or to someone else. And it was similarly "to prevent that influence which servants more especially would gain over young ladies" that the courts squashed marriage brocage contracts.[106]

Parents were also capable of making a daughter's portion depend on her obedience. Before 1753 family settlements sometimes stated that a portion was to be paid to a daughter at 18 or 21 or at her marriage, but that if she married without parental consent she was to lose all or part of her portion. Lord Petre had the power by his settlement to give to an obedient daughter any part of the portion of a disobedient one that he chose. Lord Gower by his will gave each daughter an extra £1000 but stopped it if they married without consent. And the first and second dukes of Ancaster took away their daughters' portions if they married without consent before they were 21.[107] Restrictions such as these were frequently contested in the courts. Lady Newport's daughter leapt over the wall of her mother's house by the aid of a wheelbarrow and ran away to marry without her consent. The court deprived the daughter of her portion because it was in land and because by the terms of the settlement it was to be given to another use if she disobeyed. Heneage Finch declared this case was "epidemical and concerns all the parents of England." The chief justice agreed that the principles of the decision

---

[105]John Loftis, *Comedy and Society from Congreve to Fielding* (Stanford: Stanford Univ. Press, 1959), 44–46; Namier and Brooke, *Townshend*, 29–30.

[106]H.M.C., *House of Lords MSS 1678–1688*, 276–279, *1689–1690*, 245, *1690–1691*, xv, 253–260, *1695–1697*, 547–548; John Ashton, *Social Life in the Reign of Queen Anne* (London: Chatto & Windus, 1893), 30; Henry Gally, *Some Considerations upon Clandestine Marriages* (London, 1750), 26, 73–80; *The English Reports*, XXVII, 1171. An annonymous attempt to steal an heiress in 1707: H.M.C., *Portland MSS*, V, 381–382.

[107]Essex R.O., F. 108, 1712; Staffs. R.O., D. 593/C/19/2; Lincs. R.O., 5 Anc 2/A/3, 5 Anc 8/5/21.

were "very good restraints for children and ought to be made good here to encourage obedience and discourage those who would make a prey of them." But the greater leniency of the practice of the ecclesiastical courts did force the chancellors to agree that when a portion was in money and was not left to someone else in case of disobedience, such provisions were merely *in terrorem* and did not prevent a daughter's claiming her fortune.[108] The simplest way, however, for parents to make their way around such tangles was to declare that a lump sum was provided for all younger children, that it was at a parent's discretion to decide what share each child should receive and that it was to be equally shared only if no disposition had been made before the parent's death. This became the predominant practice in family settlements after 1720.[109] Clearly what Parliament could not encompass, private persons arranged in their settlements, and the courts then regularized the principles of these settlements and enforced them. Parents had arranged to rescue their daughters from the violence of fortune hunters and the vagaries of the marriage laws. But before 1720 parents themselves were as capable of violence against those daughters as any fortune hunter when they perceived that romantic love had led a young woman into a mésalliance.

There is the case of Lady Bridget Osborne, a daughter of the duke of Leeds, who married a clergyman in 1715 and horrified her parents. They beat her, locked her away for several months, interrogated her constantly, and evidently bribed the clergyman who performed the ceremony to deny it. The Osbornes had had bad luck in this way, for an aunt (after she was widowed) had married her chaplain, much to her father's distress. But the girl's mother was experienced in getting out of such matters, for she had been bought off from a first marriage contracted when she was 12.[110] This time around, however, the duchess lost, and her daughter's marriage was upheld.

The Reverend William Williams had been recommended to be the domestic chaplain to Lord Carmarthen, Lady Bridget's brother, by her aunt's husband, who had become bishop of Hereford.[111] Lady Bridget

---

[108] Thomas Leach, *Modern Reports* (London, 1793), **I**, 308–314; West, *Reports of Cases*, 422–427.

[109] On the marriage of his daughter in 1785, Lord Hertford wrote to one of the trustees that "the essential points are the dower, the pin money and the provision for children by a proper settlement of her fortune; as to the distributing of it which your Lordship mentions, as the number of children arising from this marriage may be more or less, I do not think it important if the parents do; they may, in my humble opinion, decide the matter very properly themselves" (Warwickshire R.O., CR 114/**III**/7/vii).

[110] Verney, *Verney Letters*, **I**, 218; G. E. Cokayne, ed., *The Complete Peerage*, **VII**, 511, n.h., 512, n.c.

[111] All drawn from Notts R.O., DD. 4P/43/3.

acted as her brother's housekeeper, and Williams was thrown into her company when he helped her in the absence of the steward. After 2 months of this, Lady Bridget's younger sister, who had married the duke of Beaufort, wrote to her mother and her brother advising them that Williams be dismissed as she suspected that the two of them had fallen in love. Lady Bridget, however, calmed Williams' worries and "was pleased to say that the countess of Plymouth by marrying the Bishop of Hereford was very happy, and she thought that a Lady might be very happy in marrying a clergyman."

At this point the Osbornes began to try to inform Williams that he could not expect to get Lady Bridget's fortune. It seemed that her grandfather had not intended Lady Bridget to marry. For while he had left £15,000 to the duchess of Beaufort, who was a more handsome woman, Bridget had only £10,000, and it was tied to two conditions. If she married without her mother's consent, she lost it all, and if she died childless, her husband was obliged to give it back to the Osbornes. Her mother had indeed once said to her: "Biddy, you know your fortune is at my disposal; you shall never marry." Williams himself told her, "Certainly, Madam, the Duke of Leeds never intended you should marry for no one will venture to have you upon those hard conditions." But Bridget was able to reply that she had consulted two lawyers who had informed her that "though I marry without my Lady's consent, my fortune will not be forfeited." This bit of news Williams took as so great an encouragement that he soon arranged for them to be secretly married. Lady Bridget said she would declare her marriage in June when the household went up to London.

The couple now began to find it very difficult to meet. The suspicions of Bridget's mother were fully aroused. The duchess finally cornered her daughter and in an angry scene forced out a confession of the marriage. Bridget asked her husband "for God's sake to carry her away"; but he knew no one in the neighborhood would receive them, and the coachman betrayed their plans. They tried to lock Williams up in the steward's room, while the duchess asked him where his estate was and called him a beggarly rascal. He left the house when he was told that Bridget would be let out of the bakehouse where she was under guard only after his departure. The couple corresponded, and he unsuccessfully tried to arrange her escape. She admitted everything to her brother and burst into tears when he told her that their father, the duke of Leeds, was coming to take her and lock her away in a house at Wimbledon.

Williams eventually brought a suit to win back his wife. When she appeared in court, she and her relations denied everything, and the clergyman said he had not married them. But the Court of Delegates did not believe them and unanimously declared for Williams.[112] He lived to become a prebendary of Winchester. This tale is the most vivid instance of the conflict between patriarchy and romantic love that I have found, and it is an excellent illustration of the confidence to flout parental power and class distinctions that settlement could give a young woman. But it is also a story very much of its generation. One is almost tempted to say that it could not have occurred after 1720.

In the generation after 1720 one finds that those who had had their marriages arranged were willing nonetheless to approve the love matches of the new generation. Mrs. Delany's first marriage had been arranged and left her unhappy: the second time around she pleased herself and married a clergyman. In the course of 16 months in 1728–1729, she was able to tell her sister of four love matches and to speak of them with marked approval. Lady Bell Tufton, with £2000, wished to marry a younger son of the duke of Bolton, who had £2000 a year. Her father forbade the marriage, and Mrs. Delany said she was impatient with him "for who can judge of our happiness but ourselves." But she did not mean to approve of improvidence: "I have no notion of love in a knapsack, but I cannot think riches the only thing that ought to be considered in matrimony." Her cousin Grace Carteret she thought had a better chance of happiness than most aristocratic women, and it was because her parents "though they have as much ambition as most people ... would not force her inclinations." And Grace knew this sufficiently to say so to Lord Dysart when he courted her with her parents' consent. Mrs. Delany was so committed to the new ideal that she could approve of flouting parental power. When Ann Howe married without her mother's consent, she was turned out of doors and consoled by her husband. He took her to a house at Parson's Green, and Mrs. Delany declared it "a sweet place for lovers."[113]

Parents were increasingly inclined to allow their children to marry for love, although, like Mrs. Delany, they could still urge some degree of financial caution. Lord and Lady Hertford without seeing each other had had their marriage arranged by his father when the groom was a man of 30. But their marriage proved happy, and they acted quite differently toward their daughter. She fell in love with Sir Hugh Smithson, who was tall and handsome but poor, and from a not especially distinguished family. Lady Elizabeth was anxious to declare to her parents that she thought it her "duty to sacrifice my inclination to your commands," but she was told by them that they were "ready to

[112]*St. James Evening Post*, 7–9 March 1717.
[113]*Delany*, I, 1861, 154, 203, 173, cf. 153.

sacrifice our inclinations to your happiness, and that in a way of as much friendship and tenderness as we are capable of." They reassured her that they were not angry with her, but they asked her to take a few months to see if she could not change her inclination "without making yourself miserable." "In the end," Lady Hertford wrote, "you have only your heart to combat with, and not a stern authority." Lady Elizabeth's heart won and she married Sir Hugh in the private modern way. As husband and wife they were so inseparable that "they in some degree made themselves ridiculous" in a society which had not yet fully adjusted to the new ideals of romantic love and domesticity.[114]

The marriage arranged for social prestige and economic well-being did not, of course, disappear, but it was on the defensive. Lord Hervey had to defend his position: "I never said, if one knew anything very bad of any woman's temper or morals, that money in one scale ought to be looked upon as a balance to any good qualities you could put in the other." But he was adamant that "the fortune may be a *certainty*, and that for the rest you must take your chance, for there is no getting a wife bespoke—you must take her ready-made." Young men were still willing to have their relations arrange their marriages, but John Spencer's friends were pleased to hear as his grandmother said that he "wishes they may like one another when they meet, for I think that looks as if he was under no sort of inclination or engagement."[115] And they were right to be cautious on this score for he was marrying one of the Carteret women who were free to marry as they liked or not. A young woman could still be drawn in by her older female relatives to give her consent, but then discover as Horace Walpole said, that *"la belle n'aime pas trop le Sieur Leandre*; she cries her eyes red to scarlet: he has made her four visits, and is so in love that he writes to her every other day." This match between Lady Mary Campbell and Lord Coke proved notably unhappy. A young woman could also find that her freedom to move in society led her to fall in love with a man, then engage herself without her mother's consent, and end like Lady Caroline Fitzwalter: privately committed by herself to Lord Jedburgh and publicly promised by her mother to the duke of Leeds.[116] But even the superficially cynical, like Horace Walpole, had begun to find married love charming and to think it an advantage that English aristocratic society had over its continental counterparts. He saw the duke of Richmond sit "by his wife all night

---

[114]Hertford, 35, 100–101, 115–118.
[115]Earl of Ilchester, ed., *Lord Hervey and his Friends, 1726–38* (London: John Murray, 1950), 232; G. S. Thomson, ed., *Letters of a Grandmother, 1732–1735* (London: Jonathan Cape, 1943), 110–111.
[116]Walpole, **IX**, 36–37; Thomson, ed., *Letters of a Grandmother*, 161–162.

kissing her hand" and remarked to his friend in Florence, "how this must sound in the ears of a Florentine cicisbè's, cock or hen!"[117]

The generation after 1750 opened with the passage in 1753 of Lord Hardwicke's Marriage Act, which made marriages of persons under 21 illegal without the consent of their father or guardians (26 Geo II, c. 33). It is an act that at first may seem to go against the very trend I have been claiming existed. It certainly seemed so to some of its opponents. One of them wrote that "in private settlements the invention of mankind, alarmed by their experience of injustice and abuse, is every day at work to temper and confine the parental power"; and while no father would allow his daughter's children to be provided for at the caprice of his son-in-law, this act put the daughter's marriage in her father's power. The act also seemed to all its opponents to be aimed at increasing aristocratic power on the ground that the fathers of heiresses would now consent to marry them only to peers. John Shebbeare had a character in his novel explain that "this Act will throw all the money into the hands of the nobility, who, purchasing the boroughs, will choose what Commons they please; by which means they will become the Representatives of the Lords and not the People, the [King] will be a mere cypher, a kind of pensioner of the Lords." Finally, the act seemed intended to prevent unequal matches because of aristocratic pride of family.[118] But mésalliances, it was pointed out with great sociological penetration, were not prevented by laws but by education. "Nature hath placed your children under your inspection and care," Henry Stebbing told parents; this authority "should be employed in giving them a sober and virtuous education suitable to their rank and quality, which will naturally dispose them to set a just value upon themselves and to think themselves disgraced when offers of marriage are made to them by persons of inferior condition." Class endogamy, he said, was in any case the rule, as the evidence of their eyes would tell them. For ordinarily the poor married "among the poor, the middle rank among the middle rank, and the rich and noble among the rich and noble. The world *naturally* runs this way without the help of laws. The lower classes of men have it not in their *power* to marry above their rank, or very rarely. The rich and great have as rarely so little *pride* as to permit

---

[117]Walpole, **XVII**, 184: cf. his "is it not amazing that in England people will not find out that they can live separate without parting" (ibid., 486).

[118]*Considerations upon the Bill for Preventing Clandestine Marriages* (London, 1753), 13; John Shebbeare, *The Marriage Act* (London, 1754), 2 vol., I, 74–75; *A Letter from a Bystander* (London, 1753), 6–7.

them to marry below theirs."[119] It might seem that the trend of the previous generation was being reversed by an act that, its opponents claimed, promoted a view of marriage that made it an instrument of patriarchal and patrilineal power rather than the supreme expression of romantic attachment.

But they were wrong. First of all, their views were seriously prejudiced since satirical depiction of aristocratic family life was so often in the eighteenth century the first means of middle-class agression. We shall see this in Richardson, and we can see it here in Shebbeare's novel, if we take Mrs. Delany as our guide. She began to read him under the impression that the book was a satire against Lord Hardwicke. But she did not easily understand it: "It seems a general satire, with a good deal of humor in Fielding's way—spun out to make the most of it." And then when she finished it, she was quite disappointed as she "had heard it cried up." For the book turned out to be not against the Marriage Act but against the aristocracy: "I don't understand the policy of making all the nobility appear odious." And she wondered whether satire would be taken for reality: for "books that are written for the middling rank of people ought not to be in an ironical strain: they are often taken literally, and do more harm than good."[120]

Mrs. Delany knew that aristocratic mores had changed but that some parts of the world did not. A year before the passage of the act, she was obliged to help the duchess of Portland squelch a rumor that she was marrying her daughter to a rich man with no principles: "you know the Duchess of Portland's heart too well to believe that she can be so blinded by ambition as to sacrifice a daughter's happiness."[121] But yet this was the same duchess who refused to countenance the marriage of her brother-in-law to his mistress. For romantic love was expected to operate within the bounds of class endogamy (as it does today[122]) and the double standard. And it was because romantic love had become so acceptable that the act was finally passed. It had always seemed to fail before because it would have deprived younger sons of the means of making their fortunes. But the House of Commons, which allowed it to

---

[119]Henry Stebbing, *A Dissertation on the Power of States to Deny Civil Protection to the Marriages of Minors* (London, 1755), 47–48. It was still possible to marry without parental consent by running away to Scotland, as Lord George Lennox did, or to Guernsey, or by using a large London church for the announcement of banns (*Leinster*, II, 89–90; *Gentlemen's Magazine*, XXX, 1760, 30–31; *Annual Register*, X, 1766, 60).

[120]*Delany*, III, 1861, 321, 328. A writer like Stebbing had another axe to grind: He was a clergyman objecting to aristocratic anticlericalism and perhaps also to their social disdain for his profession. See Sir Tanfield Leman, *Matrimony Analysed* (London, 1755), 67–68.

[121]*Delany*, III, 1861, 73.

[122]W. J. Goode, *The Family* (Englewood Cliffs, N.J.: Prentice-Hall, 1964), 37–41.

pass, must have been filled, finally, with a majority of younger sons who felt, like Spencer Cowper, that there was no chance of happiness in marriage where "choice is directed by gain."[123]

The Marriage Act passed not because there was a reassertion of patriarchal power, but because men were no longer willing to tolerate the use of marriage as a means of making one's fortune, and parents were content to allow their children to marry for love. They could marry for love, but they were encouraged to do so at an adult age; and it is very likely that in England romantic marriage meant later marriage. Guardians and parents alike were convinced by the 1770s that love made marriages and that their business was to discourage precipitate decisions and to remind their wards or children not to forget entirely considerations of birth, wealth, and character.

The making of Frances Duncombe's marriage in 1775 is instructive in this regard, for she was the kind of heiress who in another age would have been married off at the earliest possible moment.[124] Her father, Lord Faversham, had married three times; all his children by the first wife died but he had a daughter by each of the other two. When he died the younger daughter went to live with her mother when she married Lord Radnor as his second wife. But Frances, the other daughter, was refused by all her relations, including her grandmother. Bishop Moss took her into his house for he was her guardian along with John Hayes, her father's best friend, and Lord Willoughby, Faversham's brother-in-law by his first wife. Shortly before Frances came of age, her mother's relatives began to show an interest in her for she was a great heiress of £57,000. Her mother's sister, Lady Ranelagh, began taking her to Almack's, where, with her approval, Frances danced with a young man called John Bowater who shortly began to court her. Bowater was the son of a man who had a fortune of £3000 a year drawn from the rents of dockyards and houses in Woolwich.

Bishop Moss resented the sudden reappearance of Frances' relations, and he would not agree to their having a hand in making her settlements. He thought Bowater too impetuous and none too bright. He felt that neither his family nor his fortune were equal to Frances's. And besides he had singled out a young man himself, "a person of great quality as well as fortune." It was Lord Folkestone, the stepson of Frances' stepmother. But Folkestone was a less than ardent lover and Frances rejected him. The bishop believed, however, that with time she

[123]Gally, *Clandestine Marriages*, 99; Hughes, ed., *Letters of Cowper*, 6. Charles Townshend (Namier and Brooke, *Townshend*, 29-30) was a younger son of the old school, but his side lost the vote.
[124]Shakespeare's Birthplace Trust: Willoughby de Broke MSS, 1650.

could be brought round to forget Bowater and to look kindly on Folkestone.

But Bowater was not to be dealt with in this way. He appealed to Lord Willoughby over the head of the bishop. Willoughby agreed with the bishop that Bowater's family and fortune were not equal to Frances' but he certainly thought his fortune was "a good one, and joined with her's, sufficient to make any people happy as far as that will do it." Willoughby was more impressed by what he thought to be Bowater's "real attachment," and feared the "danger of her liking somebody less worthy." But the bishop insisted that "she had made this acquaintance very hastily" and would only describe it as a "small attachment" or "Miss Duncombe's new attachment." The bishop decided that it would be best if the couple did not see each other for the summer months and that if by the autumn or winter "no better party should offer and she continue to like him, it would then be time enough to think of him." The bishop persuaded Hayes to agree with him, this approval eased by the latter's memory that "early marriages were ever the abhorrence of her poor Father; forty times at least has he most seriously talked to me on this head." But Willoughby was obliged to say that he doubted Bowater would agree "because it is what I would not do were I in his case," and he was mildly sarcastic about Lord Folkestone's diffidence as a lover.

The bishop nonetheless put his program into action, and extracted some sort of agreement from Bowater, which Bowater promptly broke. The bishop told Willoughby that Bowater was "rude, clamorous and ungentlemanly" and began to think of turning Frances out of doors. Willoughby warned the bishop "that as she evidently has a liking to him and he persists in his attempts to see her, if we continue to refuse it, we shall probably drive them to run away." And run away they almost immediately did. Hayes' reaction was that "until I see him disposed to make her a bad husband, I feel myself inclined to do everything I can to dispose him to make her a good one." Willoughby therefore approached Bowater on the subject of a settlement, but the young man, knowing he had the support of Frances' relatives, declared: "You wish to hear my proposals for settlements. You already have them. I never swerve from what I once propose, but as the case now stands, it must be a Master in Chancery who shall direct them." From this folly, however, Willoughby patiently persuaded him with a reminder of the notorious delays of that court, and 3 days later the articles were signed. It had all taken about 12 months—from first proposals through elopement to marriage settlement. And it might all have been less dramatic if the bishop had not had such high hopes for his ward's marriage, or if he had been more inclined to believe in love. But Frances' relatives were convinced of love's value, as were her other guardians, and in the face of their acquiescence, the Bishop had to yield. But the contest between Bowater and Folkestone had also represented a contest between the relations of Lord Faversham's second wife and those of his third. And in this generation the former had the overwhelming advantage, for they backed the young man Frances Duncombe had fallen in love with. The two families fought each other not for Frances' money, but for influence; and romantic love, not violence, decided the outcome.

Parents, like guardians, thought it their duty to represent to their daughters the claims of prudence, but consented when love was proven. When the duke of Grafton's daughter, Lady Georgiana, fell in love with a man 25 years old, of good character, and with an estate, but who still did "not seem an equal match," her father told her that if she waited 6 months and still felt the same, he would consent to the marriage. But these waiting periods—so beloved by the older generation—never worked. They either confirmed affection or drove an impatient couple into running away. Lady Georgiana had fallen in love with John Smith when she was 19; within a month after her 21st birthday, she left her father's house and married him in a London church.[125]

But love matches so grew in prestige that parents came to foster them when they thought they would contribute to a daughter's happiness. Lord Duncannon fell in love with Lady Harriet Spencer, but being a quiet man, he did not tell her. Instead he sent his father, Lord Bessborough, to make proposals to her parents. Lady Spencer answered for them that they "would never decide in an affair of this kind," but left it entirely to their daughter's determination. But in truth they liked the idea. Lady Spencer was pleased that Duncannon had had a religious education, and they liked his family. The only difficulty was his fortune, for the Bessborough estates were worth only £5000 a year, half of which the young couple would have to live on. There remained the question of Lady Harriet's feelings. Lord Duncannon was "very much in earnest indeed," but Harriet was, at first, surprised. For, as she explained, "it is impossible one should be very well acquainted with any body in the intercourse of the world, with him I was less than most people." So she did not reply at once to his proposals. She wished she could have known him better, but she was willing to try to fall in love, especially as she knew it would please her parents. Lady Spencer soon persuaded herself that "Harriet, if I can judge of anything, [is] almost as far gone as" Duncannon. And Harriet had in fact come round to think-

[125]Walpole, **XXXII**, 351, **XXXIII**, 15.

ing that "from what I have heard of him, and the great attachment he professes to have for me, I have a better chance of being reasonably happy with him than with most people I know." But she was frightened by the disparity in their temperaments. At this point Lady Spencer felt it her "duty to represent strongly to her the inconvenience of so small a fortune compared to what she has hitherto seen and experience in life." Harriet was able to reassure her with answers that were "so prudent, so sensible and so proper." But Lady Spencer had probably been won over from the first, convinced, no doubt, that the gravity that frightened her daughter was just what she needed in a husband: "I really think," she wrote, "his character will give her a better chance of happiness than a much larger fortune if they like each other as much as I suspect they do."[126] Money was no longer a principal object in marriages. Daughters were given full freedom to choose or reject their husbands, and parents counted present love and its future likelihood the strongest justification for marriage. But a young woman like Harriet was so trained to hide anything that might seem like an immodest interest in sexuality that parents could experience great difficulty in trying to decide whether a daughter was in love. Bishop Moss had declared himself to have just this difficulty with Frances Duncombe. And the authority of parents was still so great that a woman could, like Harriet or Frances Duncombe, allow a romantic marriage to be arranged for her.

It was at this point in 1784, that the young François de la Rochefoucauld visited England and wrote down for his father what he had observed of the nature of English aristocratic marriage. The English married in their later twenties, which was contrary to his French experience of earlier marriage. And he hit upon the right reason. "To have a wife who is not agreeable to you must, in England, make life a misery," he wrote. "Accordingly the Englishman makes more effort to get to know his bride before marriage; she has a similar desire, and I suppose it is on this account that marriage before the age of twenty-five is rare." But he did not notice explicitly that the difference in ages between men and women at marriage could be accounted for by the length of their education. For a woman was formed at 15, entered society with her mother, and married at 25. A man's education was not completed till he was 21, and he married at 30. Once in society Rochefoucauld noted, "the English have much more opportunity of getting to know each other before marriage, for young folk are in society from an early age . . .

[126]Earl of Bessborough and Arthur Aspinall, *Lady Bessborough and her Family Circle* (London: John Murray, 1940), 31–32, 36; Chatsworth MSS, **V**, 307.

young girls mix with company and talk and enjoy themselves with as much freedom as if they were married." After 10 years of this, they married, and Rouchefoucauld estimated that "three marriages out of four are based on affection, and one can see by experience that most of them are perfectly successful." Once married, "husband and wife are always together and share the same society. It is the rarest thing to meet one without the other....It would be more ridiculous to do otherwise in England than it would be to go everywhere with your wife in Paris." What had been ridiculous in the previous generation now seemed to a foreigner's eye the usual course. And he noticed that these marriages produced more children than in France, which was statistically correct. "I don't know what will be my fate in France," he told his father, "but at present I should find it much more to my taste to have an English wife."[127] The English Channel had become the great divide between romantic and arranged marriage.

Marriage Ceremonies

The new marriage pattern lay at the heart of domesticity—two people married for love, lived constantly thereafter in each other's company, and put great effort into the rearing of a large brood of children. Marriage ceremonies changed accordingly by generation in symbolic symbiosis, discarding first the public marriage feast and ceremony, then the symbolic bedding of the bride by her relations, and issuing eventually in the private honeymoon. In the seventeenth century marriage had been celebrated by a great feast given by the bride's father. It could spread out over several days and cost many hundreds of pounds. And the wedding night was concluded by the public bedding of the bride with much obscenity and the couple's making each other's acquaintance. By 1720 the marriage feast had disappeared. Instead the marriage took place in the evening about eight or nine, and was followed by a dinner that day and the next, some card playing, and perhaps some dancing. But only very near relations were invited.[128]

The larger world learned of the marriage through the distribution of favors and the presentation of the couple at court. Favors were large bows of fine material that were given out to those who went to visit

---

[127]Marchand, ed., *Frenchman in England*, 48–50. Rochefoucauld's estimates as to the age of marriage and number of children find statistical support in Hollingsworth, 10–19, 25–28, 29–42, 71. This must lead us to accept his estimate of the frequency of love matches.

[128]Stone, *Crisis*, 633, 651–652; Henri Misson, *Memoirs and Observations in His Travels over England*, trans. by M. Ozell (London, 1719), 349.

the bride and were sent to friends in the country. They were worn on the arm on the wedding day and on one's hat for some weeks thereafter. Early in the century they were distributed in great numbers. At the marriage of the duke of Ormond's sister, 500 were given out and everyone from the king to the meanest servant could be found with one in his hat. Sir Robert Walpole was even more extravagant when, at the moment of his wife's death, he married the mistress to whom he was passionately devoted. Over 800 favors were distributed. They cost a guinea apiece and were made of six bows of silver gauze with eight more bows of narrow gold ribbon in the middle; members of the royal family were given special favors of embroidered gold ribbon that were six times as expensive. But Walpole was the king's minister.[129] With others the distribution and wearing of favors could be used to mark society's disapproval of second marriages, or its doubts about the legitimacy of a particular marriage. Lady Mary Coke declared that it was "certainly out of all form" that Lord Burghersh should give out favors on his second marriage; but the sister of Burghersh's first wife evidently approved of her brother-in-law's new marriage, for she wore his favor. The most prestigious approval a marriage could receive was for the royal family to wear its favors. The duke of Kingston was, therefore, careful when he contracted a marriage that many thought was bigamous not only to send his relations to court wearing his favors, but also to present them to the royal family, who, alas for him, refused to wear them. The sister of the new duchess's real husband smilingly remarked that she thought she should have been sent a favor. By the 1760s and 1790s, however, even this ceremony was being contracted. Families in the first decade came to court wearing favors, but did not present any to the royal family. And in the next decade (admittedly in the case of a couple both of whom were over thirty), favors were given only to those who attended the wedding and to the aunts and uncles who had not.[130]

In the generation after 1720 privacy and discretion were increasingly emphasized. Lord Hertford married off his daughter by deciding at the end of dinner, when the servants had gone off to eat, that this was as good a time as any. He asked his chaplain to fetch the prayerbook, and the ceremony was performed before the seven people who had been at dinner. The groom's mother missed the wedding since it had originally been planned for a day or two later. The marriage was kept a secret for a few days until the settlements arrived. For the signing of the settlements was usually the signal for the marriage. Grace Granville was

[129]Misson, Memoirs, 349; Hertford, 60–61; Delany, I, 1861, 96; J.H. Plumb, Sir Robert Walpole (London: Cresset Press, 1960), 112–115.
[130]Coke, II, 10–11, III, 39–40; Delany, I, 1862, 591.

Settlement and Marriage   115

married suddenly at noon on the day the settlements were signed. The marriage in this case took place with somewhat greater ceremony. There were two bridesmen and two bridesmaids, and Lord Weymouth gave the bride away. There was a handsome family dinner for seven, and a supper at a tavern at 8:00 in the evening with a harper for music and some card playing. But the bride was still formally put to bed at night by two of her female relations. The couple went into the country the following morning to be alone for a few days. But it is unlikely that there were any tales of sexual prowess as there might have been in a previous age. Horace Walpole complained that after Lord Fitzwilliam's marriage, there were "no anecdotes of the wedding night." He supposed that Lord Lincoln, Fitzwilliams' close friend, might have been told something, but "he is discreet, I suppose by compact."[131]

Discretion about the occurrence of a marriage began to be taken to great lengths. It was a week after Lord Middlesex's marriage before it became known, and Walpole said that the bride "might have popped out a child before a single Sackville would have been at the expense of a syllable to justify her."[132] But this behavior was not peculiar to a single family. For it was one of the serious objections to the Marriage Act that it seemed to require couples to be married in the public glare of a church. Any aristocrat, though, was able to secure a licence that allowed marriage in a private house. And even a marriage in a church could be managed with no great show. Lady Georgiana Spencer was suddenly told on Sunday morning that she was to be married to the duke of Devonshire although another date had originally been set. But the celebration of the king's birthday had conveniently brought both families to town: so early in the morning they went out of town to Wimbledon church where between one service and the next, they were married "as quietly and uncrowded as if John and Joan had tied the Gordian knot."[133]

Once the marriage was performed, and the few days spent in the country over, the young couple came back to town, and accompanied by their relations, they went to court in their wedding clothes to give public notice of their marriage to the king and queen. These clothes remained, perhaps, the most elaborate part of marriage. The bride was usually married in a gown of white satin trimmed with silver, and wore jewels given to her by her husband or his family. There were also a number of other gowns made for a bride on this occasion, and the story of a

---
[131]Hertford, 100; Delany, **II**, 1861, 80; Walpole, **XXX**, 49–50.
[132]Walpole, **XVIII**, 527.
[133]Gally, Clandestine Marriages, 89; Delany, **I**, 1862, 593.

marriage was not complete without an account of the variety of their materials and colors.[134] But in keeping with the general moderation of public ceremony, Mrs. Delany declared in 1774 that the fashion of brides being presented at court in white was out.[135]

After 1750 the private family supper, the trip into the country, and presentation at court all remained part of the ceremonies of marriage. But the bedding of the bride seems entirely to have passed away. And in the 1770s there was a narrowing of the circle of those who came to the supper or went to court with the bride and groom. Lady Mary Coke was mortally offended that she and the other aunts were not invited to their nephew's marriage: "As we were excluded I did not see that we had any business to make fine clothes to go with the bride to court." And when Lord Cathcart married off his two daughters, Lady Mary noted that it was "quite in the old style; seventeen in company, a great dinner and supper, distant relations invited." The marriage trip also lost its accompanying relatives. In 1766 after Lady Betty Montagu was married, she and her husband went down into the country and were accompanied by their relations. But when in 1774 Lady Stanhope and her relations went down to Chevening with her son and his bride, Lady Mary Coke commented that as a "consequence the marriage has been celebrated in the old style: the new one you know does not admit of a third person."[136] In such an atmosphere did Lord Herbert reply to his father's suggestion in 1787 that he invite a young foreigner to his wedding: "You were certainly joking when you proposed I should ask him to my marriage, for though his family are well known to you, you must recollect that he is a very slight foreign acquaintance of mine, and that no one likes to faire spectacle de son marriage, and I have absolutely refused to let any of my nearest connections and greatest friends to be at it."[137] Marriage had become, as far as possible, an intense and private experience between husband and wife. It was no longer a public spectacle nor even a family occasion. It was the hidden pearl of domestic happiness.

This domesticity was in a real sense fostered by the compromise between kindred and patrilineage that the family settlement effected, since the settlement gave to women a degree of independence which helped them to choose a husband for love and then to live with him to some degree as an equal and true friend. It was certainly the case that

---

[134]*Delany*, **I**, 1861, 427–428, **II**, 1861, 487–488; *Walpole*, **IX**, 235, **XXX**, 49–50.

[135]*Delany*, **I**, 1862, 583.

[136]*Coke*, **I**, 205, 210, **IV**, 449, 450; John McClelland, ed., *Letters of Lady Sarah Byng Osborn, 1721–1773* (Stanford: Stanford Univ. Press, 1930), 97–98.

[137]Lord Herbert, ed., *Pembroke Papers (1780–1794)* (London: Jonathan Cape, 1950), 347.

peasant or artisan women, whose lives were affected primarily by kindred structures, enjoyed a higher status than did women among a patrilineally inclined aristocracy. This was true in medieval Europe, whether in Genoa or in England, and the absence of patrilineal structures in America will probably also best explain the higher status in the seventeenth century of American as opposed to English women. But the closer relations between husband and wife, and parent and child, that we have called domesticity cannot be seen simply as the effect of the family settlement. For even in a purely kindred society like traditional Ethiopia where both sexes had equal rights to property and divorce, the conduct of women was still subject to the patriarchal correction of a father or a husband.[138] The emergence of eighteenth-century English domesticity must therefore be seen primarily as the consequence of the replacement of patriarchal patterns of authority by egalitarian relations, however much the continuing presence of kindred structures at all levels of society may have facilitated the process. It is therefore the business of the remainder of this book to assemble the evidence for the rise of domesticity by considering, first, the changing patterns of dependency in households and then the bearing, care, and education of children.

---

[138] D. O. Hughes, "Urban Growth and Family Structure in Medieval Genoa," *Past & Present*, No. 66, 1975; "Domestic Ideals and Social Behavior: Evidence from Medieval Genoa," C. E. Rosenberg, ed., *The Family in History* (Philadelphia: Univ. of Pennsylvania Press, 1975); R. H. Hilton, *The English Peasantry in the Later Middle Ages* (Oxford, Clarendon Press, 1975), Chap. 6, read in the light of D. M. Stenton, *The English Woman in History* (London: Allen & Urwin, 1957), Chaps. 1 and 2, and Lorraine Lancaster, "Kinship in Anglo-Saxon Society," *British Journal of Sociology*, IX, 1958; Roger Thompson, *Women in Stuart England and America* (London: Routledge & Kegan Paul, 1974); Allan Hoben, *Land Tenure among the Amhara of Ethiopia* (Chicago: Univ. of Chicago Press, 1973), 61.

Figure 3.1 *Portrait of the marquess of Halifax by Mary Beale. The marquess advised his daughter: "That which you are to pray for is a wise husband, one that by knowing how to be a master for that very reason will not make you feel the weight of it . . . . Servants may be looked upon as humble friends." Copyright photograph from the National Portrait Gallery, London. Reproduced by permission.*

III

Patriarchy and Domesticity

There were in the eighteenth century two opposing models of household organization. One we have called *patriarchy*, the other *domesticity*. Patriarchy was ancient and had grown out of the organization of traditional agricultural society, but it had received a new degree of conscious articulation in the sixteenth and seventeenth centuries. It was enshrined in traditional religion. An exposition of the whole duty of man explained that the Tenth Commandment reckoned as "the possessions of our neighbour... not only his house, servants and cattle, which may all pass under the general name of his goods or riches, but particularly his wife, as a principal part of his possessions."[1] Patriarchy presumed that there was property not only in things but in persons and that ownership lay with the heads of households. It meant that some men were owned by others, and all women and children by their hus-

---

[1] Richard Allestree, *Works* (Oxford, 1727), 64.

119

bands or fathers. For reasons that are not yet very clear these presumptions were discredited by egalitarian ones in England and in the rest of European society in the seventeenth and eighteenth centuries. The clearest victories of egalitarian ideas occurred in the relationships between adult men. All forms of slavery were discredited for the first time in human history, and the three great revolutions of these two centuries put forward the idea that all men were created equal and worthy of being part of the political nation. But the abolition of slavery and the arrival of political democracy came only after another century of struggle.[2]

The relations of men to women and children changed even more slowly. The Roman church today continues to bar women from its ministry, and all men are still confident that they own their children— for have they not made them? Among the eighteenth-century English aristocracy there did appear, however, a limited degree of equality between men and their wives and children that resulted in a new pattern of household interaction— from which servants were excluded. This was domesticity. Lady Sarah Napier described it to perfection when she said of her nephew that "his aimable little wife adores him, and he doats on her and her six pretty girls: it's quite charming to see them all together, and they are so domestick you scarce see them separate."[3] This pattern of close and loving association between husband and wife, and of doting care for children, is said by Edward Shorter to have appeared among the European working class by the middle of the nineteenth century. Lawrence Stone, with greater probability, first finds it among the wealthy classes of England and America in the late seventeenth and the eighteenth centuries.[4] Stone's explanation of the

---

[2]M. I. Finley, *The Ancient Economy* (London: Chatto & Windus, 1973); Christopher Hill, *Society and Puritanism in Pre-Revolutionary England* (London: Secker & Warburg, 1964) and *The World Turned Upside Down* (New York: Viking Press, 1972); C. B. Macpherson, *The Political Theory of Possessive Individualism* (Oxford: Clarendon Press, 1962); G. J. Schochet, *Patriarchalism in Political Thought* (New York: Basic Books, 1975); John Bossy, "The Counter-Reformation and the People of Catholic Europe," *Past & Present*, No. 47; G. W. Mullin, *Flight and Rebellion* (London: Oxford Univ. Press, 1972); D. B. Davis, *The Problem of Slavery in Western Culture* (Ithaca: Cornell Univ. Press, 1966).

[3]Lady Ilchester and Lord Stavordale, *The Life and Letters of Lady Sarah Lennox 1745-1826* (London: John Murray, 1902), 383.

[4]Edward Shorter, *The Making of the Modern Family* (New York: Basic Books, 1975); Lawrence Stone, "The Rise of the Nuclear Family in Early Modern England," in C. E. Rosenberg, ed., *The Family in History* (Philadelphia: Univ. of Pennsylvania Press, 1975); cf. his "The Domestic Revolution," a critical review of Shorter in the *TLS* (28 May 1976), 637. Shorter is systematically criticized by Joan Scott and Louise Tilly in *The Family in History*. Stone suggested in the *TLS* (presumably on the basis of Peter Burke, *Venice and Amsterdam* (London: Temple Smith, 1974), and R. A. Goldthwaite, *Private Wealth in Renaissance Florence* (Princeton: Princeton Univ. Press, 1968)) that domesticity may have first appeared among the haute bourgeoisie of Florence and Amsterdam. But Goldthwaite must be

causes and consequences of these new feelings is in many ways similar to the one that will be offered here, but it is not entirely satisfactory because some of his causes are more problematical than he realizes, and because he misses the fundamental structure of traditional European kinship by failing to distinguish between kindred and patrilineage. Stone maintains that kinship ties in the sixteenth and seventeenth centuries were weakened among the aristocracy because of the state's demand for their loyalty, and among the poor by changes in the economy which loosened manorial and guild control and increased geographical mobility, while the state took on the care of the widow, the orphan, the sick, and the old. But even as this contraction of kinship ties occurred, Protestant religion entered the household and made it the center of worship and affection; yet this new intensity between parent and child, and husband and wife, sometimes strengthened rather than weakened patriarchy.

This last point is Stone's strongest. We have seen Edward Wortley use an argument from domestic affection to ensure that his control of his property would allow him to punish and reward his wife and his children. The act that controlled the marriage of minors was passed by the first generation that married for love. And, as this chapter will show, damages from a wife's lover and divorce for her adultery appeared together with the feminist tracts of the 1690s. Protestant religion certainly spiritualized the household, but, as John Bossy has shown, so did Catholicism.[5] And as we shall see in a moment, family prayers were said in aristocratic households as a means of disciplining the servants. They disappeared when those households ceased to be at the center of the local economy and grew less complex in their staffs—and after masters came to see themselves as fathers to their children but merely employers to their servants.

Stone sees that the kinship ties of the poor were loose, but by attributing this to economic change he misses the likelihood that they had always been so because of the nature of cognatic family structures. Economic change is far more likely to have affected the poor by excluding them from the patriarchal concern and control of the great households of their neighborhoods than by lessening their ties to their relations. But a commercialized economy will not in itself account for the appearance of egalitarian ideas, since Japan (with a kinship system

---

read in the light of the criticisms in F. W. Kent, *Household and Lineage in Renaissance Florence* (Princeton: Princeton Univ. Press, 1977), and it is likely that what has been observed in Florence, or in Amsterdam as opposed to Venice, is better explained by the differences between kindred and patrilineage than between domesticity and patriarchy.

[5]Bossy, *Past & Present*, No. 47.

similar to Europe's) underwent at the same time similar economic changes without producing an egalitarian ideology.[6]

Stone is certainly right to claim that landed families were disregarding the ties to an extensive cousinhood that had once existed. We have argued for this from the legitimation of cousin marriage, the changes in the ceremonies of mourning and marriage, and the role of friendship. But Stone cannot see (in the absence of the distinction between kindred and patrilineage) that the limitation of effective ties to an individual's families of orientation and procreation is a frequent characteristic of kindred societies.[7] If he had, he might have asked why the aristocracy in the late seventeenth and the early eighteenth centuries should have felt free to abandon to some degree the protection that a patrilineal ideology gave them in a kindred society. The degree of this abandonment is apparent in their strengthening of the rights of younger children and in their treatment of marriage not as an alliance but first as an act of incorporation and then of love. The answer to the question may well lie in the changing political situation of the aristocracy, for while aristocratic lineages, as Stone says, may have been brought under control in the early sixteenth century in the interest of the princely state, the aristocracy itself felt able in the late seventeenth century to relax its patrilineal ties once it had taken the reins of government into its own hands. It might then be possible to account for the appearance of aristocratic domesticity in the following way. A commercialized economy cut the patriarchal ties between aristocratic masters and their servants. Religion encouraged a particular form of family affection. And political control allowed the aristocracy to somewhat disregard patrilineal norms and permitted it to participate more fully in the egalitarian ones of a kindred society. In the class where education facilitated conscious cultural change more than in any other, the fusion of these four factors—commercialization, religion, political control, and kindred structures—may have produced that partial egalitarianism in familial relations that we have called domesticity. But as so often in historical explanation, this remains speculative. And causation is nowhere more difficult than in the history of the family. It is much easier to describe the appearance of the two major changes that European family structure has undergone in the last thousand years, or to show something of their consequences, than it is to explain why European elites should have adopted a patrilineal ideology in the tenth century and a domestic one in the eighteenth. But we at least may

---

[6]Thomas C. Smith, *The Agrarian Origins of Modern Japan* (Stanford: Stanford Univ. Press, 1959).
[7]G. P. Murdock, ed., *Social Structure in Southeast Asia* (Chicago: Quadrangle Books, 1960).

attempt an explanation for these changes in a way that we cannot approach (except perhaps on some grand evolutionary scheme) the inexplicable given that before, during, and after both of these changes European society was cognatic in its basic structure.

In this chapter, therefore, my main purpose must be to describe change rather than explain it. Its overall aim is to show the replacement of patriarchy by domesticity by considering first the structure of the aristocratic household and then the subordination of women and children. An aristocratic household was an establishment of from 30 to 50 people, composed of the head of the household, his wife, his children, and his servants. There were no other relations living in the household, partially as a result of romantic marriage. For the same reason wives took a growing role in household management, and children were shielded from contact with the servants. The great household was probably becoming less the center from which the estates were managed; its contribution to the local economy was likely to be less important in a commercial world; and its broken meats were no longer used to relieve the poor at the gates.

The social gulf between master and servant deepened when the lesser gentry ceased to serve as the household's servants of state. The master's moral control over his servants was loosened when the chaplain disappeared and family prayers went with him. Most masters might still forbid servants to marry and form families of their own, but some were changing their views under the pressure of the argument that all men had an equal right to domesticity. Servants, it was still argued, served best when they loved their masters and regarded them as fathers. But it was increasingly the case that the wage contract was the principal tie between master and servant, and to make it more effective, there was an attempt to abolish a servant's traditional perquisites. Servants, it has been said, entered contractually into patriarchal relations, and consequently their discipline was always problematical.

Patriarchal rights over women and children were established by the marriage contract. A man had no legal rights over his bastards, who were no one's children, certainly not their mothers'. They were therefore under the crown's guardianship. Domesticity, as has been said, increased patriarchal control over women and children since men believed they could not love what they did not own. But domesticity was based on the friendship of husband and wife, and friendship, as the feminist writers said, could exist only between equals. Divorce, therefore, which began as a means of punishing an adulterous wife and protecting the integrity of a lineage, became a means of releasing individuals from unhappy marriages. And while a wife was never able to claim damages from her husband's mistress as he could from her lover, a husband who philandered could hardly claim to love his wife, and she might feel justified in making it difficult for him to provide for his bastard.

Household Size and Composition

Great families (as the households of the aristocracy were called) were supposed to be centers in their neighborhood of moral influence and the relief of the poor. "A well-regulated great family," Samuel Johnson said, "may improve a neighborhood in civility and elegance, and give an example of good order, virtue and piety." But it was also Johnson who remarked that "to consider it as a duty to reside on a family estate is a prejudice; for we must consider, that working people get employment equally, and the produce of the land is sold equally, whether a great family resides at home or not; and if the rents of an estate be carried to London, they return again in the circulation of commerce; nay, Sir, we must perhaps allow that carrying the rents to a distance is a good, because it contributes to that circulation."[8] The demands of a national economy were not easily accommodated to those of a self-sufficient patriarchy. Men therefore saw the size of these great families decline without regret and were prepared to deliver the poor over to the care of the parish.

It was a common opinion throughout the century that the number of aristocratic servants was declining. Bishop Burnet was happy to see in 1713 the disappearance of the remnants of bastard feudalism and thought it "a happiness to the nation that the great number of idle and useless retainers that were among noblemen anciently is much reduced," even though he recognized that their great houses still required them to "entertain many servants to be either nuisances where they live or to set a pattern to others."[9] By the end of our period the scale of these households had been so reduced that Boswell had great difficulty in persuading Johnson that the earl of Eglinton had had a hundred persons in his house. But for once Boswell's snobbery may not have misled him. The duke of Somerset in the 1690s had a retinue of over a hundred, and the duke of Chandos in 1722 had 90. But Somerset and Chandos were exceptional in their pride and princely pretensions. The efficient

---

[8]James Boswell, *Life of Johnson* (London: Dent, 1963), **II**, 130.
[9]Gilbert Burnet, *History of His Own Time* (Oxford, 1833), 6 vol., **VI**, 219.

number of servants seems to have varied between 30 and 50 throughout the century. Nottingham had 49 in 1693, and Lord Hervey 40 in 1704. Both these men, however, had many children, a factor likely to increase the number of servants. Nevertheless, the duke of Newcastle, childless and rich, had 40 in 1734, and the bachelor earl of Lonsdale had 49 in 1787. The duke of Bedford usually had 40 servants in London, but the duke of Norfolk, Lord Gage, and Lord Hardwicke each got by with 30. But whether there were 50 servants or merely 30, these great families were extremely conspicuous in a society in which most people live in households of 4 or 5.[10]

The economic function of these great households in their neighborhoods came soon in the eighteenth century to be limited to their internal consumption. The patriarchal ideal had been otherwise. It had held, as Lord Warrington told his sons, that "good housekeeping is a thing that is highly praiseworthy, and the way to have yours so esteemed, is to let your provisions consist rather in sufficiency of that which is wholesome, than in little curiously dressed dishes, which won't suffice to fill your servants' bellies when you have done, and consequently the poor must be sent railing and cursing from your gates."[11] Lord Derby directed in 1692 that no food was to be given to strangers or beggars except by his direction, and that the meat left from dinner was not to be given away but used for supper; but his porter still distributed a daily allowance for the poor at the gate.[12] The master's table, in this world, fed the neighborhood, and its liberality could place severe financial strain on as great an estate as that of the duke of Newcastle.[13] But a master like Lord Nottingham, who rejected this part of tradition, arranged that, while his servants should have at their table all that was fit for them, there was to be no basket for the poor, so that the master might "distribute his charity in his own way."[14] The great family had turned in on itself, and the master's charity had become an individual rather than a patriarchal action. By 1740 Lady Petre was

[10]Boswell, *Life of Johnson*, II, 226; J. Jean Hecht, *The Domestic Servant Class in Eighteenth Century England* (London: Routledge & Kegan Paul, 1956), 5; C. H. C. Baker and M. I. Baker, *The Life ... of James Brydges, First Duke of Chandos* (Oxford: Clarendon Press, 1949), 176; H. J. Habakkuk, "Daniel Finch, 2nd Earl of Nottingham: His House and Estate," in Plumb, ed., *Studies in Social History* (London: Longmans, Green, 1955), 171–172; *Bristol Diary*, 90; S. Y. Nulle, *Thomas Pelham-Holles, Duke of Newcastle* (Philadelphia: Univ. of Pennsylvania Press, 1931), 184–185; Peter Laslett and Richard Wall, eds., *Household and Family in Past Time* (Cambridge: University Press, 1972), 135; G. S. Thomson, *The Russells in Bloomsbury 1669–1771* (London: Jonathan Cape, 1940), 283–289; Hecht, *Servant Class*, 5.
[11]*The Works of the ... Earl of Warrington* ed. by J. Delaheuze (1694), 25.
[12]Lancs. R.O., DDK/15/8.
[13]R. A. Kelch, *Newcastle* (Berkeley: Univ. Of California Press, 1974), 82, 190.
[14]Pearl Finch, *History of Burley-on-the-Hill* (London: Bale & Danielsson, 1901), 2 vol., 1,232.

therefore able to tell her young protege that in England, unlike France, the distribution of food was more "for necessary ostentation sake than for true charity" since the wandering poor were provided for by the poor laws.[15] The great family had become a private household.

But before we turn to consider in earnest the domestication of the patriarchal household, we must establish that these were not extended households, that is, that the master did not, in usual circumstances, have living with him either his siblings or his married children. In this, as in the relief of the poor, the English aristocracy differed from its continental peers. In France, as young Rochefoucault noticed, men and women in their early twenties entered into arranged marriages and then lived with their parents until they learned discretion in managing their lives and expenses.[16] In Florence (and probably in most of Mediterranean Europe) a man in his late thirties married an adolescent wife and received his unmarried brothers into a household that he ran himself.[17] But in England romantic marriage meant later marriage (he at 30, she at 24) and an independent household. It seems to have been assumed that the young couple were capable of sharing the superintendance of their household, and the seventeenth-century custom of spending the early years of marriage in a parent's household had quite passed away.[18] That older custom had sometimes been resorted to not only as a means of teaching household management but also because the family estates could not support three separate households when there were as many adult generations alive.[19] And whenever in the eighteenth century extension did make a temporary appearance in an aristocratic household, it was usually because of financial need.

This was the case when children lived with their parents. When in 1698 Lady Henrietta Churchill married Sidney Godolphin, their set-

---

[15]Dom John Stephan, ed., "Notes on Household Management in the 18th Century," *Notes & Queries*, **CCIV**, 1959, 171: She calculated there would be "forty in family" (169).

[16]J. Marchand, ed., *Frenchman in England 1784* (Cambridge: University Press, 1933), 49–50; cf. Claude Levy and Louis Henry, "Ducs et Pairs sous l'Ancien Regime: Characteristiques Demographiques d'un Caste," *Population*, **XV**, 1960; Arthur Young, *Travels in France*, ed. by Constantia Maxwell (Cambridge: University Press, 1950), 264.

[17] R. Burr Litchfield, "Demographic Characteristics of Florentine Patrician Families," *Journal of Economic History*, **XXIX**, 1969; cf. Piozzi, *Observations*, 36, 53, 56 (Milan), 93 (Venice); J. C. Davis, *The Decline of the Venetian Nobility as a Ruling Class* (Baltimore: Johns Hopkins Univ. Press, 1962); Robert Forster, *The Nobility of Toulouse in the Eighteenth Century* (Baltimore: Johns Hopkins Univ. Press, 1960).

[18]Lawrence Stone, *The Crisis of the Aristocracy, 1558–1641* (Oxford: Clarendon Press, 1965), 589.

[19]This was the case when the fourth earl of Leicester married in 1672 with both his father and grandfather alive; the arrangements led to a complicated family quarrel that had to be settled in Chancery in 1699 (Kent R.O., U 908/L.8). Arthur Young noticed that such extended households in France could not be attributed to financial need alone (*Travels*, 264).

tlements were quite modest, and her mother therefore "contrived it so as to make it easy for them to live with me and gave them my best apartment in my lodgings at St. James's till she had three children"—at which point her father suggested that she go live with her father-in-law.[20] A generation later, Lord Percival, in the course of one of the many unsuccessful proposals of marriage for his son, offered to give up his house in town to the young couple while keeping an apartment for himself and sharing their housekeeping expenses; but Lord Grantham declined the offer for his daughter because there would have been "too little to live on."[21]

In both of these cases what was to be shared were lodgings in London: There was no question of separate houses in the country. But in fact it was the ideal to live separately not only in the town but also in the country. When Lord Petre's heir married, he agreed in the settlement to provide the new couple with separate houses in both town and country or to give them £500 a year instead. The duke of Bedford gave Houghton House to Lord Tavistock for the country and Thanet House for London.[22] But when there was not quite as much wealth as in these two cases, a compromise could be proposed. Lord Pembroke at first told his son that he and his wife when in the country could use a smaller house near to the amenities of Wilton and that he hoped that his "grandchildren with their Papa and Mama will make Wilton, Portsmouth and Whitehall, as they please, their chief home." But then he changed his mind and thought it better that his son "make over to us any small house ye may fit up for yourselves, and take Pembroke House from us." Lord Herbert, however, was all for economy and would have none of it. He found Pembroke House in London too large; he thought it should be sold and declared that he did not "intend to have any place of any kind in the country"; but there was no question but that father and son would live in separate houses in London.[23] It was a system which struck a young French aristocrat as "in some ways contrary to nature," for "the Englishman would rather have the woman he loves than preserve the love of his parents."[24] Love and domesticity could thrive only in separate houses.

Brothers and sisters no more expected to live with each other than children did with their parents. This could be especially difficult on a

[20]K. M. Lynch, *A Congreve Gallery* (Cambridge, Mass.: Harvard Univ. Press, 1951), 75.
[21]H. M. C., *Egmont Diary*, **I**, 152, 156, 162. The Duke of Grafton gave his daughter £1000 more when she married in order "to be off their living with him" (*Walpole*, **IX**, 30).
[22]Essex R.O., D/DP F 118; Thomson, *Russells*, 370.
[23]Lord Herbert, ed., *Pembroke Papers 1780-1794* (London: Jonathan Cape, 1950), 274, 344, 346.
[24]Marchand, ed., *Frenchman in England*, 88-89.

man's unmarried sisters, but they moved out of the ancestral home nonetheless. Lady Sarah Cowper had been obliged to wage a considerable battle to be allowed to live with her brother after the death of their parents, but she promised to leave when he married, and she kept her word. Lord Halifax bought his sisters a house and furnished it when he married, and this won him Mrs. Delany's praise for setting an example to others "to do generously" by their sisters.[25] And the two eldest daughters of the duke of Richmond firmly told their younger sister that she should on no account allow her husband's sister to live with them, for "that never can do well were she an angel." They were therefore quite startled to learn a year later that their younger brother George and his wife were going to live with their eldest brother and his duchess. But, as usual, there was a financial explanation. "Though I'm sure they don't like it," one of them wrote, "my brother Richmond says it's so advantageous to George and saves him so much money." The arrangement did not last, and Lord George and his wife eventually took a house of their own.[26]

Romantic marriage might seem the cause of these arrangements to a foreigner. The English usually assigned another reason. Lord Polworth decided to stop sharing a house with his parents-in-law in the summer out of "fear of being troublesome and the dread of some disagreeable circumstance springing out of that most unmanageable and never exhausted source of family mischief, the tattling impertinence of servants." Lady Wentworth told her son that "certainly I should never desire to live with a daughter-in-law, for though themselves are never so good, yet some tattling servant or acquaintance will put jealousies into their head, to breed discontents." Servants were necessary but intruded on domestic privacy. Polworth, after being accustomed to a rambling house where he never saw the servants, moved to Southill because meeting them in the passages of a smaller house caused him to stare.[27] The reasons of the foreigner and the Englishman are therefore not so far apart; it was only that one stressed the separation of the conjugal family from the patrilineal household and the other its isolation within the patriarchal family. Insofar as their commitment to a patrilineal ideology may have disposed the English aristocracy to be

[25] Herts. R.O., D/EP 12, 48 B/3; *Delany*, III, 1861, 285.
[26] *Leinster*, I, 203, 276; cf. J. H. Plumb, ed., on the Walpoles in *Studies in Social History* (London: Longmans, Green), 186, 191. Richmond built his youngest sister a separate house on the family estate in which she and her daughter could live in decent retirement after her separation and divorce (Ilchester and Stavordale, *Lady Sarah*, passim).
[27] B. L., Add. MSS, 35, 384, f. 364; J. J. Cartwright, ed., *The Wentworth Papers* (London: Wyman, 1883), 48; Joyce Godber, *The Marchioness Grey of Wrest Park* (Bedfordshire Historical Records Society, 1968), 101.

patrilocal in the seventeenth century, the ideal of romantic marriage in the eighteenth century was strong enough to counteract this tendency; and within the patriarchal household romantic marriage certainly provided a positive motive to those who, because of the commercialization of the economy, found patriarchal relations with their servants difficult and distasteful.

The Great Family versus the Little Family

Aristocrats distinguished between their little and their great families. By the first they meant their children, and by the other, the servants; and they endowed the first with a heavy sentimental value. Mrs. Elstrob inquired about the health of the "dear little family" of the duke and duchess of Portland, and Lord Orrery said that he was bringing "all my little family with me" because "my heart cannot bear the separation."[28] But gentlemen were also cautioned in regard to their great families: "Care must not stop at your children, let it reach to your menial servants; though you are their master, you are also their father." The unreality of this doctrine, however, was nowhere better established than in the different provision that men made for their children and for their servants; for, as Bishop Fleetwood said, "to 'provide for our own' is to provide for such as have any relation to and dependence on us, such as are more ours, than any others." Servants, however, did not inherit whereas children did; or, at least, the former had to expect their provision from another father in another mansion. Fleetwood, with no trace of irony, declared that since "servitude is absolutely necessary by the appointment of the wise creator," that creator "to encourage it ... promises that they who behave themselves well in this life *as servants*, shall be looked upon and treated as *children* in the life to come, they shall have the reward of inheritance, which is what properly belongs to God's children."[29]

Parents were increasingly inclined, as the century wore on, to see the great family as a threat to the little one, to think that servants were harmful to the love and discipline between parent and child, that they were likely to destroy the sexual innocence of children, and that they might lead an adolescent into an improper marriage. There is no better example of these feelings than the long and eventually successful cam-

---

[28]*Delany*, II, 1861, 56; *Orrery Papers*, I, 263.
[29]William Darrell, *The Gentleman Instructed* (1727), Pt. i, p. 87, cited in Hecht, *Servant Class*, 75; William Fleetwood, *The Relative Duties ... Masters and Servants* (1705), 114, 386–387.

paign to get aristocratic women to give up the wet nurse. They were encouraged to nurse their children themselves since it was claimed that the nurse imprinted her personality on the child and won his strongest affections. Locke wrote his *Education* largely to persuade parents to take their children out of the hands of untrustworthy servants. For servants, he said, were indiscreet. They encouraged a child's disorderly appetites; they set bad examples; they comforted him in the face of a parent's displeasure; they made it impossible to develop in children any sense of shame; and they introduced them to debauched language, drink, and other vices. Locke valued private over public education because he thought it was the one way to keep a boy from the "taint of servants."[30] But others saw schools as means of escape from the servants and looked upon them, even for girls, "as necessary evils, which under some circumstances are inavoidable; as the cabals, the party-spirit, the fear of the governess, the secret and foolish indulgence of the maids, sometimes teach dissimulation, jealousy, resentment and revenge."[31] And if a servant did not corrupt a child's morals, he might damage his manners, for "peasantry is a disease (like the plague) easily caught by conversation."[32]

It was claimed that servants introduced children to masturbation at early ages, which was especially bad for their health.[33] And the maids were a standing invitation to experimentation. Lord Temple once recalled to Wilkes that when he "was very very young indeed my father was called in to whip me for putting my hands up the maid's petticoats; how dearly he did love me, how much he did grieve at every stroke he gave me? but my mother was peremptory, and all my vivacity could not save me."[34] At the onset of puberty these possibilities grew more probable. The duchess of Manchester dismissed a maid who debauched her only son at 13, though she did not hesitate to recommend her as a nurse in another family. But as adolescence drew on, it was the maids who needed to be advised that they ought to be especially on guard against their master's son and any promises of a settlement he might make; that they should not flatter themselves "that because such matches have sometimes happened, it will be your fortune."[35]

[30]For wet nurses, see Chap. 5; *Locke*, 130, 144, 154–155, 164, 171, 176, 187, 211, 371, 374.
[31]*Delany*, II, 1861, 46.
[32]William Darrell, *The Gentleman Instructed* (London, 1716), 16.
[33]S. A. Tissot, *Three Essays ... Third on Onanism* (Dublin, 1772), 43, 66.
[34]W. J. Smith, ed., *The Grenville Papers* (London, 1852–1853), 4 vol., I, 460: Mr. W. S. Lewis kindly supplied me with a copy of the original so that I might learn the reason for the whipping, which is omitted in the printed version.
[35]William Hickey, *Memoirs*, ed. by A. Spencer (London: Hurst & Blackett, 1913),4 vol., I, 12; Eliza Heywood, *A Present for a Servant Maid* (Dublin, 1744), 48, cf. Thomas Seaton, *The Conduct of Servants in Great Families* (London, 1720), 106–107.

Such a match was the worst evil a servant could do to his master's child, and the evil was greatest when the occasional footman ran off with the daughter of the house. For as Mr. B ____ told his sister, when he explained why he might marry his mother's maid but why she had to avoid the footmen, "a man ennobles the woman he takes, be she *who* she will, and adopts her into his *own* rank, be it *what* it will: but a woman, though ever so nobly born, debases herself by a mean marriage, and descends from her *own* rank to *his* she stoops to."[36] In such a situation, a woman like Lady Harriet Wentworth, who ran off with her Irish footman, had to content herself with the thought of "how quiet she should be in her retired station" while her relatives armed themselves with "fortitude and resignation," went into "agonies of affliction," and were "monstrously shocked" and then blooded by their physicians.[37] But before the Marriage Act of 1753 made clandestine marriages fairly difficult, masters feared not only that servants might marry their children, but that they might arrange for others to do so. It was to prevent this from happening, especially through "that influence which servants more especially would gain over young ladies," that the courts undertook to deprive servants of their profit from such ventures by denying the legality of marriage brokerage contracts.[38] Aristocratic masters were therefore in no doubt that their little families could be gravely imperiled by their great households, since a servant might steal away a child's love for his mother or his respect for his father, might debauch a son, or deprive a daughter of her station in life.

But if children had to be protected from the servants, they also had to be trained how to be their masters; for a well-conducted household was a great article in aristocratic prestige. Augustus Hervey, dazzled by Lord Temple at Stowe, could only remark: "How well he is served....I never saw so large a house so well conducted, servants that have no *embarras*, no noise, but all attention and respect: 'tis a miracle how they have formed them so, rubbed off the dirt and familiarity from the foreigners, and inattention and ill-breeding from the English ones." Lord Halifax told his daughter that she would be wiser to spend on her servants and the decoration of her house rather than on her dress for they would "make you a better figure than too much glittering in what you wear, which may with more ease be imitated by those that are below you."[39]

---

[36]Samuel Richardson, *Pamela* (Norton ed.), 447.

[37]S.C.L., WWM. R. 143-13, 132-14-1,2 (for the later history of this marriage, see W. S. Lewis, ed., *Notes by Lady Louisa Stuart* (New York: Oxford Univ. Press, 1928), 20.

[38]*The English Reports*, **XXVII**, 1171.

[39]Smith, ed., *Grenville Papers*, **III**, 89; Lord Halifax, *Complete Works*, ed. by J. P. Kenyon (Baltimore: Penguin, 1969), 293.

Running the household was increasingly the province of the wife, partly because the ideal of romantic marriage required that a woman should spend more time at home, and partly because the staff of a great household was increasingly composed of women and therefore more amenable to a mistress's direction. The contrast with aristocratic households in France or Italy was striking and was noticed. Rochefoucauld remarked that in England all the cooking and housework that were not seen were done by women but that men were used in the presence of guests. He also noted that the English had many more servants than the French; a nobleman in Paris was likely to have a mere 15 servants to the English lord's 30. Mrs. Piozzi was struck that the 8 servants in a Milanese household were nearly all men, that the household management fell to the master, and that the ladies were quite unacquainted with such matters.[40]

In England, on the other hand, Lord Halifax told his daughter that the "government of your house, family and children ... is the province allotted to your sex"; that "the economy of the house would be in some degree indecent" to her husband "whose province is without doors"; and that the establishment of order and quiet in a man's family was a better means to keep a husband than good looks, which were "not such a lasting tenure as to be relied upon." Addison in *The Spectator* made a similar but more sentimental point by contrasting Aurelia—who was always with her husband and her children and kept her family under a regular economy with her husband's aid—with Fulvia—who neglected her children and considered "her husband as her steward, and looks upon discretion and good housewifery as little domestic virtues unbecoming a woman of quality."[41] Men did in fact marry, as Lord Sunderland did, "to be free of the trouble of accounts and family concerns"; and women were careful of their households, even to excess, like Lady Hardwicke, whose children complained that she "takes too much pains in her household affairs; she is really her own housekeeper."[42]

---

[40]Marchand, ed., *Frenchman in England*, 25; Robert Forster, *The House of Saulx-Tavanes* (Baltimore: Johns Hopkins Univ. Press, 1971), 122–123; Piozzi, *Observations*, 36, 53.

[41]Halifax, *Works*, 288–290; D. F. Bond, ed., *The Spectator* (Oxford: Clarendon Press, 1965), 5 vol., I, 68–69. "If his turn of mind leads him to care and inspection of his estate, avoid to interfere with a branch of government not properly your sphere. Should he be neglectful of his family interests, supply his place with redoubled attention" (Countess Dowager of Carlisle, *Thoughts in the Forms of Maxims to Young Ladies on Their First Establishment in the World* (London, 1789), 3).

[42]H.M.C., *Portland MSS*, V, 534; *Hardwicke*, II, 565. Lord Cowper was told by his brother that "it is impracticable for you to look so narrowly into the affairs of your family as is necessary: It must be a great measure left to the diligence and faithfulness of servants ... as your Lady whose proper province it is, is entirely incapacitated by her illness" (Edward Hughes, ed., *Letters of Spencer Cowper* (Surtees Society, 1956), 21).

To prove the wisdom of Halifax's advice, there is the case of Lord and Lady Bristol.[43] After having survived 17 pregnancies in 20 years, Lady Bristol took in her late 40s to living at court. Her husband preferred the country and strongly resented her absence since he was obliged to run the household. For the last 20 years of her life, they wrangled over this question until all their passion for each other had drained away. The first signs of tension appeared in 1721 when he told her that he could not join her as planned and that "all the abatement I can feel proceeds from reflecting how very much this ungovernable family would want me had I been in a condition to leave it at the time I intended; for as it is, even the bread was left all night in the oven and utterly spoiled, and not so much as a toast left for me to eat with my chocolate." A year later he told her that "if you knew what full employment this family keeps me in, you would rather wonder how I find time from it to correspond." In the spring 2 years later he complained that he could not "say much of the good order I find things in, either within or without doors, neither indeed can it be expected where the master's and mistress's eyes are so often missing," and clearly the master's eyes were there to supervise the out-of-doors. A decade later in May he referred to his "family, which at present wants a mistress more than ever"; 5 days later he told her "your presence [was] much wanted in the family"; and in the next December he brought a more grievous charge: "After this I expect you will think a little of putting into better order your family here, which at present wants reformation so much by your long and frequent absences, that this morning after nine o'clock, when I came down into the drawing room, there was not a board of it nor a chair in it cleaned; but this is but a light circumstance compared with the dismal state of it when dear Nan was so very hopelessly ill, and I left helpless with her." He thought that she had avoided her duty to provide for the internal order and comfort of the house; she had left him helpless and had endangered the life of their daughter. When she died 4 years later, he noted it with a restraint most unlike himself.

Bristol's expectation that his wife would run the household was increased because its chief servant was a female housekeeper and not a male steward; he kept a steward for his estates but not for the house. Halifax's advice to his daughter had also presupposed a household under a housekeeper. When the chief servant was a man like Daniel Eaton, who combined the roles of land and house steward, his master

[43]*Bristol Letterbook,* **II,** 184, 242, 269, **III,** 157–158, 190.

seems to have been drawn far more into household management.[44] It would then seem likely that the more an aristocratic household was the means through which the estates of a family were managed, the less would a wife take the most active role in its supervision; and the more a great family was removed from the commercial economy of an estate, the greater would a wife's role become in the arrangement of its domesticity. The domestic ideal required that the children be separated from the servants, and that wives manage a household when the staff consisted of domestics rather than of the servants of an estate.

Household Hierarchy and Discipline

Whatever the disposition of responsibility between husband and wife, the aim of household management was to efficiently order a staff of 30 to 50 people. Servants signed contracts for wages to which they could legally be held, but the aim of the best housekeeping was to extract from them a willing service that grew out of filial loyalty to a master. Lord Cowper told his wife that "since we neither beat our servants nor fine them, the only way to govern them is to make them so content with their places, that they shall fear turning away."[45] Parents gave their children the same advice. "Let not your servants be over familiar or hail fellow with you," Lord Warrington told his sons, "neither keep them at too great a distance," for in the one case they would grow "saucy and careless," and in the other, "it does so discourage them, that it altogether chills the respect and affection that a servant usually bears to his master, and then all their duty will be turned to eye service." Warrington proposed this same mixture of distance and ease as the best means of dealing with children, and Lord Halifax similarly looked to the standards of other kinds of family duty when dealing with servants. He told his daughter that "the inequality which is between you must not make you forget that nature maketh no such distinction, but that servants may be looked upon as humble friends," or, in other words, as poor relations. "By these methods," he concluded, "you will put yourself in possession of being valued by your servants, and then their obedience will naturally follow."[46]

---

[44]*Ibid.*, **II**, 184–185 *et passim*; Halifax, *Works*, 288; Joan Wake and D. C. Webster, eds., *The Letters of Daniel Eaton* (Northamptonshire Record Society, 1971).

[45]John, Lord Campbell, *Lives of the Lord Chancellors* (Philadelphia: Univ. of Pennsylvania Press, 1851), 7 vol., **IV**, 330–331.

[46]Henry, Lord Warrington, *Works* ed. by J. Delaheuze, 26; Halifax, *Works*, 292.

The group of servants was usually coordinated by dividing them into upper and lower servants, placing them in separate departments, and separating men from women.

The servant hierarchy underwent its most drastic change when the state servants disappeared from most aristocratic households after 1720, and by the end of our period there had been, as Johnson told Boswell, "a change of modes in the whole department of life." It was this, rather than irreligion, Johnson claimed, that accounted for the disappearance of the household chaplain, as well as of the ladies- and gentlemen-in-waiting who had stood at the head of the servant hierarchy in the 1690s.[47] The third duchess of Bedford had had her attendant ladies who were not included in the ordinary salary list of servants, and Lord Derby in 1702 had six gentlemen who were. These officers had often been drawn from the minor gentry, and their disappearance deepened the social gulf between master and servant. The chaplain would most probably not have been of so high a class, but he usually stood at the head of the hierarchy, as at Knowsley. His duties were manifold.[48] The duke of Chandos expected his chaplain to read prayers in the family and preach in the chapel "when we don't go to the parish church." As the chaplain was to be "a companion to me as well as a servant in the family," Chandos also wanted someone "who would be a man of learning, and though of such behaviour and deportment as should give him the respect of the neighbourhood yet I should also wish he may be a cheerful companion." But he concluded that though "he generally dines with me, yet there is another table, which I call the chaplain's, and when my own is full, he goes there, and dines with my secretary and my steward."[49] When the chaplain disappeared from a household, family prayers went with him, and the most important of the traditional means of asserting the religious sanctions of patriarchy was destroyed.

The upper male servants who remained, after the disappearance of the state servants, were the steward, the clerks of the kitchen and the stables, the valet, the butler, the gardener, and the groom of the chambers. For most large households the ultimate authority was the steward; but as it was his task to be his master's principal man of business, overseeing the estates and the rents, there was often a house steward for daily household management who kept the accounts, made all dis-

---

[47]Boswell, *Johnson*, I, 370.
[48]Thomson, *Russells*, 224, 230; Lancs. R.O., DDK/15/24; Hecht, *Servant Class*, 34–42.
[49]Shakespeare's Birthplace Trust: Leigh of Stoneleigh MSS, Series D, Glos. Bn 18-3.

bursements for provisions, wages and liveries, and oversaw the other major domestics.[50] Responsibility for food and transportation devolved on the clerks of the kitchen and the stables. The clerk of the kitchen made up the bill of fare, delivered the food to the cook, rang the bell for meals, presided over the lower domestics as they ate, and under his mistress's eye ordered the courses on and off the main table. Increasingly he had to share his authority with such experts in the kitchen as the confectioner and the cook. By the 1770s the clerk had disappeared in Lord Stanhope's household, and the table in the servants' hall was being presided over by the cook. The clerk of the stables saw to it that the coachmen, grooms, and stableboys did their work; he provided food and medical care for the horses; and he had to be able to judge expertly among the various kinds of horses: racehorses and hunters, coach horses and hacks.[51] The valet was his master's personal attendant. He wound him up each morning and took him apart at night; he accompanied him on his shopping, his visiting, and his travels; he was expected to be accomplished in French politeness and sometimes, as with Lord Ashburnham, to be "skilled in letting blood and playing upon the music." For an unmarried master, he could double as house steward, as Lord Bristol was anxious to point out to a spendthrift grandson.[52] The butler cared for the glass, the plate, and the wine cellar. When there was neither a house steward nor a clerk of the kitchen, he directed the footmen as they waited at table, and sometimes, as at Lord Stanhope's, he had charge of all the manservants. The gardener gardened, and the groom of the chambers cared for the furniture, kept up the fires, and waited in the hall when there was company.[53]

The lady's woman, the housekeeper, the cook, and the nurse were the upper female servants. The first and last of these positions were of long standing, for a lady's clothes had always needed attention and her children, care. But the increasing number of female servants made the housekeeper a necessity and sometimes allowed her to take over most of the direction of a household. The lady's woman was "always supposed to be a person of some education who knows the world, and what is proper for her to do in her station, and to direct those under her." She was sometimes a gentlewoman. Lady Bristol's woman came from "a

---

[50]Hecht, *Servant Class*, 34–42.

[51]Hecht, *Servant Class*, 42–44; Thomson, *Russells*, 225–227; Finch, *Burley-on-the-Hill*, I, 231–232; Aubrey Newman, *The Stanhopes of Chevening* (London: Macmillan, 1969), 364.

[52]Hecht, *Servant Class*, 45–46; Robert Gunnis, "Letters of the First Lord Ashburnham," *Sussex Archaelogical Collections* (London: 1949), 9; *Bristol Letterbook*, III, 292.

[53]Hecht, *Servant Class*, 46–50; Thomson, *Russells*, 227; Newman, *Stanhopes*, 364; Finch, *Burley-on-the-Hill*, I, 230–231.

good family in Wales." With Lady Hertford's two women, the first was "a widow of gentle extraction, and her niece, Mrs. Nevinson, the second woman, was a daughter of a clergyman in the North; she was a woman of reading and parts, and though a servant, yet Lady Hertford treated her more like a companion." The nurse's experience of children allowed her to oversee the wet nurse, the rocker, and the nurserymaids.[54]

The housekeeper's role could simply be to manage the maids, as at Claremont where she had under her seven housemaids and three laundrymaids. But her role could also be much greater. Lord Bristol did not have a house steward but used a housekeeper instead. Lady Stanhope's housekeeper supervised the maids, controlled the kitchen, cared for the furniture, sent the servants to church, and yielded to the butler only in control of the footmen. A housekeeper, indeed, could become a substitute mistress and sometimes a wife. Lord Bristol at his wife's death chose as his housekeeper Mrs. Williams, who had been his wife's woman for 18 years. Lord Dorset's housekeeper (and her two sisters) managed his affairs, and 15 months before his death he married her, much to his relatives' distress. And though Lord Paget did not marry his housekeeper, he left her all he had. The cook and her scullerymaids were innovations in what had often been male kitchens, but she was always taken to be less talented than her male counterpart.[55]

The greater part of the lower servants—all that great army of chambermaids, housemaids, laundrymaids, and scullerymaids, boys in the kitchen, grooms in the stable, and workers out of doors—are of no particular interest to us. But the footman is an entirely different matter. For he was charged with more varied duties than most other servants, and he was also the hardest to control. He was a young man of good carriage and excellent physique, who could make a splendid show when decked out in his master's livery. He was usually one of a group of four to seven others, and he was often assigned to wait on some specific member of the family. Indoors he waited at table, helped in the various departments when a man's strength was needed, and stood about to lend ceremonious dignity to his master's entertainments. He delivered messages, accompanied home distinguished guests, and assisted his master or mistress when they went abroad. He seduced the

[54] Hannah Glass, *The Servant's Directory* (London, 1760), iv; *Bristol Diary*, 74; *Hertford*, 96; Chatsworth MSS, V, 523, 528; *Bristol Diary*, 90.

[55] Nulle, *Newcastle*, 184; Newman, *Stanhopes*, 364-268; *Bristol Letterbook*, II, 184-185 et passim; Brice Harris, *Charles Sackville, Sixth Earl of Dorset* (Illinois Studies in Language and Literature, 1940), 225; Lady Verney, ed., *Verney Letters of the Eighteenth Century* (London: Ernst Benn, 1930), 2 vol., I, 293-294; Hecht, *Servant Class*, 65.

daughters of the house and sometimes crept into his mistress's bed. He was a household's most conspicuous item of consumption.[56]

These strong, healthy, often underemployed young men could be quite troublesome. Lord Bristol's woes with his footmen offer excellent illustration that at the source of the difficulty was the impossibility of demanding patriarchal deference from a contractual employee in a commercial and highly politicized society.[57] Bristol once began a jeremiad to his wife by declaring: "I should not trouble you to bring me a footman, having still too much of Adam; would I could live without any servants, the bane of quiet." On another occasion he complained that his eldest son "Jack's footman is gone for refusing to make a fire even in his master's chamber, and... then as to my only footman Will, I could not help (contrary to all my resolution) chastising him for sowing sedition in my family, by asking Syer (when she was doing her duty and going to see if they behaved well at the third table), in a very jocose tone, what the old woman had to do there, and rose and shut the door against her, and have given him warning, but he begged I would not discharge him till we return to London." A year later Bristol had gotten yet another footman, but this one, John, was "ill of a fever by getting drunk since he came, and lying asleep three hours on a tomb-stone in a cold night." But it was in the late spring and early summer of 1738 that Bristol had his most extended contretemps over a servant. He had hired Richard Forster for a year to serve as his wife's footman, but before a month was out Forster had run away without giving any notice and been hired by Lord Tankerville. Bristol wrote twice to Tankerville before he got a reply to his request that as Tankerville now knew Forster "is still my servant, you will have the goodness and justice to discharge him, that he may be proceeded against according to the law." Tankerville was unsympathetic and Bristol had to write again at great length:

> On the first day of March last I hired Forster to serve as a footman to my wife at £7 per annum wages, a livery etc., who before he was hired told her that he was very desirous of serving her, and for about a fortnight behaved himself very well, till hearing your Lordship gave constant board wages and going after your place, he began to neglect her service... for which being only blamed in a very mild and civil way by her woman, he thought fit to put on his own clothes, requiring to be

---

[56]Hecht, *Servant Class*, 51–57; Thomson, *Russells*, 227–229. Sexual fantasy for middle-class writers was apt to center on the footman. One physician wrote that "hunting is a prejudicial exercise for such as long for children... the ladies are not such ill judges as not to know who can quell their heats and gratify their passions: Thus, the footman graces his master's couch" (*The Family Companion for Health* (London, 1729), 5). Another advised against having a daughter carried around by a footman for, after his rude hands, she "does not when she is bigger, start at the decent touch of a gentleman" (John Hill, *On the Management and Education of Children... by the Honourable Juliana-Susannah Seymor* (London, 1754), 172–172).

[57]Bristol Letterbook, II, 119, 222, 336, III, 202, 200–211, 213.

discharged immediately without giving any other or further warning; whereupon I sent for a constable, who carried him before Justice Margate, who having heard the case made his mittimus order to send him to the house of correction; but keeping him still in custody sent me a message by my valet de chambre signifying that he found Forster very sorry for what he had done, and that if I would forgive him he would beg my pardon for what passed, and would promise to behave better for the future; whereupon I consented to his being released . . . but the very next day at night he knocked at my door, and my porter opening of it, Forster threw his livery into the hall saying, there are my Lord's clothes, and I will never come into the house again, running away immediately.

Tankerville made some plea for Forster, but Bristol was adamant, declaring that it was "every gentleman's interest to have such notorious instances of sauciness meet with that treatment they justly deserve."

Bristol's troubles give point to every complaint lodged against servants. He had difficulty keeping a servant to his year's contract. So did other masters, and there were several unsuccessful attempts to have Parliament legislate against this "instability of continuing in their places."[58] Privately, masters could refuse to hire a servant without a character from his previous master. Lord Asburnham would not hire a valet until he had heard from the duke of Newcastle "the reason he was dismissed from that service, how long he lived there, what he is capable of and what character he has in the world as to his behavior and sobriety."[59] But there were always others like Tankerville who would hire without a character or even protect a servant from the magistrate. And since most servants could expect, like Bristol's Will, to be taken to London where the market in masters was largest, their fear of not finding an alternative service was slight. When servants did abide by their contracts, there still remained the problem of discipline when their good will could not be secured. How to keep a servant sober, how to keep him meek, and how to restrain oneself from the final satisfaction of beating him—none of these were easy matters. And they were not made easier by the English servant's rights; for it was not unheard of for servants to successfully sue a master for damages after a beating that was excessive or had caused permanent injury; and in this highly politicized society, it was necessary for Defoe to tell servants that "having the right to the liberty of an Englishman, does not make you equal to a gentleman." Patriarchal deference was difficult to maintain in a contractual society.[60]

[58] Hecht, Servant Class, 78–70.
[59] Gunnis, Sussex Archeological Collection, 9.
[60] Hecht, Servant Class, 78–80; Daniel Defoe, The Great Law of Subordination Considered (London, 1724), 30; cf. G. J. Schochet, "Patriarchialism, Politics and Mass Attitudes in Stuart England," Historical Journal, XII, 1969.

The chief attraction of Tankerville's household, however, had been his board wages, which were payments made to a servant in place of meals at his master's table. Such a payment went against the patriarchal ideal and was therefore opposed by many; and since they also made a servant independent of his master, they were lumped together with the other traditional monetary perquisites which servants received from those who dealt with their masters. All these took away what was increasingly the master's one means of ensuring dependence, namely, the payment of wages at the end of a year's contract.[61] (Bishop Fleetwood remarked that with regard to wages, "the higher we go, the better quality and fashion people are of, the more they are observed to offend against this part of justice, the less regard they have to the discharge of what is due by contract to their servants."[62]) The perquisite that was most vigorously and successfully opposed was vails, or the tips made by visitors to a household which commonly doubled a servant's wages. "There are," Thomas Seaton explained, "some offices in a family which have certain vails that belong to them by an almost universal custom, and every visitor makes an account of discharging these customary civilities, expecting that his own servants will reap the benefit of the like in their turn." This was said by the chaplain of a traditional household in 1720; but by mid-century it all seemed intolerable. "This custom," declared a critic, "has totally destroyed the reciprocal relation between master and servant, instituted by authority no less than divine. On whom does a servant where vails are taken depend, on his master? No, on the guests; as these increase the servant is willing to keep or leave his place. Can a master expect fidelity, love, or gratitude from such a servant?"[63] By the 1770s the custom had ended in most aristocratic households, and footmen had their wages doubled as a consequence.[64] But the other attempts to reduce servants to a total dependence on a master's wages failed. Payments by guests to butlers or footmen for providing playing cards, shopkeepers' commissions to servants for their master's patronage, and board wages—all these remained to prevent the servant from sinking into the dependence of the wage laborer. Neither hierarchical organization nor affection for one's servants could guarantee that they would respond with a proper pa-

---

[61]Hecht, Servant Class, 152–153, 158–170, 172–173.
[62]William Fleetwood, Relative Duties of Parents and Children (London, 1705), 399–400.
[63]Seaton, Servants, 93; The London Chronicle, **XXI**, 1767, 239, cited in Hecht, Servant Class, 163.
[64]Thomson, Russells, 228: Thomson was at some pains to explain why among the Russell servants only the footmen should have had their wages doubled in the sixties; it was, in all probability, because they stopped receiving vails cf. E. P. Thompson, "Patrician Society, Plebeian Culture," Journal of Social History, **VII**, 1974, 382–387.

triarchal deference, for they had entered into a relationship whose legal boundaries were set by a wage contract. They might, ironically, use the perquisites of the traditional household to increase their independence; but, ultimately, they lived in a society that had rejected patriarchal politics for the liberty of every Englishman.

Patriarchy and Servants

Traditional masters did not expect merely external deference and obedience to their commands; they expected, as the fictive fathers of their servants, to instill in them the principles of true religion and to control their sexuality. But as the century moved on, both of these became increasingly impossible; for the domestication of the aristocratic household caused the disappearance of the servants of state and with them the chaplain and family prayers; and the purveyors of bourgeois morality came to assert that the right to control a woman's sexuality was her father's and not her master's, that servants belonged first to their own families and only then to a master's.

Family prayers had been thought a necessity when men took on themselves the government of families since "God committed to them a charge of souls" and made every master "a priest in his own family."[65] In aristocratic society, however, the priest's profession in the early eighteenth century was one of very low prestige; no gentleman would read prayers willingly; and a chaplain was a necessity. Therefore when, as Bishop Burnet noticed, noblemen began "to neglect having chaplains in their houses," the consequence was that "the worship of God and the instruction of servants is quite neglected."[66] It was a neglect that was impractical since "this practice is the best method to make them dutiful and obedient, and serviceable in their different stations."[67] Lady Cowper, who thought that her husband undermined her authority with the servants, found that he "affirmed that all people's servants were as profligate as ours and he knew not where to get better"; but she replied that "if that were true, which I hoped not, it was a sad instance that masters were to blame in neglecting the Word and worship of God in their families whereby they should be taught their duty."[68] Religion was, after all, the best means of keeping men in their

---

[65] *A Present for Servants* (London, 1787), 10th ed., iv–x, 13–14, 60–62.
[66] Burnet, *History*, VI, 219.
[67] Robert Nelson, *The Practice of True Devotion* (London, 1791), 27.
[68] Herts. R.O., D/EP 49, 30 October 1700.

places, as even Horace Walpole agreed; he was scandalized that at a French dinner table, "though all the servants were waiting, the conversation was much more unrestrained, even on the Old Testament, than I would suffer at my own table in England, if a single footman was present."[69]

In a traditional household family prayers were an elaborate ceremony conducted twice a day. At Lord Nottingham's, the groom of the chambers cleaned the chapel, laid out the cushions for prayers, and rang the bell that assembled the household. The gentleman of the horse then marshaled in all the servants and reported those who did not attend. Lord Middleton, as a young man, had prayers at eight in the morning and ten at night, and those servants who did not heed the morning bell had to miss their breakfast. Lord Derby was stricter still for if a servant missed prayers at eleven or six, he was discharged.[70]

These three early eighteenth-century households would probably have used the Prayerbook forms of morning and evening prayer since all three had chaplains. And it was this reliance on the Prayerbook that some blamed when the practice had nearly disappeared at mid-century. It was said that whereas many of these prayers were "proper only to be read by men in orders, many families of the gentry and nobility, where there were no chaplains, began to disuse them; and nothing being substituted in their room, this was in a great many families the occasion of totally neglecting this duty." It is an intriguing explanation (and has been taken up by Canon Smyth), but it begs too many questions.[71] For there were available other forms of prayer and even High Churchmen recommended the substitution of these for the more formal liturgy. Lord Wharton's daughter at her marriage asked her father's chaplain and two other clergymen to draw up such a work for her, which was privately printed as *Prayers for Families*. Manuals like Nelson's *Practice of True Devotion* had occasional domestic prayers for servants who did not have the time for private prayers or for the public liturgy that their masters did. And John Evelyn told his grandson "not to forget morning and evening prayers for your domestics, to be constantly said by one of your chief servants, unless you be able to maintain a pious chaplain who might be useful to instruct your domestics: I would that he or yourself would use the public church prayers before dinner, but at

---

[69]Walpole, X, 176.

[70]Finch, Burley-on-the-Hill, I, 231, 228; Cassandra, Duchess of Chandos, *The Continuation of the History of the Willoughby Family*, ed. by A. C. Wood (Eton: Shakespeare Head Press, 1958), 134–135; Lancs. R.O., DDK/15/8. See also Hertford, 96.

[71]*The Life of the Reverend Humphrey Prideaux* (London, 1748), 61–65; Charles Smyth, *Simeon and Church Order* (Cambridge: University Press, 1940), 30ff.

night perhaps some other suitable after a chapter out of the new Testament."[72]

But men grew disinclined to have either chaplains or other servants say prayers—and certainly did not wish to say them themselves—not because of irreligion, but because domesticity had weakened patriarchy: The decline of the patriarchal household brought with it the death of the old family prayers. And when the Evangelicals set about to revive them, it was not the old prayers that were brought back. Whitefield tried to persuade Lord Lothian to lead prayers himself; the duke of Somerset did so occasionally under the same kind of influence; and Lord Dartmouth did so frequently—to the distress of Lord Rockingham's sister, who said she did not mind his having family prayers, but could not bear that he led them himself.[73] The Evangelical lord said prayers for the sake of his own soul and not for the discipline of his servants; he gave up household government and turned to the religion of the home.

After 1750 those aristocrats who did not take up Evangelical prayers could still be concerned with the formal religious practice of their servants, and their concern usually took the form of sending them to church. The duke and duchess of Portland were in the habit of receiving the Sacrament with their children and all their servants in the parish church. Lady Stanhope directed that as many of her servants as could "be spared are to go to church on Sundays, and to take it by turns."[74] It was said that "in all well-governed families, a maid servant has the liberty every Sunday, or every other Sunday at least, in the afternoon, of going to church."[75] But this was sabbatarianism rather than daily family religion, and to sabbatarianism the aristocracy increasingly resorted. It did so, perhaps, out of an uneasy consciousness that it was partly responsible for the decline in church attendance that

---

[72]John Howe, *The Obligation from Nature and Revelation to Family Religion and Worship* (London, 1726), v–vii; Nelson, *True Devotion*, 27, 31–32, 42–43, 158–159, 242ff; John Evelyn, *Memoirs for My Grand-son*, ed. by G. Keynes (London: Nonesuch, 1926), 8–9. Sir William Cowper told his wife that as for family prayers "we might thank the Church of England for that neglect, in former days such order was observed but laid down since that came in. I asked if he anywhere found the Church forbid it, since all might do it that pleased, and if he would come there, he would meet with frequent exhortations to it" (Herts. R.O., D/EP 49, 30 October 1700).

[73]A.C.H. Seymour, *The Life and Times of Selina Countess of Huntingdon* (London, 1839), 2 vol., I, 91, 128 n.; S. C. L.,. WWM. R; but cf. Thomas Hearne, *Collections*, X, 424. Household religion had also become impossible for the Roman Catholics, who ceased to center their lives around the patriarchal households of their gentry and turned instead to the middle classes in the towns; see John Bossy, "Four Catholic Congregations in Rural Northumberland, 1750–1850," *Recusant History*, IX, 1967, and "More Northumbrian Congregations," *ibid.*, X, 1969.

[74]*Delany*, III, 1861, 247, 316; Newman, *Stanhopes*, 364.

[75]Eliza Haywood, *A Present for a Servant Maid* (Dublin, 1744), 39.

had followed the Toleration Act.[76] For there were critics prepared to say that "family duties and instruction (if carefully minded) would have prevented much of the disorder that is in almost all parishes, which now is not so easily cured."[77] And it was certainly sabbatarianism rather than family religion that a mother like Lady Spencer tried to instill in her children.

Lady Spencer must have had some trepidations about the state of religion among the Cavendishes when her eldest daughter married the fifth duke, for the young duchess wrote to her on a Sunday some 4 months after the marriage that she was not "at all pleased with the manner I have spent this day, for after dinner I really forgot it was Sunday and proposed playing at whist." Well might the duchess have had her qualms about such a Sunday, for her mother had prescribed to her a year before what a suitable Sunday regimen might be for a married woman. Lady Spencer had recommended that Georgiana rise early, examine her conscience over the past week, be cheerful at breakfast, and then go to church. She was later in the day to give religious advice to her servants and her children, help the poor while out riding or walking, and remember that "it is a real duty to make a steady uniform attention to religion appear amiable and attractive to others." The duchess therefore realized that her mother would "be pleased to know the Duke of his own accord begged Mr. Ward to read prayers in the chapel here, which has not been done for many years." In the following weeks the young couple even took to going to the village church. Lady Spencer was delighted and declared that "if you were both to do it constantly wherever you are, you cannot imagine how much good your example would do, for there are many well meaning people who want to be kept in countenance in doing what is right." But the duchess never attained to any regularity in these matters, and 7 years later (in one of her many lamentations over not going to church) she assured her mother that she felt "the neglect sincerely, and I shall read a Blair with my servant this evening to make up for it." The duchess was content to edify herself and a single servant, and where even sabbatanianism could be forgotten, there was no chance at all for family religion.[78]

But with sabbatarianism, as with family religion, there were masters and mistresses who set out to care for the salvation of their servants, as two examples from the old school and one from the new will show. Lord Warrington supported the Societies for the Reformation of

---

[76]G. V. Bennet in Holmes, ed., *Britain after the Glorius Revolution* (New York: St. Martin's Press, 1969).
[77]*A Present for Servants* (London, 1787), viii.
[78]Chatsworth MSS, V, 10, 32, 50, 338.

Manners, put down drinking and swearing among his servants, and had family prayers. The discipline for his servants he drew straight out of St. Matthew (18:15-17), telling his sons that "if you have occasion to reprove any servant, let it first be in private, and calmly without passion, and as far as you can, convince him of his sin: if after this he commits the like offence, reprove him more sharply; and if he gives you further occasion, then reprove him before the whole Family."[79] Lord Nottingham's chaplain claimed that he had never known his master to give a servant a command that it would have been unlawful for him to comply with; and indeed, the chaplain found his Lordship's conversation "so strictly sober, and virtuous, and just; your attendance upon the devotion of your family so punctual, and your frequenting the word and sacrament at your parish church so constant [that] I had abundant reason to bless God, whose goodness allowed me to be received into that house; where all my little endeavours to promote a sense of piety, have met with the countenance of your Lordship, who is the master of it." Nottingham required as much of the other upper servants as of the chaplain, for the gentleman of the horse had been obliged to admonish those who drank, or swore or cursed, and to turn them out of the house if they could not be reformed.[80] Lady Rockingham, who was of the new school, always went to church, took the Sacrament often, and exhorted her husband for eight pages at a time to do the same. "What is the reason," she asked him, "you do not receive the comfortable Sacrament of the Lord's Supper as often as I do?" But failing here, she turned to her servants and found them more promising, or at least more pliant, material. She turned away a footman for being out late; disapproved of a maid who had two lovers at once; and most satisfyingly of all, kept track (through a hefty correspondence with her steward) of the long, drawn out death of an old servant, to whom she sent a sermon on deathbed repentance that was read to the poor old man.[81] A sense of moral responsibility for one's servants—that feeling that they were in some sense one's children—persisted, then, even after the institutional discipline of family prayers and the chaplain had disappeared; but the religious supervision of 40 individuals by an aristocratic master with many other demands on his time must necessarily have been haphazard and irregular.

The fictive fatherhood of masters received even greater challenge, however, over the question of the control of their servants' sexuality. A

---

[79] Richard Wroe, *A Sermon at the Funeral of the ... Earl of Warrington* (London, 1694), 20-21; Warrington, *Works*; Seaton, *Conduct of Servants*, ii-lv.
[80] Finch, *Burley-on-the-Hill*, I, 228.
[81] S.C.L., WWM:R, 168-79, Stw. 2, *passim*.

real father's property in his children was institutionalized in his power to appoint guardians by his will and by his right to give minors in marriage. No master ever claimed the first power, but masters did try to prevent their servants from marrying, and they usually required them to leave the household when they did. Real fathers, of course, controlled but never enjoyed the sexuality of their daughters, and a husband's patriarchal control of his wife was enshrined in his exclusive access to her sexuality. But it became necessary to tell masters that they did not have such patriarchal rights, that a master was not a husband and a man's mistress not his wife. The force of the new moral system entered boldly into a nobleman's household and told him that to be a master was not to be either a husband or a father.

In the seventeenth century a writer like William Baxter had assumed that a servant would not marry and that this was one of the advantages of his station. Bishop Fleetwood included among the benefits of servants' lives that they "generally speaking, have themselves alone to provide for; their masters have wives, and children, and relations."[82] Aristocratic masters agreed with such sentiments and were loath to hire married people. An exception was sometimes made for upper servants. Some of the duke of Bedford's upper servants were married and had houses of their own, but his lower male servants, and all of the women, were unmarried and slept in his house, the women in the attics and the men in the cellars.[83] Lord Ashburnham, on the other hand, was "not disposed to entertain married servants," and always looked for single men whether they were to serve as butler, cook, or postilion.[84] An Englishwoman abroad was struck that most of the Milanese servants were married men with children. She thought it "the comicallest sight in the world to see them all go gravely home, and you may die in the night for want of help, though surrounded by showy attendants all day."[85]

It was usually expected that if a servant married he left his master's service, for membership in two families might in the end bring on a conflict of loyalties. Maids were advised, in the days when vails were still given, to save these and to live on their salaries, as their savings would make them more attractive if they hoped to marry and leave

[82]R. B. Schlatter, *The Social Ideas of Religious Leaders 1660–1688* (London: Oxford Univ. Press, 1940), 83; Fleetwood, *Relative Duties*, 385.
[83]Thomson, *Russells*, 224, 226, 229–230 (cf. Dorothy Marshall, *The English Domestic Servant in History* (London: Historical Association, 1949), 14).
[84]G. E. Mingay, *English Landed Society in the Eighteenth Century* (London: Routledge & Kegan Paul, 1963), 229–230.
[85]Piozzi, *Observations*, 36–37.

service. And Jonas Hanway, in writing against vails, had proposed that if a preference were given to "all young persons who *have learnt some useful art* (when they offer themselves as domestics), they would be better enabled in case of marriage, to retire from service and get their bread."[86]

But a reformer like Hanway eventually came to think that the celibacy of servants was contrary to the promotion of both the religion without which the common people would "devour each other" and the "authority of parents and masters" that supported the laws. Hanway was aware that the old system of family prayers had declined, and he urged its revival; but he was unaware that the values of the conjugal family that he extolled were at variance with those of the old patriarchal system. He opposed masters who prevented their servants from marrying and enjoying the benefits of domesticity. He said that "the rights of mankind, as they regard the passions and appetites... are equal: yet... we usually reject them when they are married, tempting them to practise sinister arts and contrivances to conceal their situation." He explained that "the reason why some masters and mistresses object to married servants is that they are exposed to the temptation of being absent from home and of pilfering provisions, with a view to convey them to a wife or children." But "celibacy forced on the servant" had, he warned, "a great mixture of selfishness, pride, cruelty, and manslaughter on the part of the master or mistress." Masters who did promote their servants' domesticity were in fact better served. He proposed the ideal Sir George Friendly who "takes care of the children of his married servants," and he gave the example of the actual duke of Portland who had "hardly any servant who is not married" and than whom "no person is better served or has a completer confidence in his domestics." In Hanway's eyes, equality gave all men the right to have families of their own. The personal domesticity of a servant was the best guarantee of his efficiency in his master's household.[87]

If masters after 1750 were being urged that their servants had the right to marry, they had had to be reminded constantly in the previous generation to keep their hands off the maids. It seems likely that in the late seventeenth and the early eighteenth centuries, European masters felt increasingly free to exploit sexually their female domestic ser-

---

[86]Haywood, *A Present*, 42–44; Jonas Hanway, *Eight Letters to His Grace* ____, *Duke of* ____, *on the Custom of Vails-Giving in England* (London, 1760), 60.

[87]Jonas Hanway, *Virtue in Humble Life* (London, 1771), I, v, 85; *The Defects of the Police* (1775), 142–147; *Virtue*, **I, v, II,** 462–463, I, 32. As one might expect, Hanway was in favor of mothers' nursing their own children (*Virtue*, I, 55, II, 492–493).

vants.[88] In aristocratic households this would have been a greater possibility since there were more female servants than formerly, but it was also indicative of the breakdown of patriarchal restraints, for no good father would have seduced his own daughter. In such an atmosphere a young man might be urged to marry not only because it was inappropriate for him to descend to "the little things of housekeeping" but also because "the dull converse of servants only will either give scandal or tempt you to ramble, and make you be thought looser than really you are."[89] Servants were told that it was "exceeding shocking and unnatural" to think that male servants would be approached by their mistresses but it was very likely that a maid would be attacked by either her fellow servants or her master.[90] In such cases she should do her best to keep out of their way when their lust was up, and if this were not possible, she would find that "a steady resolution will enable you, and as a vigorous resistance is less to be expected in your station, your perseverance may, perhaps, oblige him to desist."[91] But when a maid did become pregnant, the usual response was for a master or mistress to disclaim responsibility and send her back to her parents.[92]

Nowhere was this conflict between the master's exploitation of a servant's sexuality and her parent's right to control it put with greater imaginative force and propagandistical flourish than in Samuel Richardson's *Pamela or Virtue Rewarded*. Mr. B ___'s mother had first employed Pamela, and when after his mother's death he began to give the girl gifts, her parents told her how uneasy this must make them in the case of "a designing young gentleman, if he should prove so, who has so much *power* to oblige, and has a kind of *authority* to command as your master." Their fears proved warranted; but when Mr. B ___ kissed her, Pamela bolted; whereupon he told her, " 'I'll do you no harm Pamela, don't be afraid of me.' I said, 'I won't stay.' 'You won't, hussy!' said he. 'Do you know whom you speak to?' I lost all fear and all respect, and said, 'Yes I do, sir, too well!—Well may I forget that I am your servant when you forget what belongs to a master.' " Pamela was at this point sent away from the household, which was conducted by her master's good housekeeper, Mrs. Jervis, Pamela's "third best friend."

[88]Edward Shorter, "Illegitimacy, Sexual Revolution and Social Change in Modern Europe," *Journal of Interdisciplinary History*, II, 1971, 243–250; Jacques Depauw, "Illicit Sexual Activity and Society in Eighteenth Century Nantes," in Forster and Ranum, eds., *Family and Society* (Baltimore: Johns Hopkins Univ. Press, 1976).
[89]Stephen Penton, *The Guardians Instruction* (London, 1688), 12.
[90]Seaton, *Conduct of Servants*, 143–146.
[91]Haywood, *A Present*, 45.
[92]L. G. Mitchell, ed., *The Purefoy Letters, 1735–1753* (London: Sidgwick & Jackson, 1973), 144, cf. 40, 142, 151–152.

She thought she was being sent to her parents, her two "best friends"; but she was instead held in another house supervised by Mrs. Jewkes, her master's procuress. There Pamela had two conversations with Mrs. Jewkes. On one of these occasions, Pamela began, "'Well,' said I, 'you will not I hope, do an unlawful or wicked thing, for any master in the world.' 'Look ye,' said she, 'he is my master; and if he bids me do anything that I *can* do, I think I *ought* to do it; and let him he who has his power to command me, look to the *lawfulness* of it.'" On the other occasion, Mrs. Jewkes said to her: "'My instructions are, not to let you be so familiar with the servants.' 'Why,' said I, 'are you afraid I should confederate with them to commit a robbery of my master?' 'May be I am,' said the odious wretch; 'for to rob him of yourself, would be the worst that could happen to him in his opinion.'" But Pamela would not admit such claims and asked, "How came I to be his property? What right has he in me, for such as a thief may plead to stolen goods."[93]

There it all was in a nutshell. Masters had only a "kind of authority." To enjoy a woman's sexuality was to own her, but masters had no such rights of property in their servants. These were reserved to the parents of an unmarried woman, who were her best friends, and to take them without parental consent was robbery; for they were rights that could be enjoyed only by a husband to whom they were transferred at marriage. The further incidents of Pamela's captivity bear this out. When she sought aid, the neighboring clergyman offered to marry her, but her reply to him was: "Forbear, sir.... while I have a father and mother, I am not mistress of myself, poor as they are." But this claim of parental right was one that some were loath to allow the poor. When Sir Simon Darnford heard of Pamela's situation, he remarked to his wife: "Why, what is all this, my dear, but that our neighbour has a mind to his mother's waiting maid. And if he takes care she wants for nothing, I don't see any great injury will be done her. He hurts no *family* by this." Mrs. Jewkes urged Pamela's compliance with their master's desires, telling her "to learn to know your best friend"; she warned her that Mr. B ____ had found out "a way to satisfy my scruples: It is, by marrying me to this dreadful Collbrand, and buying me of him on the wedding day for a sum of money! Was ever the like heard?—"; and then, said Mrs. Jewkes, "it will be my duty to obey my husband." But Pamela was not so easily caught and asked her parents whether "a husband can sell his wife against her own consent? And will such a bargain stand good

---

[93]Richardson, *Pamela*, 13, 16, 34, 102, 111, 129. To see *Pamela* as the story of a girl who successfully withholds her sexual favors to make a good marriage is to miss the point and unconsciously to take up the hostile aristocratic reaction to Richardson's doctrine of domesticity for all ranks of society.

in law?" For, as she implied, a husband's property in his wife was not transferable. And when Mr. B ___ offered that "you shall be mistress of my person and fortune, as much as if the foolish ceremony had passed. All my servants shall be yours," Pamela rejected him, knowing that this foolish contract made the difference between being the mistress of a man's pleasure and the lawful mistress of his house. It was only when her virtue had triumphed and he had duly wed her that she could bring herself to call him not only master but her "dearest friend" and her "best friend."[94]

Here domesticity and parental right triumphed and came to the aid of patriarchy, for Pamela spends two thirds of the novel caring for her servants and her children. It was an ideology to which aristocrats themselves had considerable commitment; but it is probable that only middle class men like Hanway and Richardson could insist on its applicability to all social classes; for that insistence was based on a presumption of equality. Pamela's fate was improbable; the much more likely reward of such a girl was to be left (as Lord Townshend left the housemaid by whom he had had three children) all that her master was free to leave by the terms of his family settlement. £50,000 in the funds rather than married gentility was the apotheosis to which such a woman might aspire.[95]

Property in Wives and Children

Equality, commercialization, and domesticity might join together to limit, and sometimes annihilate, a master's patriarchal feelings toward his servants; but it is probable that such feelings toward a man's wife and children were intensified by domesticity and that the equality of men and women was accepted only with great difficulty. It is likely that as romantic marriage displaced the arranged, regard for the symbolic property conveyed by marriage was heightened in the minds of men who could not think of loving without owning. Some such paradigm is needed to explain why there should emerge together in the

---

[94]*Ibid.*, 138, 152, 192, 188, 200, 465, 500.
[95]*Walpole*, **XXII**, 211, **XXXIII**, 149. Hanway, who clearly took his title from Richardson, had similar ideas: "If instead of guarding the indigent, whose only dowry is their virtue and their ability to labour, men triumph over the spoils of innocence....they must answer for it at the judgment seat" (*Virtue*, **I**, 88). Pamela was an unwelcome symbol to aristocrats. When Lord Salisbury married the daughter of a barber, it was said that "as the way of life he was in promised even a worse choice, his friends can hardly regret Pamela's good fortune" (Hughes, ed., *Letters of Cowper*, 39–40). Pamela was to be preferred to Fanny Hill.

1690s feminism, parliamentary divorce, and the action for criminal conversation. For feminism, maintained that women were neither weak, irrational, nor childish and were, indeed, fit to be true friends with men; whereas the other two institutions allowed the husband of an adulterous wife to claim monetary damages from her lover and to divorce her and marry again. Wives, who were encouraged, in the name of domesticity, to stay at home to mind their houses and their children and to go into company only with their husbands, could be seen as equals only with some difficulty; and men who were convinced that only possession created love were prepared to assert (in the name of a higher morality than that of mere interest) their ownership of the sexuality of their children and their wives through the law. The new sexual roles that came with domesticity sometimes reinforced the old ones from patriarchy.

Women were held to be inferior to men either because by nature they were physically weaker and less rational or because God had subordinated them to men. "The men endowed with strength," one author wrote, "terrify the women, transfer to them the laborious duties, and reserve themselves for exercises, which gratify or amuse." But this was a jaundiced account, intended to make the point that these were the ways "in the associations of savages."[96] The matter could be put more pleasantly. "Assume no masculine airs," Lady Carlisle counseled, "real robustness and superior force is denied you by nature: its semblance, denied you by the laws of decency." Men told their daughters that they recoiled when "a woman speaks of her great strength, her extraordinary appetite, her ability to bear excessive fatigue." And Lord Chesterfield told his son that civility was a woman's due since it was "the only protection they have against the superior strength" of men.[97] Women were supposed to be delicate; if they proved otherwise, they were to hide it; for men liked them best when they could protect them. But to suggest, as one writer did, that such protection could be a form of exploitation was quite exceptional.

The two ways in which such an exploitation could most easily be realized in aristocratic society were to consider women either "as domestic drudges or the slaves of our pleasures."[98] Both of these were rejected as neither English nor Christian. "Young ladies," it was protested, "are brought up as if God created 'em merely for a seraglio, and

[96] *Letters on Love, Marriage and Adultery* (London, 1789), 38.
[97] Countess Dowager of Carlisle, *Thoughts to Young Ladies*, 38; John Gregory, *A Father's Legacy to His Daughters* (London, 1774), 50–51; Bonamy Dobrée, ed., *Letters of Lord Chesterfield* (London: Eyre & Spottiswoode, 1932), 6 vol., II, 525.
[98] Gregory, *Legacy*, 6–7.

that their only business was to charm a brutish sultan."[99] And when Lady Lucy Douglas married, she was told that "when a man looks upon a wife but as an upper servant, and believes that the sole end of woman's creation was to propagate the species, his ideas qualify him more for a Mahometan paradise than for the company and conversation of a virtuous and sensible woman." Such attitudes were contrary, Bishop Fleetwood held, "to reason and decency and the design of nature, who intended them for friends and companions." But Fleetwood certainly did not think women the rational equals of men. He had to distinguish between the "love of friendship, due to merit and qualities" which was "generally paid to our equals" and the mutual love of marriage.[100]

But it was at just such a point that the feminists attacked, for "how can a man respect his wife when he has a contemptuous opinion of her and her sex?" This was Mary Astell's question, and she followed it with a description of men looking down from their own elevation on women "as void of understanding and full of ignorance and passion, so that folly and a woman are equivalent terms." Respect was impossible and contempt very likely; and no more so than when fathers taught it to their sons. Lord Chesterfield, in his anxiety to make his son into a man, could think of no better way than to class women and children together as irrational beings to be avoided. "Women, then, are only children of a larger growth; they have an entertaining tattle and sometimes wit; but for solid, reasoning good-sense, I never in my life knew one that had it"; "a man of sense only trifles with them, plays with them, humors and flatters them, as he does with a sprightly child"; "no flattery is either too high or too low for them"; they were therefore "to be talked to as below men and above children." To such a mind it was no good saying that if gentlewomen were given an education equal to that of their brothers, they would show the same equality of capacity that was to be found among animals and the lower classes.[101] For it was so evident to men of the upper classes that since "trade and merchandise, and making wars abroad, and executing justice at home" were done only by themselves, such managerial capacities were "evident indications of nature's intending to make the men superior to the women."[102] Household management did not have the prestige of a rational occupation,

---

[99]Darrell, Gentleman, 127.

[100]Reflections on Celibacy and Marriage (London, 1771), 25; Fleetwood, Relative Duties, 170, 297.

[101]Mary Astell, Reflections upon Marriage (London, 1706), 47; Dobrée, ed., Letters of Chesterfield, IV, 1209, 1224 (cf. 1305, III, 1038 but 755); Mary Astell, An Essay in Defence of the Female Sex (London, 1697), 14–16, 36–37.

[102]Fleetwood, Relative Duties, 169–170.

and when women were told that they were intended "as our companions and equals," it turned out to mean that they were "designed to soften our hearts and polish our manners."[103] Women were above servants or children, but not yet the equals of men, for they were a species of property given by God to man.

Man at the creation had had only his natural superiority of mind and strength, but at the fall (occasioned by Eve's sin) "the superiority seems to be given by the positive command of God ... in that text, 'Thy desire shall be to thy husband, and he shall rule over thee.'"[104] But it was the case that no man owned any particular woman, except through marriage; for "no man can say that this or that particular woman is subject to him, until she has made herself so by compact."[105] Women, like servants, entered contractually into patriarchal relations; and it was used as an argument against clandestine marriages that "by this means women may be married against their wills and so lose the property of their own persons: which is the most valuable of all properties."[106] A property so valuable had to be settled by marriage, for otherwise one would have to "suppose that the most desirable creatures in nature would occasion no contention where every other trifle does, where property is not settled."[107] And such an individual settlement was the guarantee of care, for "where there is a distinct property, it naturally creates love, and love maintains protection."[108] For in this society it was "impossible for men to love anything without some respect to their private interests."[109] Such were the hard opinions of the first generation of the century. By the end of our period the growth of romantic love had caused men to modify their conscious statements, but a percipient writer could see that not much had changed, for "though the idea of being property, or parts of our goods and chattels, be exploded from our philosophy and from some of our laws, it still remains in our prepossessions or customs, counteracted by a little senseless and romantic gallantry." For in 1789, in the year of liberty, fraternity, and equality for men, the double standard of sexual morality stood untouched: "the crime is always contrived and committed by the man; the punishment and the infamy are borne by the woman. These are the principles of Europe."[110]

---

[103]Gregory, Legacy, 6–7.
[104]Thomas Salmon, A Critical Essay Concerning Marriage (London, 1724), 72–73.
[105]Fleetwood, Relative Duties, 171–172.
[106]Henry Gally, Some Considerations upon Clandestine Marriages (London, 1750), 13.
[107]Salmon, Critical Essay, 36.
[108]Marriage Promoted ... by a Person of Quality (London, 1690), 9.
[109]Abel Boyer, The English Theophrastus (London, 1702), 197.
[110]Letters on Love, Marriage and Adultery (London, 1789), 64.

The double standard institutionalized men's desire to have an absolute property in women; and Keith Thomas has stressed this as being the strongest explanation of the institution—stronger than the eighteenth century's more usual statement that (as Johnson said) "confusion of progency constitutes the essence of the crime" since all property depended on the chastity of women.[111] But men could assert property in a woman's sexuality even if they did not impregnate her themselves: If they owned her children, they owned her. It is rather that aristocratic property in England was inherited patrilineally, and therefore among ordinary people with either different rules of inheritance or no property, the double standard was, as Thomas says, of less importance. The importance of patrilineage to the double standard could be recognized in the eighteenth century by observing a contrary system: "To preserve the succession in a right line, that no base child may deprive the lawful heir of his just privilege, 'tis an ancient custom in several places of the East, as well as in Africk, that the heirship of families runs all along on the mother's side, as being least liable to sophistry and imposition. So that if once the nativity be allowed, the proper father is never questioned."[112] Matrilineal societies, in other words, were not likely to have a double standard. As far, therefore, as English aristocrats thought that women were men's property, they shared the universal presupposition of patriarchy; but the institutions they threw up to protect this property were peculiar to their patrilineal customs.

Property in women was enshrined in the principles and actions of the law, and the most fundamental of these was that "by marriage the very being or legal existence of a woman is suspended or at least it is incorporated into that of her husband, under whose wing, protection and cover, she performs everything." To protect this property a man had several options open to him. He could bring an action for criminal conversation against his wife's lover in which he asked the court to award money damages. He could get a legal separation from his wife for her adultery or desertion; and if he could prove her adultery to Parliament, he could get a divorce that allowed them both to remarry. But he could not revenge himself, for it was manslaughter rather than

---

[111] Keith Thomas, "The Double Standard," *Journal of the History of Ideas*, XX, 1959; Boswell, *Johnson*, I, 347, 623, cf. *A Treatise Concerning Adultery and Divorce* (London, 1700), 15.

[112] Castamore, *Conjugium Languens* (London, 1700), 16. See also Salmon, *Critical Essay*, 36: "But farther, would not good will and benevolence we extend to our relations, everywhere be wanting, if a promiscuous use of women were allowed? How could there by such a thing as a family ... if men had none, or knew no relation they had to one another?"; *Marriage Promoted*, 9: "The whole band of civil society ... proceeds from the succession of lawful issue"; and *Reflections on Celibacy*, 19: The "conjugal state is the strongest fence of property, without which succession would be precarious, relations unknown, and society a rope of sand."

justifiable homicide to kill an adulterer taken in the act. A woman, on the other hand, could freely kill a man who tried to rape her; she could bring an action in the bishop's court for the defamation of her sexual character; she could demand protection from a husband who beat or threatened her outrageously; and she could win a separation for cruelty or desertion.[113] But she could not win a divorce because of her husband's adultery, although Christian doctrine presumed that husband and wife had such a "propriety in each the other's person" that if neither party "hath forfeited the right they had to each other by giving themselves into the power of any other person, there can be no divorce or dissolution of that bond."[114] The vindication her reputation received at the bishop's hands was nugatory; for her slanderer would be sentenced to do penance in the parish church, fail to appear there, and then be excommunicated—a punishment with no consequence—and perhaps for this reason aristocratic women did not seek it out.[115] A woman's sexuality, therefore, was as dear to her as life, for she could kill to protect it; but her honor was less dear than a man's; and she (despite the bishops) was incapable of owning a man. A man, on the other hand, clearly had property in his wife, though it was a property less dear than life. He could extract money damages from another man who invaded that property and force him into jail or exile if he could not pay. And he could punish a wife who had given to another man what she had contracted to give to him alone, by ending the marriage, breaking her reputation and keeping her property. A woman's sexuality was property but not a thing, nor yet as valuable as land or money; for a man could be hung for stealing a watch; but a husband was compensated for the loss of her sexuality with a fine from her lover and the possession of her dowry.

Both the action for criminal conversation and divorce for the wife's adultery were innovations of the 1690s. The duke of Norfolk, after his wife and he could no longer agree and she had taken a lover, tried (on the precedent of Lord Roos's divorce of 1670) three times to divorce her by act of Parliament. He finally succeeded in 1699 when her family ceased to support her because she had given evidence of their political disaffection, and when he had been able to persuade his fellow lords that only if he were free to marry could his estates and titles be prevented from going to a papist. But after the first bill had been rejected in 1691, the duke brought an action for tresspass against his wife's lover

---

[113]*Laws*, 11 ff., 53, 54, 65, 184.
[114]William Fleetwood, *Works* (Oxford, 1854), 3 vol., II, 216–217.
[115]Greater London R.O., DL/C 174, 276, 54; the case of Mary Abendon v Leah Hiam, 30 April, 26 June, and 9 November 1763.

in the court of King's Bench and was awarded damages. This set a precedent which was followed until 1857. While the duke was still attempting to get free, Lord Macclesfield tried to separate from his wife through the eccleciastical courts because she had had an illegitimate daughter. When Lady Macclesfield refused to appear in court, he brought his evidence to Parliament and was granted his divorce in 1699. Norfolk got a similar divorce in 1700, and another divorce (preceded by both eccleciastical separation and damages) was passed in 1701. In 1711 there was still another when a young man, who had been lured into marrying a prostitute, divorced his wife for her repeated adulteries. These four cases (with the one of 1670 making a fifth) were the only divorces in England before 1720.[116] The precedent had been established that a woman who bore a bastard or committed adultery could be divorced by her husband, and that the divorce by Parliament would usually be preceded by trials in the spiritual and temporal courts. There were, indeed, cries for an easier divorce that would "raise the pleasures of a married life and sink the delights of intriguing," but they were of no avail.[117] Their presence does show, however, that though divorce might have originated as the means of vindicating a man's property, it might also become the means of ending an unhappy marriage.

In the next 30 years there was a divorce every 3 years, but only two of them involved aristocrats.[118] Aristocratic scandal revolved, instead, around actions for criminal conversation. The most notorious of these arose when Lord Abergavenny sought £50,000 damages from his bosom friend for seducing his wife. The matter came to trial in 1730 although Lady Abergavenny had died 2 months before. The jury awarded £10,000. To some, like Fielding, this was monstrous, for "each wife is (when discover'd) an estate." In his play *The Modern Husband*, he put in plain language the presuppositions of such an action. "Your person is mine," says Mr. Modern, "I bought it lawfully

---

[116] George Abbot, *The Case of Impotency* (London, 1715), 2 vol., II, 59–298; Burnet, *History of His Time*, IV, 222 n; Herts. R.O., D/EP 49, 7 April 1701: Lady Cowper: "a noble Lord of celebrated virtue speaking of the D of Norfolk's death, told me that truly he had not voted for that D's divorce, but that he deceived him by assuring him his only aim was to prevent a popish succession to the family"; *The Duke of Norfolk's Case for Passing His Bill* (London, 1699); *The Trial between... Norfolk, Plaintiff and John Jermaine, Defendant, in Action of Trespass* (London, n.d.); Campbell, *Lord Chancellors*, IV, 109; H.M.C., *House of Lords MSS, 1697–1699*, 57–60, *House of Lords MSS, 1699–1702*, 175–176; B.L., 9 Ann, c. 30. Norfolk claimed he did not seek an ecclesiastical divorce because his wife's adultery was so plain: "Mary Eliot... declared, farther, that she saw Mr. Germain's y[ard] come from the Duchess reeking, slimy and limber, casting his s[perm] about the room," *The Further Depositions... in the Affair of the Duke and Duchess of Norfolk* (London, 1692), 16.

[117] Boyer, *Theophrastus*, 37–38; Castamore, *Conjugium*, 24–28.

[118] B.L., Private Act collection.

in the church; and unless I am to profit by the disposal, I shall keep it all for my own use."[119] To this mentality he opposed the ideal of romantic marriage in which a woman's preferred company was her husband and her children. In this same spirit Lord Warrington argued a few years later that to restrict divorce to the case of the adulterous wife was to deny the most fundamental ends of marriage. A man should be free to divorce a woman who was a bad mother, or one who did not sexually arouse him, or one who, especially, because of a narrow mind or a contentious nature, was no support to "the peace and comfort of a husband's mind." Divorce, in short, should be allowed whenever it was impossible to fulfill the ends of romantic marriage. But Warrington blithely assumed that it was only a husband who would ever seek this relief.[120]

This pursuit of the happy marriage must have had its influence on the flood of divorces that aristocratic society felt had burst upon it in the generation after 1750. In the 1750s there were nearly two a year; in the 1760s one a year; and in the 1770s, four a year. And this time the great aristocratic names were prominently represented. The duke of Grafton, Lord Bolingbroke, Lord Percy, and Lord Carmarthen divorced their wives; and Lady Sarah Lennox, Lady Frances Manners, and Lady Anne Vane were divorced by their husbands.[121] The Grafton divorce in 1769 was especially disturbing, since almost immediately afterward the duchess married her lover, Lord Ossory. The king told the lord chancellor that he "was desirous that something should be thought of that might be likely to prevent the very bad conduct among the ladies, of which there had been so many instances lately."[122] Others agreed, and in the next year a bill to prohibit the marriage of a divorced woman to her lover passed in the Lords but failed in the Commons. There followed 9 years in which 33 divorces were passed. Bishop Barrington then proposed to prevent an adulteress's remarriage because of "the shameful height to which the vice of adultery had risen among us, and especially in the higher ranks of life, to the great misfortune of some of the best families in the kingdom"; but this also passed the Lords

---

[119]Charles B. Woods, "Notes on Three of Fielding's Plays," *Publications of the Modern Language Association*, LII, 1937, 364–366; Henry Fielding, *Complete Works* (New York, 1967), 16 vol., X, 15, 45, 58, cf. 16, 59, 60, 69, 91 (these actions were used by all classes: *The British Journal*, 22 June 1723, 5: A turner sued a salesman's son for £ 1000 and got £ 500; the defendant, who was 18, fled to Holland). When the Duke of Beaufort sued for damages in 1744, Lord Ossory wrote: "Alas! what money will make amends for such injuries! However, of course his expenses ought to be defrayed upon this unhappy occasion" (*Orrery Papers*, II, 171–172).

[120]George, Lord Warrington, *Considerations Upon the Institution of Marriage* (London, 1739).
[121]B. L., Private Act collection.
[122]*Coke*, III, 52–53.

and failed in the Commons.[123] Clearly, it was extremely disturbing to see that divorce was being used not to prevent the imposition of a bastard heir on a noble family but to allow a woman to marry the man she loved. By 1800 Thomas Erskine, who was the most frequent counsel in such cases, was able to say that most divorces arose out of an agreement between husband and wife that they should part.[124]

In at least two of the cases of the 1760s it is clear that husband and wife parted because they had become estranged from each other, and that only after the separation did the wife find the lover for whom she was divorced and whom she then married. Lord Bolingbroke admitted that it was his drunken behavior that led his wife to leave him after 8 years of marriage and 3 children; but he thought that he then repented enough for her to return. He tried to force his wife's relatives to urge her return to him, and he got his aunt to speak to his mother-in-law. But his sister-in-law, Lady Pembroke, was highly sceptical of his repentance, and infuriated him with an accusation that he was acting a part he did not feel and was going on in the same course as before. The separation became settled. Lady Bolingbroke then fell in love with Topham Beauclerk and bore his child. Bolingbroke went to court and got damages of £500, then a separation, and finally a divorce. Lady Bolingbroke, with the consent of her family, married her lover.[125]

The duke and duchess of Grafton parted because of "disagreement of tempers" after 9 years of marriage and 3 children. The duke had openly kept a mistress for 2 years, and his wife's card playing annoyed him. She went to live with her parents and then bought a house of her own. Articles of separation were drawn up and she was given £3000 a year. In 1765 and 1766 she became fond of the duke of Portland. He lent her money and gave her advice about her children and about going to court to keep up her reputation. But then he married, and she fell in love with Lord Ossory. When she became pregnant, her husband sent to tell her that he knew of it, that he could use it in a divorce, and that she should not risk an abortion to hide it. Two weeks after the child's birth, Grafton started proceedings and in 5 months was divorced. She married Ossory, was estranged from her parents, and lived quietly in the

---

[123]*Parliamentary History*, **XVII**, 185 ff., **XX**, 591 ff. (similar attempts to restrict remarriage were made in 1800 and 1809 after similar waves of divorces; see *Parliamentary History*, **XXXV**, 250–251, 255 ff; *Parliamentary Debates*, **XIV**, 329 ff; *The Times*, 13 June 1800).

[124]*Parliamentary History*, **XXXV**, 312 ff. At the Duke of Beaufort's divorce in 1744, an attempt was made to prevent the Duchess from remarrying, but a threat from her lover prevented it (*Orrery Papers*, **II**, 171–172).

[125]Stavordale and Illchester, *Lady Sarah*, 183; Kent R. O., U 471. c. 14; *Trials for Adultery* (London, 1779–1780), 7 vol., **I**: Bolingbroke; 8 George III, c. 70; *Walpole*, **XXII**, 567. Lady Bolingbroke gave up her £500 pin money and £2000 jointure for £800 p.a. for life.

country. Young men there got glimpses of her and owned to be "much struck with the gentility and ease of her behavior as well as with her figure in general." Women continued to gossip of her. And her well-meaning relation Horace Walpole could write to her of the current crop of adulteresses with so little care that he had then to reassure her by asking whether it was just or rational "to confound yourself or to imagine that I confounded you with women who brave the public censure or level themselves to the most abandoned of their sex."[126]

Women, then, could subvert an institution intended to assert their status as property into a means of rearranging their marriages and satisfying their hearts; but they were ultimately subject to a husband's caprice; and they always knew that even their kindest relative would have regarded their conduct in another as totally reprehensible.

Divorce could be manipulated, but the double standard was an adamantine chain. The duchess of Argyll set out to protect her daughter when she fell in love with the duke of Dorset and was separated from her husband, Lord Derby. The duchess and Lady Derby undertook to organize visits to Lady Derby by other ladies, "in defiance," Walpole righteously said, "of all laws of decorum."[127] The duchess of Devonshire explained to her parents that she could call upon Lady Derby once or twice without anyone knowing, that it would be "shocking to me that the time the poor creature is in distress . . . I should entirely abandon her," and that she did not intend by this to do "anything that would endanger my reputation or set me up as a patroness of vice." But her parents persuaded her against this: "Our prudence, our tenderness, and our principles" must "get the better of your sensibility;" and she alone in her set did not go.[128] Lady Sarah Lennox, who had been divorced 3 years before, was reluctant to pass along Lady Derby's story, for she had "a constant monitor that tells me for ever, 'Would you like to have all your faults the topic of conversation?'" But she told the story nonetheless since it allowed her to say that she had recently met her former husband. He had proven generous and had "contrived to give me comfort by talking of Lady Derby's conduct just as I would wish him to talk about mine . . . and to convince me he looked upon me as his friend and one whose friendship he was pleased with." But though Lady Sarah had never had a party formed in her favor, hers was the happier lot; for she was divorced and later married happily. Lord Derby refused to divorce his wife; and her organized flouting of the

---

[126]*Walpole*, **XXII**, 269, **XXXII**, xxxi, 33–34, **XXXII**, 78–79; *Trials for Adultery*, **IV**: Grafton; N.U.L., PwF 6374a ff.; B.L., Add. MSS, 35, 384, f 305.
[127]*Walpole*, **XXXIII**, 78–69 and n.3, **XXI**, 193 and n.8.
[128]Chatsworth MSS, **V**, 236, 237.

double standard was of little use to her; for, as Lady Sarah said, she was "still most thoroughly attached to the Duke of Dorset, and if so, I suppose she will be very happy if the lessening of her visiting list is her only misfortune, and what with giving up her children, sorrow for a fault, dread of not preserving his affection, I think, she is much to be pitied."[129]

If property in women was enshrined in parliamentary divorce and the double standard, the conditions of a man's property in his children were declared by two principles of the law: First, he alone, and not his wife, had the power to appoint guardians for his children and to consent to their marriages while they were minors; second, he exercised these rights only over his legitimate children since it was marriage that gave him title to the products of a woman's womb. An illegitimate child legally was no one's child; it inherited neither property nor a surname; and its natural father could neither appoint its guardians nor restrain its marriage. But this did not mean that the child was its mother's property; it belonged, instead, to the state; and its guardian was appointed by the court of chancery. Children belonged either to men or to the crown, but not to women.[130]

A father's authority was thought to be based, in nature, on the irrationality of his children and his care for them.[131] But he was not the master of either their property, their lives, or their liberty, for they "were not tied like slaves in all cases, and with bonds that will last forever." The authority of parents, Bolingbroke said, "becomes limited when their children are able to [direct themselves] without their help, and yet continue to live in the same family. It ceases when the children go out of their family and acquire independency or even paternal dominion of their own." But parental and paternal authority were not quite the same, and the one always yielded to the other. Bishop Fleetwood explained why: "Because the father is superior to the mother, both in natural strength, in wisdom and by God's appointment,... therefore the children are especially to obey the Father in cases... where they cannot obey both parents together"; for a mother was "not presumed to have a will contrary to her husband's; and therefore the

---

[129]Ilchester and Stavordale, *Lady Sarah*, 290–292.

[130]*Laws*, 401–410, 415; Alexander Croke, *A Report of the Case of Horner against Liddiard ... with an Introductory Essay upon the ... Laws Relating to Illegitimate Children* (London, 1800). Chancery usually appointed the guardians chosen by the natural father, and if he had failed to do so, the child could choose its own guardian at 14.

[131]John Locke, *Two Treatises of Government*, ed. by Peter Laslett (Cambridge: University Press, 1970), 321–336.

child disobeys not his mother, who obeys his father's command, because the mother is to be obedient also."[132]

Fathers had been given sole (patrilineal) control of their children by the same act that abolished other feudal restraints on a man's property (12 Car.II c.24, p. viii). But in this cognatic society the sense that mothers had some natural rights remained strong, though it could be overridden. Lord Shaftesbury by his will appointed three men as his son's guardians. The boy was left to live with his mother until he was 12 when Justice Eyre, the only surviving guardian, tried to take charge of his education. The court agreed that the tutors his mother provided were inadequate and required that he be allowed to dine with Eyre, but he remained with his mother. Two years later, the countess stole a march on Eyre and married her 14-year-old son to Lady Gainsborough's daughter. For this the court held her in contempt and took the boy entirely away from her. It agreed that the countess was "guardian by nature and nurture" but it held that "the right of a testamentary guardian takes place of a guardianship by nature;... his authority... is a continuation of the paternal authority;... his interest is for the good and honor of the family; as the father was the head of the family, so the statute puts him in loco patris." Lady Gainsborough, who was also a widow, was more fortunately placed. Her husband had appointed no guardians; she was therefore the guardian of her children "by nature"; and "the marriage of her daughter belonged to her."[133] Legitimate children belonged to their mothers only insofar as their fathers allowed it.

Natural children, by the general principle of the law, belonged to no one. But neither the law, nor certainly their fathers, acted entirely on this principle. The law required fathers to support such children, and the children were forbidden to marry within the forbidden degrees of relationship as though their parents had been married.[134] Bastards had a personal kindred but belonged to no patrilineage. Nevertheless,

---

[132] Fleetwood, *Relative Duties*, 53, 59-60; Lord Bolingbroke, *Works* (London, 1844), 4 vol., IV, 183. The Marriage Act of 1753 occasioned some discussion of a minor's right to give himself in marriage. Henry Stebbing: "If a friend gives my son an estate, the estate is his and not mine; nor is he in the use of it subject to my control. Now can you tell me of anything which is more a man's his than himself?" (*An Enquiry into the Force and Operation of the Annulling Clauses in a Late Act* (London, 1754), 8). But the Act could never be repealed.

[133] Cox, ed., *Peere Williams*, I, 102-123. Lady Jersey in 1721, a year before the Shaftesbury case began, was probably more fortunate. She got the help of Lord Dartmouth, a trustee to her marriage settlement, against the attempts to control the education and marriage of her sons made by the guardian appointed by her unbalanced husband. She was careful, however, to get Dartmouth's consent when her daughter married. (Staffs. R.O., D. 1778, I, ii, 564, 582). For two other cases involving the Duke of Beaufort and Lord Holderness, see Cox, ed., *Peere Williams*, I, 702-706.

[134] *Laws*, 401-410.

fathers still brought home their bastards, gave them the family name, arranged advantageous marriages for them, and left them inheritances. But they could do these things only with the sufferance of their legitimate families, and throughout the century (but perhaps especially after 1750) a man could find any of these plans effectively opposed by his other relations, either from pride of family or the revulsion of domestic feeling.

It was common, for instance, for an illegitimate child to take its father's name. There were illegitimate Berties, Cecils, Fitzgeralds, Fitzroys, Gordons, Manners, and Walpoles.[135] Lord Pembroke and his friends were therefore surprised when Lady Pembroke in 1780 refused to consent to have the name of her husband's son changed to Herbert on the grounds that it was "an impudent thing in itself and highly improper by me." Lady Pembroke had agreed to the boy's living with them, but the memory of the way in which his father had publicly deserted her at one point for the boy's mother was evidently still present. Lady Pembroke, with the support of her own son, got her way. She may have insisted on having it solely because of her memories. But it may also have been that romantic love was making a mistress difficult to endure.[136] Lady Sarah Lennox remarked in 1760 that the previous duke of Marlborough had had women "after he was married, though he loved his wife. But that sort of love would not content me, for I have no notion of a man's loving his wife and following all those sort of people."[137]

An illegitimate child's way was, therefore, always difficult since the reaction of neither its father's relations nor the world's was certain. The Berties managed very well. Lord Albemarle had six children by his mistress and carefully provided for their education and their fortunes. His nephew the duke of Ancaster, like his uncle, never married; but he left a fortune for his daughter, who lived with his eldest sister; and the child was also remembered in her grandmother's will.[138] The Bentincks, on the other hand, refused to see Lord George's mistress even after he married her.[139] And the Finch family ended with threats to kick each other down the stairs when one sister presented a brother's natural daughter at court. Lady Isabella called it "publishing a bastard at Court."[140] Giving such children a public position made one vulnerable. Lord Orford had to patiently endure statements that he had abused "the fountain of honor by making His Majesty give a patent of honor and

[135]Lancs. R.O., Ancaster MSS; *Walpole*, **X**, 348, **XXXII**, 58, n. 1, **XVII**, 452, n. 22; Herbert, ed., *Pembroke Papers*, 44.
[136]Herbert, ed., *Pembroke Papers*, 34–35, 37–38, 44, 50.
[137]*Leinster*, **II**, 93–94.
[138]Lincs. R.O., 5 Anc 2/A/36, 2 Anc 6/16.
[139]Namier and Brooke, *House of Commons*, **II**, 83.
[140]*Walpole*, **XIX**, 389.

precedence to a bastard."[141] His son more cautiously refused to present his natural daughters at court, but he did manage to marry them all to noblemen, which was no easy feat. Lord Dysart was furious when his son married Harriet Cavendish, the natural daughter of the duke of Devonshire; and it was this perhaps that made it easier for his grandson to marry one of the Walpole girls.[142] The Herveys were distressed when their heir made a similar marriage. Illegitimate sons most probably passed more easily in aristocratic society, but even they might be snubbed. When Lord Chesterfield's son was treated unkindly, the best his father could do was to make use of the incident to say how much more "superior merit and knowledge" were necessary to him.[143]

But illegitimate children faced their greatest difficulties from their father's relations when, having no other children, he attempted to make them his heirs, in preference to his own siblings or his nieces or nephews. Lord Scarsdale's sister contested the property he left to his two natural children, and in a compromise she and her nephew shared the estate. The earl of Leicester claimed to have broken the entail on the family estates and even tried to leave Penshurst to his natural daughter. His nieces contested the will and tried to prove that he had been mad, but a compromise was arranged. And when Lord Rochford left £1100 a year to his mistress and his various children, the nephew who inherited the title contested his will.[144]

The judges could prove as difficult as relations. They denied a legacy to a child of the duke of Devonshire because the will by the duke's father had been made before the child's birth; they said that the "Earl of Devonshire could never intend that his son should go on in this course, that would be to encourage it, whereas it was enough to pardon what was past." A bastard could not inherit "until he had got a reputation of being such a one's child, and that reputation could not be gained before the child was born."[145] Children could inherit property automatically only if marriage had made them the property of their father. And since a natural child had no legal relations, if he died intestate his estate went to the crown, unless his father's relatives could get a royal warrant allowing them to inherit.[146] Legal ancestors and descendants could exist for an individual only if his father had contractually come into the ownership of his mother.

[141] Orrery Papers, II, 171-172.
[142] Violet Biddulph, The Three Ladies Waldegrave (London: Peter Davies, 1938), 28; Cartwright, ed., Wentworth Papers, 6.
[143] W. S. Childe-Pemberton, The Earl Bishop (London: Hurst & Blacke, 1924), 2 vol., I, 23; Dobrée, ed., Letters of Chesterfield V, 1961-1962.
[144] B.L., 14 Geo II, c.3; Kent R.O., U. 908/L19/5, 6, 25, 26, /L23; Cokayne, ed., Complete Peerage, XI, 55, n.c.
[145] Cox, ed., Peere Williams, I, 529-530.
[146] H.M.C., Portland MSS, V, 138-139.

Figure 4.1 Portrait of the countess of Sunderland by G. Kneller. In a letter to her husband discussing the possibility of early death she wrote "As to the children, pray get my mother... to take care of the girls and if I leave my boys too little to go school... a man can't take care of little children as a woman can... don't be as careless of the dear children as when you relied upon me to take care of them... though you should marry, for your wife may wrong them when you don't mind it. We must all die, but it's hard to part with one... in whom there was so much happiness as you, my dearest, ever were to me." Copyright photograph from the National Portrait Gallery, London. Reproduced by permission.

IV

Childbearing

    The ideal of domesticity held that it was a woman's role in life to love her husband, bear his children, and remain at home to care for them. It also held, though more tenuously, that it was legitimate for a man to take an interest in his children because they were children and not simply because they were his heirs. It encouraged him to view them as independent human beings rather than as extensions of himself. The best evidence for this is the new effort that husbands made before 1720 to ensure that their wives would survive the rigors of childbearing, and their greater success after 1750 in ensuring that their children survived infancy. Domesticity encouraged the view, in consonance with the eighteenth century's prevailing ideology, that childbearing was a natural and healthy process; and the equality of the sexes produced an effort to preserve women from the dangers of childbirth. But the still considerable power of patriarchy required that human intelligence be applied to such problems only by the rational part of creation—that is, by men. Accordingly, aristocratic men had by 1720 come to agree that in difficult cases of childbirth, men midwives should be employed, and these physicians, once given their opening, managed after 1750 to change the opinion that pregnancy was a disease.

Equality and domesticity, however, were never easy partners. For when after 1750 the latter really came into its own, it meant that aristocratic women (who had been limiting their pregnancies for the past three generations) began once more to put their lives in frequent jeopardy in order to have the large families that satisfied the domestic ideal. The domestic ideal, nonetheless, changed the evaluation placed on a woman's reproductive capacities by increasing the matrifocal emphases in the family. Women were increasingly seen (as is the case in strongly matrifocal societies) as mothers rather than as wives.[1] But a mother could care for a child only if she were alive and well; whereas a wife's most pressing duty was accomplished once she had produced an heir. It is also likely that the increasing regard paid to kindred over patrilineal ties had an effect on the status of women. In a patrilineal society like traditional China men expressed their reluctant dependence on women by treating them as polluting agents who had to be confined for a month after parturition and secluded from men.[2] In the early eighteenth century, aristocratic women underwent a similar confinement, but by the 1780s they were receiving visitors in a drawing room within a few days of delivery, and there were men among them.

Conception

A community's attitudes toward childbearing must rest, first of all, on its beliefs with regard to fertility. Throughout the eighteenth century most of the medical and scientific community held some version of the preformation theory of generation—that is, that either the ovum or the sperm contained within itself the preformed human being, which simply grew larger during the 9 months of gestation. The function of the ovaries in vertebrates was discovered in the middle of the seventeenth century, and for a generation thereafter it was usual to emphasize the female contribution. In the 1680s, however, microscopic

---

[1]Nancy Tanner, "Matrifocality," in Rosaldo and Lamphere, eds., *Woman, Culture and Society* (Stanford: Stanford Univ. Press, 1974).

[2]E. M. Ahern, "The Power and Pollution of Chinese Women," in Wolf and Witke, eds., *Women in Chinese Society* (Stanford: Stanford Univ. Press, 1975), 202–203; cf. B. S. Denich, "Sex and Power in the Balkans," in Rosaldo and Lamphere, eds., *Woman Culture and Society*, for women in another patrilineal society.

investigation revealed spermatozoa in the semen. The traditionally more important male role in generation was now reasserted by the *animalculists*, as they were called, but they were opposed by the theologians, who would not admit that God would permit such a wastage, since if spermatozoa was the germ, each must have a rational soul. In the mid-eighteenth century, preformation itself was challenged by those who pointed out that as children inherited the characteristics of both parents, men and women must contribute equally to their conception. But the challenge was soon set aside, and around 1760 a new ovist version of preformation established itself and lasted for 30 or 40 years.[3] Practicing physicians in this welter of opinion seem either to have stuck to some ovist version[4] or to have refused to have anything to say on the question.[5] After 1760, when the theory seemed more settled than it had been for some time, physicians made cautious statements such as that "after many disputes, it appears, at length, probable, that the future child, ... subsists in the ovaries of females, and that what has been styled the *act of generation*, is only the means intended by providence to supply it with life. With that view the womb and vagina are plentifully supplied with nerves, and during the communication between the sexes, seems to be endowed with a double portion of sensibility."[6]

It is difficult to say what effect these scientific theories had on the minds of that fifth of the aristocrats[7] whose marriages were childless. But it is quite probable the medical advice they would have received and the legal and social assumptions of their century would have led them to see a childless marriage as the result of a woman's barrenness rather than any incapacity of her husband. Childless marriages were dissolved only if it was shown that a husband was impotent, and a man was deemed potent if he had the power of erection, and not necessarily with his wife. When the duke of Beaufort was about to divorce his wife for adultery, she tried retorting that he was impotent and that the marriage was null on that ground. But his Grace decided to be put to the test, and Walpole, in a flutter, recounted the incident:

> T'other night was appointed for the action; the lists were at Dr. Mede's house: he, another physician, three surgeons and the Dean of Arches, all matron-like person-

---

[3]Elizabeth B. Gasking, *Investigations into Generation, 1651–1828* (Baltimore: Johns Hopkins Univ. Press, 1967); F. J. Cole, *Early Theories of Sexual Generation* (London: Oxford Univ. Press, 1930).

[4]Henry Bracken, *The Midwife's Companion* (London: 1737); Pierre Dionis, *A General Treatise of Midwifery* (London, 1719).

[5]Fielding Ould, *A Treatise of Midwifery* (Dublin, 1742); Benjamin Pugh, *A Treatise of Midwifery* (London, 1754).

[6]Alexander Hamilton, *A Treatise on Midwifery* (Edinburgh, 1781), 40–41.

[7]Hollingsworth, 45–47.

ages, were inspectors. I should never have been potent again!—well, but he was. They offered to wait upon his Grace to any *place of public resort*—"no, no, he would only go behind the screen, and when he knocked, they were to come to him, but come that moment." He was sometime behind the scenes: at last he knocked and the good old folks saw what amazed them—what they had not seen in many a day!—Cibber says, "His Grace's———— is in everybody's mouth."[8]

Similarly, when Lord Aston's daughter was declared by the midwives to be a *virgo intacta* 5 years after her marriage, her plea for a decree of nullity was denied because her husband had an impediment to his penis removed by physicians and was now capable of erection.[9]

If a man could have an erection and there were still no children, the fault then lay with his wife. But such a marriage was not null, for a woman's barrenness could never be absolutely proven. When it became apparent in the reign of Charles II that the queen would bear no children and that a Catholic would succeed to the throne, Bishop Burnet recounted that there were those who "pretended she was barren from a natural cause, and that seemed equivalent to impotence in men. But the king often said, he was sure she had once miscarried. This, though not overthrown by such evidence, could never be proved; unless the having no children was to be concluded a barrenness: and the dissolving a marriage on such an account could neither be justified in law or conscience."[10] Caleb Fleming, in a similar vein, wrote that "every man who taketh a wife, may, and ought to know, that fruitfulness is not at her pleasure, or in her power; and therefore the capacity of intercourse is all he is to expect from her, relative to propagation; which being found, consummates the contract."[11]

Fleming might think that a woman did not have fruitfulness at her pleasure, but the doctors and the quacks were certainly convinced that barrenness was a disease of which a woman might be cured. The newspapers were full of advertisements of cures. One woman advertised that "this is to give notice to the female sex that barrenness, miscarriage, and all other weaknesses and indispositions in women are faithfully and speedily cured by the gentle-woman at the Golden Key in Haydon Yard in the Minories by a very extraordinary method, and exceeding safe and pleasant medicines, many years experienced." And there were also advertisements for "vivifying drops for barrenness in women."[12]

[8]*Walpole*, **XVIII**, 185.
[9]*The Cases of Impotency... Catherine... and Edward Weld... published by John Crawford* (London, 1732).
[10]Gilbert Burnet, *History of His Own Time* (Oxford, London, 1833), 6 vol., **I**, 480.
[11]Caleb Fleming, *The Oeconomy of the Sexes* (London, 1751), 5.
[12]*The London Journal*, 14 April 1722; *The British Journal*, 26 January 1723.

Among the medical men who cared for aristocratic women it was usual to say that the state of the womb and the "animal economy" of a woman were responsible for barrenness. A healthy woman would have her periods regularly and her menstrual blood, by which a child was fed in the womb, would be of "lively red colour." A barren woman's womb was either too hard to allow the placenta to take root or too weak and relaxed to hold it in, and consequently it miscarried of children.[13] In the latter case spa waters were recommended, and it was partly for this reason that so many ladies trooped off to Bath. One writer stated that "almost every physician of credit has recommended bathing for barren women" and that he "pitied poor innocent young new married women, who have heat and stewed themselves in hot baths . . . thinking that the deficiency lay on their side . . . in hope of a great belly etc., when alas the fault was in the vile, and wicked whoremasterly husband, broke and bankrupt in his bed tackle."[14]

Women were teased on the subject of taking the waters. When Lady Caroline Fox went to Bath to recover after one lying-in, she began to fear that she was pregnant again and therefore asked her husband to keep it a "profound secret" for "it will seem very silly to leave off the waters because I'm breeding." Their husbands fared no better at Horace Walpole's hands: He noticed that "Lady Carteret is going to Tunbridge—which don't look so flaming vigorous on my Lord's part; but there is a hurry for a son."[15] And because so many families were in a hurry for a son, a woman was forced into thinking herself ill and incomplete; wondering whether she had displeased God, as did the duchess of Devonshire, or whether it was just that her womb needed strengthening; and in either case, knowing that possibly her husband—and certainly his family—would consider his choice of her a disaster.[16] The duke of Bedford grew so very uneasy when his daughter-in-law did not become pregnant that one lady remarked that "she was not surprised Lady Tavistock did not breed, for the great bustle the Duke of Bedford made was enough to put anybody out." But the young duchess of Buccleugh had an even more difficult time with her husband's relations. Her mother-in-law, Lady Dalkeith, blamed the duchess's social life when she miscarried of her first pregnancy. During her second pregnancy she became so large, people began to say she

---

[13]Dionis, *Midwifery*, 57–59; Bracken, *Midwife's Companion*, 25–27.
[14]John Quinton, *Treatise of Warm Bath Water* (Oxford, 1733), I, 63–64, 95, cited in *Walpole*, XVIII, 239 n.3.
[15]B.L., Add. MSS, 51,414, f. 40; *Walpole*, XVIII, 501.
[16]Chatsworth MSS, V, 313.

would have twins. She had a son, but the child died after a few months. Lady Dalkeith now cooled toward the duchess, and others noticed that she was dissatisfied that the duchess did not become pregnant again. The duchess, in turn, began to grow markedly cool toward her husband's family. But she was soon pregnant again and had a successful delivery. "I'm glad she is safe," wrote her husband's aunt, "but I wish it had been a son." For a living heir was the only successful termination to a great lady's labor.[17]

Contraception

To have too many children, before 1750, was as great a difficulty as to have none. From 1650 on, English aristocrats began to limit the number of their children, and the marriages made in the generation after 1720 seem to have produced the fewest children. But in the generation after 1750, the trend was significantly reversed, and by 1800 aristocrats were having the greatest number of children in 200 years.[18] The limitations had been placed out of economic concern and a regard for the health of women; they were removed after 1750 when domesticity and increasing prosperity once again made large families of children valued.

There were several methods of birth control available. There was, of course, abstinence, but there were other known means as well. First, there was the lactation cycle. Lord Clarendon urged aristocratic mothers to take up nursing their children. He admitted that this would limit the number of children, but he also thought it would save lives, "whereas the over-much haste carries both mothers and children to their untimely graves." For he was aware that many husbands prevented their wives from nursing on the ground that they were not as likely to conceive if they did so.[19] But since aristocratic women did not begin to nurse until the 1760s, this clearly was not the method used. Second, there was *coitus interruptus*: The anonymous author of *Onania* was

> assured, that there are married persons, who commit a heinous sin to God, by frustrating what he has appointed for the multiplication of our species, and are commonly such as think children come too fast, and distrust providence for their maintenance and education. They indulge themselves in all the pleasures of sense, and yet would avoid the charges they might occasion in order to which, they do

---
[17]*Coke*, I, 19, II, 150, 220, 353, 434.
[18]*Hollingsworth*, 31, 43–45, 51.
[19]Earl of Clarendon, *A Collection of Several Tracts* (London, 1727), 314–315.

Childbearing 171

what they can to hinder conception. What I mean is, when the man by a criminal untimely retreat, disappoints his wife's as well as his own fertility. This is what truly may be called a frustraneous abuse of their bodies, and must be an abominable sin. Yet it is certain, that thousands there are in the married state, who provoke and gratify their lust, as far as is consistent with their destructive purpose, and no farther.[20]

There were condoms made of the specially treated intestines of sheep which were cut to seven or eight inches and bound at the open end with green or scarlet ribbons. There were vaginal sponges.[21] And there was abortion. When Lady Clermont miscarried, the duchess of Devonshire gossiped that "to tell you the truth, as it is pretty certain Mr. Morden the apothecary was the father, I fear some wicked method was made use of to procure abortion, and this is more likely as Mr. Morden might bring the drug from his own shop."[22] All these were effective means of birth control. But there were, as well, the ineffective beliefs in magical practices and coital positions.[23]

Those who limited the size of their families did so because, as the author of *Onania* said, they distrusted providence to provide for the maintance and education of their children and preferred, as Samuel Dugard put it, that "their families should be none rather than large." When limits stopped being placed, it was because the climate of opinion had changed to agree with Lady Sarah Osborn's exclaimation in 1751 that "large families in general are more lucky than small ones." She explained that this was so because "too much anxiety is not pleasing to Heaven: I hardly ever knew it succeed. Self, self, self can never prosper, for happiness or content is not to be purchased by money."[24]

But families were also limited on the ground that excessive childbearing must be unnecessarily wearing to a woman. A mother and daughter, born in different generations, could have quite different feelings on the matter. Lady Mary Wortley Montagu, who was born in 1689 and had two children, wrote in 1749 to her daughter (who was born in 1718): "I don't know whether I shall make any court to you in saying it, but I own I can't help thinking that your family is numerous enough, and that the education and disposal of four girls is employment for a whole life." Lady Bute, who already had four daughters and two sons, quite clearly disagreed with her mother, for she went on to have two

---

[20]*Onania or the Heinous Sin of Self-Pollution* (London, 1723), 8th ed., 99–100.
[21]Peter Fryer, *The Birth Controllers* (New York: Stein & Day, 1966), 78.
[22]Chatsworth MSS, V, 233.
[23]Peter Fryer, *Private Case-Public Scandal* (London, 1966), 78.
[24]Samuel Dugard, περιπολυπαιδιας : *Or a Discourse Concerning the Having Many Children* (London, 1695), 26; John McClelland, ed., *Letters of Sarah Byng Osborn, 1721–1773* (Stanford: Stanford Univ. Press, 1930), 75.

more daughters and four more sons. But it was perhaps Lady Bute who was exceptional here.[25] For a feeling similar to Lady Mary's is reflected in Lady Caroline Fox's saying in 1759, no doubt on the basis of her own experience, that she was surprised that her sister Louisa, after 6 months of marriage, "don't breed yet," and that though she did not doubt but that she would eventually, she did not think "it signifies much whether there are many Masters and Miss Connollys. I'm glad for her she don't begin too soon."[26]

For Lady Caroline was no friend to excessive childbearing. She was born in 1723 and married when she was 21. She bore her first son 9 months and 12 days after the marriage. Over a year and a half later, after a difficult labor, she bore a second son who lived less than 3 months. With her surviving son, she now went to Bath to take the waters for her health. From there she began a correspondence with her husband by saying, "I am in a great fright, and if my fears prove true, [I] shall be vastly angry with you. You wonder what I mean, but in short I believe ... that I shall come away from Bath ... if I am breeding, which I begin to suspect a little, but I hope I'm in the wrong for 'twould be very bad for me [as] I have not yet recovered my strength from my last lying-in." Three days later she continued: "If I should be breeding, which I begin to fear very much, for today is Saturday and I ought last Sunday to have omitted my waters, I shall be with you soon. But I'm willing to flatter myself the contrary because once before I was mistaken for about ten days. I shall be most exceedingly vexed at it if I should [be breeding], for ... losing a summer's comfort again." Five days later her doubts were gone and she began to act to save her situation. "I am really very much out of humour with you," she told him, "for I begin to give it quite up. I'm certainly breeding, I took a great deal of physic yesterday in hopes to send it away, but it has only convinced me my fears prove true." It is clear that she considered the pregnancy a result of his sexual demands, and she told him that "you must let me be very cross and huffy with you very often when I come back to London, to make it up with me, for I'm very angry indeed." But since he had not moderated his appetite, she had set to work to rid herself of its product, and the following day she was able to brag of her success, writing "to tell you I am not breeding(is not that clever)." In this way she managed to get through almost two summers without a pregnancy, and she bore her third son in January 1749, when she was almost 26. This child she apparently intended to be her last—two were enough—but early in 1754 whatever system of birth control she had been using failed, and

---

[25]*Lady Mary*, **II**, 428.
[26]*Leinster*, **I**, 237.

Childbearing

the following March, at 32, she gave birth to the son who was actually her last child.[27]

A married couple who decided not to limit the size of their family did not necessarily escape long periods of sexual abstinence, for the wear and tear on a woman's health that constant childbearing caused meant that for considerable periods of her marriage a woman was recovering her health from her previous lying-in and that as part of that recovery (as can be shown from birth intervals) she did not sleep with her husband. Lady Bristol, whose pregnancies can be accurately described from her husband's diary, is an excellent illustration of the point.[28] It is convenient to begin by putting our information in tabular form.

25 July 1695 Lord and Lady Bristol married. Lady Bristol is 19.

1.	15 October 1696	Son
2.	9 December 1697	Daughter
3.	20 January 1699	Son
4.	25 December 1699	Son
5.	5 January 1701	Son
6a.	29 August 1701	miscarries of triplets
6b.	6 September 1701	

Abstinence of 8 months

7.	5 April 1703	Daughter and son
8.	6 July 1704	Stillborn son

Abstinence of 12 months

9.	24 June 1706	Son, overlaid by his nurse, August 6
10.	12 July 1707	Daughter
11.	3 June 1708	Son, died after 2 hours
12.	19 May 1709	Daughter
13.	3 July 1710	Son, died 16 July

Abstinence of 9 months

14.	12 February 1712	Son
15.	5 March 1713	Son, died 2 May from an opening in his head

Abstinence of 13 months

16.	2 March 1715	Daughter

Abstinence of 7 months

17.	25 September 1716	Daughter	Lady Bristol is 39.

---

[27]B.L., Add. MSS, 51,414, ff. 36, 40, 47, 49. Birth intervals as evidence of birth control have been used for England most notably in E. A. Wrigley, "Family Limitation in Pre-Industrial England," *EcHR*, XIX, 1966, 82–109, though his results have been criticized in T. H. Hollingsworth, *Historical Demography* (Ithaca, N.Y.: Cornell Univ. Press, 1966), 181–195.

[28]*Bristol Diary*, 200–203, passim.

Unfortunately, Lord Bristol did not actually note in his diary when he did or did not sleep with his wife; and so we must explain the method by which we feel confident in asserting the existence of these abstinences between the periods of time in which Lady Bristol had a child in almost every year: 1696–1701, 1703–1704, 1706–1710, 1712–1713. In the first of these periods the child was born in December or January, in the second in April and July, in the third in June or July, and in the fourth in March and February. Lady Bristol, in these four periods, no doubt took the usual month's lying-in after parturition, then began to sleep again with her husband and within 1 or 2 months was pregnant once more. The clearest example of this is the eleventh pregnancy in which she gave birth to a son about 9 days short of 11 months after the birth of her previous child. Therefore, if we take the periods in between the groups of annual pregnancies and subtract a period of 11 months from each, we will be safe in considering that the remainder were months of extraordinary sexual abstinence.

Next we must show that these periods of abstinence were necessary because of Lady Bristol's health. Her first child was born October 15, but the second, instead of coming early in the next November, was not born until early December. The diary offers the explanation. After the delivery in October, Lady Bristol was slow in recovering, and in January she was still quite ill. By late February she recovered enough to leave London and go down into the country, and within about a week of doing so the second child was probably conceived, and a cycle of births in January or December was begun. In 1701 she miscarried of triplets when she was probably about 4 months pregnant. It took her some time to recover, for it was a year and a half before any more children were born, and in the interval she and her husband probably did not sleep together for 8 or 9 months. There was a slightly longer recovery than usual after the birth of her twins in April 1703, for Lady Bristol was suffering from a "rheumatic pain and swelling, which fell upon her left side down to her foot." In the middle of August she was at Bath for her health; Bristol hurried there as he had been away from her for 17 days and he had "never been so long absent from her before"; they left Bath a week after his arrival, and shortly thereafter, with her health no doubt improved, her next child was conceived. This child was born dead, and it is likely that in the aftermath the Bristols did not sleep together for over a year. Between 1706 and 1710 there were five children, but two of these were so sickly that they lived for only short periods. The ill health of these children may have suggested that Lady Bristol needed more rest, and there now occurred the third major period of abstinence, this time for 9 months. After this, two sons were born in a new February–March cycle, but one of them was born with an opening in his head that eventually killed him. The child's condition and the difficulty of the labor meant another period of abstinence, this one the longest of all—13 months; and then there was another pregnancy, another period of abstinence, and finally the delivery of the last child when Lady Bristol was 39 years old. Her labors with the last few children had been quite difficult, so much so that she was delivered by a physician rather than a midwife (but her labors had often been long: 13 hours for the fourth child), and when the last child was born, Bristol noted that his wife had been "safely and speedily delivered (according to our repeated joint prayers for that purpose)."

The periods of abstinence between the groupings in which the Bristol children were born we have called extraordinary; and we have done so because it is probable that a religious man like Bristol observed certain ordinary periods of abstinence as well: that he did not go to his wife during her periods, nor during her pregnancies (we may presume that they would have known by the third month), nor in her lyings-in. Of the 20 years during which Lady Bristol bore children, it is likely, then, that her husband, either because she was menstruating, because she was pregnant, or because she was recovering from a pregnancy, did not sleep with her for 11 of those years, or more than half the total. Sexual abstinence must therefore have been common enough to make its use as a contraceptive not seem at all extraordinary, and a man who abstained from relations with his wife, either from prudential motives or at her insistence, could always turn to whores.[29]

Between 1690 and 1720 aristocratic men and women undertook by means of abstinence, abortions, or coitus interruptus to limit the size of their families, and they did so because they felt a greater obligation to provide for the independence of their younger children and to save the life and health of women. After 1750 they returned to older patterns, overconfident, perhaps, in the improvements of midwifery, certain that they were richer than ever, and driven by domesticity. Families grew to such an extent that by 1817 it had all come to seem very wicked to a spinster living at the juncture of landed and professional society. Jane Austen, having endured the deaths of too many women in childbed,

---

[29]It has been suggested that an interruption in the cycle of Margaret Boswell's pregnancies can be accounted for by the slow healing of lacerations from a difficult pregnancy. The bad health that resulted from nine pregnancies may eventually have made relations with her husband less frequent and sent him to whores (W. B. Ober, "Boswell's Gonorrhea," Bulletin of the New York Academy of Medicine, XLV, 1969, 632n.). Dame Sarah Cowper stopped having relations with her husband in her late twenties as a means of birth control and then made a religious virtue of chastity. Her husband also took to whores (Herts R.O., D/EP/F29(Lady Sarah's diary) 10 Feb. 1701, 17 Nov. 1702).

took to recommending "the simple regimen of separate rooms" and wrote of the Heywoods that "they had very pretty property—enough, had their family been of reasonable limits to have allowed them a very gentlemanlike share of luxuries and change."[30]

Pregnancy

So dangerous a business could childbearing seem that it was thought that women had to have "an inexpressible desire of children, which we rudely and wrongfully term lust; whereas such a desire essentially belongs to the chief end of marriage, and is ordained by nature to make them go through such dangers and difficulties as would be almost impossible to undergo without it."[31] But before 1750 it seemed that this natural instinct could work itself out only in disease and death. Mauriceau, in the most influential book on midwifery of its time, said that "a woman with child ... although in good health, yet ought to be reputed as though she were sick, during that neuter state, (for to be with child, is also vulgarly called a sickness of nine months) because she is then in daily expectation of many inconveniences, which pregnancy usually causes to those who are not well governed."[32] But after mid-century this attitude changed under the influence of men who became convinced that it was no more natural that women should suffer or die from childbearing than that infants should die in great numbers in their first few years. Dr. William Hunter, who was the most fashionable accoucheur of his time, was obliged, when he was called to attend Queen Charlotte in her first pregnancy in 1762, to restrain Caesar Hawkins from bleeding her, on the ground that "as labour is not a disease it does not require that the constitution should be reduced."[33] But even Mauriceau had objected to that dour view that held the pains of labour to be the consequence of God's curse on Eve, since he could

---

[30]R. W. Chapman, ed., *Jane Austen's Letters* (London: Oxford Univ. Press, 1964), 480; id., *Sanditon* in *Minor Works*, ed. by Chapman (London, 1969), 373. Lord Stanley in the 1840s was unwilling to abstain, but as he felt he had too many children, he got his wife to try abortion. See Nancy Mitford, ed., *The Ladies of Alderley* (London: Hamish Hamilton, 1967), 142–143, 185.

[31]*The Present State of Matrimony... by Philogamous* (London, 1739), 67. I have found useful guidance in Margaret Mead and Niles Newton, "Cultural Patterning of Perinatal Behaviour," in Richardson and Guttmacher, eds., *Childbearing: Its Social and Psychological Aspects* (Baltimore: Williams & Wilkins, 1967).

[32]Francis Mauriceau, *The Diseases of Women*, 1st English ed., 1672, trans. by H. Chamberlain (London, 1755), 48; cf. Brundenell Exton, *A New General System of Midwifery* (London, 1751), 19; Dionis, *Midwifery*, 120; Jean Astruc, *Elements of Midwifery* (London, 1766), p. v.

[33]John Kobler, *The Reluctant Surgeon* (Garden City, N.Y.: Doubleday, 1960), 124.

see that even the brute creation experienced them. A century later, this appeal to nature's example had grown in weight and had been reinforced by Hunter's experiments in the London hospitals. An admirer of Hunter's, who was himself in search of cures of childbirth fevers, objected that it "appears contradictory to the general plan of nature in the support and preservation of her creatures" that "this most necessary operation should itself be a disease, and should often be the source of many dangerous and fatal maladies."[34] By 1780 childbearing might still have been dangerous, but it was no longer thought that it was naturally and necessarily so.

The changes in attitude toward pregnancy can be charted in three areas: the taboos against intercourse, the influence of the mother's imagination on her unborn child, and the attitude toward miscarriages. It was thought in the early eighteenth century that a woman should not have sexual intercourse during menstruation, during pregnancy, and immediately after parturition. The taboo against intercourse during menstruation was partly founded on aesthetic considerations. Lord Rochester had sung that

> By all love's soft, yet mighty powers,
>   It is a thing unfit
> That men should fuck in time of flowers
>   Or when the smock's beshit.
> Fair nasty nymph, be clean and kind
>   And all my joys restore
> By using paper still behind
>   And sponges for before.[35]

There were those who claimed that the prohibition rested on divine law and cited Leviticus (15:24, 20:18). And there was the claim, as John Evelyn told his son, that the children who were conceived during menstruation would be born with leprosy or "the evident signs of the parents' incontinency." But Bishop Taylor had disputed the probability of this on the ground that the world would long since have been filled with monsters if it were true.[36] Daniel Defoe, however, was still maintaining the old position in 1727, but he spoke as though very few were heeding the prohibition. The one applied instance of the taboo that has turned up may possibly refer to something else: Henry Savile told Lord Halifax

---

[34]Mauriceau, *Diseases*, 151–152; Charles White, *A Treatise on the Management of Pregnant and Lying-in Women* (London, 1772), xiv.

[35]Earl of Rochester, *Complete Poems*, ed. by D. M. Veith (New Haven: Yale Univ. Press, 1968), 51.

[36]Jeremy Taylor, *Ductor Dubitantium* (London, 1660), 286–290; W. G. Hiscock, *John Evelyn and His Family Circle* (London: Routledge & Kegan Paul, 1955), 122–123.

that his son Lord Eland "from a pretended tenderness of his wife" had "obliged her to go see him at times when one would not show one's self to any creature living; how far this may defer her journey I cannot answer—she will herself give you an account of it."[37]

Intercourse during pregnancy was discouraged on the medical ground that it weakened children in the womb and "hence feeble old men, who by the benefit of nature are free from headstrong desires, often produce more healthy children, than the strongest young men, who burn with lust."[38] It was also thought to increase the possibility of abortion and it was urged that "coition (although the woman be generally more desirous of it, the first two or three months of pregnancy) is bad."[39] It was opposed as an "action very unbecoming a rational creature" since not even a "beast will suffer the male to copulate with them when they are with young"; and it was held that since the end of nature had been fulfilled in conception, a man's desire for intercourse during pregnancy was "a mere shameless use of a woman, to abate the heat of his spirits, and cool his blood; 'tis making a necessary-house of his wife."[40] But all these writers were on the defensive, and well might they be, for there was respectable medical opinion to the contrary: "as for me, my wife has brought me twenty children, to the full time; and I am convinced that husbands have it not in their power to knock children on the head, and that therefore they may make love to their wives as they please."[41]

Intercourse after childbirth also excited Defoe's indignation. But it is unlikely that husbands had intercourse with their wives sooner than the second month after parturition because of the elaborate month of lying-in that aristocratic women endured. Nicholas Blundell wrote in his diary in 1704 that "my wife's month being now out we lay together."[42] But it is possible that there was some change toward the

---

[37]Daniel Defoe, *Conjugal Lewdness* (London, 1727), 61–66; W. D. Cooper, ed., *Savile Correspondence* (Camden Society, 1858), 86.

[38]Walter Harris, *A Treatise on the Acute Diseases of Children*, trans. by John Martyn (London, 1724), 14.

[39]John Burton, *An Essay towards a Complete New System of Midwifery* (London, 1751), 282; Bracken, *Midwife's Companion*, 45.

[40]Defoe, *Lewdness*, 319.

[41]Dionis, *Midwifery*, 125. The practice of an adulterous couple is perhaps not the best evidence for normal practice, but a milliner testified that she had seen Lady Grosvenor, when she was pregnant, kneeling on a bed and the duke of Cumberland taking her from behind. The duke may have withdrawn before climax, for the milliner also saw drops of his semen falling on the carpet (*Trials for Adultery* (London, 1779–1780), 7 vol., V, 149–150: Grosvenor divorce).

[42]Defoe, *Lewdness*, 325–329; Frank Tyrer and J. J. Bagley, eds., *The Great Diurnal of Nicholas Blundell* (Lancashire & Cheshire Record Society, 1968), 69. The author of *Onania*, pp. 85ff., saw no harm in coitus during a woman's infertile periods. But a number of Puritan divines had anticipated this position, see Levin L. Schücking, *The Puritan Family* (London: Routledge & Kegan Paul, 1969), 39.

end of the century when the month's recovery was made less secluded. The probable weakening of the force of these taboos meant that sexual intercourse and a woman's reproductive capacity were seen increasingly as natural and easy things and not so much as sources of danger and ill-health.

It was proverbial that pregnant women had longings for strange things. The Spectator urged that "in every settlement there ought to be a clause inserted, that the father should be answerable for the longings of his daughter." A physician told of women eating coals, chalk, cinders, raw meat, and raw fish. He urged that these cravings should be satisfied as far as possible, for a woman's imagination was held to have a great influence on the fetus's health, and the "marks which have been so often given to children are various and everyday to be seen."[43] But by the end of our period the entire doctrine of the effects of longings and frights was doubted, and was considered on the level of belief in witches and ghosts. Cases were cited in which children were born with marks when it had not been anticipated that they would be and vice versa. Marks were explained as the result of distended blood vessels. And it was said that to alleviate the forebodings of the mother was to remove the greatest part of the evil.[44]

Physicians were hopeful that the cessation of these old fears and taboos would lessen the likelihood of miscarriage, for they held that "women of delicate form, and too great sensibility, are the most likely to miscarry."[45] It is possible that the incidence of miscarriage was lowered, or at least that the confidence of physicians in their ability to prevent them grew; for by the middle of the eighteenth century they were prepared to relinquish a piece of physiology that had protected their reputations in the past: They denied the existence of moles or false conceptions. Mauriceau had defined a mole as "nothing more but a fleshy substance, without bones, joints, or distinction of members, without figure or form, regulated and determined: engendered against nature in the womb, after copulation, out of the corrupted seed of both man and woman." He explained that women were likely to miscarry of a mole from the "latter end of the first to the end of the second month" after it had been formed. By 1754 Pugh said that he had never seen a mole and said that children were simply aborted. William Smellie de-

---

[43]D. F. Bond, ed., The Spectator (Oxford: Clarendon Press, 1965), 5 vol., III, 195-197; Harris, Diseases of Children, 12-13.
[44]Hugh Smith, Letters to Married Women (London, 1774), 3-40; cf. Daniel Turner, The Force of the Mother's Imagination (London, 1729), and J. A. Blondel, The Force of the Mother's Imagination over the Foetus (London, 1729).
[45]Smith, Letters, 50-51.

nied their existence.[46] By 1781 it could be said that physicians recognized that a mole was simply a child who had died in the early months of pregnancy with its afterbirth.[47] Nature was declared not to play such cruel hoaxes on a woman's hopes for children, and physicians were obliged to take increased responsibility for miscarriage.

Childbirth

That these writers, or indeed, any men, should have a role at all in pregnancy and parturition was what many would have denied. When men did claim a place, they did so initially because of their expertise in "unnatural" or "preternatural" births. These came about when the child presented other than its head at delivery and had either to be turned in the womb or extracted with instruments. Men midwives said that their skill in these births was greater than that of traditional midwives. They later added that they alone had an experimental knowledge of nature. The opposition to accoucheurs arose from midwives who were jealous of their craft and from those who thought female modesty must suffer if men were admitted to the delivery room. Suspiciously enough to the eyes of some Englishmen, it was the ladies of the French court who had first called in the men midwives. In England, according to Pepys, it had begun when Sir Alexander Frazier helped the ladies of the court of Charles II "to slip their claves when there is occasion;" his reputation had been unsavory.[48]

The Chamberlain family were the most famous English accoucheurs with an aristocratic practice in the early eighteenth century. Their great reputation was based on their skillful use of the forceps, which they had invented and managed to keep a family secret until the 1730s. Hugh Chamberlain had translated Mauriceau's important book on midwifery, and in 1692 he delivered the Princess Anne of a son, who died immediately.[49] In 1713 when Lady Strafford expected to lie in of her second child, she told her husband that she was "very glad Dr. Chamberlain is to be in the house, for now the time draws near, I am a much greater coward than I thought I should have been; but I must beg you to write to him yourself, for he is so proud he won't go to anybody

---

[46]Mauriceau, *Diseases*, 45–110; Pugh, *Midwifery*, 115; William Smellie, *A Treatise on the Theory and Practice of Midwifery* (London, 1764), 3rd ed., I, 128.

[47]Hamilton, *Midwifery*, 85–86.

[48]Edwin M. Jameson, *Gynecology and Obstetrics* (New York: P. B. Hoeber, 1962), 42; H. B. Wheatley, ed., *The Diary of Samuel Pepys* (London: George Bell, 1924), 3 vol., II, 230–231.

[49]Jameson, *Gynecology*, 42.

Childbearing

except the husband writes to him." It is likely that Chamberlain was not being proud but merely careful, for a husband who asked him to be there could not afterward claim that a man had violated his wife's modesty, even though the man was a doctor and had only stood by in case the midwife could not cope. A week later Lady Strafford gingerly explained to her parsimonious husband that "Dr. Chamberlain says to be always ready to come to me and not to go if he should be sent for out of town to anybody, he won't do it for less than 100 guineas. Now I am really so well satisfied in your good nature and love to me as to believe you won't deny me that request." The possibility of a son, and no doubt his good nature, opened Strafford's purse strings.[50] When they were not engaged to the exclusion of other cases, the Chamberlains did not come so high. In 1725 Lord Fitzwalter, on the birth of his first son, paid Dr. Chamberlain only 16 guineas, but Lady Fitzwalter had been well attended: There was almost as much for Sir Hans Sloane, as well as a guinea for a surgeon and 2 for the country midwife who had cared for her until they went up to town for her lying-in.[51] The Chamberlains were in great demand; and consequently when it was decided at the last moment that complications made a physician's presence necessary, they were often unavailable. Thus, "when the Duchess of Argyll was three days in labour, Dr. Chamberlain was sent for, but being preengaged to [Ladies] Abingdon and Hereford, he declined to wait upon her, whereupon the Duke of Argyll wrote to the Prince for Dr. Hamilton who was with the Princess, and he went and in a few hours she was brought to bed."[52] At the birth of the Princess Mary, Chamberlain, rather than Hamilton, was engaged to wait on the princess of Wales, but he actually did nothing, for the princess was delivered by Mrs. Crane, the midwife.[53]

Sir David Hamilton (who was one of the first physicians to specialize in women's diseases) had not delivered the princess either. When she had lain in in 1717, she had already had four children. Hamilton had cared for her during her pregnancy, and the ladies of the English court wanted him to deliver her, for he had a considerable practice among aristocratic women. When, for instance, Lady Bristol miscarried of triplets, she had been attended by a midwife, an apothecary, and Dr. Gould, who all together were paid six guineas; but when by the birth of her tenth child her health had become quite problematical, she was delivered by Hamilton for a fee of 50 guineas; and he delivered

[50]B.L., Add. MSS, 22, 226, ff. 285, 293.
[51]Essex R.O., D/D MA4.
[52]H.M.C., Portland MSS, V, 536–537.
[53]The British Journal, 23 March 1723.

her of most of her remaining children at the same fee.[54] But the princess of Wales was fresh out of Germany and not up to English ways; she modestly refused to allow Hamilton to do anything. Her husband was reluctant to have him there, and the German hag of a midwife grew angry and had to be pacified. The Prince threatened to fling out of the window anyone who tried to meddle further, and Caroline was delivered of a dead son. In her next two lyings-in she conformed to English practice to the extent of allowing a physician to attend, but an English midwife conducted the delivery.[55]

Even if a physician did not actually deliver a woman, he could find that it was rather difficult to help her before or after childbirth since her modesty could be equally compromised by a physical examination. Lady Huntingdon was somehow injured in the course of a delivery in 1713, but it was some time before a circumlocutious correspondence with her doctor made this clear to him, and then he had to assure her that he had "a near relation, a man-midwife of great experience, probity and virtue, by whom I shall at last, from a little conversation only, with your ladyship, by answering a few necessary questions, settle the matter to your future peace and security."[56] William Smellie in the 1740s still often had to depend on a midwife's examination, and it was the chapter on touching (or examination) in his *Treatise* which called down the wrath of Philip Thicknesse on "these touching gentry." Thicknesse in 1764 railed that Goody Nature "who practised the art of midwifery in every corner of the globe, for many thousand generations... was about fifty years ago, stifled in France between the featherbeds, by Messrs Doctor LaMotte and Mauriceau." He was not surprised that such a practice should have begun in France "because chastity in that country is rather an unfashionable part of high breeding and high life." But he could account for its acceptance in England "only because a few women of fashion had countenanced it and their

---

[54] P. Roberts, ed., *The Diary of Sir David Hamilton 1709–1714* (Oxford: Clarendon Press, 1975), xxv–xxx; *Bristol Diary*, 27–29 August 1701, 12 February 1712, 5 March 1713, 25 September 1716.

[55] R. L. Arkell, *Caroline of Ansbach* (London: Oxford Univ. Press, 1939), 93–96; *The British Journal*, 23 March 1723. Princess Caroline had other difficulties with English childrearing customs, for in 1736 Henry Bracken wrote that "the present Queen Caroline may be to every Lady a glorious example of nursing, or rather suckling her royal progeny: for Her Majesty's good sense would not suffer others to contribute anything for the nourishment of her children when she was herself too duly qualified; until such time as our English laws debarred Her Majesty from so doing, which (as I have been told from good hands) was no small concern to this crowned head" (*Midwife's Companion*, 203). The *British Journal* said in 1723 that a Mrs. Forrester, the wife of the earl of Drogheda's butler, was appointed wet nurse to Princess Mary, after she had been approved by the physicians.

[56] C. F. Mullett, ed., *The Letters of George Cheyne to the Countess of Huntingdon* (San Marino, Calif.: Huntington Library Publications, 1940), 32–34.

pusillanimous husbands have been afraid to forbid it."[57] But Thicknesse's prurient imagination was at work to no purpose. Aristocratic men and women had decided that the life of a wife and the successful birth of a child were more important than some ideal of female modesty. Two years after Thicknesse's book, William Hunter discreetly delivered the queen of Princess Charlotte Augusta.[58] Expert skill had triumphed, and men had found a new area of life that they felt was too important to be left to women.[59]

For women, childbirth was traditionally an intimidating affair. They prepared themselves for it in the knowledge that it was quite probable they might die. So probable was it that Lord Leicester decided not to sleep with his 18-year-old wife since a great fortune was entailed on her provided she did not die in childbed before she was 21. Lady Leicester resented such treatment and would never consent to cohabit thereafter.[60] To lie in with the greatest possible safety, aristocratic women usually went up to London, for even if they were not to be attended by a man, the London midwives and the nurse keepers who saw women through their recovery had the best reputations. And when they arrived in town, they summoned up the older women of their family.

But there could be some difficulty in deciding just when they should come. In October 1762 Louisa Bagot told her aunt Lady Guilford that she "had reason to imagine for this last month or three weeks that I was breeding and within these few days have had reason to be certain; having been once so much mistaken I was determined not to be too hasty in believing it again, but I think I may now with the greatest safety venture to affirm it by Lady Barbara's advice [her mother-in-law] to your Ladyship. She imagines I am about five months gone." Lady Guilford was still skeptical and explained to Lady Barbara that she "would be very glad if I could with any degree of convenience to myself be with her at the time she is to lie in, but as her reckoning must be so very uncertain, I much doubt if I shall be in town....I flatter myself Mrs. B will find some friend then if she should lay in before I

[57] Smellie, *Midwifery* (1774 London, ed.), II, 184–189, 214–215; [Philip Thicknesse], *Man-midwifery Analysed* (London, 1764), 3, 4, 13.

[58] Kobler, *Reluctant Surgeon*, 126.

[59] The degree of their skill should not be overdone. Burton (*Midwifery*, 254) warned parents that many men midwives were not capable of much more than hacking children out with primitive instruments. Burton himself was satirized and immortalized as Dr. Slop by Sterne. See A. H. Cash, "The Birth of Tristram Shandy: Sterne and Dr. Burton," in Brissenden, ed., *Studies in the Eighteenth Century* (Toronto: Univ. of Toronto Press, 1968), 133–154.

[60] H.M.C., *Egmont Diary*, II, 437.

come." And believing in the delicate balance of a pregnant woman's mind, she added: "I desire the favour of your not to name my not being well to Mrs. Bagot as I have not in my letters to her, as I thought it might give her some concern." Lady Guilford's stepdaughter, Lady Willoughby de Broke, was, 2 years later, almost as uncertain and explained in the middle of December that she had quickened about the twenty-third or twenty-fourth of September and that "if I go as long after quickening as I did with George I shall not lie in till quite the end of February, so I hope I shall not be the means of hurrying your Ladyship and my Father up to town before it is agreeable to you." While she waited, Lady Willoughby surveyed the town and reported that "Lady Warren has been sometime in town expecting soon to lie in, but they begin now to think it is a doubt whether she is with child." Her own reckoning proved a month off, and her man midwife wrote on January 24 to tell Lady Guilford that he "was sent for yesterday morning to Lady Willoughby who was alarmed early by the breaking of her waters without any preceding pain."[61] But Lady Guilford was in no great hurry to go up to town on either occasion. For it was a duty that even the most conscientious of women did not relish: "I am extremely pleased to find you did not attend the lit de misère," Mrs. Boscawen told Mrs. Delany when the latter's niece first had a lying-in, "for indeed, my dear madam, it is an office so painful that I dreaded it for you."[62]

The pains of childbirth were usually eased with caudle. It was a water gruel in which mace and cinnamon were boiled and which was then strained and fortified with a third or fourth part of white wine or ale. The same drink was used to stimulate labor pains. But such unnatural stimulation was disapproved of by the physicians by 1750 on the grounds that strong caudles could hardly turn around a child who was in a difficult position in the womb and that they ran the risk of flattening the child's head and killing the woman by separating the placenta and flooding her.[63]

Once a woman was delivered, she was traditionally treated as though she were recovering from a serious illness. She was fed a diet of broths and gruels. She was confined for a month to a room whose every crevice was kept shut, with the windows battened down with shutters, curtains, and blankets. The hinges of the doors were greased, and the very keyholes were blocked up. During this time she saw only the men of her family, but the ladies of her acquaintance called on her and together they drank in celebration the caudle she had taken to ease her pain. Visiting the queen to drink her caudle was a considerable social occasion. And as aristocratic women publicly advertised other stages in

---

[61]Kent R.O., U471.C.10, C.11.
[62]Delany, I, 1862, 360.
[63]Smellie, Midwifery (1764), 203–204, 390–392; Exton, Midwifery, 61–62; Astrue, Midwifery, ix.

Childbearing

their life by a visit to court (as when they entered society, were married, or sought to maintain their reputations), so the beginning of mothering was marked by a visit to the queen. Near the time of her child's baptism, a woman was churched,[64] and gave thanks for her deliverance from her pain, declaring that

> Lo, children and the fruit of the womb:
>   are an heritage and gift that cometh of the Lord.
> Like as arrows in the hand of the giant:
>   Even so are the young children.

By the 1770s much of all this had changed. The doctors outlawed caudle, and its social importance declined. A friend told Mrs. Delany that she had been to see a lying-in woman and that "by-and by she treated me with caudle, which I am old fashioned enough to *like mightily.*"[65] Women were encouraged to get out of bed sooner: William Hunter had the queen take some exercise the fifth day after her delivery.[66] But high-spirited young women may well have done the same thing in the days when recovery was made under the eyes of a nurse keeper, instead of a physician: "The first time I experienced the pain of childbearing," Mrs. Boscawen once recalled, "I concluded no woman had ever endured the like upon the like occasion, and that I could not possibly recover it, whereas I danced a minuet about my room in ten days, to insult my nurse keeper and set her a scolding for my diversion."[67] But the clearest indication of the change in ethos was the conditions under which a woman received her friends. In 1772 Lady Mary Coke went "to town to see the Duchess of Buccleugh, who is perfectly well, in her great room with all the windows open, and no one thing that conveys the idea of a lying-in Lady, but a great boy."[68] A decade later matters had gone even further, and Lady Grey told her husband, somewhat quizzically, that their daughter, Lady Grantham, who had given birth to her first son a few days before, "is to get tomorrow into the largest drawing room which is now ready for her to set in, she can then see more persons, and admit *gentlemen.*"[69] Childbearing was no longer an illness, but a natural function, and it was one in which men might take a legitimate interest.

[64]White, Management of Pregnant Women, 5–6; Guilliaume LaMotte, A General Treatise of Midwifery (London, 1746), 133; B.L. Add. MSS, 22, 226, ff. 105, 106.
[65]Delany, II, 1862, 12.
[66]Kobler, Reluctant Surgeon, 133.
[67]Delany, I, 1862, 356.
[68]Coke, IV, 85.
[69]B.L., Add. MSS, 35,376, f. 93. In late eighteenth-century Philadelphia the old ways were kept up: "near relations, intimate friends, old women, but never men or young girls" in the first week after parturition, "the rest of her family and acquaintances but no man" in the second: "ceremonious visits; and occasionally a man who has asked and obtained permission comes in with his wife" in the third; and everybody "without distinction" in the fourth: K. Roberts and A. M. Roberts, eds. and trans., Moreau de St. Mery's American Journey (Garden City, New York: Doubleday, 1947), 289.

Figure 5.1 *Portrait of Lady Mary Wortley Montagu and her son in Turkish dress by J. Vanmour. Lady Montagu was a feminist who married for love against her father's wishes and without a settlement. She gave her son cold baths for protection against rickets and, while they were in Turkey, had him inoculated against smallpox. Her husband disinherited the son in favor of their daughter and her second son. Copyright photograph from the National Portrait Gallery, London. Reproduced by permission.*

V

Mothers and Infants

The same forces that led to innovation in childbearing were responsible for more measurable changes in the care of infants, for after 1750 the death rate of aristocratic children under the age of 5 dropped by 30% in a period of 25 years. It was an unprecedented rate of change, and it was a change limited to the aristocracy and certain sections of the middle classes, like the Quakers; for the life expectancy of an aristocrat in 1752 was not achieved by the general population until 1846.[1] So radical a change requires a radical explanation. I will argue that it was neither the lessening of disease nor the improvement of nutrition that were responsible. It was rather that by 1750 aristocratic women, because of the force of domesticity, were spending more time with their infants and that the quality of that time had significantly changed. For

[1]*Hollingsworth*, 52–62, 68–70. Richard Vann has found a similar change in mortality among Quakers.

above all children require for their psychological well-being that they forge a strong bond of attachment to a single mothering figure, and it is very likely that a child who has forged such a bond will not only be happier but healthier as well, and more likely to live.[2] It is a theory borne out in the experience of other populations in the past. The decline in the Quaker death rate may be connected to the new interest in childhood that the English middle classes displayed in the money they spent on schools and entertainment. In industrial Lancashire the infant mortality rate fell when unemployed mothers remained at home, and in a Paris besieged by the Germans, maternal care seems to have had the effect of lessening infant mortality by 40%. In both these cases, the level of nutrition had declined and the incidence of disease probably increased.[3] Among eighteenth-century English aristocrats, there were certainly changes in the incidence of disease and improvements in nutrition, but it will become clear that these occurred either too late or in the wrong age groups to explain the fall in infant mortality in the years after 1750.

Infant Mortality

At the beginning of the eighteenth century the thing most typical of all children seemed to be that they were very likely to die. It was a source of perpetual woe. To protect themselves from excessive pain, parents appealed to the inscrutable will of God, and they encouraged others to moderate their affection for their children, some of whom must surely die. "On Tuesday morning about one a clock my sweet pretty son James was found dead in the bed, being overlaid by his fatal nurse," wrote Lord Bristol; "the Lord gave, and the Lord hath taken away, yet blessed be the goodness of my most merciful God, who hath left me so many alive."[4]

But Christian resignation was rare: There were, more often, bad dreams and great pain. On March 31, 1702, James Brydges had a dream. His wife was 36, and 4 of their children had died. His surviving son

---

[2]My account of attachment theory I take from John Bowlby, *Attachment and Loss* (London, Hogarth Press, 1969–1973), 2 vol. I have also been stimulated by Marion J. Levy et al., *Aspects of the Analysis of Family Structure* (Princeton: Princeton Univ. Press, 1965), and Lionel Tiger and Robin Fox, *The Imperial Animal* (New York: Holt, Rinehart and Winston, 1971), 56–68.

[3]J. H. Plumb, "The New World of Children in Eighteenth-Century England," *Past & Present*, No. 67, 1975, 64–95; Margaret Hewitt, *Wives and Mothers in Victorian Industry* (London: Rockliff, 1958), 117–118; John Spargo, *The Bitter Cry of the Children* (New York: Johnson, 1966), 43.

[4]*Bristol Diary*, 6 August 1707; cf. Henry, Lord Warrington, *Works* ed. by J. Delaheuze (London, 1694), 32–33.

Lancelot was 16 months old, and about ten o'clock on the night of the thirty-first the child was "flung ... into a high fever." His father that night dreamt as follows:

> I thought my wife and I were just come out of a wood, and a little before us was a little sort of flower garden, on each side whereof was a walk or kind of road for I thought I saw the ruts of coaches, but yet not so common but that it was green, the grass growing on it. I thought we chose that on the right, and went to the end of it, where there was a bench, on which we sat down. We had no sooner sat down, but I thought just over against us which was the road, an hackney coach stopped, and I saw light out of it Mr. Ekins dressed in white, (a gentleman who served for Highham Ferrers and died about a fortnight ago) leaving a child's coffin in it. He went and sat down on another bench not far from us, at which I was mightily surprised knowing him to have died so long before, and said [so] to my wife; but I thought she looked very earnestly on me with an unusual look and smiled; but I was much more frightened when I saw him presently after rise up and come towards us, upon which I thought we both began to pray very heartily, and when he was come to us he said something, but what I don't remember, and reaching out his hand towards me. I caught hold of my wife but was infinitely frightened when I felt her as cold as ice, and thereupon cried out, "Lord, my wife is dead, 'tis her ghost." Upon which I thought both she and Mr. Ekins smiled, and the last said, "Why, did you not know that before?" Upon this, I rose up, my heart ready to burst with grief. What became of Mr. Ekins I know not, but my wife came with me I thought to the end of the green lane, and there I thought we parted in the bitterest sorrowful manner imaginable. I went on towards the wood, at the entrance of which I found myself in the hall of an old house ... and ... as soon as I came in, I saw two young women, what became of one I know not, but the other I ran after amongst the chairs a pretty while and at last catched her, and kissed her heartily.[5]

Brydge's son died 4 days after this dream. Fifty years after Brydge's tragedy, four children of Lady Bessborough's died of a sore throat and fever. According to Walpole, her husband eventually

> fell ill of it, very ill, and the eldest daughter slightly. My Lady caught it, attending her husband, and concealed it as long as she could. When at last the physician insisted on her keeping her bed, she said as she went into her room, "Then, Lord have mercy upon me, I shall never come out of it again," and died in three days. Lord Bessborough grew outrageously impatient at not seeing her, and would have forced into her room when she had been dead about four days—they were obliged to tell him the truth—never was there an answer that expressed so much horror! He said, "And how many children have I left?"—not knowing how far his calamity might have reached.[6]

In such circumstances did physicians try to preserve life, and it was therefore revolutionary when one of them like William Cadogan

---

[5]C. H. C. Baker and M. I. Baker, *The Life ... of James Brydges, First Duke of Chandos* (Oxford: Clarendon Press, 1949), 28–29.
[6]*Walpole*, IX, 272.

came to assert that it was ridiculous to hold that infants died so frequently because it was their nature, that "infants are more subject to disease and death than grown persons." On the contrary, he said, "they bear pain and disease much better, fevers especially (as is plain in the case of the smallpox, generally most favourable to infants) and for this same reason that a twig is less hurt by a storm than an oak." Consequently when Walter Harris set out to write on the diseases of infants in 1689, the great Sydenham told him that "your little book may be of more service to the public, than all my own writings." Harris himself declared that a "perfect cure of the diseases of children" was of consequence not only "to the noble, the powerful, and the wealthy, who are desirous of having heirs, and preserving them, but to all parents of any rank." But the noble and the powerful were the most likely to experiment. Even among them, however, progress was slow, partly because the medicine of men like Harris was of no great help, and partly because, as William Cadogan put it, "the business has been too long fatally left to the management of women, who cannot be supposed to have a proper knowledge to fit them for such a task, notwithstanding they look upon it as their own province, what I mean is a philosophic knowledge of nature." Women, he said, presumed upon the "examples and transmitted customs of their great grandmothers, who were taught by the physicians of their unenlightened days."[7]

But, in the end, it was these much contemned women who came to listen to the advice of the learned. Freed from some of the restraints of patriarchy and emboldened by the ideology of domesticity, they ignored their mothers and challenged their husbands. They subscribed to the physicians' books, and the diseases of their children very often provided the practical experience on which those books were founded. But if changes in male sexual roles allowed physicians to take an interest in childrearing, the changes in female roles were of greater significance on two grounds. For, first of all, the new science of pediatrics often had no great effect, and, second, it seems likely that the mothering role of aristocratic women was the real cause of the change. What needs to be explained are the means by which biological mothers became nurturing mothers. For the fact that aristocratic mothers were once discouraged from undertaking the intimate care of their children is the best of evidence that biology was not destiny. When these women changed, it was because their culture had changed. It is likely that these

---

[7]Walter Harris, *A Treatise on the Acute Diseases of Children*, trans. by John Martyn (London, 1742), 3; William Cadogan, *An Essay upon Nursing* (London, 1750), 6–7, 3n; cf. George Armstrong, *An Essay on the Disease Most Fatal to Infants* (London, 1799 ed.), 154–155.

cultural changes depended, in turn, on changes in family structure which allowed women to accept the eighteenth-century appeal to empiricism, nature, and sentiment in the care of their children. For the fall in the aristocratic death rate was one of the finest fruits of the Enlightenment.

Children and Disease: Cold Bathing and Inoculation

An eighteenth-century physician would probably have seen two diseases—rickets and smallpox—as the two greatest causes of infant mortality. Rickets had been diagnosed by English physicians during the Civil War. In the two generations following the Restoration they set about its cure. They were driven by the insistent evidence of the bills of mortality, which showed it to be ever so great a danger to children between the ages of 9 and 18 months.[8] A mid-eighteenth-century compendium described its symptoms as follows:

> The child at the beginning is seized with an aversion to motion, or exercise of any kind; the joints grow feeble and weak, and the flesh soft and flaccid; the head is over large, and the child's capacity exceeds its years. The belly is hard and very prominent; the bones of the arms and the legs grow crooked, and are knotty at the joints; a cough comes on and difficulty of breathing; the pulse is low and languid, and an hectic fever carries off the child.[9]

To deal with a condition to which the natural softness of infants made them seem especially prone, it was necessary to come up with a regimen for hardening the body; and exercise and cold bathing were hit upon as the answer.

The rage for cold bathing seems to have got under way in the 1690s; physicians looked to the practice of the ancient Stoics and the modern Irish; and Locke in his *Education* declared that "every one is now full of the miracles done by cold baths on decayed and weak constitutions for the recovery of health and strength, and therefore they cannot be impracticable or intolerable for the improving and hardening the bodies of those who are in better circumstances." The historians of cold bathing claimed that rickets had appeared when the practice of immersion at baptism was discontinued, and that if children were

---

[8] J. C. Drummond and Anne Wilbraham, *The Englishman's Food* (London: Jonathan Cape, 1939), 182–192.

[9] John Theobald, *The Young Wife's Guide* (London, 1764), 44–46.

bathed every day in cold water for the first 9 months of their first year, they would avoid both rickets and convulsions.[10]

Locke's reference to those who were "in better circumstances" was very much to the point, for it was a consistent medical opinion that rickets was to be found more often among the rich than among the poor since the latter were sooner exposed to the harshness of the world and thereby strengthened.[11] But it seemed a hard doctrine to many an aristocratic mother. Lady Mary Wortley Montagu in 1714 had a son 14 months old, over whom she was "in abundance of pain" for the child was very weak and apparently had rickets. She told her husband that the boy was "almost never out of my sight" and that a "Mrs. Behn says that the cold bath is the best medicine for weak children, but I am very fearful and unwilling to try any hazardous remedy." She thought her husband's interest in the child insufficient—"you mention your little boy with so slight a regard, I have no mind to inform you how he does"—but she screwed up her courage and consulted a doctor who recommended bathing the child nine times in a cold spring. She took him the first time herself "with a beating heart" and afterward thanked God that "he appears to gather strength since." The treatment seemed to continue along well, but a month later she still asked her husband to consult Dr. Garth on the matter. She added that she hoped "you love the child as well as I do, but if you love me at all, you'll desire the preservation of his health, for I should certainly break my heart for him."[12]

At the end of our period the remedy no longer seemed quite so hazardous, but it was still modified by tender mothers. Mrs. Delany told her niece that with regard to a daughter who was 5 months old, she approved "extremely of your wrapping her up *warm*. It will be time enough to harden her." Lady Grantham had her children stop cold bathing entirely during the winter months.[13] But, unfortunately, none of this was much to the point. For rickets is caused by a deficiency in calcium, which could not be remedied by plunging a child into cold water. But the prevalence of the disease helps to make more comprehensible the feeling that children were naturally weak. And it also helps to explain the prevalence of swaddling, for this was thought to prevent a child's weak bones from being bent. It is impossible to say,

---

[10]Reginald Lennard, ed., *Englishmen at Rest and Play* (Oxford: Clarendon Press, 1931), 75–76; Locke, 120.
[11]Drummond and Wilbraham, *Englishman's Food*, 189, 322.
[12]*Lady Mary*, I, 209–212, cf. 216.
[13]*Delany*, I, 1862, 407; Joyce Godber, *The Marchioness Grey of Wrest Park* (Bedfordshire Historical Records Society, 1968), 114.

however, whether the abandonment of swaddling between 1720 and 1750 represents any real success in dealing with rickets.

Rickets, however, inspired in aristocratic parents nothing like the horror that smallpox did. In the late seventeenth century as the plague died out, smallpox epidemics grew in intensity; and in the early eighteenth century the intervals between epidemics notably decreased; for while there were no major outbursts of the disease between 1681 and 1710, there were peaks in 1714, in 1716, and in 1719. It was seen as a child's disease, but yet one that could strike an adult very hard; when it did not kill, it often disfigured badly; and for aristocrats—trained, both male and female, to dominate with their personal presence—this was a disaster. The attacks of the disease were made without regard for rank, and it was even thought that the rich, with constitutions weakened by luxury, were especially subject to it.[14]

By the second decade of the eighteenth century, however, there was a group of London physicians and some aristocrats as well who were aware that there were effective means of protection against smallpox in other parts of the world. When in the spring of 1721 there was a new epidemic, Dr. Walter Harris, who had previously written on the diseases of aristocratic children, published a report on Chinese inoculation.[15] Almost immediately it became a guarantee of aristocratic patronage to claim knowledge of a new foreign method. There was a Captain Dover, who had come "home with *Agripulca* ship in the Queen's time." He now set up as a doctor to treat smallpox with a regimen of quicksilver and cold baths. Lady Dupplin told her aunt that a number of mothers and grandmothers turned from the fashionable doctors like Chamberlain, Mead, and Freind and put their daughters under Dover's care. "None of these ladies," she wrote, "were given over by the physicians, which amazed all reasonable people that they should be put into the hands of such a quack." It was clearly a panic, but coolness soon prevailed, and the competent experiment was distinguished from the fraudulent.[16]

One aristocratic woman led the way. Lady Mary Wortley Montagu had survived an attack of the disease herself, but she had lost her beloved brother to it. She was, however, an intrepid woman, something of a feminist, and sufficiently bold to make a runaway marriage for love in a generation when most marriages were arranged. When she accom-

---

[14]Genevieve Miller, *The Adoption of Inoculation for Smallpox in England and France* (Philadelphia: Univ. of Pennsylvania Press, 1957), 26–34.
[15]*Ibid.*, 23–24, 49; Robert Halsband, "New Light on Mary Wortley Montagu's Contribution to Inoculation," *Journal of the History of Medicine*, **VIII**, 1953, 390–405.
[16]H. M. C., *Portland MSS*, V, 616–617.

panied her husband, the English ambassador to Turkey, she discovered the Turkish practice of inoculation and became confident of its efficacy. In March of 1718 she had her 5-year-old son inoculated, and the operation was a success. An account was published in 1722 of the operation, and it helped to start the practice in that year among other aristocrats. But while Lady Mary was much consulted by those who decided to inoculate their children, she was unable to persuade her own sister to inoculate her nephew. She did succeed in getting her dead brother's son inoculated.[17]

Lady Mary's example was not the only cause of this great innovation. Experiments in inoculation were first made in England on criminals and orphans, and these were observed with careful interest by Princess Caroline. In April 1722 Lord Sunderland took the plunge. He already had four grown sons by his second wife. His third wife had 2 1/2 years previously born him a son, and it was this child he ventured. Two weeks later two princesses were inoculated. Sunderland's son died 4 days after this and was buried with his father, who had died 2 days before. There was great anxiety for the princesses, and the death of Sunderland's son put an end to further experiment. By the middle of May confidence was restored. Lord Berkeley had his heir (who was 6) and his daughter inoculated on May 15; he had been a widower for nearly 5 years as his wife had died in 1717 of smallpox. On May 17 two of Lord Townshend's sons by his second marriage (there were already a grown heir and three sons by a first marriage) were inoculated, one of them coming to town from Eton. Through the next several years aristocratic children were inoculated in growing numbers: two daughters of Lord Strafford, the children of Lord Hervey, the duke of Kent's daughter, and the children of the widowed duchess of Portland. It can be seen, though, that there were limitations to the willingness to experiment; it was usually the younger sons, or the daughters, or the children of a second or third wife who were ventured rather than the heir.[18] For instance, when Lord Waldegrave (born 1715) died in 1763 of smallpox, Horace Walpole wrote of him that "his brother and sister were inoculated, but it was early in the practice of the great preservative, which was then devoutly opposed, he was the eldest son and weakly," and he was therefore not inoculated.[19]

In the 1730s and 1740s the practice of inoculation continued to spread. Lady Hertford in 1741 remarked that it "is at present more in

---

[17]*Lady Mary*, I, 181–184, 338–340, 392–393, II, 15, 25–27, 49.
[18]Miller, *Inoculation*, 96–110; *The London Journal*, 9 June 1722.
[19]*Walpole*, XXII, 126–127.

fashion than ever: half my acquaintance are shut up to nurse their children, grandchildren, nephews or nieces." She wished to see her own 15-year-old son inoculated, but "at his age, it must be either a voluntary act, or left undone." Lord Beauchamp was unwilling, and the result was fatal: He died 3 years later of smallpox while on his travels in Italy and left his family without an heir.[20] In 1750 there were still entire families that had not been inoculated, for in that year Lord Dalkeith died after a 3-day attack of smallpox, and previously three of his uncles, an aunt, and his only brother, whose "limbs fell off, as they lifted the body into the coffin," as well as his eldest son, aged 4, had all died of the same disease.[21] When inoculation was used in this decade, the preparations were still elaborate. Mrs. Boscawen's 4-year-old son had his hair cut off for the event but was spared being purged and bled. The child was inoculated in both arms while his mother held him, and he took 2 months to recover.[22] Still another decade later, in 1761, there were those who found that inoculation was not necessarily effective: "Lord Carmarthen had been twice inoculated," Lady Kildare told her husband. "The last time he had the regular smallpox fever, his arm ran, and a few pimples appeared, but did not stay out the right time. However, Sir Edward Wilmot and all the physical people agreed he would never have it. Upon this assurance [his parents] ventured to put him to Westminster School, where he caught the very worse sort, naturally, and died the day before yesterday."[23]

The 1760s, however, saw a great flourishing of the art of inoculation under the direction of members of the Sutton family. Older women especially found the new process shocking. In 1768 Lady Holland's first grandchild was successfully inoculated when she was 6 months old. Lady Holland did not approve. "What tempted them," she asked, "to inoculate the child so young? Was it Mr. Sutton's fashionable inoculation, which will spread the distemper all over England, his patients all going into the air, be the weather what it will, with the smallpox out upon them?" But she added, "he has had most amazing success, so *il n'y a pas le mot a dire*, but it seems odd."[24] If one was not a patient of the Suttons, inoculation continued to be done between the ages of 4 and 5. In 1762 Lord Hardwicke asked that his grandson and heir be told when he was 5 years and 4 months old that his inoculation

---

[20]Miller, *Inoculation*, 123–152; Lady Hertford and Lady Pomfret, *Correspondence* (London, 1805), 3 vol., **III**, 190; *Hertford*, 343.
[21]*Walpole*, **XX**, 137.
[22]Cecil Aspinall-Oglander, *Admiral's Wife* (London: Longmans, 1940), 161, 167, 170, 179.
[23]*Leinster*, **I**, 103–104; cf. H.M.C., *Dartmouth MSS*, **III**, 164.
[24]*Leinster*, **I**, 535 (cf. *Delany*, **II**, 1862, 157–158).

"will make him a big man and enable him in a little while to ride a pony"; and in 1765 when Lady Twysden took a house in Jermyn Street to have her son and daughter inoculated, she noted in her diary that "William was 4 years, 10 months and 21 days old when he was inoculated."[25]

It is therefore unlikely that Dr. Razzell was right in attributing the fall in the aristocratic death rate to the effects of inoculation, for that fall occurred principally among children under the age of 5, and they were not usually inoculated.[26] These children may possibly have benefited from living in less infected atmospheres, since their older siblings and their servants were more likely to be inoculated. The servants of a great household were often a source of infection. Twenty-two of the duchess of Northumberland's servants were once taken ill together, and the duke and duchess of Montagu fled their house the day after a servant's death. Mothers made an effort to employ servants who were immune, but a man would often say anything for a place. Mrs Boscawen was much chagrined when a footman died of smallpox after having said that his parents had assured him he had had it. She was more careful with the nurse maids: She had them inoculated under her eye.[27] But the infants were uninoculated, and when they began to survive in unprecedented numbers, it must have been for some reason other than being better protected from disease.

The adoption of inoculation by aristocratic parents does show a new sensitivity to their children. In France, where the ideology of domesticity did not begin to make much of an appearance until after 1750, inoculation failed to be taken up in the early decades of the century, although all of the needed information was available. And when inoculation did eventually begin to make its way in France, it seems to have come hand in hand with domesticity.[28] In England, women like Lady Mary Wortley Montagu, who led the way, were heavily influenced by domesticity. Lady Mary was one of the few women to make a romantic marriage before 1720, and she did her best to develop her husband's interest in his children. In the generation after 1720 most parents came to feel that their principal duty toward their children lay

---

[25]*Hardwicke*, II, 598; Kent R.O., U 49, F 4/1: 18 March 1765.

[26]P. E. Razzell, "Population Change in Eighteenth-Century England: A Reappraisal," *EcHR*, XVIII, 1965.

[27]*Coke*, II, 42, 130; Aspinall-Oglander, *Wife*, 105, 170.

[28]This is what the evidence cited in Miller (*Inoculation*, 180, 205, 217–219) suggests, but she tends to attribute success in England entirely to the royal family and the Royal Society (193). Her tendency to ignore the parents of the children who were inoculated seems to be a consequence of her desire to limit the role of Lady Mary Wortley Montagu.

in protecting them from ill health and from the loss of sexual innocence. To this end (as the next chapter shows) they tried to reorganize the great public schools, where infection of both kinds was even more likely than in a great household. But it is far more probable that they managed to delay sexual knowledge than that their precautions were of much use to the physical health of their children. It was more likely, and more simply, the new intensity of parental concern that did the greatest good.

Mother's Milk, Wet Nurses, and Artificial Foods

If the introduction of cold bathing after 1690 and of inoculation after 1720 cannot be used to account for the dramatic fall in mortality that began in 1750, there is an alternative to be considered—that these two generations did see effective changes in nutrition. But when one deals with the feeding of infants there is the difficulty that two things are being done at once: The body is receiving the nourishment it needs for growth and for warding off disease, and the child is also establishing its most important human attachments. When a child is deprived of either of these benefits from its feeding, it is likely that its chance of physical survival is severely limited and that as it grows to be an adult, its physical or mental health will be impaired.[29] For physical nourishment before 1750 the only effective food that convention allowed aristocratic children to receive was human milk, but another convention of extremely long standing forbade aristocratic women to nurse their children and instead required them to bring a wet nurse into their houses. Aristocratic children were therefore likely to be mothered by at least two women, and consequently their attachment to either figure was not likely to be as strong as it might have been had there been only one.[30]

Dissatisfaction with this system in the late 1680s resulted in the introduction of what was called bringing a child up by hand.[31] It eliminated the wet nurse and it required, as Lady Sarah Pennington said, a "mother's close inspection" since it was "almost impossible to make the lower class of people who are hired to take the care of children,

---

[29] See, generally, John Bowlby, *Attachment and Loss*, Levy, *Family Structure*, and Tiger and Fox, *Imperial Animal*.

[30] Bowlby, *Attachment*, I, 357.

[31] J. E. Illick in Lloyd deMause, ed., *The History of Childhood* (New York: The Psychohistory Press, 1974), 336 n. 30.

believe the utility of this uncommon method."[32] It probably increased the attachment of aristocratic children to a single mother figure and to their actual mothers since it seems to make no psychological difference to a child whether he is fed by breast or by hand. But before 1750 it did make a nutritional difference because of the refual to use cow's milk and the inadequacy of other substitutes. It was estimated by a knowledgeable physician that hardly one child in three survived dry nursing.[33] The only viable alternative to the wet nurse before 1750 was the mother herself. But it would seem that though aristocratic women did eventually start to nurse their children, they did not do so until the late 1760s, or well after the fall in mortality had begun. Changes in infant feeding, whether from its nutritional or psychological consequences, will therefore not account for the fall in mortality.

When aristocratic women employed wet nurses, they were doing what mothers do in most developed societies—appointing a deputy. It was a custom which by 1700 was at least of 700 years standing among aristocratic women in England.[34] It had apparently been introduced at the same moment that the aristocracy adopted a patrilineal ideology—a further confirmation that in patrilineal societies men are inclined to see women as wives rather than as mothers. But it was also a custom which had been preached against at least since the Reformation, though to little effect; for save for a few aristocratic Puritans in the early seventeenth century, it had all fallen on deaf ears.[35] The preaching continued in the eighteenth century, and then, with the widespread appearance of domesticity and the lessening of patrilineal ties, it bore fruit more abundantly. But before this is shown, the practice of the old system must be explained.

A wet nurse was a woman of lower social rank who, since she had recently had a child and was supplied with milk, was paid to give up

---

[32]Lady Sarah Pennington, *Letters on Different Subjects* (London, 1767), 4 vol., III, 124–126.

[33]Bowlby, *Attachment*, I, 346; Cadogan, *Nursing*, 28. In wet-nursing, servant maids rather than wet nurses were a mother's helpers: "If you happen to be in a family where the mistress either suckles or brings up an infant by hand at home, part of the duty of a nurse will fall to your share, and to use the little innocent with any harshness, or omit giving it food, or any other necessary attendance, is a barbarity which nothing can excuse (Eliza Haywood, *A Present for a Servant Maid* (Dublin, 1744), 16)."

[34]Bowlby, *Attachment*, I, 241; J. C. Russell, "Aspects Demographiques des Débuts de la Féodalité," *Annales: E.S.C.*, XX, 1965, 118–127.

[35]C. H. George and K. George, *The Protestant Mind of the English Reformation, 1500–1640* (Princeton: Princeton Univ. Press, 1940), 294–295, n 103; R. B. Schlatter, *The Social Ideas of Religious Leaders 1660–1688* (London: Oxford Univ. Press, 1940), 32, n. 1; Michael Walzer, *The Revolution of the Saints* (Cambridge, Mass.: Harvard Univ. Press, 1965), 192; Lawrence Stone, *The Crisis of the Aristocracy, 1558–1641* (Oxford: Clarendon Press, 1965), 592–593.

the care of her own child and to nurse instead the child of her social superior. There are four things that we should know about the wet nurse: her qualifications; how she was recruited; why she was employed; and why she was opposed.

It was thought that a woman's milk was converted blood, and therefore the physical characteristics that were sought in a nurse and the regimen that was prescribed for her once she had been hired were all intended to ensure that she had a plentiful and healthy supply of blood. A nurse, it was thought, ought not to have an itch or an ulcer, for that was proof that her blood was corrupt. Her complexion should be fresh and clear, but it was better not to take anyone with red hair and freckles and to settle, instead, for a wholesome brown color, for this indicated that her natural heat was in its full force and vigor. Her teeth should not be rotten, her breath should be fresh, and she should not squint. It was best for her to have a large square breast, but not a fat one, for fat carried away the best part of the blood. She should be between 25 and 35, for in that decade the human body enjoyed it best temperature. She should have been delivered 3 or 4 months before she was engaged, and her pregnancy should not have ended in a miscarriage. If her child had been a son, that was so much the better, for the physical composition of a boy demanded less of his mother's blood than did a girl's. A woman who had borne two or three children would have a breast which was larger and contained more milk than a woman who had had just one. The milk, if it was good, would be white, have a good smell, and be of a moderate consistency.

Once she was hired, a nurse's diet had to be attended to. A diet of white bread, veal, mutton, and poultry either boiled or roasted, and ripe fruit such as figs, raisins, apples, and pears would keep her body open and her bile equally distributed. Pickles and spices and salted or seasoned meats, on the other hand, would cause her milk to become heated and acrimonious. Her milk would become too thin if she ate summer fruit, drank water, or exercised after dinner; it would be too thick if she ate beef, pork, peas, cheese, or hard-boiled eggs. The milk could be dried up altogether if she did not eat, took violent exercise, suffered from insomnia, or fretted. Its amount could be increased by taking broth and by exercising her arms before eating, for that would bring more blood into her breasts. As for strong drink, she could take a little wine to ease her digestion, but certainly not cider or sherry. And finally she was not to sleep with her husband, for if she did, her milk might be soured, or her periods begin again, or—worst of all—she could conceive a new child whose growth would take away her best blood. To ensure against this last point she was expected to live in her master's house, and preferably she was not to see husband at all.[36]

The state of a nurse's mental and physical health was always a source of anxiety, in addition to the condition of her blood, for it was strongly felt that any illness she contracted would be passed on to the child. When in the spring of 1727 the nurse to Lord Cardigan's second son fell and broke her arm, the boy was not allowed "to suck for 5 or 6 days, for these things are always attended with a fever." And on another occasion Lady Mary Coke reported disapprovingly that "the nurse that suckled Lady Charles Spencer's youngest child is gone melancholy mad, and has prevented her going to Addenbury; but I heard of her at all public places, so I imagine she is not so much alarmed as many people would be under the terrible apprehension that the child may be affected."[37]

The recruitment of wet nurses was usually in the hands of a woman's mother or mother-in-law, or of her aunt or sister. They, in turn, made use of the connections of the London nurses and accoucheurs to find suitable women or they dug out a nurse that some relation had previously used. A woman from the country was preferred, but if at the last moment a woman's planning proved inadequate, a nurse could be gotten from a London lying-in hospital. But the first business was to secure a nurse keeper for the lying-in. Some advance planning was necessary as these women were often in great demand. Lady Lincoln, with a lying-in or two behind her, grew somewhat casual and left the arrangements till the last moment. Her mother, Lady Katherine Pelham, wrote to tell her of the difficulty in getting the right keeper, saying that "Lady Halifax would not part with Mrs. Collins till her month was up, 'twas most natural to think she would not." Another nurse, "having heard Nurse Collins was to be with you, has engaged herself for about the time you would have [need] of her." But there was yet a third "whom Mrs. Graham gives an extreme good character of; she will inquire if she is engaged, and let me know, and then I will send to know if you would have her if she is to be had." When this part of the business was arranged, Nurse Collins' connections were called into play; and Miss Pelham told her sister that their mother

> had been at Chelsea this morning with Nurse Collins to see the wet nurse and her children. Mama says she seems a very clean decent looking woman, she is about four or five and twenty years old, is no beauty, but has a wholesome brown complexion, and good teeth; her children look clean and healthy, Mama took her unex-

---

[36]*The Nurse's Guide* (London, 1729), 29–35; Theobald, *Guide*, 11–13.
[37]Joan Wake, *The Brudenells of Deene* (London: Cassell, 1953), 224–225; Coke, II, 401.

pectedly, for she did not know anything of her coming, therefore could not be prepared; she says she had the smallpox when she was a child, and the woman whose servant she was told Nurse Collins, she would not have taken her had she not been convinced she had had them ... , that her sisters were very well known about there, as very good sort of people, and employed by a great many persons in that neighbourhood. The woman was born either there, or at Kensington, Mama is not sure which place; I conclude you know she is a widow.

The woman was the ideal: she was of the correct complexion and the best age; she was effectively inoculated against passing on diseases; her breasts would have been in excellent condition from previous nursing; her children were living proof of the excellence of her milk; her moral character was vouched for; and she had no husband to get her pregnant again.[38]

A woman bearing her first child was likely to be more anxious about the whole business and would seek advice early. As Louisa Bagot was an orphan, she wrote her aunt that she was "about five months gone" and that "your goodness will make you glad to give me some advice concerning what I ought to do about a nurse, whether I ought not to write immediately to engage one, and who you would advise me to have." Lady Rockingham, who had had no children of her own, was apparently not very forthcoming. Louisa's mother-in-law took over and saw to the London nurse and the wet nurse as well, and when Louisa was in about her eighth month, she told her aunt that "the woman I have taken for my wet nurse has been brought to bed this month, and Lady Barbara writes me word, that she and her child, which is a very fine one, are both very well." The timing could be difficult, but in this case the wet nurse's milk would have been flowing long enough, and the child whose care she was to surrender testified to the value of her milk.[39]

An aristocratic woman did not nurse her child when it was thought that her health would not bear the strain or that her ill health would be passed on to the child; when the older women in her family persuaded her that it was not the thing to do or when she felt that it would destroy the shape of her breasts; or when her husband positively forbade her to do so. It was claimed that some women were too weak to bear the strain of nursing, for it would rob them of their own nourishment. Delicate women, William Buchan said, were "subject to low spirits, hysteric fits, or other nervous disorders"; such a frame of mind made a woman a bad nurse, and it was "rare to find a woman of fashion free from [these

---

[38] N.U.L., NeC 3090, 3051.
[39] Kent R.O., U471.C.10.

disorders]."[40] In this, as in so many other aspects of childrearing, "habit and prejudice" played their part, especially when new wives were "advised from [nursing], at first, by their older relations or friends, either on the mistaken idea of their health, or on the score of fashion.[41]

The fashion was to have fine breasts, and women went through elaborate procedures to drive back the milk by applying to their breasts lint or hareskins which had been treated with ointments. Breasts cared for in this way often became inflamed or developed tumors or cancers; but all this was endured, for the breasts (as is usual in such situations) had become less symbols of maternity than objects of adult sexual attraction; and the decolletage of eighteenth-century portraits unavoidably proclaims that women were wives and not mothers.[42] This decolletage, in women of virtue, was reserved, of course, for a husband, and the eighteenth-century sources are quite free in suggesting that husbands used their authority to forbid a woman's nursing for the sake of "the indulgence of our selfish inclinations." "A man cannot be conversant in life," wrote James Nelson, "and not see that many a sensible woman, many a tender mother, has her heart yearning to suckle her child, and is prevented by the misplaced authority of a husband."[43]

The critics of wet nursing were usually members of the professions, and the parents of the children for whom they sought to care would certainly have disapproved of their daughters' marrying them. It is not surprising, then, to find that there is at times a degree of social hostility in their comments. Michael Underwood described the employment of wet nurses as a sacrifice of the children of the poor in order that their mothers might nurse the children of the rich, and he approvingly noticed that under the patronage of the queen a plan to care for the children of wet nurses was "meeting with all the support that could be wished for from families of rank." Jonas Hanway saw the practice as a typical instance of the corruption of aristocratic family life, and Henry Brooke in his novel represented it as part of their unfeeling stupidity.

---

[40]Cadogan, Nursing, 17; William Buchan, Domestic Medicine (London, 1772), 2–3.
[41]William Moss, An Essay on the Management, Nursing and Diseases of Children (London, 1794), 462.
[42]Gilbert Burnet, History of His Own Time (Oxford, 1833), 6 vol., III, 320 n; Richard Steele, The Tatler (London, 1709–1711), No. 15; Trials for Adultery (London, 1779–1780), 7 vol., IV, 22 (Duchess of Grafton); John Pechey, A General Treatise of the Diseases of Maids, Bigbellied Women, Childbed Women, and Widows (London, 1696), 184; Hugh Smith, Letters to Married Women (London, 1774), 76; Margaret Mead and Niles Newton "Cultural Patterning of Perinatal Behaviour," in Richardson and Guttmacher, eds., Childbearing: Its Social and Psychological Aspects (Baltimore: Williams & Wilkins, 1967), 180n; cf. Jean Astruc, Elements of Midwifery (London, 1766), 62.
[43]Smith, Letters, 70, 77, 82; James Nelson, An Essay on the Government of Children (London, 1753–1763), 43; cf. John Tillotson, Works (London, 1728), 3 vol., I, 488–489.

James Nelson blamed the bad example that women of rank set to those beneath them by not nursing their own children. And it is significant that when Dr. Hill set out to impersonate a gentlewoman, he tried to persuade his reader to nurse by pointing out that it could hardly do a child much good to receive his first impressions from one who was so very much beneath his station in life. Defoe stated the inconsistency, with greatest point, of gentlewomen who allowed their "heir to drink the blood of a slave or drudge, the blood of a clown or a boor" but "scorned to marry 'em among citizens or tradesmen however personally accomplished, however furnished with wit, beauty, modesty, breeding or fortune."[44]

It was held to be best for the health of mother and child if she nursed herself. The nurse was likely to pass on her diseases to the child, including the venereal infections which gave a child scrofula; and a nurse who was sexually inconstant would probably soon conceive again, causing her young charge to be troubled with rickets, watery gripes, and diarrhea. The mother's milk, on the other hand, would be of the right age for a child, purging it at first and then becoming more nourishing at the correct moment. The mother, even if she was weak and sickly, would reestablish her own health by nursing, and she certainly would be more likely to avoid fevers and inflammations of the breast if she nursed for at least the first few weeks. As for the shape of her breasts, there was no cause for alarm: they were not spoiled by suckling but by fat.[45]

So much for the body; but the critics were equally concerned with the effect that wet nurses had on the relationship of mother and child, and of one sibling to another. Archbishop Tillotson preached that "this course doth most certainly tend very much to the estranging and weakening of natural affection on both sides; . . . both on the part of the mother and of the child. The pains of nursing as well as of bearing children doth insensibly create a strange tenderness of affection and care in the woman." Walter Harris, on whom the Archbishop relied for his technical knowledge, claimed that if children put to a wet nurse survived, their mothers were likely to "suffer a deserved punishment" by finding their children "more cool towards them, but warm and

---

[44]Michael Underwood, *A Treatise of the Disorders of Childhood* (London, 1797), 11–12; Jonas Hanway, *Virtue in Humble Life* (London, 1771), 2 vol., II, 55, 492–493; Henry Brooke, *The Fool of Quality* (London, 1765–1766), Chaps. 1–3; Nelson, *Government of Children*, 46–47; [John Hill], *On the Managerment and Education of Children . . . by the Honourable Juliana-Susannah Seymour* (London, 1754), 149–150; Daniel Defoe, *The Compleat English Gentleman*, c. 1728, ed. by K. D. Bülbring (London: David Nutt, 1890), 7. (*The Spectator*, No. 246, [12 December 1711], held that it was one of the most unfortunate instances in which those of lower rank imitated their betters).

[45]Smith, *Letters*, 78–80; Cadogan, *Nursing*, 17, 18, 27; Armstrong, *Diseases*, 127.

affectionate towards the Nurse who took them up, and performed the duties of a real mother." The child was also likely to take on a good deal of its nurse's "natural inclinations and irregular passions" and of her "manners and disposition." Jean Astruc and Henry Brooke, in their different ways, both claimed that brothers nursed by different women were likely to grow up to love neither each other nor their parents.[46]

The moral obligation of a mother to nurse her child had been stressed before, but the obligation had usually been put as the positive command of God, with proof texts out of Lamentations (4:3–4) or Job (39:13–18). In the eighteenth century the stress fell far more on the naturalness of nursing. Lord Shaftesbury wrote that in nature, unlike human society, there was "no failure in the care of offspring."[47] And at the end of our period it was said that a mother's nursing was the "manner nature has intended" for infants to be fed, that only a "strange perversion of human nature could first deprive children of their mother's milk."[48] It was within this frame of reference that Tillotson declared that he thought himself obliged to tell women that "this is a natural duty; and because it is so, of a more necessary and indispensible obligation than any positive precept of revealed religion; and that the general neglect of it is one of the great and crying sins of the age and nation."[49] This combination of Christian duty and natural obligation, after it was fortified with the ideologies of empiricism and domesticity, eventually caused aristocratic women to turn their backs on 700 years of tradition when they began to nurse their children in the 1760s. But in the two generations before that decade there was the alternative of dry nursing for those who found the wet nurses distasteful.

It was usually a man who decided that a child was to suck neither its mother nor a nurse, but was instead to be brought up by hand. In the first half of the century it was typically the father who decided to have his heir brought up by hand either because he disapproved of nurses but was not willing to allow his wife to nurse, or because he had been told that his wife was too weak to do so. In the second half of the century, dry nursing was more typically the suggestion of a physician who was pessimistic about the likelihood of persuading an aristocratic woman to nurse.[50] In the earlier period there were two great difficulties

---

[46]Tillotson, Works, I, 488–489; Harris, Diseases, 18–19; John Astruc, Treatise on All Diseases Incident to Children (London, 1746), 18–19; Brooke, Fool of Quality, Chaps. 1–3.

[47]Astruc, Diseases, 20; Lord Shaftesbury, Inquiry Concerning Virtue (London, 1699), 99.

[48]Pennington, Letters, III, 124; Smith, Letters, 63.

[49]Tillotson, Works, I, 488.

[50]Armstrong, Diseases, 123; Smith, Letters, 78; Underwood, Disorders of Childhood, III, 2; Moss, Management, Nursing and Diseases, 62.

Mothers and Infants   205

to overcome, namely, finding a sufficiently nutritious substitute for human milk, and then, discovering an efficient means of giving it to the child. Neither of these difficulties were solved until after the middle of the eighteenth century. Physicians first recommended dry nursing in the late seventeenth century. In 1688 at the birth of the Prince of Wales, on whom the fate of a kingdom hung, the queen's physicians decided that the infant prince should be brought up by hand. Lady Powis, who was his chief dry nurse, explained the details of the regimen to the duchess of Beaufort, 15 days after the prince's birth: "We dare not give it a drop of food, but by the doctors' orders, and what it has had hitherto, has been only plain water-gruel, without any bread or spice; and his drink, water boiled and poured upon a very small proportion of anniseeds." Despite this diet, Lady Powis said that he was a strong and healthy child, and that she could not "discern anything to ail him but wind." But the experiment was eventually thought a failure; he was given a wet nurse 2 months after his birth, and thrived.[51]

Other examples of bringing up a child by hand have less happy endings. Young Lady Brooke, after a 6-hour labor, was delivered of her first son in 1717, and Sir David Hamilton, visiting her directly after, pronounced her free of dangerous symptoms, though a little low in spirits. Her husband had previously announced his intention that the child was to be brought up by hand. Lord Hertford, his brother-in-law, tried to dissuade him, but to no avail. And Lady Brooke's sister wrote to their mother a little while after that "the little boy thrives purely and is not to suck, for my Lord Brooke will not so much as think of it, and indeed considering how well the child is without it, it is better (I hope) to let him go on as he has begun."[52] That doubtful hope proved fatal, and the child died an infant. The duke of Buckinshire was another experimental father:

> He would not let it suck from the apprehension he had that there was no sound woman to be met with, nor be fed with a spoon, because he designed the Duchess, when she was well enough, should give it suck herself. So he had the invention of a sucking bottle, which was so managed, in short, the child was starved. Then they were in hunt for a nurse. Mr. Walpole had a child at nurse, that nurse got herself recommended there, the Duke examined her breast himself and told her he liked her but would see the child that sucked her, which she brought without asking Walpole's leave. And the Duke made her nurse the child and he examined it all over stark naked and found it without any spot, so he said he would have her. She went

---

[51] *Orrery Papers*, I, 5–6; H. C. Foxcroft, ed., *A Supplement to Burnet's History of My Own Time* (Oxford: Clarendon Press, 1902), 275; cf. B. C. Brown, ed., *The Letters of Queen Anne* (London: Cassell, 1935), 39–40.
[52] Hertford, 29–30.

with joy to her master Walpole and told him all that had passed and beg[ged] pardon she had gone without his leave. He said he would not have her lose her place, but charged her to tell the Duke, that all the soundest nurses in England could never [make] a child of his sound, and if he had a mind to have a sound one, there was no way but to desire him to get it. The child was opened and Lady Dorchester [the Duchess's mother] said they could see nothing but that it was starved.[53]

It is a sad story (though it was told as a joke), but it is an excellent illustration of two points. It shows the inadequacy of the new system and the consequent need to fall back on a wet nurse; this was sometimes done soon enough to save a child's life, but more often not. It also shows the interest that a father could bring himself to take in the most minute details of childrearing when he felt that his heir was in danger and his house likely to be extinguished.

Fifty years later, in 1767, Lady Henrietta Grey, who had already borne a son and heir, tried to bring up her second child by hand, but the girl died less than 3 weeks after her birth. Lady Grey's brother, the duke of Portland, told his own wife that the actual cause of the child's death was not being acknowledged, and it is clear that for him dry nursing was still a disreputably dangerous thing for a parent to undertake.[54] It is likely, however, that Lady Grey had merely been unfortunate; for by 1767 it is probable that the greater part of medical opinion would have held that if a woman was not to nurse herself, the next best thing was dry nursing. Those who made this recommendation were aware of the great differential between the mortality rates of the children of the poor and those of men of fortune which had occurred after 1750. Medical opinion had changed because it felt that certain important changes had been made in traditional dry nursing. In the 1750s the exiguous diet of water pap on which the Prince of Wales had been fed was supplemented with cow's milk diluted to the consistency of human milk. By the 1760s diluted milk had driven out water pap, and in the following decade undiluted milk came to be used. Ass's milk was also recommended, for it seemed closer to human milk, but it was rare and expensive. By 1780 milk pap as well as water pap was discountenanced in favor of warm cow's milk, which was always to come from the same cow. These diets were not only more nourishing, they also could be more efficiently given to a child after the invention of Hugh Smith's milk pot. And fresh milk was becoming more easily available in Lon-

[53]B.L., Add. MSS, 31,143, f 590 (Printed in J. J. Cartwright, ed., *The Wentworth Papers* (London: Wyman, 1883), 153).
[54]N.U.L., PwF10, 547.

don, where most children were delivered.⁵⁵ But the combination of a nutritious diet and a mother's close attention, both of which dry nursing gave, came too late in the century to cause the decline in mortality; and the literary sources, in any event, never convey the impression that the practice was ever widespread.

Wet nurses were by the middle of the eighteenth century morally unsatisfactory to many aristocrats. But the alternative of dry nursing seemed irresponsibly dangerous. Those aristocratic values that stressed the banality of childrearing and resulted in a certain emotional distance between parent and child were too firmly entrenched to be shaken by those who advocated that gentlewomen should be their own nurses. It was also rather difficult to demonstrate that masses of children were dying because the manner in which they were fed was emotionally or physically unsatisfactory. But once before, in the panic of a smallpox epidemic when their children died like flies, it had been possible on the basis of carefully observed experiments on the poor to persuade aristocratic parents to take the extreme course of inducing a temporary illness in a child in order to make him permanently immune to smallpox. In the 1740s two physicians, William Cadogan and William Hunter, set in train another series of medical experiments, using the poor as guinea pigs. Cadogan, working with the children of the foundlings hospital, and Hunter, working at the lying-in hospital, both came to recommend on the basis of their experience in those places that a mother who nursed was taking the surest means of protecting her own health and of ensuring her child's life.⁵⁶

In 1753, 5 years after Cadogan had published his book, James Nelson wrote still another appeal to aristocratic women to nurse, but as he was not "insensible how little probability there is that my advice herein will be followed by persons in high life," he gave an account of the work of Cadogan and Hunter.⁵⁷ Nelson, however, was overly pessimistic. In the very year in which he published his book, the Princess of Wales had a conversation with Mrs. Pinckney from Carolina that shows the direction in which the minds of aristocratic women were tending. Mrs. Pinckney wrote that the princess had asked her a number of

---

⁵⁵Armstrong, Diseases, 154–155; Nelson, Government of Children, 64–65; Pennington, Letters, III, 124–126; Smith, Letters, 126–128, 140–141, 203–204; Moss, Management, Nursing and Diseases, 63–65, 89–93; Underwood, Disorders of Childhood, III, 2–3, 71–74; M. W. Beaver, "Population, Infant Mortality, and Milk," Population Studies, XXVII, 1973, 243–254. Beaver suggests that the availability of milk may have helped to lower infant mortality among the London poor.

⁵⁶Cadogan, Nursing, passim; Nelson, Government of Children, 47–53.

⁵⁷Nelson, Government of Children, 45.

domestic questions, among them "if I suckled my children. I told her I had attempted it but my constitution would not bear it. She said she did not know but 'twas as well let alone, as the anxiety a mother was often in on a child's account might do hurt." But Mrs. Pinckney, after mentioning that "we had Nurses in our houses," criticized the English for "putting their children out to nurse, we had no such practices in Carolina." The Princess was "vastly pleased" at this and said that she thought "it was a very good thing, the other was unnatural." So the matter stood in 1753.[58] In another decade such women were actively nursing, and by 1784 a knowledgeable physician declared that "ladies of rank are every year becoming converts to this maternal duty" and that there was therefore less occasion for bringing children up by hand.[59]

It is unfortunately not possible to say precisely how many women nursed. It is possible to discover when and under what circumstances they began by constructing two case studies from literary evidence. The women of the Lennox and the Spencer families wrote to each other extensively on these subjects over two or three generations. Their experience will show that networks of mothers and daughters and of sisters and sisters-in-law encouraged each other to innovate. The particular innovation of breast feeding will prove to have come too late to be responsible for the fall in mortality, but it will appear that by 1750 these women were full converts to domesticity. They were in love with their husbands; they were deeply interested in their children; and they spent great amounts of time in their company. I will be obliged to argue that after 1750 aristocratic children began to survive infancy in unprecedented numbers because the quality of their attachment to their mothers had markedly improved, and that the improvement occurred because most aristocratic women had become converts to domesticity. Children survived less because they were immune from disease or better nourished, and more because they were better loved.

Two Case Studies: The Lennoxes and the Spencers

The wife of Charles Lennox, the second duke of Richmond, was married to her husband in 1719 when she was 13 and he was 18. There is a story that the marriage was arranged to settle a gambling debt between their fathers. The young couple did not live together for 3

---

[58]H. H. Ravenel, *Eliza Pinckney* (New York: Scribner's, 1896), 151–152.
[59]Underwood, *Disorders of Childhood*, III, 2, 9.

years while Richmond made his tour of Europe. On his return he saw his wife in a box at the theater, and without knowing who she was, fell in love with her. Their arranged marriage was transformed into a love match. Nineteen years later they could still edify Horace Walpole who wrote to his friend in Italy that at a dance "the Duke sat by his wife all night kissing her hand: how this must sound in the ears of a Florentine cicisbe's, cock or hen!"[60] Their sexual life continued actively all their marriage, and they did not practice birth control. In the 28 years between 1722 when they began to live together and 1750 when the duke died, the duchess was pregnant 27 times. It is likely, however, that 15 of these 27 pregnancies ended in miscarriages, and of the 12 which she brought to delivery, only 4 daughters and 2 sons lived to maturity. Her first child, Caroline, was born in 1723. Eighteen months later there was a son who died at birth; 14 months after that, a daughter who died at 3; 6 months later there was a child who lived a few months. For over 4 years there were no further births; there were miscarriages, and then there was a son who died within a few months of his birth. A year later a daughter, Emily, was born. Three years later a son, Charles, who lived to succeed his father, was finally born after 15 years of marriage and 13 years of childbearing. Another son, George, came almost 3 years after. And then at intervals of 2, 4, 1, and 5 years, there were four more daughters; the first died at 2 of smallpox, and the last died when she was nearly 20; the other two, Louisa and Sarah, eventually married.[61]

The duchess of Richmond had borne her last child when she was 44. Her eldest two daughters were married by then and between them had given her five grandchildren by the time she bore her last child. Her husband died in August 1750, 5 months after the last child's birth, and the duchess herself died a year later of a broken heart. She left behind three young daughters aged 8, 6, and 1 1/2. These girls were sent to live with their sister Emily in Ireland until they reached their early teens, when they went to Caroline in London to make their entrance into the world. Caroline and Emily belonged to one generation of parents; George and Sarah to another (for the 7 years between them was negated by the different ages at which men and women married); Charles and Louisa never had children of their own.

The duchess and her children represented three generations of parents. Her annual pregnancies make it very likely that she used wet nurses for her children, but her close devotion to her husband also

---

[60]Earl of March, *A Duke and His Friends* (London: Hutchinson, 1911), 2 vol., **I**, 34–35, 64–66; *Walpole*, **XVII**, 184, **XX**, 125.

[61]Sir Egerton Brydges, ed., *Collins's Peerage* (London, 1812), 9 vol., **I**, 208–211.

makes it likely that she spent a good deal of time with her children in the new domestic fashion. When her two eldest daughters began to enter society, she brought them to share her interest in the foundling hospital in which some of the first observations of the effects of nursing were made.[62] These two daughters, Caroline and Emily, did not nurse themselves, but they felt guilty about it, and they were extremely close to their children in other ways. But their younger sister Sarah did nurse, and Emily's daughter and daughter-in-law nursed almost as a matter of course. Caroline had no daughters, and as an older woman, she was skeptical when her granddaughter was inoculated at the unprecedented age of 6 months. But since the operation succeeded, she kept her mouth shut, and with good reason, for as a young mother she had herself been notorious in some aristocratic circles for her innovations in childrearing.

Caroline had run away at 21 and been married to Henry Fox, who her father described as "infinitely beneath her" but yet a man who by "his merit and talent is bound to make a name for himself in this country.[63] She deliberately limited the number of her children, and three of her four sons survived infancy. She and her husband gained some notoriety for the laxity with which they raised their children. Indeed, her nephew Lord Ophaly observed to her from time to time that her house was "reckoned such a house of liberty for children," but she countered that she did "maunder, and they laugh at me and mind me notwithstanding." Her husband certainly enjoyed and encouraged the companionship of his sons, for she told her sister that her 10-year-old son Charles "never leaves his Papa when there are any of the lawyers or people that talk over this business with him, and is *au fait* of it all as much as anybody but the law people are." She was especially fond of her youngest son, whose conception had probably been an accident. His two older brothers had left the nursery by the time of his birth so that he was raised by himself. When he was 6, his mother declared that she and Fox intended "Harry to be a clergyman," and that as "his brothers approve it, so won't set him against it, and as he is taught to think so from his youth perhaps he will like it." Lady Caroline was anxious to keep him out of the army: She would have "none of my children of the murdering trade, I thank God." At 7 "dear little Harry" was a pleasant little child; and when Rousseau's *Emile* had just come out, his mother noted that "he really works very hard all day out of doors, which is very wholesome and quite according to Monsr. Rous-

---

[62]John Brownlow, *Memoranda or Chronicles of the Foundling Hospital* (London, 1847), 208–209.
[63]March, *A Duke*, II, 650.

seau's system; he eats quantities of fish, and is so happy and so pleased all day." But Lady Caroline never found Rousseau entirely practical, for, as she said, "there is certainly a small objection to putting his scheme of education into practice, viz, that it's impossible—there are also a number of contradictions in his book, but it is immensely pretty." She related that "at night we depart a little from Monsr. Rousseau's plan, for he reads fairy-tales and learns geography on the Beaumont wooden maps." Much against her inclinations, she eventually decided to send him to school. It was the only way to avoid servants, to keep him from growing pert, and to provide him with the knowledge that a man needed for business and pleasure, since neither the boy nor his mother cared for the idea of having a tutor at home. Her principal objection to a school, aside from the pain of parting, was that Harry would lose there "his health and perfect innocence." But the difficulties she was encountering with her two eldest sons, one of whom had recently married and the other of whom was gaining his reputation for extravagance, left her increasingly skeptical about all systems of childrearing, for "education," she said, "may spoil or mend manners a little, but as they are born, so I am convinced they remain, with regard to good nature or good hearts."[64]

Lady Caroline's sister Lady Emily had at least two suitors before she was quite 15. She rejected one, and forthrightly told her mother she wished to marry the other. Four months after her fifteenth birthday she married Lord Kildare, who later was created duke of Leinster, and by him she had 19 children, of whom 12 survived infancy. At Leinster's death she married the clergyman who tutored her children and thereby created something of a furor. By this second husband she also had children, not all of whom survived.[65]

In 1755 one of Lady Kildare's children died, a "poor dear sweet pretty little babe," and she found it a grievous experience. She sought comfort in thinking "how much happier the poor little thing is than it ever in all probability would have been in this world" and "how much less a misfortune it is to lose them at such an age than any other." After the child's death the group of attendants had to be paid off. She saw to it that the wet nurse and the person who had sat up with her to tend the sick child were given five and two guineas, respectively. The others— the doctor, the nurse keeper, the women who drew her milk, and the clergyman who churched her—were paid by Lady Caroline. But this business was no aid to understanding her feelings. She told her hus-

---

[64]Leinster, I, 217–218, 251, 285, 343, 354, 339, 387, 309, 514, 555.
[65]March, A Duke, II, 606–611; Leinster, I, 15.

band that she would not have thought it possible to grieve so for "an infant that I could know nothing of," and she explained to him that "it really convinces me there is a great deal more in what is called nature or instinct than I ever imagined before, for what else but such an impulse could make one feel so much for a poor little thing that does but just exist, as one may say."[66]

To have a child die was not the only pain of childbearing, however. "Sweet siss," Lady Caroline told her, "I do feel vastly sorry you should lead so uncomfortable a life as continually breeding and lying in makes you do"; but Caroline evidently did not suggest her own solution of birth control, for she added, "I don't wonder it wears your spirits, but some thing[s] there must be." And though Lady Kildare might complain, she felt compensated. She told her husband after one difficult delivery that "Nurse Martin and Doctor Carter both give me hopes that I may be right in two or three days again, as the three months from the time of being brought to bed will be out." "I wish it may be so," she added, "but I fear otherwise; however I have resolved not to grumble! After all, are not my pretty babes a blessing? When I look round at them all, does not my heart rejoice at the sight, and overflow with tenderness? Why, then, repine? They are good, they are healthy, they are pretty: God Almighty bless them; if they gave me pain, they now make up for it by giving me pleasure."[67]

This note of pleasure she struck again and again, and she embodied it in practice by spending a great deal of time in the company of her children and by her anxiety that they should be raised by the best and latest methods. She employed a large staff to assist her, and this, to some, seemed inconsistent. Her brother Richmond, when she would not leave her children to come to town, complained that "She don't suckle them, she don't wean them herself, and she can't cut the teeth for them—why won't she come?"[68] The nurses did, on occasion, get in the way of her feelings for her children. As a young mother of 19 she wrote of her first two sons:

> William is a sweet little child, too, in a different way. He is not so lively or active as George is by a good deal, but he is forward enough both as to his walking and talking, for he says several words and walks quite alone. As for his little person it is fat, round and white.... He is the best natured little creature that can be and excessively passionate already, but puts up his little mouth to kiss and be friends the next minute. He is vastly fond of his nurse and does not care twopence for me; so, as you

[66]Leinster, I, 5, 27, 17.
[67]Ibid., I, 289, 159.
[68]Ibid., III, 69–70.

may imagine, I cannot for my life be as fond of him (tho' in reality I love him as well) as of George, who is always coaxing and kissing me, and does not care for any body else.[69]

George, who was the eldest son and the first child, was 2 1/2 years old. William, the second child, was 17 months old. Clearly both children, despite the use of wet nurses, had become attached to their mother. The difference in their behavior can probably be explained in terms of the different stage of attachment behavior that each child had reached. The younger was still in the second phase, which usually begins at 6 months, when the child acquires some degree of mobility but must still depend ultimately on the mother to maintain proximity. For William, the nurse was usually closer, and so his affection for her was greater than for the mother he could not control. George had entered the third stage of attachment in which the child maintains proximity as much as the mother. He had more fully transferred his attachment to his mother, for Lady Kildare was usually not too far off. Twelve years later, when there were a great many more children to care for, she was still not too far away. She told her husband that the two nurses of that time were "the best play-fellows for children I ever saw; they invent some new diversion every night, they play and romp in Lady Kildare's dressing room, and I sit in the India paper drawing room, so that I have them or not just as I like. Henry naked is the dearest little being on earth."[70]

With her first son, William, Lady Kildare had set out on a course independent of the accepted wisdom about childrearing as represented by the older women of the aristocratic community; and she did so with a confidence derived from her knowledge that she was with her children more constantly than anyone else. When William was 6 months old, she told her mother: "If I allowed him to be set upon his feet, he would begin to walk, for sometimes when I set him upon his feet, he steps very prettily"; but she decided not to do so as she was convinced it was not good to put them on the ground too soon. Her mother-in-law, the dowager Lady Kildare, wrote her that she "hears word he is so forward, she wonders I won't try him on his feet." But the younger woman replied that she was determined not to do so until he was much stronger. In addition, she said to her own mother: "In things that can do no harm I always have and I always shall manage them quite my own way, [she was trumpeting a bit: she had only been married a year and a

---

[69]Brian Fitzgerald, *Emily Duchess of Leinster* (London: Staples Press, 1949), 29; cf. Bowlby, *Attachment*, I, 243-244.
[70]*Leinster*, I, 151.

half], for I think those who are with them and see them constantly, are much the best judges of their constitution."[71]

It was not, however, only her mother-in-law's traditional wisdom that caused her difficulty. Her husband, when George and William were 7 and 6 years old, told her that "the sooner you put our dear little boys to school the better." She did not have enough confidence to withstand his opinion. But she did not spare him her feelings: "My sweet boys leave me tomorrow. I feel as if I should bear this parting as well as I did the last summer; I have reconciled and accustomed myself so much to the thoughts of not living with them, that it don't appear new to me to part with them, still looking on the first time they left me as giving them up once for all, and every time I see them only as so much got."[72]

With the remainder of her children she arranged that she should not have to part with them, and she used the authority of Rousseau to lend her support. She and her sister both read *Emile* when it came out in 1762, and we have seen how Lady Caroline half heartedly applied the theory to her youngest son. But Lady Kildare was a much less conventional woman than her eldest sister and had the soul of a true enthusiast. She thought of asking Rousseau to become the tutor of her children, and and when that came to nothing, she set up for them an environment according to the master's prescriptions. The children rose at 5:00 in the morning and in the summer went to make hay; in the winter they weeded the gardens and burned the weeds afterward in great bonfires. They bathed at least once a day, and sometimes as often as three times, except when the snow in winter made it impossible. The older children did some lessons in the early morning, and at 9:00 they all had breakfast. The older ones worked again till 1:00 while the younger ones romped. There was more exercise from 1:00 until 3:00; then they dressed for dinner and sometimes visited their grandmother. After dinner there was play, and bathing, and more schoolwork until 5:00. They supped at 7:30 and went to bed an hour later. Mr. Ogilvie, who ran all this, she married as her second husband.[73]

Both Caroline and Emily were aware that they were radical in their methods of childrearing. What made them so? They were both quite religious. Emily went to church on a Saturday morning and was told by the verger that she could not go to her own seat as it "was not ready, for that no *quality* was ever expected at Church of a week day." Caroline,

---

[71]March, *A Duke*, II, 647.
[72]*Leinster*, I, 28, 60.
[73]Fitzgerald, *Emily*, 102, 128, 134–140.

after having "had sacrament, prayers, very good preaching all comfortably in our own chapel," said that she was the "happier and the better for it," for "however tender-hearted or good-natured one may be, piety makes one think more and exert oneself more to be useful to one's fellow creatures, at least I think so." They were both very tenderhearted: One eloped at 21, and the other entered into a mésalliance with a clergyman at 43. They both believed in the existence of a natural instinct that drove women to love their newborn children and that was the basis of vice and virtue. They read the latest books and recommended to each other's serious attention Voltaire and Rousseau, Richardson and Crebillon. They both took great pleasure in the company of their children, so much so that their younger sister Sarah once said to Emily that she would give a good deal to convey to their sister-in-law (Lord George's wife) "a small share of your pleasure in your children's company which you could spare and which she wants; she never loved their company as children, but she does not grow to like it as women; this astonished me as much as it vexes me—it is something very particular." Their children probably benefited in very material ways from this combination of domesticity, religious duty, and intellectual curiosity—from these great exemplars of England's Christian Enlightenment. And the greatest of these benefits must surely have been an extended life span. For whereas only 50% of the duchess of Richmond's children survived to maturity, over 63% of Lady Emily's did, and 3 out of Lady Caroline's 4. But neither Caroline nor Emily had broken away from wet nurses, and this was heavy on their consciences. For in 1760 Caroline denounced Lady George to Emily when that poor sister-in-law was

> brought to bed of a fine large girl, who I hope will do well, though it runs a great risk, poor thing! she having provided no wet nurse; one was to be got from the lying-in hospital yesterday. They must, you know, in that case take what they can get, and a nurse got in such a hurry and in London I'm afraid the chance is much against. I feel very angry at her. I own I was pretty near as young as her, and yet I think I was anxious to provide a good nurse. I think it is a duty and the only way one can justify to one's mind not nursing one's child oneself.[74]

Lady Sarah, the youngest of the surviving sisters, was the first to undertake nursing her own child. In December 1768 she gave birth to a daughter, and on Christmas Eve Lady Caroline reported that "Sal is charming well, her rash gone off, but she won't be completely happy till she has suckled the babe. I grieve to see her immoderate fondness for it. It's very well now, thank God, though it alarmed us for the first

[74]*Leinster*, I, 61, 357, II, 225, I, 301–302.

day." Four days later the child was not doing well; Dr. Hunter (who had conducted the experiments in breast feeding at the lying-in hospital) was consulted, and he said the child had "lost the instinct by being kept so long from the breast." Lady Caroline had at the very beginning of the experiment asked that a wet nurse should be engaged, just in case such an eventuality should arise, but her sister had overruled her. Lady Sarah had plenty of milk, but her nipple could not be drawn out, and there was yet no adequate nipple case to help the mother and child. She, by "drawing it various ways," finally got the nipple out, but the child would not then take it. Three weeks after the child's birth, Lady Sarah gave up and the child was given a "clean good nurse, sucks, and sleeps and thrives; God send it may go on so doing, for she doats upon it."[75]

This was the case of a passionate young woman who had decided to nurse her child and had sought the best expert advice. Her older sister, who had had her last child 14 years before, had encouraged her; but she knew the experiment to be a risky one and had asked for the insurance of a wet nurse; and being still so full of the old pessimism with regard to infant mortality, she was distressed that in the midst of a dangerous experiment her sister did so little to guard herself against the pain that must accompany the child's probable death. But Lady Sarah was all for recklessness in the affairs of the heart. She had seemed before her marriage to her husband "to court him more than he does her, in a free way," and he evidently never fully responded to her.[76] Eight weeks after the experiment of nursing failed, a greater scheme had come to grief: The child had not been her husband's, and she went off with her lover, to the desolation of her friends. The daring of her older sisters did not extend to flouting of the double standard. For while her siblings did not give her up, Lady Caroline remarked that she was glad their parents "could not look out of their graves to see that sight," that it would be better to be dead than so disgraced.[77]

It was only in the following decade that nursing began to assume the air of the commonplace. Emily's daughter, Lady Bellamont, nursed her own child. The older women continued their interest in the latest books on childrearing: They circulated William Buchan's *Domestic Medicine* among themselves and liked it, for they found it moderate and sensible. Emily's daughter-in-law, the young duchess of Leinster, became pregnant in 1777. The older women gathered around, and from

---

[75]*Ibid.*, I, 559–563 (cf. Underwood, *Disorders of Childhood*, III, 8).
[76]*Ibid.*, I, 119.
[77]Coke, III, 205.

the family home where she had retired to recoup her reputation, Sarah teased Emily: "Pray, are you going to teach the little Duchess to lie in? You certainly have a competent knowledge of that business." After his aunts had soothed the duke's worries about the delicacy of his wife's constitution, it was decided that she would nurse her own child. One woman in the family, however, was not to be told: the duke's grandmother, the dowager Lady Kildare, for her sympathies had not crossed the great divide and she was likely to "toss up her nose and say, 'Lord, ma'am, what a fancy! How should she know how to nurse a child?'"[78] For this divide set apart those who held that the best in childrearing practices was to be found in the slow accumulated knowledge of the older women, from those of another generation who used the confidence acquired from domesticity to ignore their older relations and reach out for the latest experimental knowledge—which, they would have said, confirmed a mother's natural instinct.

When we turn from the Lennoxes to the Spencers, we shall cover only two generations of women on either side of mid-century. The first Lady Spencer bore her husband an heir and four daughters: Georgiana (born 1757), who married the duke of Devonshire; John (born 1758), who succeeded his father; Harriet (born 1761), who married Lord Bessborough; Charlotte, who was born in August 1765 and died in September of the next year; and Louisa, who was born and died in the first few days of April 1769. Lady Spencer, whom Walpole called the goddess of wisdom, combined the old and the new in the rearing of her children. She carefully passed on a recipe for pap that she had from her mother-in-law, and it is worth quoting to show how that noxious concoction was sometimes made:

> Take a white half-penny role, such as are sold at country bakers, piqued at each end, and let all the crust be pared off very thin (that is the outward crust of all), and then put the rest of the roll into a pint of very fine spring-water, which must boil till it looks like a jelly, it must then be strained into a china or earthen bowl through a lawn sieve. This if rightly done, will be of the consistency of a jelly when it is cold; it is to be taken out in small quantities as is wanted, to be warmed and mixed with a little milk, and the milk should be mixed into every cup-full, when it is warmed, and not into the whole quantity.[79]

On such a diet (and, presumably, a wet nurse) she brought up her first children. By the late 1760s, however, when her fourth child was born, she was affected by the latest opinions and nursed the girl herself.

---

[78]*Leinster*, III, 220, 132, II, 217, III, 234.
[79]*Delany*, I, 1862, 357.

When a year later the child died, it was said that nursing the child herself had made her "remarkably fond" of her.[80] Her fifth child died too soon for experimentation.

When her eldest daughter married the duke of Devonshire in 1774, Lady Spencer told her that she hoped their correspondence would be "like a comfortable conversation with the friend of one's heart," and from their letters we are able to reconstruct something of the way in which the young women of the family dealt with their infants in the 1770s. Five months after her marriage the duchess became concerned that she was not yet pregnant. Her mother tried to reassure her that this would "in the end be better for your health" and that without starting to have children for another year, she might still have two or three children by the time she was as old as her friend Lady Betty Stanley, whose pregnancy had caused her some heartburning. Lady Spencer also told her that it would not do to mention her regrets to any other woman and especially not to her husband.[81] For the entire Cavendish family was poised, awaiting the young woman's performance, and a year later, when at 18 she miscarried, her husband wrote to his brother-in-law the duke of Portland that his "Duchess has not been as lucky" as Portland's, who had just given birth to her third child.[82] Motherhood was a duty, and it conferred status. To be barren, from whatever cause, was somewhat shameful. For 6 years the poor duchess was not pregnant again; in that period her younger brother and sister both married and had children; her tensions came out in the "hysteric fits" that she had in the mornings,[83] and by evening—no doubt in compensation—she plunged into the swirl of high life, to her religious mother's increasing distress.

In 1781 her sister, Lady Bessborough, had her first child, a son. Lady Bessborough decided to nurse, and the duchess wrote wistfully, "what would I give to see her suckling him." Lady Spencer replied that Harriet "makes an excellent nurse, and my grandson I assure you is a very stout little gentleman." The child was healthy, and his mother's only complaint was the "soreness of her breasts occasioned by his biting too hard, which puts her to a great deal of pain, but will I hope decrease as she gains strength." (The child was christened a month later, and his father insisted, to the Spencers' delight, that the child bear Lord Spencer's name ahead of his own, and that he be called by it.)

[80] Coke, I, 74.
[81] Chatsworth MSS, V, 26, 42B, 97.
[82] N.U.L., PwF2700.
[83] Lady Ilchester and Lord Stavordale, *The Life and Letters of Lady Sarah Lennox 1745–1826* (London: John Murray, 1901), 261.

Lady Spencer grew uneasy about the nursing eventually, and Lady Bessborough gave up and a nurse was hired. The child thrived, and when he was 11 months old, Lady Spencer reported that she had ridden over to "Rowhampton, where I found John on his bread and milk and vastly well."[84]

Lord Althorp, the duchess's brother, married in March 1781, and in the usual fashion, his wife was pregnant 6 months later and bore a son on May 30, 1782. (It is no wonder the duchess was distressed.) But the child was sickly and his mother, apparently, did not nurse him. His father showed great interest in his son and examined him "accurately whenever he has an opportunity and now and then measures him, he says he is grown this week"; but a skeptical grandmother added that "I really think he thrives, though it will be some times before I shall build much hope upon his poor diminutive carcass."[85]

The duchess had still provided her husband no heir of any kind on which to build his hopes. She had begun to think that what her mother would have described as her life of dissipation was depriving her of children, for she said she was tempted to believe that God denied her children "till I deserve them." Lady Spencer rose to the occasion and prescribed a regimen of early rising, serious reading, and economy which the Duchess tried to follow in 1782. But being the ingenuous woman that she was, she admitted to her horrified mother that she had read *Les liasons dangereuses* and Rousseau's *Confessions*, and in a long "religious dissertation" she showed that she was familiar with what Lady Spencer called "all the artful meanings and sophistical arguments of the most dangerous writers against Christianity." In December she went off to Bath in search of fruitful waters. She was successful, and Lady Spencer told her to stay away from London and its disturbances or she should "only think you love a play or an opera better than a child." Lady Spencer was quick to use the opportunity of the approaching danger of childbirth to attempt a moral reformation (as she had used previous illnesses of her daughter), and when the duchess was 3 months pregnant she wrote to Lady Spencer:

> I really have the strongest wish and intention to receive the sacrament before I lie in, both in mark of thankfulness to God for the blessing he has granted me, and besides though I do not apprehend much danger in the lying-in, from an idea that there is a probability one should die. But I must put it off till all danger of miscarriage is quite over, for though I hope I have no grievous or heavy sin to repent of, yet I have follies enough, and those of a kind that are interesting to my feelings in such a degree that I

---

[84]Chatsworth MSS, V, 355, 356, 358, 374, 376, 389.
[85]*Ibid.*, V, 400.

dare not venture the apprehending of them just now—my feelings have ever an amazing connection and power over my frame....

And so this poor badgered woman, full of guilt that her pursuit of pleasure had hindered her from fulfilling her great natural function, and yet believing that the strong feelings that had driven her into those follies were not to be ignored, carefully carried her burden, and on Saturday morning the twelfth of July 1783 was delivered of a daughter.[86]

As one might have expected, she had decided to nurse the child. Indeed she was so "taken up with ... the prospect of nursing her child herself" that, according to Lady Sarah Lennox, she talked "as if her whole happiness depended upon succeeding."[87] But even this she was not allowed to do in peace. For the Cavendishes were not satisfied; they wanted an heir; and when Lord John Cavendish, the leader of the clan, was carried to see the girl, "it happened at a moment when she was throwing up her milk, which thought quite right for her, made her look [low] and Lord John teased me with saying, all his kind of jokes, that a dairymaid was a better nurse than a fine lady, etc." But Lord John was not overly concerned about his great-niece's health; it was rather that he found domestic affections a tiresome impediment to lineal ambitions; for, as her husband explained to the duchess, what made his uncle "abuse suckling is their impatience for my having a son and their fancying I shan't so soon if I suckle." Her husband's prolific sister, the duchess of Portland, also came to visit and told her to drink porter to fatten the little girl, and Lady Sefton and the duchess of Rutland (her sister-in-law's aunt) said Lady Lincoln's child was fatter. It was a series of comments that left the duchess feeling overwhelmed by her husband's hostile relations, and they undermined her self-confidence as a nurse. At night, depressed, she wrote her mother a plaintive account of the whole business, but when sleep and the child's good looks had relieved her depression the following morning, she added to her letter: "Pray don't let anybody know I write you all this—but my heart was so full last night I could not help it—she is charming today and indeed looks fat and I am sure I shall be a very good nurse to her—but how can one help being anxious."[88]

Three weeks after this disturbing visit from the Cavendishes, the duchess carried her 6-week-old daughter down to Chatsworth. She

[86]*Ibid.*, V, 313, 442, 448 (the last two are printed in Earl of Bessborough, ed., *Georgiana* (London: John Murray, 1955), 56–57), 453, 459, 472, 208, 484, 509.
[87]Ilchester and Stavordale, *Lady Sarah*, 356.
[88]Chatsworth MSS, V, 516.

wrote to her mother, in a happier mood, that she "never saw Georgiana look better—her cold is gone and she sucked in the night without wrangling." The duchess remained diligent and anxious. "Here we are and as usual [I am] the most nervous of beings. I fancied I had hit the child's head against a door, which I certainly did—but she never cried or left off sucking—'tis now fast asleep and we have examined her head twice and rubbed it all over, so that I think I cannot have hurt her, but I shall not take her through a double door again in a hurry." Her nursery staff included a head nurse and a rocker, who was to have been made into a nursery maid but had to be dismissed. "You know I would bring the rocker with me meaning, as she was poor, to keep her whilst I suckled—she was only rather dirty till last night, when she was quite drunk—my dear little girl sleeps now in bed with me after her first suckling as it is too cold to move her and rocker was to turn her dry and lay her down to sleep—I perceived that she made the bed stink of wine and strong drink whenever she came near it and that Mrs. Smith was always watchful and telling her to leave the child, this rather ashamed me, but this morning I learnt she had been so drunk as to sit down and vomit," and so she was dismissed. The duchess had been well trained in guilt, and it was a difficult training to set aside. She worried that her inexperience would hurt her child, but she had kept on an unsatisfactory servant because she found her poverty moving; and in doing this, she once more placed herself in a position to be disapproved of by an older woman, though the woman was only a servant. And then, of course, she wrote an account of the whole business to Lady Spencer. But through it all, she continued to nurse. She gave Lady Spencer, to whom a properly arranged schedule was a supreme good, an account of the way in which her day revolved about the child: "I get up at about ten but with suckling and dressing am seldom down till twelve; I breakfast and drive out till time to dress for dinner—after dinner the child keeps me till she goes to sleep, and then two pools at commerce till supper," and after supper, to bed and more nursing. Reynolds painted the child in her mother's arms, and William Dent designed a carriage for her. But there was to be a decade and yet another daughter before the Cavendishes got a son out of the duchess and were satisfied.[89]

The duchess seems to have not met with much opposition from older women in her decision to nurse; some of her female in-laws, in the face of her period of barrenness, may have doubted her strength to undertake the business and been unkind enough to say so; but Lady Spencer, though she might want a nurse as reassurance in the case of a

---

[89]Ibid., V, 522, 523, 528 (in part in Bessborough, ed., *Georgiana*, 63), 532.

daughter who found the business difficult, had, after all, nursed a child herself. It was rather from her husband's male relations that she met with difficulty. The selfishness of fathers in preventing their wives from nursing, which was so often complained of, may have arisen from a dissatisfaction with not being able to sleep with them when they nursed (for, presumably, the medical objections to sex for a nursing woman applied equally to mothers and wet nurses), but more probably, as in the case of the Cavendishes, the taboo was ignored, and what was feared was a woman's physiological incapacity to conceive during lactation. The production of an heir might be impeded, and the property of a husband's family in his wife's sexuality would be squandered in an excess of emotional indulgence.

The duchess bore a certain emotional likeness to the Lennox sisters. Like them, she had been raised with a strong sense of religion and duty. She was full of romantic passion and ardor, and her family approved of marriages for love.[90] She was interested in books and the anatomy of the emotions. She enjoyed children; she trusted natural instinct; and she was convinced that inexperience was nothing in the face of instinct. She was not, perhaps, entirely conventional. Like Lady Sarah she was willing to go the extent of disregarding the double standard. But by the late 1760s and the 1770s a woman did not have to be so extreme to decide to nurse her child. There was no hint of unconventionality about Lady Spencer, or Lady Bellamont, or the young duchess of Leinster. It would seem instead that young women who had been born in the 1740s in families where domesticity was valued, were by the 1770s being encouraged by their own mothers to nurse their children. Mrs. Boscawen, for instance, bore her children in the former decade. At that time she disapproved of early marriages; she delighted in her children and took great care of them; she was very much in love with her husband and found him sexually exciting, and she once confessed to him that she preferred "her husband's company to all the world." But despite all this, she was quite unsympathetic when she learned in 1748 that an acquaintance intended to nurse her own child. "I can't think but she will make a bad nurse," she told her husband, "at least, I know I would not hire her." But by 1774 Mrs. Boscawen had experienced with everyone else the great sea change. The second of her daughters had married in the previous year, and at her grandson's birth she told Mrs. Delany that her daughter made

---

[90]See Chap. 2 for Lady Spencer's attitude toward her younger daughter's marriage.

an exceeding good nurse, and was obliged to-day to invite another child to breakfast beside her own, who was under suspicion of having overeat himself yesterday—but it is a great addition of fatigue to the poor mother, I perceive, (for I never saw till now the beginning of this very natural proceeding), and she is so often roused when she seems sleepy, but as she bears all with the greatest patience, and never makes a complaint, I hope all will agree with her, so as to leave her none to make, were she so inclined.[91]

Mrs. Boscawen had never seen a woman begin to nurse before because her wet nurses, and those of her other daughter, had always been women who had already started to nurse. But she was willing to give up the opinion she had held 25 years before because even she had become convinced by the argument from nature. Domesticity and nature had conquered together 700 years of aristocratic convention. Enlightenment had trimphed over feudalism.

By 1780 a knowledgeable physician could estimate that most aristocratic women were nursing themselves, and that when they did not, they preferred to bring a child up by hand to using a wet nurse.[92] Between 1765 and 1780 aristocratic society had dramatically changed its habits in this regard. That it could be done over so short a span of time as 15 years is an excellent illustration of the speed with which such practices could gain ground among a group that read the same books, used the same doctors, and visited each other in London. But breast feeding came too late to explain the fall in mortality that began in 1750. The one certain change we know of in aristocratic childrearing at that point was that mothers spent more time than ever with their children; that they used this time to try various experimental schemes; and that they were encouraged by domesticity to place the highest possible value on the company of their children. It has indeed been claimed (with some exaggeration) that the medical literature can be used to show that there was an abrupt change at 1750 in the oral, anal, and sexual behavior of infants and in the degree of dependence that was encouraged and of aggression that was allowed.[93] But the difficulty with such catalogs of change is that they are made on the basis of

[91]Aspinall-Oglander, *Wife*, 245, 232, 123 et passim; Delany, II, 1862, 7. The Spencer connection may be followed into the eighties when Lady Bessborough told her mother in 1786 that her sister-in-law "Lady Fitzwilliam and Lord Milton are perfectly well, she has suckled him several times without the least pain" (Earl of Bessborough and Arthur Aspinall, *Lady Bessborough and Her Family Circle* (London: John Murray, 1941), 38).

[92]Underwood, *Disorders of Childhood*, III, 2–12. See also H. Meister, *Letters Written during a Residence in England* (London, 1799).

[93]Alice Ryerson, "Medical Advice on Childrearing, 1550–1900," *Harvard Educational Review*, XXXI, 1961, 302–323.

Freudian theories of secondary drive, that is, that children first need to have these bodily drives satisfied and then strike up relationships with those who provide their satisfaction. It is, however, more to the point to view the formation of a single intense relationship as a child's primary need, and to see all its actions—crying, smiling, babbling, clinging, eating, and defecating—as means to this end. (This theory of attachment, like eighteenth-century opinion, disbelieves in the importance of childhood sexuality.)[94] Eighteenth-century opinion was certainly capable of observing the growth of attachment through such channels. Locke, for instance, could say that "we may observe, that, when children are first born, all objects of sight . . . are indifferent to them" but that by 6 months a child "will not come to a stranger . . . because having become accustomed to receive its food and kind usage from only one or two, that are about it, the child apprehends, by coming into the arms of a stranger, the being taken away from what delights and feeds it."[95] It is therefore in this light that the changes in such practices as toilet training or swaddling must be seen. And since these changes went against the traditional practice of nurses and had to be imposed and directed by aristocratic women, they are my last piece of evidence that by 1750 aristocratic mothers were more successfully attaching their infants to themselves as sole mother figures, and that it was this rather than immunity to disease or better nutrition that was probably responsible for the fall in the death rate after 1750.

Attachment, Innovation, and Maternal Supervision

Modern studies have shown that infants cry for a variety of reasons: from hunger, pain, and anger. Eighteenth-century writers certainly noted all three reasons. Locke wrote that there were two kinds of crying: A child cried as a means to obtain mastery and from pain. He said that "these two, if carefully observed, may by the mere looks and actions, and particularly the tone of their crying, be easily distinguished; but neither of them must be suffered, much less encouraged," not "only for the unpleasant and the unbecoming noise it fills the house with," but also because allowing one would encourage their passions, and not preventing the other would let slip an excellent opportunity "to harden them against all sufferings."[96] Many women pre-

[94]Bowlby, *Attachment*, passim.
[95]Locke, 222.
[96]Bowlby, *Attachment*, I, 289–296; Locke, 215–218, 224, 375–378.

sumed that continual crying was natural in children, and that they cried most often when they were hungry. When Lord Bristol traveled with his daughter and his nurse, he remarked that even "Lady Louisa behaved herself so well as not to cry (but whimpered only when she wanted the bubby)." Dr. Cadogan complained that as a result a child was "accordingly fed, ten, twelve or more times in a day or night," and that it would be found that a child "never cries but from pain" and that "a child (I mean this of a very young one) that is hungry will make a hundred other signs of want."[97] After mid-century it is probable that this automatic feeding when a child cried went out of favor; there were indeed complaints that some parents "among some few families of quality" were going to the opposite extreme and starving their children;[98] and aristocratic women like the duchess of Devonshire clearly only nursed at stated times in the day. Rocking in a cradle was another way to quiet crying. Most medical writers were opposed to the cradle, feeling that children should be exercised a great deal, and one of them declared that "he was an ingenious man who invented a mousetrap, though none but a fool first thought of a cradle."[99] But a wise doctor like Underwood recommended cradles because they were "so like what all children are used to before they are born, being then suspended and accustomed to ride, as it were, or be gently swung in a soft fluid, upon every motion of the mother and even during her sleep."[100] Some aristocratic women must have agreed: the duchess of Devonshire had in her nursery a servant called the rocker. Children were sometimes allowed to cry because it was thought that tears dissipated the superfluous moisture of the brain and that crying opened and dilated the lungs. Nursing and rocking and allowing a child to cry were all positive responses. But when the pattern of a child's crying indicated anger, it is likely that the child was sometimes whipped, thought the defensiveness with which this was recommended must indicate that there were many who thought such a practice barbaric.[101]

Children instinctively grasp, cling, and reach, and by the time they are 5 months old the mother becomes the consistent object of this behavior. In the early eighteenth century a child was usually well swaddled at birth, and this must have limited the development of early grasping. At 2 or 3 months its arms were unwrapped, but the right hand

---

[97]Pennington, Letters, IV, 8–9; Bristol Letterbook, II, 2; Cadogan, Nursing, 19.
[98]Buchan, Domestic Medicine, 23; Hill, Management and Education, 32.
[99]Smith, Letters, 103.
[100]Underwood, Disorders of Childhood, III, 107.
[101]Nurse's Guide, 48; John Pechey, A General Treatise of the Diseases of Infants and Children (London, 1697), 13; Nelson, Government of Children (1763), 151.

was given greater freedom than the left, and the discouragement of left-handedness lasted even after swaddling went out of practice. Cadogan in 1748 was the first physician to recommend that a child not be swaddled.[102] Rousseau, 14 years later, praised the example of England where "the senseless and barbarous swaddling clothes have become almost obsolete."[103] Aristocratic children were among the first to experience the change since they were delivered in London. William Smellie had saved the life of a child that had been bound too tightly by a country nurse and reported the nurse's response: She said "in her own excuse [that] she was told London nurses dressed them so as to give them fine shapes. I told her the danger of that practice, and that they now dressed them very loose, to prevent spoiling their natural shape, which was much better and handsomer than artificial ones."[104] Since children were carried and tossed about a great deal more than in the previous century as part of the preventive medicine against rickets, they were allowed much greater scope for clinging. But an aristocratic mother as late as 1748 could be torn between a traditional sense of decorum and her enjoyment of her child. "The child is pure well," the duchess of Leeds wrote when he was nearly a year, "and says Mama quite plain, kisses me violently at night, at no other time without he is bid."[105]

Nurses in dealing with infants were expected to "be merry and cheerful, and [to] smile often to divert the child." And it was the nurse who usually encouraged a child's babbling. Babbling, however, was heavily discouraged on the ground that children were to be spoken to as rational creatures; but one suspects that nurses and mothers paid no heed to these admonitions.[106]

All the activities so far described, from feeding to babbling, occur in the first 6 months of a child's life, when he is dependent on his mother or his nurse for the maintenance of proximity. After these first 6 months, the autonomy of the child increases, and thereafter it is as much he as his mother who maintains proximity. The desire for proximity has by then become focused on a particular person, and the eighteenth century was aware of the marked change: Locke described it, and James Nelson advised that at 6 months a child should be accus-

[102]Bowlby, Attachment, I, 277–280; Nurse's Guide, 4, 49–50, cf. Hill, Management and Education, 100; Pechey, Diseases of Infants, p. 9 on right-handedness; Cadogan, Nursing, 10–12.
[103]J. J. Rousseau, Emile, trans. by B. Foxley (London: Dent, 1914), 28n.
[104]William Smellie, A Treatise on the Theory and Practice of Midwifery (London, 1764), 1774 ed., 354–355; cf. Underwood, Disorders of Childhood, III, 35–37; Cadogan, Nursing, 19, 24; Moss, Management, Nursing and Diseases, 55–58.
[105]K. M. Lynch, A Congreve Gallery (Cambridge, Mass.: Harvard Univ. Press, 1951), 98.
[106]Pechey, Diseases of Infants, preface; Pennington, Letters, IV, 3; The Common Errors in the Education of Children (London, 1744), 14.

tomed to other arms or faces lest its mother or nurse become its slave. The great milestones along this way of autonomy are weaning, toilet training, and walking.[107]

The age of weaning changed markedly over the course of the century as a result of the theories of physicians. In the 1690s there were those who weaned at 10 or 12 months, but the usual recommendation was that a child should be suckled until he was 1 1/2 or 2 years old, and this held true through the first three decades of the eighteenth century.[108] When Mary Lovett's son was 17 months old she wrote to her father, Lord Fermanagh, in 1707: "I should be very glad my boy were weaned, if he be not, my mother desires it should be on Good Friday, I think there is an old wife's saying on that." A year later she said that she had weaned her second son when he was just over a year, and "he thrives very well."[109] Cadogan, in 1748, recommended weaning at a year and said that it should be done by "insensible degrees." But there were physicians at the same time, and later, who were prepared to say that a healthy child might be weaned at 3 or 4 months.[110] Lady Betty Smithson weaned her son at 6 months in 1743. And in 1767 the duchess of Portland began to wean her son when he was 10 months and 3 weeks old; she said that it "makes me in a little fuss but I hope he will get very well over it as he has been perfectly quiet. I did not intend to have done it quite so soon, but it was the advice of the learned." Two days later she added that the child had "got over his weaning vastly well without the least trouble and I never saw him better." It is likely, then, that from 1740 on, children were weaned between 3 and 12 months and never later, and that their mothers often took an active role in supervising the process.[111]

Locke was the eighteenth-century's great authority on toilet training. He thought that going to stool regularly had great influence on one's health, and that an individual's disposition in this regard also affected his personality, for "people that are very *loose*, have seldom strong thoughts or strong bodies." On the basis of an experiment he conducted he recommended that each morning after breakfast a child was to be "set upon the stool, as if disburthening were as much in his power, as filling his belly; and let not him, nor his maid know anything

---

[107]Bowlby, *Attachment*, I, 243–244; Locke, 222; Nelson, *Government of Children* (1763), 174.
[108]Pechey, *Diseases of Maids*, 11 (recte 10); *Nurse's Guide*, 56–58.
[109]Lady Verney, ed., *Verney Letters of the Eighteenth Century* (London: Ernest Benn, 1930), 2 vol., I, 200, 203.
[110]Cadogan, *Nursing*, 24; Nelson, *Government of Children* (1763 ed.), 57; Moss, *Management, Nursing and Diseases*, 297–437.
[111]Hertford, 243; N.U.L., PwF10, 577–578; Underwood, *Diseases of Childhood*, III, 98–99.

to the contrary, but that it is so." Locke was trying to combat the use of physic to bring on bowel movements, for it was usual for nurses to purge every day if the bowels had not moved by a stated time. But Locke gave no indication of the age at which the training was to begin.[112]

As long as children were swaddled, training could not have begun much before they were a year old, and swaddled infants were often left in their excrement because it was thought that "clean linen and fresh clothes draw and rob them of their nourishing juices." In 1753 Nelson suggested that it was possible to train children at 5 or 6 months, but he did not necessarily recommend it. In the next decade Lady Pennington maintained that a child who was properly attended could be trained, beginning at the end of his first month, to be "perfectly cleanly." Underwood knew of three or four instances of children trained in this way, "one of which was in the family of a Lady of rank, whom I was some years ago attending. I was myself there a witness to the good effects of holding a little pan under an infant of only four months old, as it lay across the nurse's lap, which I was assured had been her practice from the month, and that the Lady had obliged her nursery-maids to do the like with her two former children." But Underwood, like other physicians, recommended beginning at a year with Locke's system and that in difficult cases suppositories of cloth or paper daubed with oil should be used rather than purging.[113] The result must have been that the aristocratic child, unswaddled and controlling his bowels at ever earlier ages, was able to follow his mother and his nurses with greater ease and less embarrassment after the middle of the century.

But a child is best able to control his proximity to his mother or nurse when he can walk or crawl to her. There was a tendency in the early eighteenth century to encourage a child to walk sooner than it would if left entirely to its own pace, and to support it by leading strings or a go-cart when it did begin to walk. By mid-century both practices were discountenanced. It was recommended instead that children should crawl about on a carpet and not sit for long periods of time in a chair.[114] We have seen how firmly Lady Kildare insisted on following these new ideas and disregarding her mother-in-law's ad-

[112]Locke, 133–136; Harris, *Acute Diseases*, 40–47.
[113]Cadogan, *Nursing*, 12; Nelson, *Government of Children* (1753), 119; Pennington, *Letters*, III, 130–132; Underwood, *Disorders of Childhood*, I, 65, III, 31–32, 147; Buchan, *Domestic Medicine*, 142. Boswell wrote "Tuesday 11 October: From this day follow Mr. Locke's prescription of going to stool every day regularly after breakfast (F. A. Pottle, ed., *Boswell in Holland 1763–64* (London: McGraw-Hill, 1962), 43)."
[114]*Nurse's Guide*, 49–50; Smith, *Letters*, 152–154; Nelson, *Government of Children* (1753 ed.), 120.

vice.[115] The child was allowed his own forms of movement, even if it meant crawling, instead of being forced into adult modes of locomotion that he could not fully control.

Therefore, in the 1740s and 1750s it is likely that the opportunities for an infant under 6 months to use clinging as a means of attaching himself to a mother figure were much increased by the disappearance of swaddling. On the other hand, adults probably felt that they should be less responsive to a child's crying. At the same time, by not feeding a child on demand but rather on schedule, it is likely that the trauma of weaning was lessened. For under the old system, by the time a child was weaned at 18 or 24 months, his capacity to control his food supply would have become a vital part of his attachment, and its sudden frustration at weaning would greatly have disturbed the entire organization of his attachment to his mother figure.[116] But by 1750 the infant over 6 months was not only freed from the traumas of weaning but was controlling his crawling and walking without adult intervention. All these changes that cluster just before mid-century could be executed only by an aristocratic mother's personal supervision. Maids and nurses were not likely to be convinced of the efficacy of the new ways. If a child was to be left unswaddled, if he was to be fed on schedule and weaned at 10 months, if he was to be taught to control his bowels and was not to be purged on schedule, or if he was to walk by his own power and not with leading strings—if any of these things were to happen, a mother would be obliged to come in and assert her authority in the face of her deputies. By this assertion, it is likely that she indicated to her child that she was his sole mother figure and thereby attached him more firmly to her. In this process it is also probable that the child's relationship with others became more satisfying. For a child strongly attached to a single figure tends to show a discriminated interest in others, whereas a child who is weakly attached because he has had to deal with a succession of mother figures tends to confine all his social behavior to one person. It is also likely that now when an aristocratic mother used deputies, they remained such. For a child will form his principal attachments to parents who see him but a few hours a day if they are able to interact with him on a more satisfying level than the nurse who may provide him all of his routine care.[117] And that aristocratic women were increasingly able to achieve such a level of interaction is the probability toward which all the evidence leads.

---

[115]See supra, 219.
[116]This is a point made in M. D. S. Ainsworth, Infancy in Uganda (Baltimore, 1967), 413.
[117]Bowlby, Attachment, I, 307–317, 346.

Childhood Experience and Adult Life

I have been arguing that the most dramatic and measurable change in the life of aristocratic children—the fall in the death rate after 1750—was a consequence of a marked but less measurable change in the quality of their attachment to their mothers. To completely make the case, it should be possible to show that the insecure attachment that resulted from mothering by a succession of figures had an effect on adult life. The classic eighteenth-century case that is available does not unfortunately, suit our purposes in two respects—the individual was not an aristocrat, and his nurse did not live in his parents' house—but Samuel Johnson's experience is of interest nonetheless. For it has been cogently argued that Johnson's entire life was governed by his fear of abandonment that arose from being put out to nurse. Most of his life he struggled against attacks of melancholia, and he did not manage to free himself from them until after his mother's death. Johnson also had his physical health affected, for it was from his nurse that he caught scrofula.[118] But unfortunately there is no easy evidence that aristocrats as a whole suffered from depression.

There is better evidence that aristocratic women suffered from hysteria. A modern case has been made that such women are reacting to the experience in childhood of an attachment figure who was either inaccessible or unresponsive. It also seems that women are more likely than men to respond to such an experience with an extreme dependence or anxious attachment, whereas the male response is more likely to be a detachment acted out aggressively.[119] Eighteenth-century physicians mistook the etiology of hysteria, but their observation of its incidence and its symptoms was acute enough. The physical symptoms of headaches, vomiting, and spasms were likely to be accompanied by feelings of anxiety, anger, and jealousy. There was a tendency to make it a physical disease by attributing it to the disorders of the womb, and this is, after all, not so much worse than the classical Freudian explanation of penis envy. But there were some who stressed its psychic origins since both men and women were observed to suffer from it. Even these observers did notice, however, that patients were predominantly women, and that among women, the adolescent and the newly widowed (or those who were losing or had recently lost their male attachment figure) were the majority. Marriage was therefore a tra-

---

[118]George Irwin, *Samuel Johnson: A Personality in Conflict* (Auckland: Auckland Univ. Press, 1971).

[119]Bowlby, *Maternal Care*, 35; Bowlby, *Attachment*, II, 226.

ditional remedy. But this was likely, as Bernard Mandeville said, to perpetuate the condition with hysteric mothers bringing up melancholic daughters. Physicians also claimed that the rich were more likely to be hysteric than the poor, and city women more likely than peasants. It was a plausible claim, for it was the aristocrat and the urbanite who made the most frequent use of wet nurses, and their children were therefore the most likely to suffer from attachment difficulties. Physicians also used hysteria as a reason to persuade aristocratic women that they were not strong enough to nurse their children. Thus it is likely that hysteric women were married to be cured and were then persuaded that their illness prevented them from nursing and thereby delivering their own children from the insecurity of a diffuse attachment to mother and nurse.[120]

If, as it was suggested, Englishmen tended to be melancholic and Englishwomen hysteric, they were both likely to overeat. And the strongest evidence of the effects of maternal deprivation among aristocrats is probably to be found in their eating habits and in the medical therapies dependent on those habits. Modern children when they are separated from their mothers tend to overeat in compensation,[121] and a good case can be made that eighteenth-century aristocrats were encouraged to overeat as children and continued to do so as adults. Their doctors, in their theory and treatment of disease, recognized this but were usually discreet enough not to say so, for they knew the defensive hostility they would encounter if they did.

Those physicians who encouraged mothers to nurse were also convinced that children ate far too often, and the limitation of children to eating only two, three, or four times a day was one of the great changes in childrearing that occurred after mid-century.[122] John Locke imputed "a great part of our disease in England, to our eating too much flesh, and too little bread," and he observed that "if we look into the houses of those, who are a little warmer in their fortunes, there eating and drinking are made so much the great business and happiness of life, the children are thought neglected, if they have not their share of it."[123] Physicians certainly held early in the century that most diseases were caused by the food one ate; and this is of interest since a society's theory of disease often reflects the malfunctioning of its childrearing

---

[120]Ilza Veith, *Hysteria: The History of a Disease* (Chicago: Univ. of Chicago Press, 1965), 114, 117–118, 123–126, 129–133, 141–142, 154, 157, 164, 172, 174, 179; Buchan, *Domestic Medicine*, 2–3.
[121]Bowlby, *Attachment*, I, 218–219.
[122]Cadogan, *Nursing*, 20; Buchan, *Domestic Medicine*, 23; Hill, *Management and Education*, 32–40; Smith, *Letters*, 102.
[123]Locke, 127, 141.

practices. The most influential writer on childhood diseases, Walter Harris, maintained that all ill health in childhood was to be diagnosed as the result of a child's food turning acid and that a doctor should proceed on the information he received from the nurse as to the state of the child's hiccups, its vomit, and its stool.[124] As a grown man, Lord Hervey (who was probably suffering from gallstones) found that all physicians "jog on in one beaten track; a vomit to clear your stomach, a glister to give you a stool, laudanum to quiet the pain, and then a purge to clear your bowels, and what they call 'carry it off.'" Hervey eventually put himself under the care of Dr. George Cheyne, who maintained that a third of the complaints of the higher ranks were caused by overeating. Cheyne was greatly vilified for saying this "Attacks made upon me by ignorance, intemperance, and gluttony," he said, "are innumerable and incredible"; he was called a leveller and accused of destroying all orders, ranks, and property. Cheyne's great remedy was to place his patients on a special diet and to give them almost no medicine, though even he could not do entirely without vomits and purges. Hervey related that at Cheyne's direction he lived "for three years together" eating "neither flesh, fish, nor eggs, but lived entirely upon herbs, roots, pulse, fruits, legumes, and all these sort of foods which, before I left off meat and wine, I could never eat of," and that as a consequence he had enjoyed good health.[125] With others of his patients, Cheyne recommended drinking milk as part of their special diet.[126] It is therefore not too much to suggest that aristocrats, deprived at birth of the emotional satisfaction of being suckled by their mothers and thereby firmly establishing their first human relationship, sought to compensate in adult life by making eating "the great business and happiness of life." They thereby ate themselves into their graves. As infants when

---

[124]Harris, *Acute Diseases*, 5–9.

[125]John, Lord Hervey, *Somce Materials towards Memoirs of the Reign of King George II*, ed. by Romney Sedgwick (London: Eyre & Spottiswoode, 1931), 3 vol., III, Appendix II, 965–966, 987, I, xviii–xx, III, 968–970.

[126]C. F. Mullett, ed., *The Letters of George Cheyne to the Countess of Huntingdon* (San Marino, Calif.: Huntington Library Publications, 1940), *passim*; cf. J. M. W. Whiting and I. L. Child, *Child Training and Personality: A Cross-Cultural Approach* (New Haven: Yale Univ. Press, 1953), Chap. 8, for a discussion of the relationship between a society's theory of disease and the malfunctioning of its childrearing practices. Physicians other than Cheyne also had to face hostility. "Abstemiousness has been caused to a pernicious extreme by the present age," wrote Vicesimus Knox. "Dr. Cheyene's books contributed to introduce it, and Dr. Cadogan's pamphlet on the gout rendered it universal among valetudinarians. Asthentic or nervous diseases have in course multiplied" (*Personal Nobility* (London, 1793 ed.), 90). And in 1771 a friend wrote to the duke of Newcastle that he was very sorry to hear from the duke of Kingston "that your Grace has not been well, which he attributes to your having read Dr. Cadogan's book on abstinence; but we determined to come to Clumber on purpose to burn that foolish book (N.U.L., NeC 3241)."

they were dependent and unable to find any satisfactory substitute, they simply died.

The universal remedy of purging was resorted to in cases of psychic disturbance as well as of physical disease. There is the melancholy case of Lord and Lady Cowper.[127] They had married for love in 1732, and in the first 6 years of marriage, Lady Cowper gave birth to a daughter and then to a son. But in the year following her son's birth, Lady Cowper went into deep depression. She felt that her husband had treated her badly for some time, but she refused to name any particular thing he had done, and instead she simply insisted that his "whole behavior to her is unkind and that she will never forgive it." Cowper was convinced that her behavior was nothing "else but vapours," which had been brought on by an inactive life. In short, she was hysteric. (The vapors were thought to arise from lack of exercise, and horseback riding was prescribed as a cure.) But he had great trouble persuading her relations of his diagnosis. He therefore consulted Richard Mead, a fashionable doctor who sometimes treated mental patients. Mead diagnosed the case as "distraction of the mind" and explained that this was "no more than the mind's being so fixed and habituated to one particular thought or passion, that it cannot be diverted from it or attend to any other." (Freud noted how easy it was to confuse the symptoms of hysterical and obsessional neuroses.) His prescription was "actions [that] will be suitable to the thought with which the mind is possessed." This meant "such evacuations as are proper in such cases; that is, by bleeding, vomiting and purging at such intervals as her strength will bear, (and her Ladyship is not at all weak) to bring her spirits into a right course." The purging was intended to break her will and destroy her obsession. "I should by this means hope," Mead concluded, "that she will be brought to hearken to the counsel of her friends, which now makes no impression, and that then, upon representations made to her of the ill consequences of her present deportment, she may come again into that way of life which will make your Lordship and herself happy."

The treatment did not work. Cowper began to detach himself from his children on the ground that this was the way to prevent spoiling them like their mother. He moaned to his sister that he had now "nothing else to do but ramble up and down the world to divert myself as I

---

[127]Herts R.O., Panshanger MSS, Box 19, Shelf 226, Box 51; Edward Hughes, ed., *Letters of Spencer Cowper* (Surtees Society, 1956), 6, 20–21, 66, 68. My interpretation of Lady Cowper's condition is drawn from N. K. Wenner, "Dependency Patterns in Pregnancy," in Masserman, ed., *Sexuality of Women* (New York: Grune & Stratton, 1966); F. T. Melges, "Postpartum Psychiatric Syndromes," *Psychosomatic Medicine*, **XXX**, 1968. These were brought together in Bowlby, *Attachment*, **II**, 360.

think I can never hope ever to live at home again with the pleasure I once proposed." His dream of domesticity had been shattered. But he did not in fact ramble: He stayed at home and mourned, ate too much, and, as his friends teased him, grew fat and lazy.

Lady Cowper was probably suffering from postpartum depression, and the aggressive way in which she had tried to force her husband to support her dependence reflected her lack of confidence that such support could be expected. Her pessimism probably had its roots in an unsatisfactory relationship with her own mother. It is also possible (as it has been suggested about nineteenth-century American women) that she found in hysteria the means of resolving the conflict between her roles of passive wife and active mother.[128] In either case the only therapy available was a regimen of purging, and that regimen, alas, was probably a reflection of the inadequate bonds of attachment from which aristocratic society suffered before 1750. The system was self-reinforcing and self-perpetuating at most points. Detachment led to further detachment. But Cowper did have one other bond to fall back on. His ties to his sister were quite close. They had clung together when Cowper, at 14, had had to endure within 4 months the death of his father and then of his mother; and so he now adjured her, "my sister, continue to love me as long as I deserve it and make you happy in this world."[129] Sibling solidarity could partially compensate for the loss that had to be endured when domesticity did not prove strong enough to break the cycle of detachment. But for Cowper's children there was probably no relief. The detached son and husband had become the detached parent.

The story of the Cowpers shows why it was so difficult to break out of the old system—it was self-perpetuating and self-protective at most points. But Cowper's actions also show that aristocrats were aware that domesticity was the means to break down the old walls of detachment. The most visible proof that those walls did come down is the dramatic fall in infant mortality after 1750. For if it cannot be shown that infants were either better protected from disease or better nourished than previously, we are left to conclude that it must have been that they were better loved. Domesticity drove mothers to spend more time with their children, and the vogue for experimentation that domesticity encouraged guaranteed that the quality of that time would be changed, even though the routine care of children was still provided by servants.

---

[128]See Carroll Smith-Rosenberg, "The Hysterical Woman: Sex Roles and Role Conflict in 19th-Century America," Social Research, XXXIX, 1972, 652–678. Smith-Rosenberg raises the possibility that, while domesticity may have lessened hysteria by providing more satisfying attachments in childhood, it may also have contributed to its incidence by containing within itself two contradictory roles for adult women: the passive wife and the competent mother.

[129]Herts. R. O., Panshanger MSS, Box 51.

I have also been arguing in this last section that the old system bred up unhappy adults—women who were hysteric and men who were melancholy or violent. It should be possible to show that this syndrome also changed, but it is difficult to do. By way of a single suggestion, however, I would take the change in the male code of honor. For the dueling code was the clearest institutionalization of a male agressiveness that probably had its roots in childhood detachment. In the eighteenth century, those who opposed this code were also proponents of domesticity (the best example is *The Spectator*); and in the course of the nineteenth century, dueling disappeared—not, I would suggest, because the aristocracy had turned bourgeois, but because male aggression had lessened. If this was so, it is also likely that hysterical dependence among women declined, and that new possibilities for action and autonomy were opened for upper-class women. But be this all as it may, it is certain that aristocratic children after 1750 survived in unprecedented numbers and that they were better loved and cared for by their mothers. Taken together, these changes indicate that in the last generation of the old regime, English aristocratic children were being treated more nearly as the equals of adults. As grown men and women they may have missed the sweetness of life, but as children they had entered upon the pursuit of happiness.

Figure 6.1 *Portrait of Samuel Parr by G. Dawe. One of the two principal surrogate fathers whom Lord Dartmouth provided for his sons in the various experimental schools to which he sent them. Copyright photograph from the National Portrait Gallery, London. Reproduced by permission.*

VI

Fathers and Children

Patriarchal ideas arranged human beings in a hierarchy of rationality—men first, women second, and children last—and the hierarchy was maintained by varying degrees of separation between these groups. Domesticity threatened this hierarchy by requiring the constant and intimate association of all three groups, and it thereby also raised the possibility of their equality. Women, however, had less to lose by associating with children than did men, for men drew the line of full rationality between themselves and women. "Women," as Chesterfield put it, "are to be talked to as below men and above children." Consequently it was easier for a woman than for a man to dismiss as merely vain those who found the first book of Rousseau's *Emile* childish and thought themselves "lowered by so much attention to our childhood."[1] It will come, therefore, as no surprise that aristocratic

---

[1] Bonamy Dobrée, ed., *Letters of Chesterfield* (London: Eyre & Spottiswoode, 1932), 6 vol., **IV**, 1224; *Leinster*, **I**, 354.

237

men managed less well than their wives in the new atmosphere after 1750. Before 1750 men positively avoided their infant children. After 1750 their fear of children was moderated and some fathers began to take a close interest even in the first year of childhood. But fathers never managed to associate very closely with their daughters at any age, and they avoided their sons until they were about 7. They acted as they did for the same reason in both cases—a girl's education was conducted wholly by her mother, and boys were under women's care until they went away to school, so much so that for the first 4 or 5 years they were clothed in an adaptation of women's clothes.

The difference in the education of boys and girls after the age of 7 was founded on their supposed difference in rationality, and on the need to train boys to compete and to dominate. Boys were sent away to schools where, before 1750, they associated with groups of their peers from which almost all adult companionship—male or female—had been excluded. It was a training that probably produced a high degree of self-sufficiency. But this near total separation from their parents also probably engendered great hostility. It was a hostility acted out in the violence of school life, and it caused the revolts led by the adolescent boys against school hierarchies from which they were almost fully isolated. After 1750, aristocratic fathers, under the influence of domesticity, began to try to provide their sons with surrogate parents either by restructuring the great public schools or by sending them to small private schools. It probably lessened the severity of a boy's reaction to his separation from his parents,[2] and it is certainly the best evidence of the extent to which even aristocratic men were affected by the new currents of feeling. But the extent to which any man could associate closely with women and children was severely limited by the means by which masculine identity was forged. For separation from, and denigration of, women and children were crucial to the formation of a boy's gender identity in childhood and to the development of heterosexual behavior and the internalization of the homosexual taboo in adolescence.

---

[2]H. G. Hansburg, *Adolescent Separation Anxiety* (Springfield, Ill.: Charles C Thomas, 1972). This work applies attachment theory to adolescence by arguing that adolescents need to separate themselves from their parents as a means of forming adult identities, and yet cannot do without adult attachment figures. When they are separated from adults they are likely to lose self-love and be less concerned about intellectual life; they will often react with anger and violence; but they are likely to have a high degree of self-esteem and assertiveness. Institutionalized children suffer less from separation when provided with surrogate parents (see 8, 56–57, 60–63, 71–73, 75, 78, 95–98, 119, 124, 138).

The Male Role and Childrearing

At the beginning of the eighteenth century, men were prepared to say that nature had given the care of children to women as a means of balancing the power that men had because of their superior rationality. Lord Halifax told his daughter "that for the better economy of the world the men, who were to be the lawgivers, had the larger share of reason bestowed upon them," but that in compensation "the first part of our life is a good deal subjected to you in the nursery, where you reign without competition, and by that means have the advantage of giving the first impressions." Men were obliged to be abroad on public and private business; women, Lord Warrington wrote, were "by nature appointed to a more domestic life"; and therefore "the care and education of children, both with respect to their bodies and minds, is by nature given all along to the mother in a much greater proportion than to the father." But Halifax's book came out in 1688, Warrington's in 1739; and the generation's difference had changed the context of their remarks. Halifax told his daughter that "you may love your children without living in the nursery"; he warned her that it was ill-bred to make them the topic of her conversation; and he concluded that "though a woman of quality ought not to be less kind to them than mothers of the meanest rank are to theirs, yet she may distinguish herself in the manner, and avoid the coarse methods, which in women of a lower size might be more excusable." Warrington, on the other hand, wrote his book to persuade the world that a man should be able to divorce a woman who had not provided the proper degree of domesticity by morally supporting her husband and teaching her children to love him. Both men did agree, however, that mothers were especially charged with their daughters' education. Halifax wrote that boys should be left "to the father's more peculiar care," and told his daughter that she could "with the greater justice pretend to a more immediate jurisdiction over those of your own sex." For Halifax's world was very much one of distance and hostility between the sexes. Warrington simply said that there were some parts of a daughter's education that it "would be indecent for the father to have any regard to." And here he must have had puberty and adolescence in mind, when a boy would be safely away at school, but a girl would be at home with her parents.[3]

Before 1750 fathers were prepared to step in and assert their authority at what they considered crucial points in early childhood. They

---

[3] Lord Halifax, *Complete Works*, ed. by J. P. Kenyon (Baltimore: Penguin, 1969), 277–278, 290–291; George, Lord Warrington, *Considerations upon the Institution of Marriage* (London, 1739), 6–7, 22.

were especially inclined to do so when they might claim to have reason or expert opinion on their side. Fathers sometimes undertook to decide whether a child was to be nursed by a wet nurse or by his own mother or whether he was to be brought up entirely by hand, and when he was to be weaned. In this they were certainly encouraged by physicians who resented the exclusiveness of women in these matters. William Cadogan recommended that every father "have his child nursed under his own eye, to make use of his own reason and sense in superintending and directing the management of it; nor suffer it to be made one of the mysteries of the *Bona Dea*, from which men are to be excluded."[4]

There is a revealing correspondence in this regard between Lord and Lady Orrery. In the last week of March 1741, Orrery wrote to his wife, asking that she wean their infant daughter Kitty, before she came to him, for she would find that "Dr. Barry is of the opinion that she may well be weaned about May." A week later he repeated his request. Lady Orrery evidently protested, and in mid-April Orrery said he could not consent to her coming unless the child was weaned. Then he rolled out his full artillery: "Let me meet you as a husband, though I stay a month longer for the happiness. Consider what it is to be banished for so many months. Consider I love only you. Consider—oh! consider nothing at all but obey me. You promised it at marriage, I now put you to the execution of that promise. Dr. Barry will tell you that the girl has been suckled long enough: Believe him if you will not regard me, and wean her my dear, wean her." Orrery had his way, and his wife weaned the child at the end of May. But she did not cease, to his distress, to tell him of her fears. He could only reply in early June that "seriously Dr. B. told me a child ought not to be suckled too long—but I recall all I've said if she runs the least hazard." And lest she doubt his love in the midst of so strong an assertion of his authority, he assured her that he could not "bear to hurt our child." Expert opinion, the marriage vow, and much coaxing had given him his way over a mother's traditional views and instinct.[5]

Although a husband might on occasion intervene in his wife's arrangements for their children, her disappearance, whether from

---

[4]William Cadogan, *An Essay upon Nursing* (London, 1750), 28: cf. William Buchan, *Domestic Medicine* (London, 1722), 6.

[5]*Orrery Papers*, II, 162–167. William Pitt wrote in reply to a request of Dr. William Hunter that "I certainly wished to have continued Nurse Caruthers about my boy until he had been older, and more particularly at this time that he is every day cutting more teeth, but upon reading the account your letter gives of the melancholy situation of poor Lady Maynard, I could not hesitate in giving my consent to part with Nurse Caruthers" (J. M. Oppenheimer, *New Aspects of John and William Hunter* (New York: H. Schuman, 1946), 124).

death, divorce, or psychic withdrawal, left him helpless. As quickly as possible he farmed out his children to a grandmother, a sister, or a sister-in-law; or went through the tiring process of remarrying; or sent them off to school, sometimes girls as well as boys. There were women who thought this a natural response. Mrs. Delany said it was "indeed a sad thing for children to lose a mother; the wisest and best fathers cannot make up that loss to them. As women are designed by Providence to be more domestic, they are endowed with the proper *talents* and *patience* to train up their children—men have not the attention that is necessary for so great a work." But it is unlikely, especially before 1720, that many men regarded it as a great work. When Lady Mary Wortley Montagu's mother died (probably in childbirth) her father sent his four children to live with his mother, and Lady Mary later explained that he was a "young father, who, though naturally an honest man, was abandoned to his pleasures, and (like most of those of his quality) did not think himself obliged to be very attentive to his children's education." Lord Dorset, at his wife's death in 1691, actually made a settlement in which he gave his mother-in-law the custody of his daughter, and he sent his son to live with her.[6]

Men who started out with good intentions soon found that their interest waned. Lord Bridgewater, at his wife's death, told his mother-in-law that he had "no other thoughts but to tend my children," but his daughter was soon taken into her grandparents' household. Lady Bridgewater's sister, before her own death, with clearer eyes as to her husband's virtues, told him: "as to the children, pray get my mother, the Duchess of Marlborough to take care of the girls, and if I leave my boys too little to go to school—to be left to servants is very bad for children, and a man can't take the care of little children as a woman can." And she asked him not to be as "careless of the dear children as when you relied upon me to take care of them."[7] But if there was no grandmother available, a man had no choice but to send his children to school or to marry again, reluctant though he might be. It took Lady Cowper 6 months after her sister's death to persuade her brother-in-law to send his daughter to school, and when she succeeded, she promised to care for her niece in the holidays.[8] Lord Orrery, after his wife's death, told a lady that his little daughter was "the tender object of my heart; and whilst I remain single, cannot be placed so directly under my eye."

---

[6]Delany, III, 1861, 57; Robert Halsband, *The Life of Lady Mary Wortley Montagu* (New York: Oxford Univ. Press, 1960), xiii, 1–3; Kent R.O., U269.T 69/8, A9/3.
[7]David Green, *Sarah Duchess of Marlborough* (London: Collins, 1967), 193, 199.
[8]Delany, III, 1861, 383.

While this might indeed seem an argument for a second marriage, he knew that "the name of a stepmother is dreadful, and methinks bringing my poor child under the conduct of a mother-in-law will be like inoculating her, I shall mean it for her preservation, but perhaps destroy her."[9]

Lord Cowper's first wife did not die, but her disordered mind left her husband in much the same situation. His daughter was 8 and his son 3. He told his sister that the "education of young ladies is no small charge, but as I have her I am inclined to endeavour to breed her up as she ought to be and to keep her from idleness," for he thought idleness to be at the root of her mother's difficulties. His son he could get rid of more conveniently, for he intended to "inoculate him in the spring, and after that send him out that I may have no hand in spoiling him."[10]

The daughter of a woman who had been divorced for adultery was often sent to school, for her father was embittered and her mother hopelessly compromised. But in a more amiable separation, the duke of Grafton allowed his wife to keep with her their eldest son (who was 6) until he was put to school in a few months time, and he told her he was willing that during the holidays the boy should stay with her as "from his post" (he was secretary of state) "he would not find time to attend to his education." But Grafton kept with him the youngest child—the duchess's "poor little unknown one"—who was not quite 17 months old, and he hoped that she would think that "he makes fully up for keeping him, by giving up the other." She must be aware, he said, of "the light he must appear in without the care of anyone of his children." There was never any doubt, though, that the Graftons' only daughter would remain with her mother. This arrangement lasted till the duchess took a lover.[11]

Grafton claimed in 1765 that public opinion required a secretary of state to take care of an infant. But Lord Kingston in 1692 had farmed out his children for the sake of his pleasures. The difference was no doubt one of personality, but the times had also changed. For after 1750, Grafton was no isolated example. John Spencer went into the nursery to measure his son whenever he had the opportunity; and Henry Fox told a friend that "Charles is playing by me and surprizes me with the *eclat* of his beauty every time he looks at me."[12] Fathers might not take a very active role in the daily care of their small children, but some of them had become able to delight in their company.

---

[9]*Orrery Papers*, I, 147.
[10]Herts, R.O., Panshanger MSS, Bx 51, 22 November 1741.
[11]*Walpole*, XXXII, 33, XXII, 269; N.U.L., PwF 6374a.
[12]Earl of Ilchester, *Henry Fox* (London: John Murray, 1920), 2 vol., II, 175.

Nursery Life and Gender Identity

Adult men found the nursery years of life the most threatening, probably because it was the period in life in which males and females were most nearly treated alike. (It is, unfortunately, the least well documented period of the aristocratic life cycle: The child between 2 and 7 tends to disappear from the sources.) This is not to say, of course, that female children were as acceptable as male. On the contrary, a woman's joy in giving birth was complete only if the child was a boy. If she was old-fashioned there were traditional signs by which she might predict during pregnancy whether her child was to be a boy. Boys were considered healthy, strong, and cheerful and supposedly had a preference for lying on the right side; they caused their mothers to look and do likewise. A girl, of course, had all the opposite effects, and was in fact the left-handed gift of Providence.[13] When Lord Dartmouth's daughter was with child, his brother-in-law told him that he was glad to hear she was "so well and that your grandson is so brisk." But in case the guess proved wrong, Lord Aylesford added, "I hope you will have a plentiful issue of that happy pair; so if this should prove a girl, the next may make amends for the disappointment. I can assure Sir Walter that girls are apt to come before they are invited."[14] If a child did come out a girl, there was nothing left for her mother to do but apologize. Lady Strafford told her husband that she wished "at my heart I could wish you joy of a son, but as it has pleased God it is a daughter. I hope nevertheless that you will love it."[15] And Lady Buckinghamshire was "so miserable at having a third daughter that ... she fretted herself ill," and the following year, at the birth of a fourth daughter, the poor woman gave up and died.[16]

These attitudes probably had an unconscious effect in the attention paid to boys over girls with a result reflected in the mortality rates. For male mortality was somewhat lower than that of females until 1750; and between 1700 and 1750, when the male expectation of life at birth increased by about 4 years, that of females remained almost stationary.[17] The old attitudes and the new toward children in general, and toward girls in particular, were nicely illustrated in the duchess of Portland's disapproving remark when she was told that her sister-in-

---

[13]Pierre Dionis, *A General Treatise of Midwifery* (London, 1719), 114–115; Nicholas Culpeper, *A Directory for Midwives* (London, 1681), 103; N. Venette, *The Pleasures of Conjugal Love Explained* (London, 1740), 80–88.
[14]Staffs, R.O., D. 1778, I, ii, 583.
[15]B.L., Add. MSS, 22,226, f. 93.
[16]Coke, II, 229.
[17]Hollingsworth, 56–57, 70.

law's child had died at 3 weeks of age: that she was sorry that "lady Harriet has lost her child as I daresay she will be very much so, though I think since it was so young, and a *girl* it signifies but little to her."[18]

But it was usual to say that no difference was to be made between boys and girls in matters such as food, sleep, and toilet training, and there is no indication that there was any. In exercise and bathing there was a differentiation, for boys were encouraged to go out in the sun and to bathe in the open, whereas modesty and a regard for their complexions prevented girls from doing either. It is likely that the feeling that children were delicate and had to be hardened by the regimen of the nursery must have been the earliest inculcation in children that men were superior to women; for when Locke came to recommend that children be allowed to sleep a good deal, he said that "of all that looks soft and effeminate, nothing is to be more indulged children than sleep."[19]

In regard to discipline, it was sometimes said that there was a tendency to indulge an eldest son. But women seem to have been more conscious that it was the first child, whether male or female, who was likely to be spoiled. Ann Clavering said that her sister Lady Cowper "designs, before she has another little one, to spoil this girl, for that I think is often the fate of the first child."[20] But for this very reason Mrs. Boscawen thought it was better to begin with a girl, for a spoiled woman could do less harm than a man. "The first is generally tant soit peu enfant gate," she wrote; but she explained that "it is of much less consequence to spoil a girl than a boy, for he being armed with power will make his caprice be felt, whereas she being born to obey, will be reduced to submission sooner or later." Fathers like Halifax or Warrington took for granted that any parent with many children would prefer one to the others. They simply counseled that the knowledge be kept from the child. But they did not presume to say whether the child would be a girl or a boy, the eldest or a younger.[21]

Discipline in a nursery, whatever the slight differences as applied to different children, always had the same purpose. The child was not to be spoiled. His will was to be broken, and he was to be made obedient to his parents. The easiest way to accomplish this was to use a

---

[18]N.U.L., PwF 10548.

[19]*Locke*, 117, 131, 344–346; John Hill, *On the Management and Education of Children . . . by the Honourable Juliana-Susannah Seymour* (London, 1754), 66–83.

[20]James Nelson, *An Essay on the Government of Children* (London, 1763 ed.), 191; H. T. Dickinson, ed., *The Correspondence of Sir James Clavering* (Surtees Society, 1967), 8.

[21]*Delany*, **I**, 1862, 359–360; Halifax, *Complete Works*, 291; Henry, Lord Warrington, *Works* ed. by J. Delaheuze (London, 1694), 32–33.

child's natural awe (or fearfulness) to instill a sense of shame. When this was not enough, parents before 1750 resorted to various degrees of whipping, and after 1750, they were likely to stand a child in the corner.

At the beginning of the century, the behavior of children was often compared to that of the other subordinate classes in the patriarchal scheme. Since children were irrational like women, Locke declared that "shame in children has the same place that modesty has in women"; and since they were dependent, Bishop Fleetwood preached that they owed their parents "all external honour and civility"—their behavior was "to be submissive, dutiful, and mannerly, and such as becomes inferiors towards their betters." Children, like servants, were to be treated with a combination of love and discipline. "Children are to be governed neither wholly by love nor altogether by fear," Lord Warrington wrote for his sons' benefit; "for by a right temperature of both you may lead them which way you will." If a father was "easy and familiar," he won his children's love and devotion. But if he treated them with "too much awe," he risked losing "a great deal of pleasure and satisfaction that is to be had in children." But Warrington, true to his time, disapproved any public expression of family warmth: "Care is to be taken that before company they may know their distance."[22]

When a child proved obstinate, the final means of subduing him was whipping. This was, indeed, the only condition under which Locke approved of whipping. He was in general opposed to it as a short and lazy way of correction that taught a child to avoid pain but did nothing to instill a sense of shame. But when obstinacy made whipping necessary, it could be a lengthy process. He told of a mother who beat her daughter eight times in one morning "till she had bent her mind"; and he explained that "whenever you come to that extremity, 'tis not enough to whip, or beat them, you must do it ... till with submission and patience they yield to the correction, which you shall best discover by their crying, and their ceasing from it upon your bidding."[23]

But children were also whipped under less extraordinary conditions. Mrs. Boscawen wrote to her husband when he was at sea that their younger son had "not forgot the whipping. He says he was a naughty boy in coats, but now he is a man he's sure Papa won't whip him." Mrs. Boscawen did not hesitate to whip the boy herself, nor to use the threat of a whipping, as when she recounted that "today he

---

[22]Locke, 155; William Fleetwood, *The Relative Duties of Parents and Children* (London, 1705), 9; Warrington, *Works*, 32 (children), 26 (servants).
[23]Locke, 148–150, 177–179, 216, 346.

would not eat milk for breakfast, but the rod and I went to breakfast with him, and though we did not come into action nor anything like it, yet the bottom of the porringer was finally revealed."[24] Lord Cowper assured his wife that "the presence of one of us here is necessary in respect of the children; your sister is prudent, but they don't stand in awe of her, and there was no living till the birch was planted in my room, where some little action has diminished it."[25]

There was the occasional story of cruelty: Lady Abergavenny who "killed her own child, about seven years old; she having been a great while whipping it, my Lord being grieved to hear it cry so terribly, went into the room to beg for it, and she threw it with such force to the ground she broke the skull." And there was impatient and inefficient correction: Lady Bristol was told that all her children were well "and very good except Felly, who was grown very naughty ... that I was obliged to whip him before I was one hour in the house; but I doubt he found it in so superficial a manner that he'll be a little better for it; his eyes are so like yours that whenever they weep whatsoever is then asked, must of course be complied with."[26] But all these incidents occurred before mid-century, and it is probable that as the century wore on, beating was used less and less. Certainly a tender mother like Lady Kildare, who was in agonies when a friend told her teasingly that her son had been whipped at school, would not herself have whipped her children.[27]

After 1750 parents were still concerned about spoiling their children. Mrs. Delany's niece worried in 1772 that her aunt might think she was spoiling her child. Mrs. Delany reassured her, but then asserted that "an early obedience saves infinite chagrin to parents and children." It could be arranged "so cautiously as hardly to be perceived by the little pupil till it gains such ground as to become a habit." Even so, Mrs. Delany had told her sister 20 years before that "a perverse, injudicious manner of contradicting and thwarting them, and very severe correction for trifles, does them I believe almost as much harm as a universal indulgence."[28] It was just such an indulgence that the duchess of Portland feared when she told her husband that their eldest

---

[24]Cecil Aspinall-Oglander, *Admiral's Wife* (London: Longmans, 1940), 123–124, 161, 179.

[25]John, Lord Campbell, *Lives of the Lord Chancellors* (Philadelphia: Univ. of Pennsylvania Press, 1851), 7 vol., **IV**, 312.

[26]J. J. Cartwright, ed., *The Wentworth Papers* (London: Wyman, 1883), 243; *Bristol Letterbook*, **II**, 128.

[27]Lady Sarah Pennington, *Letters on Different Subjects* (London, 1767), 4 vol., **IV**, 22; *Leinster*, **I**, 75, 84, 91.

[28]*Delany*, **I**, 1862, 468, **II** 1861, 618.

son at 10 "from not having been treated so much as a child, as he ought to have been, has none of the timidity and backwardness so amiable in youth, and which all would have, if properly brought up, for I am well convinced that it was designed by Providence that shyness in our first years should be a check upon our actions till we had gained experience and judgment."[29]

But aristocratic attitudes toward children's fearfulness was becoming more empathetic, and there was perhaps a growing reluctance to use fear as a means of discipline. Lady Louisa Connolly explained in 1776 that her brother the duke of Richmond because he was not used to children "don't understand how very easily they are made afraid of one. I find nothing so difficult as directing children, and yet prevent the great awe they naturally have of those that care for them; unless you quite spoil them, all children have a great deal of it."[30] This more empathetic attitude may explain why Bishop Fleetwood in his day should have thought aristocratic children more obedient and less rude than those of meaner people who were treated with a great and dangerous liberty, whereas Samuel Richardson, a generation later, should have denounced aristocrats as badly educated because they did not have their wills broken in childhood.[31] Aristocrats did not in fact give up instilling awe in children or trying to keep them from being spoiled. But by 1750 they were pursuing these ends in a domestic rather than a patriarchal context.

It was under such conditions that mothers turned from whipping to standing a child in a corner. Lady Caroline told her husband that "yesterday [he] was so naughty, I was obliged to make him stand in a corner, and hide his face until he grew good again which was in about a minute; 'tis such a good natured little rogue that spoiling him can't do much harm." And when Mrs. Pinckney told the Princess of Wales that "Princess Caroline (the youngest of all) was very humble," the Princess of Wales "said she was a pretty good girl; then addressed her. Have you ever been in the corner, my queen? No ma'am, says the pretty creature, never in the corner. I'm afraid you have, says the Princess upon which Prince Frederick says, No ma'am she was never in the corner but that sister has."[32]

Aristocratic parents thought they had identified two contradictory characteristics in children. Children were willful (or irrational), and

[29]N.U.L., PwF 10708.
[30]*Leinster*, III, 233.
[31]Fleetwood, *Relative Duties*, 14–15; Samuel Richardson, *Pamela*, 1740 (Norton ed.), 254, 470.
[32]B.L., Add. MSS, 51,414, f. 19; H. H. Ravenel, *Eliza Pinckney* (New York: Scribner's, 1896), 150.

they were naturally fearful. Parents were urged to respond to these characteristics with a combination of love and the withdrawal of love (or with fear). And the aim of this discipline was to prepare them for the disappointments of the adult world: "For if they never meet with contradiction," Mrs. Delany said, "till they are of age to engage in the great concerns of life, how will they be able to sustain the contradictions, disappointments and mortifications they must encounter in the world."[33] The adult fear of spoiling children was clearly connected to a pessimistic evaluation of the world. If a child was not encouraged to depend on the constant good will of his parents, he would not be disappointed when the good will of his adult companions was not forthcoming. But ironically enough, children who are disciplined through the withdrawal of affection are, according to modern studies, very likely to be dependent and anxious about separation.[34] It is unlikely, therefore, that aristocratic self-reliance was formed in the nursery. It is much more likely that it was a result of the experience of institutional separation in the schools. And since women did not go to school, they were likely to be more dependent than men. Here was another reason for a man to avoid the nursery. It was the kingdom of the dependent ruled by the dependent. It was the rule of the irrational by the irrational, in an age when reason was a code name for self-reliance. It is no wonder that Locke advocated shame in children only as a "proper guide and encouragement of children till they grow able to judge for themselves, and to find out what is right by their own reason."[35] And neither he nor almost any eighteenth-century man would have thought women notable for their reason.

Brothers and sisters in the nursery were encouraged to be decent to each other. Parents were anxious to avoid making an older child jealous of a newborn sibling. It was here that the roots of sibling solidarity were planted. But because of sexual roles it was easier to interest a sister in her brother than the other way round. Lord Harcourt told his own sister that his 5-year-old son, after the birth of a second sister (the other had come when he was 2), was beginning "to be a little more reconciled to his sister; but he says that his mama and sister are very lazy to lay a bed so much as they do in this fine weather."[36] A mother could worry about jealousy even in a much older child. Louisa Bunbury had been an only child for 14 years when her mother remarried and had a son. Her mother was relieved to say that "Louisa is doatingly fond of it, which

[33] *Delany*, II, 1861, 618.
[34] John Bowlby, *Attachment and Loss* (London: Hogarth Press, 1969–1973), 2 vol., II, 237–244.
[35] *Locke*, 156.
[36] E. W. Harcourt, ed., *The Harcourt Papers* (Oxford, 1876–1905), 12 vol., III, 35.

you may guess is a very pleasant circumstance, for as I am not one of those who know how to nurse and make a fuss with a little child, she is always pressing me to attend more to it, and wondering how I can be so little taken up with it, which you see entirely precludes all idea of jealousy...which you know people are but too apt to create in young minds where it would never come of itself."[37] It is a case in which a woman of great psychological penetration had used a daughter's interest in babies to get through well what might have been a difficult situation. And the same interest could be made use of in a much younger child. Lady Harriet Somerset at the age of 2 "assumed a higher office, that of comforter to her little brother, Edward," who at 10 months was being weaned. Mrs. Boscawen, in what she called a "grandmother's story," reported that Harriet "calls him 'mine boy,' and is most carefully occupied to amuse him under his misfortunes, charging her own nurse to 'take care of mine boy!' "[38]

Brothers and sisters were punished for striking each other. Mrs. Delany approved when her sister corrected her daughter for hurting her brother, but she also said that she did not "suppose the dear child meant the harm she did; but if children are not put upon their guard, accidents might prove fatal." On another occasion Mrs. Delany summarized this point of view by remarking that "next to inculcating right religious principles the most material work is to make brothers and sisters *perfectly well-bred towards* one another. I see many sad disagreements arise in many families merely from want of *good* manners." Children were discouraged from telling tales on each other. Locke thought that they should be trained to give their possessions freely to each other, for this would make "brothers and sisters kinder and civiller to one another, and consequently to others." He added that after such generosity had been established, parents might proceed to inculcate that stricter sense of property upon which a child would ultimately found his sense of justice; and in these two ideas he was followed by others.[39]

Although Mrs. Delany declared the religious education of children "the most material work," it is practically the hardest kind of informa-

---

[37]Lady Ilchester and Lord Stavordale, *The Life and Letters of Lady Sarah Lennox 1745–1826* (London: John Murray, 1902), 344. It is perhaps worth noting that in an attempt to apply Lloyd deMause's grand scheme of Whiggish pessimism to the eighteenth century, B. W. Lorence entirely misinterprets Lady Sarah's letter (see B. W. Lorence, "Parents and Children in Eighteenth-Century Europe," *History of Childhood Quarterly*, II, 1974, 11–12).
[38]*Delany*, II, 1862, 324.
[39]*Ibid.*, III, 1861, 34, 58; *Locke*, 213–215; Nelson, *Government of Children*, 224; William Giles, *A Treatise on Marriage* (London, 1771), 88.

tion to come upon. Mothers were expected by some to instruct their children. Lady Dalkeith disturbed her sister because she "greatly neglects the most material part of her children's education: the instructing them in the principles of religion." But Lady Dalkeith seemed "unaccountable" in other respects. She saw her children only 1 hour in the day although she was fond of them. But whoever taught the children religion, it is likely that they used something of the method recommended by Anthony Heasel for the use of nurserymaids. When children began to speak it was time to teach them short prayers and to read a little to them each day from the Bible so that "they will become in love with religion, even before they understand it." Before they began to learn to read and write, they could memorize a verse at a time from the Psalms. It is likely that for boys this would be the only time of intense religious training, for the public schools had a bad reputation in this regard. And it is also possible that as a girl's entire education was conducted by her mother, this would account, in part, for the greater religiosity of women.[40]

Boys and girls were taught to read together and at the same age. Mary Astell pointed out that they showed no difference in capacity at this task, and that the differences in learning in later life was due to boys' going away to school at 6 or 7. She claimed that children began to be taught to read once they could talk; and this was what Locke recommended.[41] Since a child who could talk easily at 18 months was thought exceptional, and since some children had only begun to say "yes" and "no" plainly at 24 months,[42] it is unlikely that teaching began before the end of the second year. Actual examples put it in the third.[43] The skills of reading and writing were probably fully acquired by 7 or 8. Locke advised that reading be made a game and not a chore. To that end, boxes of letters or cubes with the alphabet on them were used, and both parents seem to have taken a hand in the teaching. The eldest brother was encouraged to teach his younger siblings, and they, in turn, began to read by emulation. Locke, at the beginning of our period, complained of a paucity of books for children, but as part of the growing interest in childhood, there appeared about mid-century the

---

[40]Coke, II, 153, 170–171, 181; Anthony Heasel, *The Servants Book of Knowledge* (London, 1773), 59–60.

[41]Mary Astell, *An Essay in Defence of the Female Sex* (London, 1697), 36–37; Locke, 174, 255–260.

[42]Examples of speaking: Coke, II, 429, III, 82; Joan Wake and D. C. Webster, eds., *The Letters of Daniel Eaton* (Northamptonshire Record Society, 1971), 101.

[43]Examples of reading: Joyce Godber, *The Marchioness Grey of Wrest Park* (Bedfordshire Historical Records Society, 1968), 115; Joan Wake, *The Brudenells of Deene* (London: Cassell, 1953), 226; Aspinall-Oglander, *Wife*, 92.

beginnings of a children's literature.[44] But this joint education of boys and girls did not last long, for boys sometime between 7 and 11 were taken away from their weeping mothers and sent to school by their fathers, while their sisters remained at home to be educated by their mothers.[45]

But before boys were delivered by their schools from the religiosity, dependence, and relative equality of the nursery which they found so threatening as men, there was an earlier symbolic differentiation from their mothers and their sisters. This was a boy's breeching. For all children were dressed at a year in what was called a coat. It looked rather like a woman's dress, except that boys had theirs cut a little shorter than girls. A boy remained in this coat until some time between his third and his fifth birthday (or 1 to 3 years after his gender identity would have been fully formed) when he was put into a man's breeches.[46] It was a transition that a woman was likely to resist, but one that her sons and her husband would urge upon her. "For you must remember," Locke wrote, "that children affect to be men earlier than is thought, and they love breeches, not for their cut, or ease, but because the having them is a mark of a step towards manhood."[47] As with weaning, women were inclined to postpone the step: The duchess of Portland told her husband a month before their son's third birthday that she could "by no means agree with you that William would look as well in breeches as in petticoats."[48] The 5-year-old son of Lady Lincoln was driven to take matters into his own hands. Knowing that his father approved the change and that his mother had promised him his breeches but that in a hot July they still had not arrived, he "contrived to make it as convenient as possible by cutting his frock and petticoats to a kind of Highland standard, that his knees and thighs might have as little embarrassment as possible." He declared "he will be a girl no longer"; he thought it "an indignity to remain on the same footing with little John," which was what he called his younger brother; and in his parents' absence he began to be masterful with the servants, for "there not being quite so much salad as was wanted, he turned about of his own accord to the underbutler and told him that 'as his Pappa and

---

[44]J. Harvey Darton, *Children's Books in England* (Cambridge: University Press, 1958); Percy Muir, *English Children's Books 1660–1900* (London: B. T. Batsford, 1954).

[45]Weeping mothers: Lady Granville, *Lord Granville Leveson Gower* (New York: Dutton, 1916), 2 vol., I, 3–4, *Leinster*, I, 28, 60. See also Stephen Penton, *The Guardian's Instruction* (London, 1688), 68.

[46]Phillis Cunnington and Anne Buck, *Children's Costume in England* (New York: Barnes & Noble, 1965), 108–113.

[47]Locke, 172, cf. 181.

[48]N.U.L., PwF 10708.

Mamma were well served when they were here, he saw no reason why there should be any neglect in their absence.' "[49] This boy was almost ready to go to school. For manliness, adult status, and the power to command all finally required separation from women.

Parental Roles and School Reform

Even after 1750 the aristocratic child experienced a number of separations before he went away to school. For parents who lived in the world were obliged to go away, and it was evidently thought imprudent to take young children to Bath or London. But it was a necessity whose consequences could leave a mother uncomfortable. Lady Grantham was disturbed to find that her children were shy of their parents when they returned from being away.[50] But other parents seem to have reacted as if separation were a matter of course. Lady Stamford in 1781 spent the summer with her husband and their 9 children in the country. At the end of August the two eldest sons left to go to school, and at the beginning of November the Stamfords moved on to their second house where, as she told her brother, they intended to remain "three or four days to settle our four younger children, then to proceed with the three eldest girls to Bath."[51]

But despite earlier separations, going away to school was an unprecedented move for a boy. It did not become easier with time, but it came to be stoically accepted. Lady Gower told her son that "all your sisters were sorry to part with you, but I believe that little Sue found out that I, of all the family, felt most like herself, so she shed tears with me in the powdering-room without restraint." James Brudenell wrote to his brother that he was "glad to hear your son George is so well settled at school. If he follows the example of his father and two uncles, he will cry heartily every time he returns to school from home, but that will do him no harm. His tears will soon be dried up when he gets among his play-fellows."[52] Once a boy went away to school, it was his peers and not his family who were the center of his ordinary life. This was an experience ordinarily limited to boys. It was certainly the part of childhood that most clearly separated boys from girls. And it was the point at which fathers forcefully entered into the socialization of their sons.

---

[49]N.U.L., NeC 3130–3132. See also Godber, *Marchioness Grey*, p. 115; Aspinall-Oglander, *Wife*, 56; Kent R.O.: U 49. F 4/1: 18 March 1765; *Leinster*, III, 530.
[50]Godber, *Marchioness Grey*, 114.
[51]N.U.L., PwF 4624, 4632.
[52]Granville, *Leveson Gower*, I, 3–4; Wake, *Brudenells*, 292–293.

The aim of a boy's education was to teach him to compete and to win by being best. It was a business that could not begin too soon. Lord Chesterfield told his son that "now that you are past nine years old, you have no time to lose." Its aim was perfection. "I'm so strongly inclined to think you perfect as I wish to see you," Lord Hervey told one son. And he later said to his wife about another that he had "a more than ordinary passion to see [the first fruit of our love] perfectly accomplished, and thereby first among mankind too." The means of "this perfection which you promise me to aim at" were, as Lord Chesterfield said, "*first* to do your duty towards God and man; without which, everything else signifies nothing; *secondly* to acquire a great knowledge; without which you will be a very contemptible man, though you may be a very honest man; and, *lastly* to be very well bred; without which, you will be a very disagreeable unpleasing man, though you should be an honest and a learned one." To attain those three ends, a boy needed to be attentive and competitive. "I know many old people," Chesterfield said, "who thought they have lived long in the world, are but children still as to their knowledge of it, from their levity and inattention." To grow old quickly was a virtue—for "considering the care I have taken of you, you ought to be at thirteen what other boys are at sixteen."[53]

If any of this should seem a father's special instructions to a bastard with his way to make in the world, there is the pious Lord Dartmouth's comment to his eldest son that he had "been looking into Lord Chesterfield's *Letters* since you left us, and I find so many wise, so many excellent things on the subject of *attention*. "You know," he continued, "how anxiously I want you to be—everything that can be desired in a man and a Christian. I want you to have competent, useful and accurate knowledge; polite good humoured and engaging manners; and above all, a heart faithfully and sincerely devoted to God."[54] Dartmouth was impressed by the stress on attention, though he reordered its aims. The duchess of Portland was as keen on competition as Chesterfield. She asked her elder son to "tell Neddy I rejoice in his advancement and dare say his emulation will increase every day." But Chesterfield was more fortunate than the duchess, for he could appeal to his own example and say that "when I was your age, I should have been ashamed if any boy of that age had learned his book better, or played at any play better than I did; and I would not have rested a moment till I had got

---

[53]Dobrée, ed., *Letters of Chesterfield*, II, 454, 505, III, 605, 741, II, 504, cf. III, 696, 698; *Bristol Letterbook*, I, 374, II, 5.
[54]Staffs. R.O., D. 1778 v. 853.

before him."⁵⁵ To an outsider like Burke, aristocratic success might seem all uncontending ease and the unbought grace of life. But aristocratic parents encouraged no such delusions in their children.

There was no complete agreement among parents as to whether a private or a public education best answered the ends they wished to encompass. One writer defined the difference between the two systems: "By what I call public, I mean an education in a school where all comers are admitted; and by a private one, an education in the house, and under the eye of the parent, or in a boarding-school where none but boarders are received."⁵⁶ Education at home, when it occurred, was limited to eldest sons, and after 1720 it seems to have disappeared almost entirely. A private school could vary in numbers of students from 10 to 100. The great public schools like Eton and Westminster had enrollments of 300 to 500. Most aristocratic parents sent their sons at some point to a public school. Of the aristocratic families 25% sent all their sons to Westminster School with utter regularity; another 24% sent all their sons to Eton; and a further 8% oscillated between the two. The 16% who sent their sons to lesser public schools like Winchester, Harrow, Rugby, and Bury St. Edmunds were almost never faithful to only one of them and usually made use at some point of Eton or Westminster. This accounts for nearly 75% of all aristocratic families. Of the remainder, a very few were Roman Catholic and sent their sons abroad; others, considering the imperfections of the school registers, may in fact have been at a public school; but the 20% that is left must either have educated their sons at home or at a private school.⁵⁷

It was agreed that no one could educate a boy so well as his father, but it was clear that no father would. Lord Thurlow told Lady Gower with regard to her son's education that "though as you know I have always been ready to believe that nobody *could teach* him as well as my Lord, I have never been much disposed to think that he would."⁵⁸ It was something, of course, that mothers did regularly for their daughters, with the help of visiting masters or a governess. But no

---

⁵⁵N.U.L., PwF 753; Dobrée, ed., Letters of Chesterfield, II, 431.

⁵⁶John Clarke, An Essay upon the Education of Youth in Grammar Schools (Dublin, 1736), 97. An account of the debate over private versus public education is in G. C. Brauer, The Education of a Gentleman (New York: Bookman, 1959), Chap. 7.

⁵⁷The registers are: G. E. Russell Barker and A. H. Stenning, The Record of Old Westminsters, (London: Westminster School, 1928); 2 vol ; R. A. Austen-Leigh, The Eton College Register 1698–1752 (Eton: Spottiswoode, 1927); id., The Eton College Register 1753–1790 (Eton: Spottiswoode, 1921); G. A. Solly, Rugby School Registers: 1 April 1675–October 1857 (Rugby: George Over, 1933); S. H. A. Hervey, Biographical List of Boys... Bury St. Edmunds from 1550 to 1900 (Bury St. Edmunds: Paul and Mathew, 1908); W. T. J. Gunn, The Harrow School Register 1571–1800 (London: Longman, 1934); the names for Winchester are culled from a variety of references.

⁵⁸Granville, Leveson Gower, I, 2.

matter what help was hired, the principal responsibility was the mother's; her conversation was her daughter's real education; and when one sister fretted to another that her daughters were missing the polish of London's drawing and dancing masters, she was told that it was a vulgar error to imagine that "anything your girls could learn of their masters would be half so much advantage to them as being with Louisa and you in that sort of quiet way you seem settled in at Castletown. I should think nothing so desireable for a girl."[59]

When a boy was educated at home, the principal responsibility fell to a tutor. Mothers preferred to have a clergyman, from the notion, as one put it, that "the profession of divinity is generally a restraint upon the vivacity of youth."[60] Men, on the other hand, preferred another kind of tutor, and the courts once declared that the tutor chosen by his mother for the earl of Shaftesbury "might be a good scholar, and a pious man, and yet it would not necessarily follow, that he was a proper governor to attend the young Earl to Court, or to noble families, or at the exercises of dancing and riding, which it was fit his Lordship should be acquainted with."[61] Such a man would be unlikely to be able, as Locke said, to give his pupil that good breeding "which sets a gloss upon all his other qualities, and renders them useful to him, in procuring him the esteem and good will of all that he comes near." But whoever the tutor was, mothers like Lady Sunderland were prone to interfere; the boy was likely to have no company his own age; and the servants probably played too great a role in his life.[62]

When a boy was educated at home, it was usually because he was the heir. Lord Cardigan was taught at home and then went up to Oxford in 1725 when he was 13, but his three younger brothers were sent to Winchester. Similarly, Lord Bristol educated his eldest son at home and at Cambridge, but sent all the younger ones to school. In both these families, the eldest son was sent to school in the next generation.[63] By 1735 it was something of an anomaly when the duke of Somerset de-

---

[59]*Leinster*, I, 355. For governesses and masters, *ibid.*, I, 483, II, 187–188, III, 221; William Gilpin, *Memoirs*, ed. by W. Jackson (Cumberland and Westmoreland Antiquarian and Archaeological Society, 1879), 118–119. See also *Lady Mary*, II, 428: "The education and disposal of four girls is employment for a whole life." Mothers often gave daughters their lessons in the morning. And some aristocratic women had great reputations as educators (Mary Lepel, *Letters* (London, 1821), 88; Ilchester and Stavordale, *Lady Sarah*, 236, 270, 272, 354).

[60]B.L., Add. MSS, 35,376, f. 285.

[61]S. C. Cox, *Reports of Cases . . . in . . . Chancery . . . Collected by William Peere Williams* (London, 1826), 3 vol., I, 106.

[62]Locke, 190 ff.; J. P. Kenyon, *Robert Spencer, Earl of Sunderland, 1641–1702* (London: Longmans, 1958), 20; cf. *Leinster*, I, 514; Brauer, *Education*, 215–216; Clarke, *Grammar Schools*, 103.

[63]Wake, *Brudenells*, 273, 255; *Bristol Diary*, 99 et passim.

cided to educate his only son at home. The duke (who was born in 1684) had himself been educated at home and then sent to the university when he was 13. But John Cowslade, who was brought into the household to lessen the isolation of the duke's son, later recalled that "Lord Beauchamp's way of life was very contracted; all the other boys of his rank were at school." For by 1720, private domestic education had pretty much disappeared, and the heir was being educated like his younger brothers.[64]

The great schools preferred by the majority of aristocrats were criticized throughout the century on a number of grounds. Some fathers exerted themselves to force change on the schools, but the changes were not made permanent until Thomas Arnold formed them into a system in the early nineteenth century. In this the English were quite unlike the French. By 1690 aristocratic schools in France had been conducted for some time on principles that were only sporadically introduced in eighteenth-century England. In the schools of the Jesuits and those of Port Royal, a new idea of childhood had been institutionalized. Children were weak and innocent. It was the task of rational men to protect them from pollution by life, and particularly from adult sexuality. They were to be strengthened by the development of their character and reason. They were not to be left to servants nor were they to be pampered. At school, they were not left alone, and their modesty was protected by separate beds and decency in conversation and reading. The school was small; there was a master for each class; and each class had its own room. Students came from a single social class. Masters were morally responsible for their pupils. Pupils lodged in houses where a master oversaw their morals as well as their lessons. The child was secluded from his family and from society at large, and in his school was molded on the pattern of an ideal human type.[65] Each of these principles had their advocates in England. Many of them were realized for a time in one of the great continuing public schools or in one of the more emphemeral private schools. But the system as a whole was never introduced, and this is curious. For the English aristocracy was certainly more forward than the French in adopting a new system of caring for infants. It may be that in England the absence of organized

---

[64]Hertford, 15, 93, 97. Another example of the change after 1720: Earl of March, *A Duke and His Friends* (London: Hutchinson, 1911), 2 vol., I, 34–37, II, 449, 691–694, 706. It is difficult to know what Nicholas Hans means when he says that one-fourth of the sons of peers were educated at home: I would doubt this for any period between 1690 and 1780 (*New Trends in Education in the Eighteenth Century* (London: Routledge & Kegan Paul, 1951), 20–29).

[65]Philippe Ariès, *Centuries of Childhood*, trans. by Robert Baldick (New York: Vintage Books, 1965), 113–119, 173–174, 182–186, 205, 253–254, 276–285.

bodies of schoolmasters living under a religious rule accounts for the failure to change the school system. Or it may have been that English religion was more confident that the family was the ideal agency of moral formation than was French Catholicism with its Tridentine suspicion of domestic and familial religion.[66] Vicesimus Knox certainly wrote that "instruction in religious and moral principles ought to come from a parent. For this reason it is, perhaps, that in many schools there has been no provision for it, and that boys have been well acquainted with the classics, and at the same time ignorant of the most obvious doctrines of religion."[67]

By 1690 the English public schools had become places where boys associated only with each other without any adult companionship or supervision outside of the hours of class. Cut off from their parents and ignored by their masters, the boys turned hostile and vented their feelings in violence against each other, in attacks on adults, and in organized rebellions against their masters. At Westminster there were too few assistant masters to adequately teach the boys, and the formidable headmaster Busby (who set a pattern of sadistic violence that was followed for another hundred years) had from avarice taken more sons of gentlemen than he could manage in his own house. There were so many holidays begged by visitors to the school that often half the week or more was spent in idleness and "all manner of vice" crept in to fill the time. Boys were able to play truant for over a week without anyone noticing. The bigger boys tyrannized the smaller, "sending gentlemen's sons on their errands to fetch them strong drink," "sometimes flinging them on the ground, dragging them by the hair, treading them under foot, only to show their authority," and demanding money from them as well. All this, it was said, not only taught "lads of generous education to be base and servile spirits, but also shows children the method of ill husbandry and running into debt." The boys had taken to wandering about at night since they were not supervised, and Knipe, the assistant master, had "quite ruined that school by his neglect to lie in the College."[68] This state of anarchy did not last, but the violent temper of the boys remained throughout the century. There were several attempted and one successful rebellion under Samuel Smith in his 24 years as headmaster after 1764. Violence against any outsider who strayed into the territory was endemic. In 1722, 3 lives were lost in a battle against boys from other schools who had been aided by some

[66]John Bossy, "The Counter-Reformation and the People of Catholic Europe," *Past & Present*, No. 47.

[67]Vicesimus Knox, *Liberal Education* (London, 1785 ed.), 357.

[68]J. D. Carleton, *Westminster School* (London: Rupert Hart-Dans, 1965), 17–20, 23 n. 10, 33.

hackney coachmen. And in 1779, 6 boys were tried and sentenced for assaulting a man who they had beaten and wounded after theatening to "rip him up" if he would not kneel down and ask their pardon.[69]

Conditions at other schools were no different. Lord Ashley complained that although his brother had spent 7 years at Winchester, he could not construe a Latin sentence. Instead he had learned to drink. The masters, who apparently did not teach, were indulgent, and at a later date allowed the boys to keep horses and dogs. Rugby had its rebellions. But it was Eton that was the home of organized rebellion.[70]

There were serious outbreaks at Eton in 1729, 1743, 1768 and 1783, not to speak of lesser attempts. In 1729 the school was described as being in "a state of anarchy," and the headmaster's weakness was blamed.[71] In 1743, when there was another rebellion, the master was blamed for not punishing a son of Lord Cholmondeley who "was an equal aggressor but being of more quality has got his pardon."[72] The rebellions of 1768 and 1783 are better described, and in both cases it is clear that the source of trouble lay in the feeling of the older adolescents that they should not be subject to the same discipline as the younger boys.[73] At the end of the rebellion in 1768 George Grenville, whose son had been one of the leaders, proposed a series of reforms which show that he was acutely aware of the psychological difficulties that grew out of the separation of adolescents from all adult companionship. He argued that boys in the sixth form "must be treated with that regard to their manliness as will pleasingly distinguish them from lesser boys; yet considering their youth, there must be bounds to the distinctions and indulgences." These boys should stand and take off their hats to the provost in church or in school, but not at a distance. They should help in the discipline of the younger boys and be allowed greater freedom of movement outside the school. They should dine at the masters' table so "that they may gradually associate with men, and be above combining in mischief with lower boys." And once a month or more they might meet with the masters for 2 hours "in a clublike sociable manner." Grenville concluded that parents on their part could help by not giving their sons too much money and by inculcating

[69]John Sargeaunt, *Annals of Westminster School* (London: Methuen, 1898), 200; *The London Journal*, 7 July 1722.

[70]Benjamin Rand, *Life ... of Shaftesbury* (London: Swan Sonnenschein, 1900), 281–283; Sir William Fraser, *The Sutherland Book* (Edinburgh, 1892), 3 vol., I, 438–439; W. H. D. Rouse, *A History of Rugby School* (London: Duckworth, 1898), 150, 182 ff.

[71]Bristol Letterbook, III, 49–50.

[72]Herts. R.O., Panshanger MSS, Box 51, I, 53/13.

[73]H. C. Maxwell Lyte, *A History of Eton College (1440–1898)* (London: Macmillan, 1899), 302, 339, 346–349, 358–359.

"principles of obedience and reverence to the rules and governors of the school; that by early learning to conform, they may hereafter better know how to direct." Whether his ideas had any effect is difficult to say—the next rebellion, at any rate, was not as grave.[74]

The rebellions continued into the early nineteenth century, with the masters returning violence for violence. Thomas Keate, the last of the unreformed headmasters, was notorious for the evident sadistic pleasure he took in flogging.[75] Men who endured brutal schooldays thought it only right that their sons should too. A clergyman wrote to a friend that he had heard that his friend's 7-year-old son had just entered Eton and "been victorious in three engagements." "I pray God he may be so in every concern in life," he piously continued. "However, he is blooded, and you have entered him charmingly. The misery of a private education is not to be expressed."[76] Individuals were blooded at their first hunt, and boys were to be similarly initiated into their first venture into male society. Boys also learned to endure their floggings and to be amusing about them. "Dear little Lord Fordwicke," who was 11, entertained his relations on his summer holiday by "acting the second master's flogging the boys, he says Mr. Dampier has a much heavier hand than the headmaster. He likes Eton extremely well."[77] These school floggings sometimes could not be given up in adult life. The old roué in Shadwell's *The Virtuoso* explains why he has come to the brothel to be flogged: "I got so used to it at Westminster School that I have not been able to do without it since."[78] These places of violent peer competition no doubt produced men of independent self-assurance, but perhaps they also produced men of impoverished hearts, with little love even for themselves.

There is little evidence, however, that parents were disturbed by the violence of the schools. They worried instead that their sons would be introduced to sex at too early an age or that they would become ill, for sexual innocence and good health were the qualities of a happy child. Lady Holland remarked that her son Harry was "well and happy though at school," but she hoped "he won't lose his health and perfect innocence."[79] But it was notorious that the morals of a public school were bad. Boys were introduced to masturbation; they could be drawn

---

[74]C. F. Mullett, "George Grenville and Eton in the 1760's," *Huntington Library Quarterly*, V, 1941–1942, 379–381.

[75]Maxwell Lyte, *Eton*, 384–391, 402–409.

[76]R. W. Ketton-Cremer, *Felbrigg* (London: Rupert Hart-Davis, 1962), 160.

[77]Herts. R.O., Panshanger MSS, Box 51, 57/53.

[78]Ivan Bloch, *Sexual Life in England Past and Present* (London: Francis Aldor 1938), 364.

[79]*Leinster*, I, 514.

into homosexual behavior; and once they were past 14 or 15 they were likely to run after whores.

In the late seventeenth century Lord Rochester had sung of schoolboys' "frigging" as universal and unending. But by the first decades of the eighteenth century, masturbation was being denounced as a moral and physical evil that produced a dire train of consequences. Schoolmasters were told to have "a strict eye over their scholars (amongst whom nothing is more common than the commission of this vile sin, the older boys teaching it the younger, as soon ever they arrive to years of puberty), tell them the heinousness of the sin, and give suitable correction to the offenders therein, and shame them before their schoolfellows for it."[80] Teachers were recommended to keep their students occupied, for "labour and employment brings down the powers of the body and dries up the springs of vicious inclinations."[81] But it was pointed out that in a public school, where the boys did not live under the master's roof, all his endeavours "to preserve the innocence, and secure the virtue of a promiscuous flock, that all, or most of them, are no longer under any management of his than during school hours, are in danger of being blasted, and rendered ineffectual by their mixing with vicious company."[82] This campaign against masturbation was not motivated only by a desire to keep adolescents innocent children; it was also that sublimation of the sexual drive in the young would lead to adult achievement: "Irregular and intemperate passions indulged at a boyish age, will blast all the blossoms of the vernal season of life, and cut of all hope of future eminence."[83]

The evidence for homosexual behavior is slighter, but then society's disapproval was greater. A Harrow master was dismissed "for making love to the boys." William Cowper, drawing presumably on his memories of Westminster, wrote

> See womanhood despised, and manhood shamed
> With infamy too nauseous to be named,

---

[80]Earl of Rochester, *Complete Poems*, ed. by D. M. Veith (New Haven: Yale Univ. Press, 1968), 45; *Onania or the Heinous Sin of Self-pollution* (London, 1723), 8th ed., v.

[81]*The Crime of Onan* (London, 1724), 2 vol., I, 17–19, II, 32.

[82]Clarke, *Grammar Schools*, 97–101.

[83]Knox, *Liberal Education*, 329–330. Advice on how to avoid masturbation: Robert Nelson, *Instructions for the Conduct of a Young Gentleman* (London, 1718), 17–19; id., *The Practice of True Devotion* (London, 1791), 26, 33, 39, 43, 113, 122, 124–131, 252; George Stanhope, *A Sermon Concerning Temptations* (London, 1703), 11–12. It is perhaps indicative of seventeenth-century attitudes that when around 1648, Hobbes tried to teach geometry to the 20-year-old Duke of Buckingham, he found him inattentive: "at length Mr. Hobbes observed that his Grace was at masturbation—his hand in his codpiece." Aubrey, who recounted this (c.1669), therefore advised ending formal education by 18 at which age he expected sexual interests to predominate (J. E. Stephens, ed., *Aubrey on Education* (London: Routledge, 1972), 160 n.1, 20, 28).

Fops at all corners, lady-like in mien,
Civeted fellows, smelt ere they are seen....

And it must have been uneasiness at such a possibility that moved Henry Fox (who knew something of his brother's attachment to Lord Hervey) to tell his son that "one thing you know I much wanted to see—your hair cut to a reasonable and gentleman-like shortness. You and some Eton boys wear it as no other people in the world do. It is effeminate, it is ugly, and it must be inconvenient."[84]

The alternative to homosexual behavior was, Cowper said, whores and drunkenness. Headmasters were inclined to be tolerant. Dr. Markham received back into Westminster a boy who had contracted a disease from a whore. He told him he would take no notice of the matter, asked him to keep it a secret from the other boys, and said that "many lads have met with the same mischance and afterwards proved and turned out good men."[85] Westminster boys were especially blessed in this regard because of the opportunities London afforded. It was said that Lady Townshend kept a dormitory for Westminster boys in her dressing room. When Lord March turned 15, his brother-in-law recommended taking him away from Westminster. March's father wondered why; he was pleased with son's school record and had hoped he would complete the sixth form; but then he realized that March must be either in danger of drunkeness or marriage to a whore; and so he withdrew him from the school. March had in fact fallen in love with a woman of the town.[86]

Fifteen was a difficult age for a boy to be at school. Lord and Lady Holland sent their eldest son to Geneva at that age because they believed that "at his dangerous time of life, it's the best place he can be in." Lord Malton had previously gone there probably for the same reason. And Lady Holland assured her sister that it was better for Lord Ophaly, her 16-year-old nephew, to suffer from ennui than to be diverted, "as the diversions and dissipations of that age are dangerous both to health and morals."[87] Lord Richard Cavendish at 16 left Newcome's school because he "was grown a monstrous great fellow and ... was tired of school." The difficulty was to know what to do with him.

---

[84]Lord Herbert, ed., *Henry, Elizabeth and George (1734-80)* (London: Jonathan Cape, 1959), 288; William Cowper, *Works*, ed. by R. Southey (London, 1854), 8 vol., VI, 185; Ilchester, *Henry Fox*, II, 171.

[85]Richard Pares in Pares and Taylor, eds., *Essays Presented to Sir Lewis Namier* (London: Macmillan, 1956), 97.

[86]Errol Sherson, *The Lively Lady Townshend* (London: William Heinemann, 1926), 30; March, *A Duke*, II, 706.

[87]*Leinster*, I, 287, 418; S. C. L., WWM.M2: cf. Dobrée, ed., *Letters of Chesterfield*, VI, 2646.

He was still too boyish for Cambridge and it was dangerous to leave him in Derbyshire where "our neighbours should make too much of him and spoil him." So he was sent to live in an obscure but pleasant place with two clergymen in succession as his tutors.[88] But it was these "overgrown boys," as Lord Clarendon said, who were "the true foundations from whence all those reproaches of dissoluteness and debauchery flow." They incited the rebellions, and they excited sexual desire. For the schools were not yet the closed institutions they became in the nineteenth century.[89] Isolation and games were not yet available to enforce sublimation, and even in the nineteenth century, sublimation sometimes lost out to homosexual behavior. Eighteenth-century parents were just discovering childhood and learning to enjoy its innocence. They really wished that adolescence could be skipped.

The eighteenth century might try to control adolescent sexuality through religious restraints, but it was notorious that the religious training in the public schools was formal and unimpressive. Lord Chesterfield decided that his godson's tutor "should be desired to teach him his religious and moral obligations, which are never heard of nor thought of at a public school."[90] This is certainly what the duchess of Portland found to be the experience of her two sons at Eton in 1725. She appointed a tutor to supplement their education, "for there is nothing but Greek and Latin to be learnt there." And she agreed with him "that those that are not good Christians can't be good men and am sorry that they have neglected to instruct them so much as they ought to have done."[91] In the next generation, matters were still much the same. Lady Rockingham wrote to her sister-in-law to say how pleased she was with their young nephew Lord Fitzwilliam:

> from an accidental opportunity I had of finding his sentiments to be so right upon the subject I so often talked over with you: Friday, being a bad day, we could not go out; and after breakfast, my Lord, being gone upstairs, his little Lordship remained with me, and Hugh [Wentworth].... By some chance ... the Roman Catholic religion became the topic, and consequently, the Protestant: the whole led me to ask him in what manner he had considered or been instructed in his religion; that I supposed his private tutor [at Eton] being a clergyman, he had done it; he answered no, that the private tutors had so many pupils it was impossible; that indeed they had a sort of

---

[88]Chatsworth MSS, V, 4; cf. *Leinster*, II, 295.

[89]Earl of Clarendon, *A Collection of Several Tracts* (London, 1727), 319. For the nineteenth-century schools see Ian Weinberg, *The English Public Schools* (New York: Atherton, 1967); Phyllis Grosskurth, *The Woeful Victorian* (New York: Holt, Rinehart and Winston, 1964), Chap. 2; cf. Malcolm Seaborne, *The English School* (Toronto: Univ. of Toronto Press, 1971), 81–84, who points out that at Eton in 1775 boys were placed in forms not by age but by knowledge of the curriculum.

[90]Dobrée, ed., *Letters of Chesterfield*, VI, 2437.

[91]N.U.L., PwC 18, 17.

catechism which they got by heart; and then of his own accord lamented very much the impossibility of gaining a sufficient knowledge of those matters in a great school; and begun to describe how he would have boys (I suppose he meant his own sons) educated and fully instructed in their religion before they were sent to public schools; in short, he talked vastly well, showing throughout his idea of religion's being the basis of everything, and instead of what we feared, (a sort of indifference to such grave advice), agreed entirely with me as to the necessity of being fully acquainted with one's religion before one's entry into life, in order to practice it afterwards....

Lady Rockingham did not stop at conversation. She suggested that her husband's old tutor should guide Fitzwilliam's religious studies, since her husband, the boy's guardian, was "rather timid in choosing proper books for that purpose, though...thoroughly capable of it." She herself gave the boy Addison's *Evidences of the Christian Religion* "to read while his nightcap is putting on."[92] But clearly most boys received no serious religious training after the nursery. The clergymen in the public schools were occupied in other ways, and it was only the exceptional father, like Lord Dartmouth, who would undertake it himself.

If schools were a threat to a boy's morals, they were also dangerous to his health. Parents seem to have gone to more trouble to secure the latter, with perhaps the reasonable justification that more could be done. Their sons were usually protected after 1720 from at least one disease since they went to school already inoculated against smallpox, but there were other diseases. In 1746 there was a wave of scarlet fever in London. All the boys in one of the boardinghouses at Westminster came down with it. At this point, the duchess of Richmond began to wonder whether she should not withdraw her eldest son. But the headmaster pointed out that the infected boys were quarantined and that all of London was infected. A friend told her that boys caught it by playing in the dew and overheating themselves, and this was just what she was afraid her son would do if he were sent home to the country. She compromised. Lord March stayed at school, but went home to his parents' London house each evening at 5:00.[93] In the previous year a report on Winchester school made to Lord Sutherland had praised it precisely for its healthiness. Winchester had "the best and wholesomest air in Britain"; the town had physicians and apothecaries as good as anywhere; and the woman who ran the boardinghouse had a "great reputation as to her care and skill about children."[94] Indeed, if a school was to be successful after 1750, it had to offer two things: first, a

[92]S.C.L., WWM. R. 169-51a,b.
[93]March, *A Duke*, II, 606-607.
[94]Fraser, *Sutherland*, I, 438-439.

boardinghouse in which there was a woman to care for sick boys and a master to tend to their morals; and then a healthy atmosphere. Westminster school was as capable as any school of providing the first, but it was located in London; and the consequence was that by the beginning of the nineteenth century, Harrow, in the countryside, had taken Westminster's place next to Eton.[95]

Early nineteenth-century schools like Rugby deliberately tried to make their students socially homogeneous. Arnold refused to admit the great families.[96] But in the eighteenth century the social heterogeneity of a place like Westminster caused only minor distress.[97] It is possible to make calculations of the social class of the boys at Westminster under three headmasters: Freind (1711–1732); Nicoll (1733–1752); and Smith (1764–1787). Aristocratic boys who went to Westminster (comprising 25% of their own social class) represented only 6 or 7% of the school's entire attendance. When they were placed with the sons of the gentry, boys from landed society accounted for 25% of the entire school. Boys from mercantile and professional families formed from over 25% to nearly 33% of the school. The remaining 40 to 50% of the school has not been identified explicitly as to class, but it is very likely that it consisted of the sons of small tradesmen or artisans. These were the day boys who lived at home and not in one of the boardinghouses; they stayed for only 1 or 2 years, rather than 5 or 10; and they did not go up to the university.[98] Instead of complaining about the mixed situation, parents circulated among themselves lists of the noblemen at school. The duchess of Northumberland noted in her diary that the "number of boys at Eton July the 23, 1755 was 466 of which noblemen 41. Number of boys 1756, 408, whereof noblemen, 38." And a list sent home in 1765 gave 52 noblemen at Eton.[99] These lists promoted the prestige of the school and made it clear that a boy could push his way forward by the acquaintance he made there. Lady Holland said that Lady Fawkener could not do better for her son than to send him to a public school since he was otherwise poorly provided for. She explained that "the intimacies he makes there, such as Ophaly and Lord Fitzwilliam, and perhaps Charles, may be of vast use."[100] And even a boy who did not need financial support later benefited in his politics from such friendships. Lady Rockingham told her son that "Lord Huntington is catched

[95] F. H. Forshall, *Westminster School Past and Present* (London: Wyman, 1884), 114, 119.
[96] T. W. Bamford, "Public Schools and Social Class 1801–1850." *British Journal of Sociology*, XII, 1961, 228.
[97] Brauer, *Education*, 207 (the slightness of his evidence).
[98] Russell Barker and Stenning, *Old Westminsters*, I, and II.
[99] James Greig, *The Diaries of a Duchess* (London: Hodder & Stoughton, 1927), 8; Essex R.O., D/D By /F 19.
[100] Leinster, I, 235.

up and lives in the D[uke] of N[ewcastle]'s pocket; one should have thought that possibly the early acquaintance at School and the intercourse you had abroad might have induced him to have favoured whatever side you took."[101]

The English public school was a place attended by the majority of aristocratic boys. It provided a separation from the adult world by which a boy competed with his peers, acquired useful knowledge, and built his self-esteem and independence. But that this separation also engendered a violent hostility against the world seems to have disturbed fathers in only one respect—it produced bad manners. "Westminster School," Chesterfield wrote, "is, undoubtedly, the seat of illiberal manners and brutal behaviour."[102] The social heterogeneity of the schools seems not to have bothered them at all. Four things were disturbing: early sexual indulgence, the lack of religious instruction, the mixture of ages, and the danger of disease. All four of these were tied to the size of the great schools. Parents who disapproved of them before 1750 attempted to improve matters by sending their sons to small private schools. But after 1750 fathers took the lead in trying to develop within the great schools themselves smaller units in which something of the aura of a private school might be maintained.

Domesticity in the School: Parental Surrogates

As an alternative to the public school, or as a partial replacement, parents before 1720 began to use small private schools. These schools were usually in one of the London suburbs. Their ideal size was 10 or 12 pupils, but the number could climb to 20 or 30,[103] and in one case it reached 100. The curriculum was more varied than at a public school, for French and arithmetic were taught as well as Greek and Latin. The surroundings were physically better. There were playing fields and, in some cases, gardens for the boys to work in. The schoolmaster's wife with her care for the children's health was a great attraction. Some students stayed at these schools from age 7 to 16, but most schools seemed to have specialized in boys beneath the age of puberty. Because the numbers were small, the master's moral supervision was close. But the smallness of the schools also cut down competitive excellence, so that a boy who transferred to a public school often found difficulty in keeping up with the more accomplished Latinity of his contemporaries.

---

[101]S.C.L., WWM. R. 169-158.
[102]Dobrée, ed., *Letters of Chesterfield*, IV, 1494.
[103]Clarke, Grammar Schools, 102, 104; C. P. Moritz, *Journeys of a German in England in 1782*, trans. and ed. by R. Nettel (London: Jonathan Cape, 1965), 65-67.

These schools effectively answered two of the major complaints against the public schools: Children in private schools were healthier and they were not likely to be exposed to adolescent sexuality.

Many of the schools lasted only as long as an impoverished clergyman was obliged to make his living in that way. The more successful survived for several generations, with the mastership passed down from father to son or son-in-law. The most famous of these were a school at Marylebone run by the de la Places and one at Hackney run by the Newcomes. Marylebone was founded in 1703. By 1711 it had a considerable reputation, so much so that when Lord Ruglen thought of sending his son to Westminster school, thinking it the best, he found that his wife's mother and aunt objected and proposed Marylebone instead because it was "freer from vice; he would get the French tongue with his Latin, and would not be so much exposed."[104] The school was also valued because it was not ruled by the brutal discipline of the public school. When Thomas Lyttleton was moved from Eton to Marylebone in 1728, his relations supposed that he would "make more improvement under the care of M. LePlace than under the rod of Dr. Bland."[105] In its early days, it was usually described as a "French school," and it is possible that it was deliberately modeled on the reformed schools of seventeenth-century France. Many boys seem not to have spent all their school days there. George Hervey was there for 4 years and then went to Westminster. Twenty years later John St. John also spent 4 years at Marylebone, and then moved to Eton.[106] It was said that after 1750 boys were taken as soon as they had been breeched and left when they were 12 or 13.[107] If a boy remained there until 14, he found, like Lord Lyttelton when he was sent to Eton in 1758, "that he was kept so backward at Mary[le]bon that he will never be able to get into the sixth form at Eton."[108] There was possibly a tendency to leave boys longer at such a school after 1750, but the reasons for sending them there remained the same. For when the duke of Grafton decided to send his eldest son there in 1766 at the age of 6, he chose Marylebone because of his concern for the boy's health.[109]

Hackney school, with its ample playing fields and periods of recreation, also had a reputation for health. There were plays in English as

---

[104]H.M.C., *Portland MSS*, V, 76.

[105]Maud Wyndham, *Chronicles, of the Eighteenth Century* (London: Hodder & Stoughton, 1924), 2 vol., I, 7.

[106]Kent R. O., U471. F4., p. 4 (notebook of Dudley North); *Bristol Diary*, 16 April 1727 (schoolbills), 4 April 1732; Kent R.O., U 471. A57.

[107]*Memoirs of . . . the Rev. Dr. Trusler* (Bath, 1806), 36, 27.

[108]Wyndham, *Chronicles*, II, 285.

[109]N.U.L., PwF 6374a.

opposed to Westminster's Latin plays. By the 1770s the period of attendance had lengthened; a boy entered at 6 and stayed until 16, and then, like Lord Richard Cavendish, left school for good. It also had grown to almost 100 pupils. And perhaps because of this size, and the presence of older boys, its moral control seems to have broken down. Charles Bosanquet at any rate, later recalled that "the habit of swearing was so inveterate that I never got rid of it. It was a most profligate, abominable school."[110]

Many of these schools were short-lived. Lord Hervey sent his son to one run by a Mr. Valet at Hampstead in 1714.[111] Lord Chandos and his brother went to one at Isleworth in 1717 before going to Westminster school.[112] Lord Cowper sent his son in 1744 to a school at Chelsea run by L'Herondell.[113] But the preference for all these schools was usually founded on the same reasons. Wandsworth school taught French, there was a good master and a woman who was a good nurse, and the influence of servants was avoided. Lady Holland told her sister that she thought it "the best nursery for delicate children in the world."[114] When the duchess of Devonshire went to visit the school at Putney in which Lord Villiers and Lord Brook were pupils, she noted that it was in "a charming situation, the house is next to the duke of Norfolk's, there is a large garden and playfield, and the rooms are very large and airy."[115] And when Lord Chesterfield's godson went home from his school of 25 boys (it was kept in a great house with a large garden), the boy's father was asked not "to let him play out of your sight with any boys older than himself, who might, perhaps teach him boy's tricks; whereas at present, I am sure he is perfectly pure, in word, in deed, and I verily believe in thought." But, significantly, Chesterfield also feared that the boy was too childish for his age, and therefore proposed sending him for 4 years to Westminster school where he would learn "to shift for himself and bustle in the world," as well as acquire enough of the classics for a man of quality.[116] Clearly the difficulty parents faced was to know how to balance the sexual innocence and good health of the private school against the self-esteem and sound knowledge of Westminster or Eton.

---

[110]John Gore, ed., *The Creevey Papers* (New York: Macmillan, 1963), 266–270; Chatsworth MSS, V, 4.
[111]*Bristol Diary*, 6 Feb 1714.
[112]Shakespeare's Birthplace Trust: Leigh MSS, Series D., Glos. Papers, Bn 21-1: 19 July 1717.
[113]Herts R.O., Panshanger MSS, Bx. 51, 68/1.
[114]*Leinster*, I, 166, 339–340.
[115]Chatsworth MSS, V, 248.
[116]Dobrée, ed., *Letters of Chesterfield*, VI, 2645, 2652, 2663, 2815.

Before 1750 if a father wished his son to have close supervision and to enjoy good health at school, he sent him to a private school. When the great public schools became aware of this, they tried to adapt themselves to these demands. The evidence is best for Westminster. At the beginning of the century a nobleman's son who went to Westminster usually lived in the headmaster's house, but the numbers eventually became so large that there was no supervision. Sometime after 1711—but not too long, significantly, after the foundation of Marylebone school—a new boarding system was introduced. Older women called dames undertook to take in pupils from the school. They sometimes arranged to have an assistant teacher or usher aid them in supervising the boys, and sometimes the ushers themselves ran boardinghouses. By the 1730s the dames' houses were officially registered with the headmaster, and there were from 15 to 20 of them, with from 6 to 19 boys in a house.[117] But the situation in these houses was still often riotous. One 11-year-old boy, after his first night in Mrs. Jones's house wrote home: "If you don't let me come home, I die—I am all over ink, and my fine clothes have been spoilt—I have been tossed in a blanket, and seen a ghost."[118]

To one of these houses the duke and duchess of Portland in the 1740s and 1750s sent their two sons, Lord Titchfield and Lord Edward. Tichfield went first and boarded at Mrs. Watts's house. He took with him a manservant, but not a private tutor—which some aristocratic boys did. He did very well scholastically, and was first the captain of his form and then of the entire Under School. He kept both his parents well informed of his progress, and they were encouraging and pleased. When he was promoted into the Shell (the name of one of the forms), his father congratulated him "upon your getting your remove with so much honour; I hope and don't doubt but you'll go through the School in the same way, as you are sure nothing can give your Mamma and me greater pleasure than always to see you act like a man of honour and quality." His parents visited him occasionally, and his mother was anxious that he dine each Sunday in some fashionable London house.[119]

Two years before Titchfield left the school "with as great a reputation as ever any young nobleman" made, his younger brother joined

---

[117] Sargeaunt, *Westminster*, 158; L. E. Tanner, *Westminster School* (London: Country Life, 1934), 19, 27–29.

[118] Carleton, *Westminster*, 30–33. In 1717 Lord Chandos was entered at Westminster "and went to board at Cousin Graham's." (Shakespeare's Birthplace Trust: Leigh MSS, Series D, Gls. Papers, Bn 21-1).

[119] N.U.L., PwF 717, 719, 723, 728, 731, 732, 743, 1167.

him there.[120] It was a difficult position for the younger boy. His parents urged him on, but when he was promoted his mother sent her congratulations in a letter to the elder son—"I shall write to him tomorrow to congratulate him upon it if I can get time." She did worry about Edward's health. When he recovered from a cold in August, she told Titchfield that she hoped Neddy was "seasoned for the winter and have no more, though that I think is a pretty hard thing to answer for considering the heats he often puts himself in at play, and then cooling off in the cloisters." But the duchess was reconciled to it all, for "he must do as other boys do and take his chance."[121] The duchess's attitude in this regard was that of the older type of parent. So, perhaps, was her urging one son to complete with the other. Another mother at the same time worried about sending two sons to the same school since "whichever excels may raise an emulation and prevent the love I wish to subsist between them."[122] The duchess, however, told her son she hoped "his emulation would increase every day."

The duchess was of a piece with the boardinghouse and the headmaster. After Titchfield left, Edward boarded with Mrs. Morell and had two or three rooms to himself. Jeremy Bentham was in the same house and recalled that in the rest of the house there were three beds to a room and two boys to a bed.[123] But aristocratic parents were being urged to give each child his own bed;[124] some boys insisted upon it,[125] and by the end of the century a character was made to say in a novel that as a boy he had "been educated at a public school, and never recollected without shuddering the hour when his youthful modesty first had shrunk from sharing his bed with a stranger."[126] The headmaster was William Markham. In keeping with the spirit of the times, Markham had taken some trouble to rearrange the grounds of the school so that the boardinghouses might be more closely grouped together and the boys have a compact playground. But to Bentham's sharp eye, "his business was rather in courting the great than in attending to the school." There was not much moral supervision from such a man. It was he who counted a boy's contracting venereal disease a pec-

---

[120]*Delany*, III, 1861, 291.
[121]N.U.L., PwF 753, 1191, 756.
[122]*Delany*, III, 1861, 485.
[123]Jeremy Bentham, *Works*, ed. by John Bowring (Edinburgh: W. Tait, 1843), reprint 1962, 11 vol., X, 26–30.
[124]Nelson, *Government of Children* (1753 ed.), 261.
[125]*Leinster*, I, 172.
[126]Mary Brunton, *Self Control* (1811), cited in R. P. Utter and G. B. Needham, *Pamela's Daughters* (New York: Macmillan, 1936), 84.

cadillo.[127] And he certainly courted his aristocratic pupils. The duchess of Portland wrote to Titchfield that "if Dr. Markham asks you to dinner you should go, and if it is of a Sunday you should send your excuse to Lady Stair, and when you see her, tell her that as he asked you several times and you have been engaged, we desired the next time you would go."[128]

Markham's rearrangement of his schoolyard apparently acted as a spur to other headmasters. In the same decade, Dr. Burton at Winchester constructed a new building to house "gentlemen's children." He told Lord Bute that if his sons were sent there, he would find that "rules and confinement are established as secure them from all temptations to idleness," that they were prevented from going into the town, and that they were "at all times subject to the Master's eye even in their diversions."[129] At Eton there was also rebuilding in this decade to move all boardinghouses within such bounds as the masters approved, and boys were forbidden to have their servants eat with them in the houses.[130] But Westminster, being in London, was perhaps less able to isolate boys from the town and from their families. The duke of Beaufort and his brother, for instance, spent each weekend with their grandmother and returned to school early on Monday morning. But their grandmother did notice that "they have a decent custom there, that when a boy is not well enough to go into school, it is concluded he is not *able* to go out of his house, and *there* he must stay."[131] It is clear that at Eton, Westminster, and Winchester, at the considerable expense that building entailed, headmasters were attempting by the 1750s to provide some degree of the supervision available in private schools. But these masters found that by the 1770s fathers were prepared to make even greater demands on the traditional organization of the schools.

When Lord Darnley sent his sons to Eton after 1775, they lived in the boardinghouse kept by one of the assistant masters, the Rev. John Norbury. Norbury's house had been in existence for many years, but the demands that Darnley's concern for the health, religion, and knowledge of his sons placed on the master were quite novel. They were demands that other fathers were making at other public schools, and if left unsatisfied, they might cause a boy to be withdrawn.

[127]Carleton, *Westminster*, 30–33; Pares, in Pares and Taylor, eds., *Essays*, 97.
[128]N.U.L., PwF 756.
[129]Old Wykehamists, *Winchester College 1393–1893* (London: Edward Arnold 1893), 90.
[130]*Leinster*, I, 172.
[131]*Delany*, III, 1862, 39, II, 1862, 358.

By the time Darnley's sons arrived at Eton, it had, like Westminster, developed a series of boardinghouses. In 1766, for instance, there were 13 boardinghouses, 3 run by men and 10 by women. In the 1750s there were about 40 aristocratic boys in the school and 50 in the next decade. In the last years of the decade, we can see something of the way these boys were grouped. Sets of brothers with a servant often shared a room, and groups of cousins might live together in a single house. Lord Ophaly, his brother, and their servant lived in one room of Mrs. Milward's house, and their two Fox cousins lived in another with their servant. In Mr. Bland's house, Lord Fitzwilliam and his cousin Lord Melbourne lived together in a few rooms that Lord Suffolk had previously occupied with the sober man who had been his servant. In the same house Lord Archer had an apartment composed of two rooms and three little studies. Groups of brothers sometimes had an entire house to themselves. This was the case with the two sons of Lord Gainsborough, as well as with the boys of the Marlborough and the Conway families. But the last two sets of boys ate with boys from one of the full-scale boardinghouses, as did Lord Milsington, who lived with one of the assistant masters. These different accommodations were a source of prestige among the boys, and the sons of Lord Cowper and Lord Lothian were held in contempt for the poor rooms they had at Mrs. Bernardiston's. But these houses were places where boys slept or ate, their supervision came from their private tutors, who had pupils drawn from various houses and who were themselves either masters in the school or individuals who made a living solely from private tuition.[132] Norbury, to whom Darnley sent his sons, was an assistant master who kept a boardinghouse as well as serving as a private tutor. One of his pupils recalled that "he kept us tight to our business by almost hourly inspection of both lessons and exercises."[133] But Norbury had 50 pupils to attend to, and we have already seen that Lord Fitzwilliam complained that though these men were often clergymen, the number of their pupils prevented their giving any sort of religious guidance to a boy.

Lord Darnley's expectations of Norbury were novel, but he seems to have gotten what he wanted. His eldest son, Lord Clifton, who entered when he was 8, stayed until he went up to Oxford at 17. Darnley, in contrast to the duchess of Portland, was extremely protective of his

[132] Maxwell Lyte, Eton, 328; Leinster, I, 172, 183; Esme Wingfield-Stratford, The Lords of Cobham Hall (London: Cassell, 1959), 203–204; Austen-Leigh, Eton Register 1753–1790, xxvi.
[133] S.C.L., WWM. R. 169–51a,b.

son's health. Clifton did not leave Norbury's house to go to the schoolroom when the weather was bad, but said his lessons to Norbury instead. After the boy caught a cough and recovered from it, Darnley told him to "take care you do not heat yourself by walking too fast, or too much, or by running or by eating." His mother told him that the apothecary said it was not good for children to be out after 5:00 in the evening, and that while she was "far from wishing you to conform to nursery rules, yet I wish you to be a little cautious after that time." Norbury was careful to inform Darnley when the servants fell ill, so that the boy could be sent home early. When Clifton's younger brother joined him, his health became as much a topic of concern. And when both boys caught whooping cough, a second servant was sent to mind them, and meticulous reports were relayed home.[134]

Darnley also worried about the roughness of his son's schoolfellows. The boy was allowed to play cricket whenever Norbury consented to it, but Norbury's son had to accompany him "to prevent mischief." Darnley frequently heard horror stories of violence at school and passed them on—a boy who had died from injuries after just 14 days at school—and he himself had seen at Eton a boy with his arm in a sling. The boy's mother worried, on the basis of their fighting at home, how her sons would get on together at school. She told Clifton that she would be uneasy "if Papa sends Edward to you, if you do not write that you have made a resolution not to hurt him, but on the contrary to take care of him, to advise him, and to keep him as much as you can from hurting himself, or being the means of making you riotious and making you angry." Once both boys were under his care, Norbury reported when they were violent at football and bruised their shins; and Darnley warned them to be less violent or be forbidden to play.[135]

Darnley worried about his son's religion and his morals, as well as his scholastic achievement. He checked to see that the boy said his prayers, read the Bible, and went to church. He recommended that he read *Don Quijote* rather than *Gulliver's Travels* and explained that in general he wished him to read "such books as tell only the truth." When Darnley heard that the boy had nearly been flogged for playing in the morning, he told him that he hoped he was "of that disposition, and have such an aptitude to learn what is properly put to you, that [you] will not deserve such coarse correction." Darnley grew furious when the boy lied and said that he has his father's permission to have a second roll for breakfast; and he was

[134]Wingfield-Stratford, *Cobham Hall*, 196, 201, 206, 210, 211, 212–219, 221–222, 233–234.
[135]*Ibid.*, 201, 202, 208, 238.

even angrier when the boy ran up debts for extra food. "I had flattered myself," he wrote, "you were free from this vice. But vicious company, evil communication, I fear has warped your good intentions." Both boys were obliged to send their school exercises home, and Darnley kept them and criticized them. And he always requested that they bring home a list of the school so that he might see where they stood in its rankings. For Darnley wished his sons to compete—Clifton told him that he was going to Oxford "to perfect my education and to become, as far as my poor abilities will make me, a polite and gentlemanlike scholar, but far from a pedant." And for this reason, no doubt, Darnley sent his sons to a public school. But he was, nevertheless, also determined to see that they were protected from the violence of the school, that their health was not endangered, and that their religious and moral principles were maintained. To these ends he was quite prepared to see them not treated like the others. And he managed to persuade the head of his sons' boardinghouse to be a moral director to them in a way that their private tutor was not—to give them all the benefits of a private school in the midst of Eton. This was a new breed of father.[136]

Darnley's view of life at a public school was quite unlike that of the second duke and duchess of Portland who had thought that a boy in such a school "must do as other boys do and take his chance." Darnley's contemporary, the third duke of Portland, despite his own great success at Westminster, broke his family's tradition and sent his sons to a private school.[137] The school had been set up in 1772 at Ealing by Samuel Goodenough, a clergyman who was a former undermaster at Westminster. After much discussion of the number of pupils, he had begun with 10 on the ground that "the greater the number was, provided it did not exceed that which I was able to take complete care of, it would be the better for the scholars." He charged £ 100 a year, and did all the teaching himself, except for masters for French, dancing, and fencing. He soon found that he could teach two more, and with the consent of the parents, the number of pupils was increased to 12. The boys were a very aristocratic lot: Besides Portland's sons, there were those of Lord Willoughby de Broke, Lord Weymouth, and Lord Albermarle.

Goodenough sent reports to Portland at Christmas and Easter, and he was always willing to fall in with Portland's pedagogic suggestions.

[136]*Ibid.*, 196, 197, 198, 199, 207, 223, 228, 234, 238, 239, 269.

[137]John Nichols, *Illustrations of the Literary History of the Eighteenth Century* (London, 1817–1858), 8 vol., **VI**, 245–256; N.U.L., PwF 1283, 1286, 10708, 4195, 4196, 4201–4204, 4212, 4213, 4217, 4227, 4231, 4242, 4249, 4250a, 1282.

He agreed with him that the boys should appear "in public or in large companies to remedy the solitariness of private education, which if totally uncorrected would produce in boys of some casts, an idle sheepishness." He took his advice about beginning Lord Titchfield's training in making Latin verses. Goodenough's curriculum was the traditional classical one, and he always indicated the state of a boy's knowledge by saying what form of Westminster school he would be prepared to enter. Portland usually asked that his sons bring home their schoolbooks in the vacation so that he could see their progress for himself and so that they should lose no time. At least once Goodenough was nervous about this intervention with his pupils. Explaining that he did not know "what assistance your Grace might produce in the country," he sent Portland three pages of commentary on some grammar books the latter had requested. He did this unasked, he said, because he was "conscious that all teaching, unless it proceed upon principle, is troublesome and unfruitful."

Goodenough was much firmer in turning back attempts by Lord Titchfield to use his father's authority as a lever against the master's control of discipline. When Titchfield had his father send Christmas presents to the servants at school, Goodenough asked that in the future all such gifts first go through his hands, for he feared that otherwise his servants might be "enticed to do things which may in the end prove prejudicial to my pupils." On another occasion he was obliged to ask Portland not to be persuaded by Titchfield to take the part of a French master whom Goodenough had felt obliged to dismiss because he had "bent his whole thoughts how he may indulge and artfully practice upon my young people's sensibility to a degree highly improper." And when Goodenough did not take seriously enough an injury to Titchfield's foot, he had to explain to the duke that Titchfield was "always in a prodigious bustle if the least matter affects him." Goodenough was afraid the boy would "readily become a most attentive valetudinarian," and therefore took to joking "with him upon his exquisite feelings in this respect."

Titchfield from his private school had a free and easy relationship with his father. He perhaps did not see as much of him as he would have liked. As a boy of 9 he wrote "I hope you will come and see me soon," and 2 years later he remarked that he was "glad to hear by Mamma's letters that you was well and would write to me soon, but I cannot say that I have received one letter of yours for the three letters I have written to you." The boy might not have had the sort of independence that a public school gave, but he was perfectly at ease with an indulgent father. His mother feared that he was too much at ease and had been spoiled. She thought it was "out of all proportion that a child of ten years of age, who rides perhaps six weeks out of twelve months, should have the notion of keeping six horses for his own use." She would have preferred him to have the shyness of his age, and blamed his "not having been treated so much as a child as he ought to have been,"when he did not.

Titchfield was sent to a private school not because he was to learn something other than Greek and Latin, nor was he sent there because he was to avoid other boys. Goodenough once reported that he was "a very great favourite with all his companions, which I look upon to be the best criterion that a boy's manners and temper are as they ought to be." Titchfield's younger brother was certainly not sent there in order to be freed from competition with his older brother. "By Easter next he will be equal to the business of the first form at Westminster, which will be an improvement great as can be expected," Goodenough reported. "Nevertheless," he added, "he has an inattention and a sort of giddiness about him which I do not remember to have been in Lord Titchfield at his age." Attention, knowledge, and self-confidence were still the goals of aristocratic education. But a man like Portland (who had himself achieved them effortlessly in a public school) had decided by 1775 that his children's health and their morals had to be secured as well, and that this could be done only in a school of one master and 12 pupils. Such a school might risk making them hypochondriac or manipulative, but that had to be hazarded, and it was most probably the constant paternal intervention that such a school allowed that was its chief attraction. Fathers had turned experimental in the education of their sons just when mothers had taken their final step and begun to nurse. The example of the most persistently innovative father I have found—Lord Dartmouth—must close my case and, I trust, give final conviction.

Lord Darnley managed to inject the supervision of a private school into Eton. The duke of Portland turned away from his own Westminster school to private education. Lord Dartmouth and his father had both gone to Westminster, but Dartmouth sent none of his eight sons there. Instead, he experimented with a number of forms ranging from private tuition in a clergyman's house to small public schools of 200 students. His first three sons he sent to Harrow, which was then a school of 200, and he managed, for a time, to arrange for them within that school the atmosphere of a private school. When this failed, he sent them to a private school of 40 to 60 students run by Samuel Parr, a former master from Harrow. When Parr closed the school and took up the headmastership of two grammar schools in quick succession, Dartmouth entrusted his fourth and his fifth sons to Parr as his private pupils. The fifth, sixth, and seventh sons were sent to another private school of 40 students, kept by William Gilpin at Cheam. The seventh son went on from Cheam to Rugby, a school of Harrow's size. The eighth son began at Rugby, and then moved on to a school for 7 students that Parr had opened.

Dartmouth, like Darnley, was strongly religious and was the greatest feather in the cap of the Evangelical party. It is likely that the religiosity of both men had something to do with the type of education they sought for their sons. Evangelicals like William Cowper strongly disapproved of public schools on a number of grounds: They mixed boys of great differences in age; there were too many pupils for masters to oversee, the boys were made to compete excessively; their morals were corrupted; and most of all, they created a distance between a boy and his father. The boy home from school became "shy and strange" with his father:

> *Alas, poor boy!—the natural effect*
> *Of love by absence chilled into respect.*

Cowper proposed, instead, a tutor, or the education of two boys at most in a clergyman's house.[138] Dartmouth never quite tried either of these, though he did approach the latter once. But his aim in all his experiments was to provide his sons with surrogate fathers, and to keep down detachment between his sons and himself.

When his fifth son, Henry, was still too young to go to school, Dartmouth began a correspondence with him during his absences from home. He called it "our small correspondence" because it was written on sheets two inches by four. Dartmouth delighted in his sons's appearance. He told him "Whenever I look at you I cannot help thinking of an animal that is found in some countries which they call a spider monkey: they tell us it has long thin legs and arms, so have you; it has a very black face, so have you—sometimes I am sure it goes on four legs, sometimes on two, so do you. It is all chattering or squealing, so are you. It loves pies and custards, and all manner of trash, so do you. In short the resemblance is so strong I cannot forbear laughing when I think of it." The greater part of the correspondence was more serious. It was full of the happiness of heaven and the terrors of the damned: Men were on a journey and their bodies were temporary houses; self-denial was necessary; but, over all, there was the love of God for his children.

[138]Cowper, Works, VI, 163–185.

With an older son, the tone changed, but the concern was the same. He told Lord Lewisham that he was always "racking my brain to know whether I have omitted anything that can be of real service to you." He was afraid of preaching too much: "I have some fear of tiring you with my advice and instructions, and of defeating my own purpose by the most lamentable of all disasters, creating a shyness between a dutiful son and an affectionate parent." For the aim of it all was to succeed "in my endeavour to persuade you of the sincerity of my affection for you, and to say the truth, I make no doubt I have."[139]

When he sent his three eldest sons to Harrow, Dartmouth chose a place that was only doubtfully a public school in some persons' minds. "Harrow, I think can hardly be called a public school," Mrs. Pinckney wrote in 1761.[140] Noblemen's children boarded with the headmaster, but conditions were bad. There was one bed for every two or three students. Food was plain and insufficient and had to be supplemented by individual purchases. Younger boys were bullied and frightened. Drinking and gambling were common. And there were pitched battles between the boys and the neighboring farmers. But Robert Sumner became headmaster in 1760, and under him conditions changed and the school grew. He eventually set up a system of boardinghouses, but when he did so, he waged a great battle to bring under his control the man in whose house Dartmouth had placed his sons in order to give them more than the ordinary boardinghouse life.[141]

Dartmouth had presumably chosen Harrow because it was healthy. Only one boy died there from disease between 1753 and 1763. But Dartmouth was anxious to ensure that his sons were under constant supervision when they were not in school. The Rev. Samuel Glass undertook to run a boardinghouse where this could be arranged. It was a very aristocratic house with the children of Lord Radnor, the heir of the duke of Grafton, and boys from the Manners and the Conway families. The boys had gardens to work in and were taught natural science by Glass. But Glass was not an easy man to deal with. In May 1765 Lord Lewisham fell into a pond which served as Glass's water supply, and his brother had to pull him out by the heels. Dartmouth asked that the pond either be drained or at least be enclosed by a fence. But in a series of letters that varied between obsequiousness and insolence, Glass temporized. It was not until January 1766, and after other

---

[139]Staffs, R.O., D 1778, V, 557, 871, 853.
[140]Ravenel, *Eliza Pinckney*, 210.
[141]E. W. Laborde, *Harrow School* (London: Winchester Publications, 1948), 40-43; P. M. Thornton, *Harrow School and Its Surroundings* (London: W. H. Allen, 1885), 145-152.

parents had complained as well, that the pond was drained. In 1767 Dartmouth told Glass that he wanted each of his sons to have a separate bed. Glass replied that there was not room enough for two beds and that only brothers were allowed to sleep together. But he eventually provided a larger bed, and with this Dartmouth decided to be content.

In 1768 the crisis that destroyed the boardinghouse arose. Sumner, the headmaster, issued a regulation that all boys, including those in Glass's house, were to attend the daily roll call and sit in the gallery at church. Glass decided to resist this, and he persuaded Dartmouth and Radnor to support him. Dartmouth said that the regulation would "defeat the purpose with which I entrusted my children to you, which was that they might be immediately under your own inspection, and that you might be at all times accountable for them to me, except during the school hours." But Sumner would not compromise and dismissed Glass. At this point Glass decided to open a private school at Harrow for his pupils. He told Dartmouth that in such a school, though his sons might not become exact classical scholars, they would learn "more about things, though they might not be quite so accurate in their knowledge of words," and he proposed to spend more time on science and less on making Latin verses. But Sumner prevented Glass from opening his school by appealing to his exclusive legal right to teach at Harrow.

Dartmouth at this point began to consider alternatives. He thought of sending his sons to Westminster, and the headmaster of Eton wrote to him recommending his school. Glass decided to open a private school 8 or 9 miles from Windsor and rented a house to that end. He did this thinking he was certain of the support of Dartmouth and Radnor. But Dartmouth changed his mind and decided to send his sons back to Harrow. He placed them in a house run by Mrs. Hodsdon and agreed to their obeying Sumner's regulations. Glass and Radnor taxed him with inconsistency. Glass tried to appeal to Lord Lewisham behind Dartmouth's back. But Lewisham sent the letter to his father—"to consult you, being the best friend I have upon earth, what answer you would have me make." To Glass, Dartmouth replied that he thought himself "quite at liberty to consult the welfare of my children in their future destination, and therefore shall undoubtedly send them to Harrow or elsewhere, as upon the most attentive consideration of all circumstances shall appear to me to be best for them, and most to my own satisfaction."[142]

[142]Staffs. R.O., D 1778, V, 832, 833, 834; H.M.C., Dartmouth MSS, III, 187.

Dartmouth had probably decided to leave his sons at Harrow because he respected the assistant master, Samuel Parr. When Sumner died 3 years later in 1771, Dartmouth supported Parr for the headmastership. But the governors gave it to someone else, and Parr left Harrow and opened a school at Stanmore. All but 1 of his 40 students there followed him from Harrow. Among them were Dartmouth's three sons, who were soon joined by their younger brother, Heneage. Parr took a special interest in Heneage as he was destined to be a clergyman. He told Dartmouth: "I dare not tell you an untruth upon such a subject, but if a sound understanding and an upright heart are the most proper qualifications of a Christian teacher, Mr. H. Legge is likely to become a real and distinguished ornament" to his profession. When Parr gave up this school Heneage remained as his pupil, Parr assuring Dartmouth that he would care for the boy's morals and his wife would care for his health.[143]

Dartmouth was by now fully committed to private education. With Parr no longer keeping his school, he sent his fifth, sixth, and seventh sons to William Gilpin at Cheam. Gilpin had taken on the school in 1752. The number of students had previously fallen to 15; but his innovations soon raised it first to 40 and then 80, with a waiting list for those who could not be accomodated. His wife cared for the health of the boys and helped to win over their parents. But it was Gilpin's system that was famous. He preferred to have only boys who had not reached puberty. The discipline of the school was based on "a code of laws with punishments annexed to each transgression." Corporal punishment was never used "except for vice or obstinate idleness," and by vice he meant masturbation. Cricket was encouraged "as a manly exercise." Boys were allowed to go out alone, but they were forbidden to visit anyone, and they were required to stay within certain bounds. They planted gardens and were allowed to trade their produce with each other. Particular attention was given to "notions of religion as well as morals." Gilpin did not try for exact classical scholarship, but rather for a sympathetic understanding of Latin and for fluency in English.[144]

Each year Gilpin sent home with his boys a written report of their progress. In 1774 he told Dartmouth that it was "a very great task upon me in many cases to stand between truth on one side and indelicacy on

---

[143]Warren Derry, *Dr. Parr* (Oxford: Clarendon Press, 1966), 11–33; H.M.C., *Dartmouth MSS*, **III**, 195, 214, 230–232; Staffs. R.O., D 1778, **V**, 850.

[144]Gilpin, *Memoirs*, 122–135.

the other: for truths of so serious a kind, as the bad behaviour of children, require at least a selection of terms." So with great circumlocution, he explained that Henry had a tendency of "gracing a story with the marvellous. He is a very great favourite with us all, and very deservedly; and my conscience rather checks me for mentioning anything *privately* to your Lordship, which I never had cause enough to mention to him." Two years later he explained that he was not interested in "being thought to give the last finishing to a classical education." He therefore recommended to men like Dartmouth, who wanted their sons to be accomplished scholars, that they send them to a tutor or a public school for a year or two before they went up to the university. But the truth was that Gilpin did not like older boys, for their awakening sexuality distressed him. He explained that he had "been so often mortified with boys when they come to the age of right and wrong, that I have long wished to have no connection with them." But he added that with Dartmouth's sons he was so far "persuaded they are boys of great purity of manners." Shortly after this, Gilpin retired, and his son took over the school. Dartmouth's sons stayed for a while and then left in 1780, one to go to sea and the other to Rugby school which had just been reorganized by a new headmaster. The eighth and last son joined his brother at Rugby, but when Samuel Parr began to teach privately again, Augustus left to become one of his seven pupils.[145] Dartmouth in his quest for the health, good morals, and sound learning of his sons was always prepared to try one more new school. A public school was tolerable if it was small and his sons well supervised, but supervision in such a school was always a difficulty. Cheam was better; its health and morality more certain—though his sons did catch scarlet fever there. But best of all was Parr's teaching, for it fostered not only health and morality but sound scholarship as well.

From these developments it should be clear that the history of the relationship of aristocratic men and their children is the history of boys at school. The culmination of three generations of change came in the 1770s when fathers, who continued to insist on a radical separation from their sons, nonetheless worried about the danger of creating a "shyness" between themselves and those sons. The separation was still necessary because it was the means of instilling in a boy that requisite degree of self-esteem that came from classical knowledge and competition with his peers. But the violent hostility that adolescent separation once engendered in boys was lessened by providing surrogate parents in

---

[145]Staffs. R.O., D 1778, **V**, 871; H.M.C., *Dartmouth MSS*, **III**, 228; Staffs. R.O., D 1778, **V**, 917; Rouse, *Rugby School*, 130–147; Derry, *Dr. Parr*, 57–60.

Male Sexual Behavior and the Limits of Domesticity

Under the influence of domesticity, aristocratic men in the course of the eighteenth century came to show an interest in two activities that had been previously defined as predominantly or exclusively feminine. They became concerned about childbearing and the education of children. But in both cases they were able to do so only through the agency of a surrogate: The physician delivered their wives, and the clergyman educated their sons. The physician and the clergyman were protected from any loss of masculine status because they could claim to be applying reason to the management of women and children; but the aristocratic man's role in such affairs had no rational justification since fatherhood was not a profession. Even aristocratic women had been told by Lord Halifax that they stood to lose their status as aristocrats if they were too free with their children. Aristocratic men stood to lose even more—their manhood as well as their gentility.

The adult man's fear of identification with women and children had been forged during the formation of his gender identity in childhood with its rites of passage of coats to breeches, and nursery to school. And it was confirmed in the differences in the development of male and female sexual orientation after puberty. Girls were never separated from the adult companionship of their mothers, and after 15 they were likely to move entirely in a social world of adult men and women. For them puberty and heterosocial behavior arrived together. The need to preserve virginity meant, however, that they did not engage in heterosexual behavior, and it is even likely (as has apparently been the case with Western women until recently) that they often did not masturbate until after marriage, if ever.[146] Boys, on the other hand, are very likely to have masturbated once they reached puberty at school, and to have done so with the support of their peers. Parents and schoolmasters tried, as the century wore on, to prevent this, either because they wished to extend the sexual innocence of childhood as far into adolescence as possible, or because they viewed sublimation as a means of maintaining that attention to education without which any

---

[146] This model of sexual development among Western peoples I take from J. H. Gagnon and W. S. Simon, *Sexual Conduct* (Chicago: Aldine Press, 1973).

later achievement in politics or the professions was impossible.[147] But once a boy had left school, his father was very likely to accept his experimentation with prostitutes. His only concern was disease. Chesterfield begged his son to wear condoms whatever the "probability or even attestations of health, nay, of untouched virginity itself." And when the duke of Newcastle's son failed in such precautions, the father's agent undertook to have the surgeon "alarm him a little with the many inconveniences that may result from the frequent use of mercury" in order to make Lord Thomas "more prudent."[148]

The aristocratic man began with individual sexual fantasy and then moved on to whores. His real difficulty lay in making the transition to heterosocial behavior with women of his own class. Young Marlow in Goldsmith's play declared that it was "the Englishman's malady" to be impudent enough among "females of another class" but to become a trembling idiot in the "company of women of reputation." A "modest woman," he said, was "the most tremendous object of the whole creation." Chesterfield tried to wean his son from such gaucherie by presenting hatred for "your modest woman's company" as part of the English booby's equipment. Instead, in a famous passage, he recommended that the neophyte in heterosociality seek out the company of some "veteran woman of condition" who, being flattered by a young man's attention, would "point out to him those manners and attentions that pleased and engaged them when they were in the pride of their youth and beauty." Women were conscious that at least in this one area of adult life they were the teachers. Men learned complaisance from women, Mary Astell said, and without that quality a man was unfit for society, though he might be brave, intelligent, and honest. "With us men show in a manner the reverse of what they are to one another," she wrote; "they let their thoughts play at liberty, and are very careful of the expression, that nothing harsh or obscene can escape 'em that may shock a tender mind or offend a modest ear."[149]

But independence and aggression rather than tenderness and attachment were the bases on which men built their identities as males

---

[147]The connection between childhood innocence and masturbation is made by R. P. Neuman, "Masturbation, Madness and the Modern Concepts of Childhood and Adolescence," *Journal of Social History*, VIII, 1974–1975, 1–27. But because he uses a Freudian model of sexual development, rather than arguing (as do Simon and Gagnon) that gender roles are formed in childhood but sexuality after puberty, he goes too far in saying that the new idea of childhood caused parents to disregard infant sexuality. He also ignores the connection between sublimation and achievement.

[148]Dobrée, ed., *Letters of Chesterfield*, V, 1931; N.U.L., NeC 3278.

[149]Oliver Goldsmith, "She Stoops to Conquer," in *Collected Works*, ed. by Arthur Freedman (Oxford: Clarendon Press, 1966), 5 vol., V, 129–130; Dobrée, ed., *Letters of Chesterfield*, IV, 1396, 1491; Astell, *Defense of the Female Sex* (1721 ed.), 123–127.

and through which they channeled their sexual behavior. The result was that while in women the strongest of sexual taboos was against intercourse outside of marriage, in men it was against homosexual behavior. In Christian morality, adultery and homosexual behavior were equally sinful for men and women. But in the law and by custom, a woman was disgraced and divorced for adultery, while a man was ostracized for effeminacy and hung for sodomy. European society in the eighteenth century was unique in the world in condemning all forms of homosexual behavior on the grounds that it was unnatural or nonprocreative and had called down supernatural fire on Sodom and Gomorrah. It was at one with the world in condemning homosexual behavior when it caused an adult man to lose his status. The world solved this problem by requiring that the passive role in male homosexual intercourse be taken either by an adolescent or a transvestite male. Europe simply classified all men who were not exclusively heterosexual as juvenile and effeminate. Homosexual behavior in women, by contrast, was likely to be viewed by men with an amused or excited tolerance, for such women had come up in the world and were acting aggressively, like men. But homosexual behavior for men could safely occur only in the protective environments of the homosexual subcultures of large cities like London or Paris, or in royal courts and aristocratic cliques.[150]

By the 1690s in England, however, public opinion was so little overawed by majesty that it would not tolerate even the rumor of homosexual behavior at court, as William III learned at some cost; and the Societies for the Reformation of Manners actively terrorized the London subculture. Aristocrats like Lord Hervey or Lord George Germain might successfully combine marriage and love affairs with men with only minor inconvenience as they moved in a discreet homosexual network; or they might choose to live abroad where a gentleman's position allowed a greater degree of freedom. Still they might be

---

[150]Randolph Trumbach, "London's Sodomites: Homosexual Behavior and Western Culture in the Eighteenth Century," *Journal of Social History*, **XI**, 1977, 1-33; A. N. Gilbert, "Buggery and the British Navy," ibid., **X**, 1976, 72-98; Louis Crompton, "Homosexuals and the Death Penalty in Colonial America," *Journal of of Homosexuality*, **I**, 1976, 277-293. See also Caroline Bingham, "Seventeenth-Century Attitudes toward Deviant Sex," *Journal of Interdisciplinary History*, **I**, 1971, 447-472. A most revealing case of female homosexual behavior: *The Annual Register*, **IX**, 1766, 116, 144. The parallel between sodomy and adultery was noted and the inequality of their punishment partially justified: "Q. Which is the greater sin, sodomy or adultery, and why are both not punished with death? A. Of these two very heinous sins the former is the worst, because a guilt of so unnatural a dye, agreeable to what we meet in *Rom* 1.27. But as sodomy is punished with death, so adultery is very worthy of the same punishment. But we must leave the political part of it to the wisdom of our lawgivers" (*The British Apollo*, 19-21 May 1708).

blackmailed, like Charles Fielding, before leaving England or vilified in the press after death, like Lord Cowper; or when discovered they might have their wives taken away, like Lord Bateman, and, like William Beckford, be permanently ostracized. But none of them, at least, ran the risk of the foot soldier and the footman in London or the sailor in his ship, who might be exposed in the pillory, whipped, or hung for sodomy. In other parts of Western society in the eighteenth century, in France, Italy and America, there was some public questioning of this taboo on the ground that it was similar to the belief in sorcery that had recently been exploded among the Euopean elites. But in England, though some hoary bits of sexual misinformation, like the belief in moles or false conceptions, might be compared to witchcraft by enlightened opinion, the taboo on homosexual behavior was not allowed to be publicly questioned. Blackstone justified the existing law by citing the story of Sodom. John Cleland's book was prosecuted for its homosexual scene. And Thomas Cannon had to flee abroad after all the copies of the little book in which he had compared ancient and modern pederasty were destroyed. English society stood firmly by its belief that any sexual act that might reduce a man to the level of a child or a woman ought to be extirpated. The internalization of this homosexual taboo, the formation of gender identity, and the development of heterosexual behavior all placed severe limits on the aristocratic man's interest in childrearing and his commitment to the egalitarian relations that were part of domesticity.

It is likely nonetheless that in the generations after 1750 aristocratic boys had quite different relations with their fathers than previously, and the difference may be seen in their later behavior. The possibility has already been raised that stronger attachment between mothers and sons may have been responsible for lessening the extent of aggression in adult men. Improved relations with their fathers probably had the same effect. And it is more certain that the presence of parental surrogates in the schools cut the level of adolescent violence. These surrogates and the new relationship between fathers and sons that they represented may also have increased aristocratic concern for the life of the mind, since it seems that children show more such concern when educated in a domestic setting than in an institutional one.[151] It is certain that as young men at the university after 1780, these boys showed an unexpected independence and seriousness in their studies.[152] And if it is true that Charles Townshend had a difficult and

[151]Hansburg, *Separation Anxiety*, 98.
[152]Sheldon Rothblatt, "The Student Sub-Culture and the Examination System in Early 19th Century Oxbridge," in Stone, ed., *The University in Society* (Princeton: Princeton Univ. Press, 1974), 2 vol., I, 247–305.

distant father and in emulation of that parental role conceived his disastrous policy toward the American colonies,[153] then it is not too much to say that it was in emulation of a different role that the men of Lord Althorp's generation piloted through Parliament an act that satisfied the clamors of the middle classes even as it left most real power in aristocratic hands. Personal gentleness, intellectuality, and an effective paternalist politics were bred in the domesticated households of the aristocracy in the generation after 1750.

[153]This is the theme of Sir Lewis Namier and John Brooke, *Charles Townshend* (London: Macmillan, 1964).

Conclusion

The principal change that the aristocratic family experienced in the three generations between 1690 and 1780 was the increasing importance of domesticity. By another name—the nuclear family—it has often been put forward as one of the contributing factors in industrialization, but this is a conceptualization that has confused the emotional climate of the household with its size. Clearly, English aristocrats were able to hold and practice the ideal of domesticity even though they lived in households of 50 people and sent their sons away to schools of 500. They saw their little families threatened by the great household and the great school, and they sometimes tried to decrease the size of the latter, but their houses could hardly operate with fewer servants. Nonetheless, mothers were able to make their presences strongly felt in nurseries staffed by many servants, and fathers did the same, if less successfully, in the great schools. But if domesticity does not require suburban seclusion to flourish, it is difficult to say in what way aristocratic domesticity can have contributed to industrialization.

It is slightly easier to suggest that domesticity contributed to political stability, by contrasting its progress among the English and continental nobilities. It can help provide, perhaps, a new answer to that old question, Why did England have no revolution? For it seems likely that romantic marriage and the close association of parents with their children had made little headway in France or Italy. Patrilocal residence, arranged marriage, and cicisbeatura—these were what an Englishman saw when he looked at the continental nobility after 1750, and he was either surprised or shocked. For he lived in a society where the possibility of social mobility (its actuality is another question) and the increasing equality of men and women made impossible the patriarchal dominance that was enshrined in the family patterns of the continental nobilities. It is therefore possible that the English nobility could more easily deal with the political demands of equality because they had internalized egalitarian patterns of behavior in their families.

The easy acceptance of enlightened ideas in England and their frequent cohabitation with religion may also be partly explained by aristocratic family patterns. For English aristocrat women, who were the usual channels of religious influence, seem in many instances to have been more open to innovation than were their husbands. The changes in family patterns perhaps made them freer of traditional authority; egalitarianism may have encouraged them to see the life of reason as less of a male preserve than it was so often claimed to be; and they had been long accustomed to rely on their feelings. They could combine religion, sentiment, nature, and empiricism all in one fine blend with the result that in ideas as in politics there was no revolution in England, only a gradual displacement of the old by the new.

Family patterns may have helped the English aristocracy to deal more efficiently with change than did their peers on the Continent, but those patterns set them apart from other social groups within English society. At the end of the seventeenth century, most Englishmen within their households were probably committed to patriarchal ideals of authority, but they diverged significantly in the organization of their kinsmen. The nobility preferred patrilineage, whose common-law rules had their origins in medieval aristocratic practice. The laborer or the yeoman turned to his kindred whose rules survived in the canon-law courts and were probably a reflection of the egalitarian practice of the medieval peasant community. The behavior of a clergyman like Ralph Josselin is revealing. He divided his property equally among his sons and his daughters. He avoided his mother-in-law. His strongest kinship ties were to his own siblings and to his wife's. And he treated his servants as part of his household. Here is the combination of kindred and patriarchy one expects. As far as Josselin moved in an aristocratic direction, he also acted as expected. He knew more about his father's than his mother's family, and outside the circle of his siblings and siblings-in-law, his closest ties were to his paternal uncles.[1] Josselin died in 1683. A century later, in a somewhat lower social class (the small tradesmen of London) the family of Francis Place provides for the 1770s the same pattern of limited ties to kindred and patriarchal authority. Place met only one of his grandfathers, knew none of his aunts or uncles, and said that in his father's "opinion coercion was the only way to eradicate faults, and by its terror to prevent their recurrence."[2] Kindred ties and patriarchal households for the poor, patrilineage and patriarchy for the mighty—that was the traditional pattern. And when the pattern changed, it was the aristocracy who led the way. For it is likely (as Samuel Richardson's shocked disapproval of aristocratic children shows) that it was the aristocracy who first came to deal moderately with their children and wives, and that as part of this moderation they also came to favor the ties of kindred over those of patrilineage. This we can best show by summarizing generation by generation the pattern that the preceding chapters have traced.

In the generation between 1690 and 1720, there occurred the first signs of the decline of patriarchy and the appearance of domesticity. The great households stopped giving to their neighborhoods the broken meats from their tables, and they became less the microcosms of the social structure when the lesser gentry ceased to serve as their officers. Family prayers, which were the most regular means of supervising the moral conduct of servants, began to disappear from many households, and some masters felt free to overstep patriarchal barriers by seducing their servants. But servants still put on mourning at deaths in their masters' families, and they usually remained unmarried. Household management was seen by many as the province of a man's wife, although most servants were still male, but an aristocrat's patriarchal powers were reaffirmed in two important ways. For the first time he was able to divorce a wife whose adultery threatened the integrity of his patrilineage, and he was able to secure money damages from her lover for poaching on his patriarchal preserve. But within the very decade of these innovations, some aristocratic men and women produced a literature which accepted class patriarchy—the subordination

---

[1] Alan Macfarlane, *The Family Life of Ralph Josselin* (Cambridge: University Press, 1970), 105–160; cf. G. C. Homans, *English Villagers of the Thirteenth Century* (Cambridge, Mass.: Harvard Univ. Press, 1941), 109–222.

[2] Mary Thale, ed., *The Autobiography of Francis Place (1771–1854)* (Cambridge: University Press, 1971), 17–33, 34, 39, 59, 61–62.

of the peasant to the gentleman—but questioned the subordination of women to men. It was not a position that won much favor in its generation; but together with the granting of divorces (which at first seems to act against it), there begins to be a case that marriage was becoming less of a transaction of property whether in wealth or in women, since divorce seems to be most prevalent in those societies where marriage least involves the exchange of property. But most marriages were still arranged. It was eccentric to expect to marry for love. And it proved impossible to pass an act that would have given parents control over the marriages of their minor children since most younger sons were still prepared to contemplate the stealing of an heiress as the means of making their fortunes. On the other hand, the professional matchmaker was outlawed: Marriages were to be made by friends and not for a commission. The younger children that a marriage produced were better provided for. Younger sons were sometimes given annuities and sometimes portions, which were probably worth more. Daughters were also given portions (or inheritances) rather than dowries negotiated at their marriage; they were, therefore, less likely to be used as pawns in the making of alliances; and the courts tended to squash clauses that made their portions dependent on their marrying with parental consent. These provisions for younger children (which sometimes had to be inserted into settlements originally made before 1690) have to be placed in a wider context. For the family settlement did more than provide for younger children against the interests of their eldest brother; the settlement also provided for a man's wife and children at the expense of the males of his patrilineage who, by the rules of intestate inheritance, had a decided interest in his estate.

The emotional results of these inroads on patriarchy and patrilineage by freer marriage and a more nearly equal division of inheritance can be seen in the experiments in childrearing that began to appear. The 1690s saw the publication of the first pediatric treatises. They also saw two innovations in the care of children's health. Cold bathing was introduced as a means of curing rickets. And those fathers who were dissatisfied with the use of wet nurses (but who could not bring themselves to have their wives nurse) encouraged the practice of rearing children entirely on artifical foods. With older children, concern for their physical and mental health took the form of sending them to small French schools instead of to the great public schools, since at the former their health was better guarded and their moral innocence left uncorrupted. It can be seen that in the very first generation of the century there had appeared, at least in embryro, all those changes that were to come to their full time in the next two generations.

Conclusion

The generation between 1720 and 1750 can sometimes seem the hardest of all to bring into focus. All the changes except for one are less dramatic than those found in the other two generations. The exception, of course, is inoculation, and it was perhaps the most daring innovation in all three generations. Parents undertook to make their children deliberately ill as the best means of saving their lives. It was accepted partly because of the prestige that scientific experiment held for this generation, and partly because there were physicians who were becoming systematic in their observation of childhood behavior. But the final explanation of its acceptance must rest with the state of mind of aristocratic parents. This was the first generation in which romantic marriage became truly prestigious, and people who made such marriages began to take for granted that a husband and a wife took most pleasure, first of all, in each other's company and then in the care of their children. This new evaluation of marriage can be seen in a number of other ways. Younger sons stopped using marriages to make their fortunes for several reasons. There were fewer of them to provide for since their parents had limited the size of their families. They were now given portions rather than annuities. And some younger sons benefited from the systematic exploitation of the resources of the state. Within marriage, women were allowed to inherit property independently of their husbands, and widows had their property protected from a second husband. It was proposed that a man should be allowed to divorce his wife not only because she had committed adultery, threatened his patrilineage, and disregarded his patriarchal rights, but because she did not provide him with the domesticity he desired. It is perhaps no coincidence that it was this generation that saw the full-scale attacks on London's homosexual subculture, for it was the first that could be very much threatened by the male identification with women or children that homosexual behavior represented. Sexual patriarchy was no doubt still solidly entrenched, but domestic patriarchy was dying. Chaplains disappeared from great households and with them family prayers; it was asserted that servants were first of all the children of their parents and only then dependents in a master's family.

But the dramatic results of the changes in this middle generation came at the very beginning of the next. The Marriage Act was passed in 1753 because even younger sons now agreed that one married for love and not for money, and by 1784 it was estimated that three marriages in four were romantic rather than arranged. The dramatic fall in the death rate of infants began around 1750, and most mothers were nursing by 1780. But it is likely that these changes at mid-century had occurred neither because children were better nourished or because they were better protected from disease, but because aristocratic women in the generation before had become convinced that they should spend more time with their children and that the temper of that time should be more openly loving. In the generation after 1750 even fathers made their way into the nursery, and men entered the rooms of lying-in women. But fathers made their best response to the spirit of their generation by the educational innovations of the 1770s. They set about improving the boardinghouse system that had grown up at the public schools in the previous generation. They experimented with small private schools. And they provided their sons with surrogate fathers, trying to cut down the pain of separation while turning out independent men, but men less violent and more loving. In this atmosphere, aristocrats became disregardful of more distant kinsmen like cousins; and a mother told a daughter who had not yet had children that to relations other than her parents, her husband, and her siblings she owed no more than what she would give to anyone.

These are the changes generation by generation. Some things remained constant throughout. Eldest sons were always preferred to their other siblings, and land usually went to the male heir of a title rather than to daughters. In this way the identity and power of the patrilineage was maintained. First-cousin marriage and the prohibition against the deceased wife's sister were symbolic guarantees that aristocratic marriage was an act of incorporation rather than an alliance, thereby maintaining aristocratic power in the face of the other classes of society. In this way the aristocrat was given another set of ties on which to draw, namely the solidarity of his siblings and his siblings-in-law. These things remained constant and secured the eighteenth-century aristocrat in his own day. Those things that changed also gave him the most innovative family structure of any group in his society. And this openness to innovation perhaps secured the dominance of his class in another age. For domesticity was the most valuable legacy that the eighteenth-century aristocrat gave to the Victorian lord.

APPENDIX **A**

Kinship Terminology

The two accompanying tables list the individual and collective terms for describing relations in the eighteenth century. They are based mainly on my own reading. Examples crop up in quotations throughout of the body of the text. But I have also tried to add system by consulting the *Oxford English Dictionary*. In the first table, listing terms for individuals, the basic distinctions are generation, consanguinity versus affinity, and sex. The least important of these is sex since all terms except husband and wife are the same whether the speaker (Ego) is male or female. Children and parents were very frequently distinguished by sex. Aunts and uncles and nieces and nephews could not be referred to without indication of sex since there were no sexually neutral terms for such individuals, and there was no collective word at all. Cousins were usually distinguished by generation and not by sex: Sexual differentiation became possible only when older cousins were called aunt or uncle. Aunts and uncles were, on the other hand, seldom differentiated by generation. Relations made by Ego's marriage were usually given the status of relatives by blood, though they could be distinguished as in-laws. Relations made by the marriage of aunts and uncles were similarly treated, though it was far rarer to refer to an uncle-in-law than to a mother-in-law. Relations made by the second marriage of one's parent, on the other hand, were almost always differentiated from consanguineal relations, usually by the *in-law* suffix, and less frequently by the *step* prefix, which Samuel Johnson claimed was commonly used only for stepmothers. Stepsiblings were the relations most likely to be given consanguineal status. The spouses of one's children were usually given consanguineal status, and the *O.E.D.* notes an instance of a man calling the mother of his daughter's husband "sister."

Family and *friend*, with or without their various modifiers, were the most common collective terms. A family might mean either the members of a household, a group of parents and children, or the descendants of a common ancestor. The meanings of friend and their importance are dealt with in Chapter 1. *Kinsman/woman* and *kindred* were common early in the century but had become unfashionable by mid- century.

It is worth noting, finally, that certain equivalencies common in the sixteenth and seventeenth centuries (*O.E.D.*) disappeared in the eighteenth: *cousin* used for 'uncle' or 'niece'; *brother* for 'uncle,' 'nephew,' or 'cousin'; and *nephew* or *niece* for 'grandchild.'

Table A.1
Individual Kinship Terms in the Eighteenth Century

	Consanguineal	Affinal
III	great-grand father/mother/parent(s)/ uncle/aunt	
II	grand father/mother/parent(s) grand/great uncle/aunt cousin/uncle/aunt (= grandparent's first cousin)	
I	father | parent(s)/best friend mother	(parent's spouse) mother-in-law/stepmother/mother father-in-law/stepfather/father
		(spouse's parents) father/father-in-law mother/mother-in-law
	uncle (Fa/Mo Bro) aunt (Fa/Mo Si)	uncle/uncle-in-law aunt/aunt-in-law

cousin/cousin once removed/second cousin/uncle/aunt/Welsh uncle (= parent's first cousin)

Ego		husband/best friend wife/best friend
	brother sister	brother/brother-in-law (WiBro, SiHus) sister/sister-in-law (WiSi, BroWi)
	brother/half-brother sister/half-sister (= one parent in common)	(children of parent's spouse) brother-in-law/step-brother/brother sister-in-law/step-sister/sister

cousin/first cousin/cousin german/brother (= child of aunt/uncle)
cousin/second cousin (= child of cousin once removed)

I	son | child/children daughter	(children's spouses) son/son-in-law daughter/daughter-in-law children/children-in-law
		(spouse's children) son-in-law/stepson/son daughter-in-law/stepdaughter/daughter
	nephew (Bro/SiSo) niece (Bro/SiDa)	
II	grand son/daughter/child/children grand/great nephew/niece	
III	great-grand son/daughter/child/children/nephew/niece	

295

Table A.2
Collective or General Kinship Terms

---

kinsman / kinswoman | kinsmen   kindred

family

friend(s)
friends and relations
friends and relatives
friends and connections

connection(s)

relation(s)
relative(s)

APPENDIX **B**

Sources for the History of Settlement

I have reconstructed from wills, settlements, Private Acts, and legal proceedings fairly complete histories of settlement for 30 families. I have assembled substantial but fragmentary information for an additional 7 families, and I also have 20 individual settlements for as many families. My conclusions are based on total of 265 deeds, wills, and settlements. The families and my sources of information are shown in Table B.1.

Table B.1
Histories of Settlement and Sources of Information for 57 Aristocratic Families

Familes	Sources[1]
1. Earls Cowper	Hertfordshire R.O.
2. Earls of Essex	Ibid.
3. Lords Monson	Lincolnshire Archives Office
4. Dukes of Ancaster	Ibid.
5. Earls of Cardigan	Ibid., copies.
6. Earls of Derby	Lancashire R.O.
7. (two familes)	
8. Lords Middleton	Nottingham University Library
9. Lords Arundell of Trerice	Ibid.
10. Dukes of Newcastle	Ibid.
11. Earls of Lincoln	Ibid.
12. Dukes of Portland	Ibid., and Nottinghamshire R.O.
13. Lords Willoughby de Broke	Shakespeare's Birthplace Trust
14. Lords Leigh	Ibid.
15. Earls of Warwick	Warwickshire R.O.
16. Marquesses of Hertford	Ibid.

(continued)

[1] See List of Abbreviations (p: xvii).

Table B.1 (continued)

Families	Sources[1]
17. Dukes of Norfolk	Sheffield Central Library
18. Marquesses of Rockingham	Ibid.
19. Dukes of Devonshire	Chatsworth
20. Lords Petre	Essex R.O.
21. Earls Gower	Staffordshire R.O.
22. Earls of Leicester	Kent R.O.
23. Lords Teynham	Ibid.
24. Dukes of Dorset	Ibid.
25. Earls of Hardwicke	British Library
26. Earls of Rockingham	Kent R.O.; South Carlton; Lincs. R.O.
27. Dukes of Beaufort	Private Acts; Staffordshire R.O.; H.M.C., House of Lords MSS
28. Earls of Strafford	Private Acts
29. Lords Montfort	Private Acts
30. Lords Chedworth	Private Acts
31. Lords Bernard	H.M.C., House of Lords MSS; Private Acts; Staffordshire and Essex R.O.
32. Earls of Stamford	Private Acts
33. Lords St. John of Bletsoe	Bedfordshire R.O. calendar
34. Earls of Abingdon	Private Acts
35. Earls of Leicester	Ibid.
36. Lord Byron	Ibid.
37. Dukes of Chandos	Ibid. and Shakespeare's Birthplace Trust
38. Lords Arundell of Wardour	Ibid.
39. Lord Boston	Lincs. R.O.
40. Duke of Rutland	Private Act
41. Earl of Exeter	Ibid.
42. Lord Hyde	MSS.
43. Earl of Westmoreland	MSS.
44. Lords Trevor	Private Act
45. Duke of Grafton	Ibid.
46. Duke of Manchester	Ibid.
47. Earl of Winchelsea	Ibid.
48. Earl of Portsmouth	Ibid.
49. Duke of Leeds	Ibid.
50. Earl Fitzwilliam	Sheffield Central Library
51. Earl of Harrington	Private Act
52. Earl Powis	Ibid.
53. Dukes of St. Albans	Ibid.
54. Earl Ashburnham	Ibid.
55. Viscount Torrington	Ibid.
56. Earl of Carlisle	Staffordshire R.O.
57. Earl of Aylesford	Ibid.

Bibliography

Abbot, George, *The Case of Impotency*, 2 vol. London, 1715.
Ahern, E. M., "The Power and Pollution of Chinese Women," in Margery Wolf and Roxane Witke, eds., *Women in Chinese Society*. Stanford: Stanford Univ. Press, 1975.
Aldridge, A. O., "The Meaning of Incest from Hutcheson to Gibbon," *Ethics*, **LXI**, 1951, 309–313.
Allestree, Richard, *Works*. Oxford, 1727.
Alleyne, John, *The Legal Degrees of Marriage*. London, 1775.
Ambler, Charles, *Reports of Cases . . . in Chancery*. London, 1829.
Annual Register. London, 1759–.
Argyll, Duke of, *Intimate Society Letters of the Eighteenth Century*. 2 vol. London: Stanley Paul, 1910.
Ariès, Philippe, *Centuries of Childhood*. Translated by Robert Baldick. New York: Vintage Books, 1965.
Arkell, R. L., *Caroline of Ansbach*. London: Oxford Univ. Press, 1939.
Armstrong, George, *An Essay on the Diseases Most Fatal to Infants*. 1779 ed. London.
Ashton, John, *Social Life in the Reign of Queen Anne*. London: Chatto & Windus, 1893.
Aspinall-Oglander, Cecil, *Admiral's Widow*. London: Hogarth Press, 1942.

Aspinall-Oglander, Cecil, *Admiral's Wife*. London: Longmans, 1940.
[Astell, Mary], *An Essay in Defence of the Female Sex*. London, 1697, 1721.
Astell, Mary, *Reflections upon Marriage*. London, 1706.
Astruc, Jean, *Elements of Midwifery*. London, 1766.
Astruc, John, *Treatise on All Diseases Incident to Children*. London, 1746.
Atkyns, J. T., *Reports of Cases ... in ... Chancery in the Time of Lord Chancellor Hardwicke*, 3 vol. London, 1794.
Austen, Jane, *Mansfield Park*. 1816. Edited by R. W. Chapman. London: Oxford Univ. Press, 1966.
Austen, Jane, *Sanditon*, in *Minor Works*. Edited by R. W. Chapman. London: Oxford Univ. Press, 1969.
Austen-Leigh, R. A., *The Eton College Register 1753-1790*. Eton: Spottiswoode, 1921.
Austen-Leigh, R. A., *The Eton College Register 1698-1752*. Eton: Spottiswoode, 1927.
Baker, C. H. C., and Baker, M. I., *The Life ... of James Brydges, First Duke of Chandos*. Oxford: Clarendon Press, 1949.
Bamford, T. W., "Public Schools and Social Class 1801-1850," *British Journal of Sociology*, **XII**, 1961, 224-235.
Baron and Femme. London, 1719.
Beaver, M. W., "Population, Infant Mortality, and Milk," *Population Studies*, **XXVII**, 1973, 243-254.
Befu, Harumi, "Patrilineal Descent and Personal Kindred in Japan," *American Anthropologist*, **LXV**, 1963, 1328-1341.
Behrman, C. F., "The Annual Blister," *Victorian Studies*, **XI**, 1968, 483-502.
Benedict, Ruth, *The Chrysanthemum and the Sword*. New York: Houghton Mifflin, 1946.
Bentham, Jeremy, *Works*, 11 vol. edited by John Bowring. Edinburgh: W. Tait, 1843, Reprint 1962.
Berkner, L. K., "The Stem Family and the Developmental Cycle of the Peasant Household: An Eighteenth-Century Austrian Example," *American Historical Review*, **LXXVII**, 1972, 398-418.
Bertie, Peregrine, *A Memoir of Peregrine Bertie*. London, 1838.
Bessborough, Earl of, *Georgiana*. London: John Murray, 1955.
Bessborough, Earl of, and Arthur Aspinall, *Lady Bessborough and Her Family Circle*. London: John Murray, 1940.
Biddulph, Violet, *The Three Ladies Waldegrave*. London: Peter Davies, 1938.
Bingham, Caroline, "Seventeenth-Century Attitudes toward Deviant Sex," *Journal of Interdisciplinary History*, **I**, 1971, 447-472.
Blackstone, William, *Commentaries on the Laws of England*, 4 vol. Oxford, 1768.
Bloch, Ivan, *Sexual Life in England Past and Present*. London: Francis Aldor, 1938.
Blondel, J. A., *The Force of the Mother's Imagination over the Foetus*. London, 1729.
Blount, Charles, *The Miscellaneous Works*. London, 1695.
Boissevain, Jeremy, "Patronage in Sicily," *Man*, **I**, 1966, 18-33.
Bolingbroke, Lord, *Works*. 4 vol. London, 1844.
Bond, D. F., ed., *The Spectator*, 5 vol. Oxford: Clarendon Press, 1965.
Bond, R. P., "Mr. Bickerstaff and Mr. Wortley," in Charles Henderson, ed., *Classical, Medieval and Renaissance Studies*, 2 vol. Rome: Edizioni di Storia e Letteratura, 1966.
Bossy, John, "The Counter-Reformation and the People of Catholic Europe," *Past and Present*, No. 47, 1970, 51-70.
Bossy, John, "Four Catholic Congregations in Rural Northumberland, 1750-1850," *Recusant History*, **IX**, 1967, 88-119.

Bibliography

Bossy, John, "More Northumbrian Congregations," *Recusant History*, X, 1969, 11-34.
Boswell, James, *Life of Johnson*, 2 vol. London: Dent, 1963.
Bowlby, John, *Attachment and Loss*, 2 vol. London: Hogarth Press, 1969-1973.
Bowlby, John, *Maternal Care and Mental Health*. New York: Schocken, 1966.
Boyer, Abel, *The English Theophrastus*. London, 1702.
Boyer, Paul, and Nissenbaum, Stephen, *Salem Possessed*. Cambridge, Mass.: Harvard Univ. Press, 1974.
Bracken, Henry, *The Midwife's Companion*. London, 1737.
Brauer, G. C., *The Education of a Gentleman*. New York: Bookman, 1959.
The British Apollo. London, 1708-1711.
The British Journal. London, 1722-1731.
Brooke, Henry, *The Fool of Quality*. London, 1765-1766.
Brooke, John, *The Chatham Administration*. London: Macmillan, 1956.
Brown, B. C., ed., *The Letters of Queen Anne*. London: Cassell, 1935.
Brownlow, John, *Memoranda or Chronicles of the Foundling Hospital*. London, 1847.
Brunton, Mary, *Self Control*. London, 1811.
Brydges, Sir Egerton, ed., *Collins's Peerage*. London, 1812.
Buchan, William, *Domestic Medicine*. London, 1772.
Bullough, D. A., "Early Medieval Social Groupings: The Terminology of Kinship," *Past and Present*, No. 45, 1969. 3-18.
Burke, Peter, *Venice and Amsterdam*. London: Temple Smith, 1974.
Burnet, Gilbert, *History of His Own Time*, 6 vol. Oxford, 1833.
Burton, John, *An Essay towards a Complete New System of Midwifery*. London, 1751.
Cadogan, William, *An Essay upon Nursing*. London, 1750.
Campbell, Lord, John, *Lives of the Lord Chancellors*, 7 vol. Philadelphia: Univ. of Pennsylvania Press, 1851.
Carleton, J. D., *Westminster School*. London: Rupert Hart-Davis, 1965.
Carlisle, Countess Dowager of, *Thoughts in the Forms of Maxims to Young Ladies on Their First Establishment in the World*. London, 1789.
Cartwright, J. J. ed., *The Wentworth Papers*. London: Wyman, 1883.
The Case of His Grace Peregrine Duke of Ancaster. London, n.d.
The Cases of Impotency ... Catherine ... and Edward Weld ... Published by John Crawford. London, 1732.
Cash, A. H., "The Birth of Tristram Shandy: Sterne and Dr. Burton," in R. F. Brissenden, ed., *Studies in the Eighteenth Century*, Toronto: Univ. of Toronto Press, 1968.
Castamore, *Conjugium Languens*. London, 1700.
Chandos, Cassandra, Duchess of, *The Continuation of the History of the Willoughby Family*, Edited by A. C. Wood. Eton: Shakespeare Head Press, 1958.
Chapman, R. W., ed., *Jane Austen's Letters*. London: Oxford Univ. Press, 1964.
Chesterfield, Lord, *The World*. London, 1755.
Childe-Pemberton, W. S., *The Earl Bishop*, 2 vol. London: Hurst & Blackett, 1924.
Christie, Ian R., *The End of North's Ministry 1780-1782*. London: Macmillan, 1958.
Clarendon, Earl of, *A Collection of Several Tracts*. London, 1727.
Clarke, John, *An Essay upon the Education of Youth in Grammar Schools*. Dublin, 1736.
Clay, Christopher, "Marriage, Inheritance and the Rise of Large Estates in England, 1660-1815," *Economic History Review*, XXI, 1969, 503-518.
Cleland, John, *Memoirs of a Coxcomb*. London, 1751. Reprint 1926.
Cokayne, G. E., *The Complete Peerage*, 12 vol. London, 1910-1959.
Cole, F. J., *Early Theories of Sexual Generation*. London: Oxford Univ. Press, 1930.
The Common Errors in the Education of Children. London, 1744.

Congreve, William, *The Way of the World*, in *Complete Plays*. Edited by Herbert Davis. Chicago: Univ. of Chicago Press, 1967.
Considerations upon the Bill for Preventing Clandestine Marriages. London, 1753.
Cooper, W. D., ed., *Savile Correspondence*. Camden Society, 1858.
Cork and Orrery, Lady, ed., *The Orrery Papers*, 2 vol. London: Duckworth, 1903.
Cowper, William, *Works*. Edited by R. Southey, 8 vol. London, 1854.
Cox, S. C., *Reports of Cases ... in ... Chancery ... Collected by William Peere Williams*, 3 vol. London, 1826.
The Crime of Onan, 2 vol. London, 1724.
Croke, Alexander, *A Report of the Case of Horner against Liddiard ... with an Introductory Essay upon the ... Laws relating to Illegitimate Children...*. London, 1800.
Crompton, Louis, "Homosexuals and the Death Penalty in Colonial America," *Journal of Homosexuality*, I, 1976, 277–293.
Culpeper, Nicholas, *A Directory for Midwives*. London, 1681.
Cumming, Elaine, and Schneider, D. M., "Sibling Solidarity: A Property of American Kinship," *American Anthropologist*, LXIII, 1961, 498–507.
Cunnington, Phillis, and Buck, Anne, *Children's Costume in England*. New York: Barnes & Noble, 1965.
[Darrell, William], *The Gentleman Instructed*. London, 1716, 1727.
Darton, J. Harvey, *Children's Books in England*. Cambridge: University Press, 1958.
Darwin, G. H., "Marriages between First Cousins in England and their Effects," *Journal of the Statistical Society*, XXXVIII, pt. 2, 1875, 153–179.
Davies, G., ed. *Memoirs of the Family of Guise*. Camden Society, 1917.
Davis, D. B., *The Problem of Slavery in Western Culture*. Ithaca: Cornel Univ. Press, 1966.
Davis, J. C., *The Decline of the Venetian Nobility as a Ruling Class*. Baltimore: Johns Hopkins Univ. Press, 1962.
Davis, J. C., *A Venetian Family and Its Fortune 1500–1900*. Philadelphia: American Philosophical Society, 1975.
Davis, N. Z., "The Reasons of Misrule: Youth Groups and Charivaris in Sixteenth-Century France," *Past and Present*, No. 50, 1971, 41–75.
Day, R. A., *Told in Letters*. Ann Arbor; Univ. of Michigan Press, 1966.
Defoe, Daniel, *The Compleat English Gentleman*. Edited by K. D. Bülbring. London: David Nutt, 1890.
Defoe, Daniel, *Conjugal Lewdness*. London, 1727.
Defoe, Daniel, *The Great Law of Subordination Considered*. London, 1724.
deMause, Lloyd, ed., *The History of Childhood*. New York: The Psychohistory Press, 1974.
Denich, B. S., "Sex and Power in the Balkans," in M. Z. Rosaldo and Louise Lamphere, eds., *Woman, Culture and Society*. Stanford: Stanford Univ. Press, 1974.
Depauw, Jacques, "Illicit Sexual Activity and Society in Eighteenth Century Nantes," in Robert Forster and Orest Ranum, eds., *Family and Society*. Baltimore: Johns Hopkins Univ. Press, 1976.
Derry, Warren, *Dr. Parr*. Oxford: Clarendon Press, 1966.
Dewes, Simon, *Mrs. Delany*. London: Rich & Cowan, n.d. G. E. Cokayne, ed., *The Complete Peerage*, 12 vol. London, 1910–1959.
Dickinson, H. T., ed., *The Correspondence of Sir James Clavering*. Surtees Society, 1967.
Dionis, Pierre, *A General Treatise of Midwifery*. London, 1719.
Dobrée, Bonamy, ed., *Letters of Chesterfield*, 6 vol. London: Eyre & Spottiswoode, 1932.
Drummond, J. C., and Wilbraham, Anne, *The Englishman's Food*. London: Jonathan Cape, 1939.

Duby, Georges, "Lineage, Nobility and Chivalry in the Region of the Mâcon during the Twelfth Century," in Robert Forster and Orest Ranum, eds., *Family and Society*. Baltimore: Johns Hopkins Univ. Press, 1976.
Dugard, Samuel, *The Marriages of Cousin Germans Vindicated*. Oxford, 1673.
Dugard, Samuel, περιπολυπαιδιας : *Or a Discourse Concerning the Having Many Children*. London: 1695.
The Duke of Norfolk's Case for Passing His Bill. London, 1699.
R. H. Eden, ed., *Reports of Cases in . . . Chancery from 1757 to 1766*, 2 vol. London, 1827.
Embree, J. F., *Suye Mura*. Chicago: Univ. of Chicago Press, 1939.
The English Reports. London, n.d.
Erikson, E. H., *Childhood and Society*. New York: Norton, 1963.
Evelyn, John, *Memoires for My Grand-son*. Edited by G. Keynes. London: Nonesuch, 1926.
Exton, Brudenell, *A New General System of Midwifery*. London, 1751.
The Family Companion for Health. London, 1729.
Farber, Bernard, *Comparative Kinship Systems*. New York: John Wiley, 1969.
Farber, Bernard, *Guardians of Virtue*. New York: Basic Books, 1972.
Farber, Bernard, *Kinship and Class*. New York: Basic Books, 1971.
Fielding, Henry, *Complete Works*, 16 vol. New York, 1967. Reprint.
Finch, Pearl, *History of Burley-on-the-Hill*, 2 vol. London: Bale & Danielsson, 1901.
Finley, M. I., *The Ancient Economy*. London: Chatto & Windus, 1973.
Finley, M. I., *The World of Odysseus*. New York: Viking Press, 1965.
Fitzgerald, Brian, ed., *Correspondence of Emily, Duchess of Leinster*, 3 vol. Dublin: Irish Manuscripts Commission, 1949–1957.
Fitzgerald, Brian, *Emily Duchess of Leinster*. London: Staples Press, 1949.
Fleetwood, William, *The Relative Duties of Parents and Children*. London, 1705.
Fleetwood, William, *Works*. 3 vol. Oxford, 1854.
Fleming, Caleb, *The Oeconomy of the Sexes*. London, 1751.
Ford, John, *Two Discourses Concerning the Necessity and Dignity of the Institution of Marriage*. London, 1735.
Forshall, F. H., *Westminster School Past and Present*. London: Wyman, 1884.
Forster, Robert, *The House of Saulx-Tavanes*. Baltimore: Johns Hopkins Univ. Press, 1971.
Forster, Robert, *The Nobility of Toulouse in the Eighteenth Century*. Baltimore: Johns Hopkins Univ. Press, 1960.
Fox, J. R., "Kinship and Land Tenure on Tory Island," *Ulster Folklife*, **XII**, 1966, 1–17.
Fox, Robin, *Kinship and Marriage*. Harmondsworth: Penguin, 1967.
Foxcroft, H. C., ed., *A Supplement to Burnet's "History of My Own Time."* Oxford: Clarendon Press, 1902.
Fraser, Sir William, *The Sutherland Book*, 3 vol. Edinburgh, 1892. 100 copies.
Freedman, Maurice, ed., *Family and Kinship in Chinese Society*. Stanford: Stanford Univ. Press, 1970.
Freeman, J. D., "On the Concept of the Kindred," *Journal of the Royal Anthropological Institute*, **XCI**, 1961, 192–220.
Freeman, S. T., *Neighbors*. Chicago: Univ. of Chicago Press, 1970.
Freud, Sigmund, *Inhibitions, Symptoms and Anxiety*, 1926, in *Complete Works*, Vol. 20. Translated by J. Strachey. London: Hogarth Press, 1959.
Friedl, Ernestine, "Dowry, Inheritance and Land Tenure," in Jack Goody, ed., *Kinship*. Harmondsworth: Penguin, 1971.
Fry, John, *The Case of Marriages between Near Kindred*. London, 1756.
Fryer, Peter, *The Birth Controllers*. New York: Stein & Day, 1966.

Fryer, Peter, *Private Case–Public Scandal.* London, 1966.
The Further Depositions . . . in the Affair of the Duke and Duchess of Norfolk. London, 1692.
Gagnon, J. H., and Simon, W. S., *Sexual Conduct.* Chicago: Aldine Press, 1973.
Gally, Henry, *Some Considerations upon Clandestine Marriages.* London, 1750.
Gasking, Elizabeth B., *Investigations into Generation, 1651–1828.* Baltimore: Johns Hopkins Univ. Press, 1967.
A General Abridgement of Cases in Equity, 2 vol. 1793.
The Gentleman's Magazine. London, 1731 _____.
George, C. H., and George, K., *The Protestant Mind of the English Reformation, 1500–1640.* Princeton: Princeton Univ. Press, 1940.
Gibson, Edmund, *Codex Juris Eccleciastici Anglicani,* 2 vol. London, 1713.
Gilbert, A. N., "Buggery and the British Navy," *Journal of Social History,* X, 1976, 72–98.
Giles, William, *A Treatise on Marriage.* London, 1771.
Gilpin, William, *Memoirs,* Edited by W. Jackson. Cumberland and Westmoreland Antiquarian and Archaelogical Society, 1879.
Glass, Hannah, *The Servant's Directory.* 1760.
Godber, Joyce, *The Marchioness Grey of Wrest Park.* Bedfordshire Historical Records Society, 1968.
Goldsmith, Oliver, *Collected Works,* 5 vol. Edited by Arthur Freedman. Oxford: Clarendon Press, 1966.
Goldthwaite, R. A., *Private Wealth in Renaissance Florence.* Princeton: Princeton Univ. Press, 1968.
Goode, W. J., *The Family.* Englewood Cliffs, N.J.: Prentice-Hall, 1964.
Goodwin, Albert, ed., *The European Nobility in the Eighteenth Century.* New York: Harper & Row, 1967.
Goody, Jack, ed., *The Character of Kinship.* London: Cambridge Univ. Press, 1973.
Goody, Jack, ed., *Kinship.* Harmondsworth: Penguin, 1971.
Goody, Jack, Thirsk, Joan, and Thompson, E. P., eds., *Family and Inheritance.* London: Cambridge Univ. Press, 1976.
Gore, John, ed., *The Creevey Papers.* New York: Macmillan, 1963.
Granville, Lady, *Lord Granville Leveson Gower,* 2 vol. New York: Dutton, 1916.
Green, David, *Sarah Duchess of Marlborough.* London: Collins, 1967.
Gregory, John, *A Father's Legacy to His Daughters.* London, 1774.
Greig, James, ed., *The Diaries of a Duchess.* London: Hodder & Stoughton, 1927.
Grosskurth, Phyllis, *The Woeful Victorian.* New York: Holt, Rinehart and Winston, 1964.
Gunn, W. T. J., *The Harrow School Register 1571–1800.* London: Longman, 1934.
Gunnis, Robert, "Letters of the First Lord Ashburnham," in *Sussex Archaeological Collections.* London, 1949.
Gutman, H. G., *The Black Family in Slavery and Freedom, 1750–1925.* New York: Pantheon, 1976.
Habakkuk, H. J., "Daniel Finch, 2nd Earl of Nottingham: His House and Estate," in J. H. Plumb, ed., *Studies in Social History.* London: Longmans, Green, 1955.
Habakkuk, H. J., "Landowners and the Civil War," *Economic History Review,* XVII, 1965, 130–151.
Habakkuk, H. J., "Marriage Settlements in the Eighteenth Century," *Transactions of the Royal Historical Society,* XXXII, 1950, 15–30.
Halifax, Lord, *Complete Works.* Edited by J. P. Kenyon. Baltimore: Penguin, 1969.
Halsband, Robert, ed., *The Complete Letters of Lady Mary Wortley Montagu,* 3 vol. Oxford: Clarendon Press, 1965–1967.

Bibliography

Halsband, Robert, *The Life of Lady Mary Wortley Montagu*. New York: Oxford Univ. Press, 1960.

Halsband, Robert, "New Light on Mary Wortley Montagu's Contribution to Inoculation," *Journal of the History of Medicine*, VIII, 1953, 390–405.

Hamilton, Alexander, *A Treatise on Midwifery*. Edinburgh, 1781.

Hammel, E. A., *Alternative Social Structures and Ritual Relations in the Balkans*. Englewood Cliffs, N.J.: Prentice-Hall, 1968.

Hans, Nicholas, *New Trends in Education in the Eighteenth Century*. London: Routledge & Kegan Paul, 1951.

Hansburg, H. C., *Adolescent Separation Anxiety*. Springfield, Illinois: Charles C Thomas, 1972.

Hanway, Jonas, *Eight Letters to His Grace ———, Duke of ———, on the Custom of Vails-Giving in England*. London, 1760.

Hanway, Jonas, *Virtue in Humble Life*, 2 vol. London, 1771.

Harcourt, E. W. ed., *The Harcourt Papers*, 12 vol. Oxford, 1876–1905. Privately printed.

Harris, Brice, *Charles Sackville, Sixth Earl of Dorset*. Illinois Studies in Language and Literature, 1940.

Harris, F. R., *The Life of ... Earl of Sandwich*, 2 vol. London: John Murray, 1912.

Harris, Walter, *A Treatise on the Acute Diseases of Children*. Translated by John Martyn. London, 1724.

Haywood, Eliza, *A Present for a Servant Maid*. Dublin, 1744.

Heasel, Anthony, *The Servants Book of Knowledge*. London, 1773.

Hecht, J. Jean, *The Domestic Servant Class in Eighteenth Century England*. London: Routledge & Kegan Paul, 1956.

Helmholz, R. H., *Marriage Litigation in Medieval England*. London: Cambridge Univ. Press, 1974.

Herbert, Lord, ed., *Henry, Elizabeth and George (1734–80)*. London: JonathanCape, 1959.

Herbert, Lord, ed., *Pembroke Papers 1780–1794*. London: Jonathan Cape, 1950.

Herlihy, David, "Family Solidarity in Medieval Italian History," *Explorations in Economic History*, VII, 1969–1970, 173–184.

Hertford, Lady, and Pomfret, Lady, *Correspondence*, 3 vol. London, 1805.

Hervey, Lord, John, *Some Materials towards Memoirs of the Reign of King George II*, 3 vol. Edited by Romney Sedgwick. London: Eyre & Spottiswoode, 1931.

Hervey, S. H. A., *Biographical List of Boys ... Bury St. Edmunds from 1550 to 1900*. Bury St. Edmunds: Paul and Mathew, 1908.

Hervey, S. H. A., ed., *The Diary of John Hervey, First Earl of Bristol*. Wells: Suffolk Green Books No. 2, 1894.

Hervey, S. H. A., ed., *Letterbooks of John Hervey, First Earl of Bristol*, 3 vol. Wells: Suffolk Green Books No. 1, 1894.

Hewitt, Margaret, *Wives and Mothers in Victorian Industry*. London: Rockliff, 1958.

Hickey, William, *Memoirs*, 4 vol. Edited by Alfred Spencer. London: Hurst & Blackett, 1913.

Hill, Christopher, *Society and Puritanism in Pre-Revolutionary England*. London: Secker & Warburg, 1964.

Hill, Christopher, *The World Turned Upside Down*. New York: Viking Press, 1972.

[Hill, John], *On the Management and Education of Children ... by the Honourable Juliana-Susannah Seymour*. London, 1754.

Hilton, R. H., *The English Peasantry in the Later Middle Ages*. Oxford: Clarendon Press, 1975.

Hiscock, W. G., *John Evelyn and His Family Circle*. London: Routledge & Kegan Paul, 1955.
Historical Manuscripts Commission, *Dartmouth Manuscripts*. London.
Historical Manuscripts Commission, *Egmont Diary*. London.
Historical Manuscripts Commission, *House of Lords Manuscripts, 1678-1688, 1689-1690, 1690-1691, 1692-1693, 1695-1697, 1697-1699, 1699-1702, 1704-1706, 1712-1714*. London.
Historical Manuscripts Commission, *Portland Manuscripts*. London.
Hoben, Allan, *Land Tenure among the Amhara of Ethiopia*. Chicago: Univ. of Chicago Press, 1973.
Hollingsworth, T. H., *Historical Demography*. Ithaca, New York: Cornell Univ. Press, 1966.
Hollingsworth, T. H., "The Demography of the British Peerage," Supplement to *Population Studies*, XVIII, 1964.
Holmes, Geoffrey, ed., *Britain after the Glorious Revolution*. New York: St. Martin's Press, 1969.
Holmes, Geoffrey, *British Politics in the Age of Anne*. London: Macmillan, 1967.
Homans, G. C., *English Villagers of the Thirteenth Century*. Cambridge, Mass.: Harvard Univ. Press, 1941.
Home, J. A., ed., *The Letters and Journals of Lady Mary Coke*, 4 vol. Edinburgh: David Douglas, 1889-1896.
Horwitz, Henry, "Parties, Connections and Parliamentary Politics, 1689-1714: Review and Revision," *Journal of British Studies*, VI, 1966, 45-69.
Horwitz, Henry, *Revolution Politics*. Cambridge: University Press, 1968.
Howe, John, *The Obligation from Nature and Revelation to Family Religion and Worship*. London, 1726.
Hughes, D. O., "Domestic Ideals and Social Behavior: Evidence from Medieval Genoa," in C. E. Rosenberg, ed., *The Family in History*. Philadelphia: Univ. of Pennsylvania Press, 1975.
Hughes, D. O., "Urban Growth and Family Structure in Medieval Genoa," *Past and Present*, No. 66, 1975, 3-28.
Hughes, Edward, ed., *Letters of Spencer Cowper*. Surtees Society, 1956.
Hughes, H. S., *The Gentle Hertford*. New York: Macmillan, 1940.
Hunt, David, *Parents and Children in History*. New York: Basic Books, 1970.
Ilchester, Earl of, *Henry Fox*, 2 vol. London: John Murray, 1920.
Ilchester, Earl of, ed., *Lord Hervey and his Friends, 1726-38*. London: John Murray, 1950.
Ilchester, Lady, and Stavordale, Lord, *The Life and Letters of Lady Sarah Lennox 1745-1826*. London: John Murray, 1902.
Irwin, George, *Samuel Johnson: A Personality in Conflict*. Auckland: Auckland Univ. Press, 1971.
Jameson, Edwin M., *Gynecology and Obstetrics*. New York: P. B. Hoeber, 1936.
Johnstoun, James, *A Juridical Dissertation Concerning the Scripture Doctrine of Marriage Contracts and the Marriages of Cousin-Germans*. 1734.
Jones, E. L., and Woolf, S. J., eds., *Agrarian Change and Economic Development*. London: Methuen, 1969.
Keesing, R. M., "Kwaio Fosterage," *American Anthropologist*, LXXII, 1970, 755-775.
Kelch, R. A., *Newcastle*. Berkeley: Univ. of California Press, 1974.
Kent, F. W., *Household and Lineage in Renaissance Florence*. Princeton: Princeton Univ. Press, 1977.
Kenyon, J. P., *Robert Spencer, Earl of Sunderland, 1641-1702*. London: Longmans, 1958.
Ketton-Cremer, R. W., *Felbrigg*. London: Rupert Hart-Davis, 1962.

Knox, Vicesimus, *Liberal Education*, 1785 ed. London.
Knox, Vicesimus, *Personal Nobility*, 1793 ed. London.
Kobler, John, *The Reluctant Surgeon*. Garden City, New York: Doubleday, 1960.
Laborde, E. W., *Harrow School*. London: Winchester Publications, 1948.
LaMotte, Guillaume, *A General Treatise of Midwifery*. London, 1746.
Lancaster, Lorraine, "Kinship in Anglo-Saxon Society," *British Journal of Sociology*, IX, 1958, 359–377.
Laslett, Peter, *The World We Have Lost*. 2nd ed. New York: Scribner's 1965, 1971.
Laslett, Peter, and Wall, Richard, eds., *Household and Family in Past Time*. Cambridge: University Press, 1972.
The Laws Respecting Women. London, 1777.
Leach, Edmund, "Complementary Filiation and Bilateral Kinship," in Jack Goody, ed., *The Character of Kinship*. London: Cambridge Univ. Press, 1973.
Leach, E. R., *Rethinking Anthropology*. London: Athlone Press, 1971.
Leach, Thomas, *Modern Reports*. London, 1793.
Leman, Sir Tanfield, *Matrimony Analysed*. London, 1755.
Lennard, Reginald, ed., *Englishmen at Rest and Play*. Oxford: Clarendon Press, 1931.
Lepel, Mary. *Letters*. London, 1821.
A Letter from a Bystander. London, 1753.
Letters on Love, Marriage and Adultery. London, 1789.
Levine, D. N., *Wax and Gold*. Chicago: Univ. of Chicago Press, 1965.
Levy, Claude, and Henry, Louis, "Ducs et Pairs sous l'Ancien Regime: Characteristiques Demographiques d'un Caste," *Population*, XV, 1960.
Levy, Marion, et al., *Aspects of the Analysis of Family Structure*. Princeton: Princeton Univ. Press, 1965.
Lewis, H. S., "Neighbors, Friends and Kinsmen: Principles of Social Organization among the Cushitic-Speaking Peoples of Ethiopia," *Ethnology*, XIII, 1974, 145–157.
Lewis, W. S., et al., eds., *Horace Walpole's Correspondence*. New Haven: Yale Univ. Press. 1937–.
Lewis, W. S., ed., *Notes by Lady Louisa Stuart*. New York: Oxford Univ. Press, 1928.
The Life of the Reverend Humphrey Prideaux. London, 1748.
Litchfield, R. Burr, "Demographic Characteristics of Florentine Patrician Families," *Journal of Economic History*, XXIX, 1969, 191–205.
Llanover, Lady, ed., *Autobiography and Correspondence of Mary Granville, Mrs. Delany*, London, 3 vol. 1861; 3 vol. 1862.
Locke, John, *Educational Writing*. Edited by J. L. Axtell. Cambridge: University Press, 1968.
Locke, John, *Two Treatises of Government*. Edited by Peter Laslett. Cambridge: University Press, 1970.
Loftis, John, *Comedy and Society from Congreve to Fielding*. Stanford: Stanford Univ. Press, 1959.
The London Journal, 1719–1744.
Lorence, B. W., "Parents and Children in Eighteenth-Century Europe," *History of Childhood Quarterly*, II, 1974, 1–30.
Loveland, R. L., ed., *Shower's Cases in Parliament*. London: Stevens & Haynes, 1876.
Lynch, K. M., *A Congreve Gallery*. Cambridge, Mass.: Harvard Univ. Press, 1951.
McClelland, John, ed., *Letters of Lady Sarah Byng Osborn, 1721–1773*. Stanford: Stanford Univ. Press, 1930.
McCullough, W. H., "Japanese Marriage Institutions in the Heian Period," *Harvard Journal of East Asiatic Studies*, XXVII, 1967, 103–167.
MacFarlane, Alan, *The Family Life of Ralph Josselin*. Cambridge: University Press, 1970.

Macpherson, C. B., *The Political Theory of Possessive Individualism*. Oxford: Clarendon Press, 1962.
Manley, Mary de la Riviere, *Secret Memoirs... from the New Atalantis*. London, 1709.
Manners Sutton, H., ed., *The Lexington Papers*. London, 1851.
March, Earl of, *A Duke and His Friends*, 2 vol. London: Hutchinson, 1911.
Marchand, J., ed., *A Frenchman in England 1784*. Cambridge: University Press, 1933.
Marriage Promoted... by a Person of Quality. London, 1690.
Marshall, Dorothy, *The English Domestic Servant in History*. London: Historical Association, 1949.
Martinez-Alier, Verena, *Marriage, Class and Colour in Nineteenth-Century Cuba*. London: Cambridge Univ. Press, 1974.
Marvick, E. W., "The Character of Louis XIII: The Role of his Physician," *Journal of Interdisciplinary History*, IV, 1974, 347–374.
Mauriceau, Francis, *The Diseases of Women*. Translated by H. Chamberlain, 1672. London, 1755.
Maxwell Lyte, H. C., *A History of Eton College (1440–1898)*. London: Macmillan, 1899.
Mead, Margaret, and Newton, Niles, "Cultural Patterning of Perinatal Behaviour," in S. A. Richardson and A. F. Guttmacher, eds., *Childbearing: Its Social and Psychological Aspects*. Baltimore: Williams & Wilkins, 1967.
Meister, H., *Letters Written during a Residence in England*. London, 1799.
Melges, F. T., "Postpartum Psychiatric Syndromes," *Psychosomatic Medicine*, XXX, 1968, 95–108.
Memoirs of... the Rev. Dr. Trusler. Bath, 1806.
Miller, Genevieve, *The Adoption of Inoculation for Smallpox in England and France*. Philadelphia: Univ. of Pennsylvania Press, 1957.
Mingay, G. E., *English Landed Society in the Eighteenth Century*. London: Routledge & Kegan Paul, 1963.
Misson, Henri, *Memoirs and Observations in His Travels over England*. Translated by M. Ozell. London, 1719.
Mitchell, L. G., ed., *The Purefoy Letters, 1735–1753*. London: Sidgwick & Jackson, 1973.
Mitford, Nancy, ed., *The Ladies of Alderley*. London: Hamish Hamilton, 1967.
Moritz, C. P., *Journeys of a German in England in 1782*. Translated and edited by R. Nettel. London: Jonathan Cape, 1965.
Moss, William, *An Essay on the Management, Nursing and Diseases of Children*. London, 1794.
Muir, Percy, *English Children's Books 1660–1900*. London: B. T. Batsford, 1954.
Mullett, C. F., "George Grenville and Eton in the 1760's," *Huntington Library Quarterly*, V, 1941–1942, 374–381.
Mullett, C. F., ed., *The Letters of George Cheyne to the Countess of Huntingdon*. San Marino, California: Huntington Library Publications, 1940.
Mullin, G. W., *Flight and Rebellion*. London: Oxford Univ. Press, 1972.
Murdock, G. P., ed., *Social Structure in Southeast Asia*. Chicago: Quandrangle Books, 1960.
Nakane, Chie, *Japanese Society*. Berkeley: Univ. of California Press, 1970.
Nakane, Chie, *Kinship and Economic Organization in Rural Japan*. London: Athlone Press, 1967.
Namier, Sir Lewis, *The Structure of Politics at the Accession of George III*. London: Macmillan, 1961.
Namier, Sir Lewis, and Brooke, John, *Charles Townshend*. London: Macmillan, 1964.
Namier, Sir Lewis, and Brooke, John, *The House of Commons, 1754–1790*, 3 vol. London: Her Majesty's Stationery Office, 1964.

Neel, James V. et al., "The Incidence of Consanguineous Matings in Japan," *American Journal of Human Genetics*, **I**, 1949, 156–178.
Nelson, James, *An Essay on the Government of Children*. London, 1753, 1763.
Nelson, Robert, *Instructions for the Conduct of a Young Gentleman*. London, 1718.
Nelson, Robert, *The Practice of True Devotion*, London, 1791.
Neuman, R. P., "Masturbation, Madness and the Modern Concepts of Childhood and Adolescence," *Journal of Social History*, **VIII**, 1974–1975, 1–27.
Newman, Aubrey, *The Stanhopes of Chevening*. London: Macmillan, 1969.
Nichols, John, *Illustrations of the Literary History of the Eighteenth Century*, 8 vol. London, 1817–1858.
Norton, J. E., ed., *The Letters of Edward Gibbon*. 3 vol. London: Cassell, 1956.
Nulle, S. Y., *Thomas Pelham-Holles, Duke of Newcastle*. Philadelphia: Univ. of Pennsylvania Press, 1931.
The Nurse's Guide. London, 1729.
Ober, W. B., "Boswell's Gonorrhea," *Bulletin of the New York Academy of Medicine*, **XLV**, 1969, 587–636.
Old Wykehamists, *Winchester College 1393–1893*. London: Edward Arnold, 1893.
Onania or the Heinous Sin of Self-Pollution. London, 1723.
Oppenheimer, J. M., *New Aspects of John and William Hunter*. New York: H. Schuman, 1946.
Ould, Fielding, *A Treatise of Midwifery*. Dublin, 1742.
The Oxford English Dictionary.
Painter, Sidney, "The Family and the Feudal System in Twelfth Century England," *Speculum*, **XXXV**, 1960, 1–16.
Pares, Richard, and Taylor, A. J. P., eds., *Essays Presented to Sir Lewis Namier*. London: Macmillan, 1956.
Parliamentary Debates. London.
Parliamentary History. London.
Pechey, John, *A General Treatise of the Diseases of Infants and Children*. London. 1697.
Pechey, John, *A General Treatise of the Diseases of Maids, Bigbellied Women, Childbed Women, and Widows*. London, 1696.
Pehrson, R. N., "Bilateral Kin Groupings," in Jack Goody, ed., *Kinship*. Harmondsworth: Penguin, 1971.
Pehrson, R. N., "The Bilateral Network of Social Relations in Könkämä Lapp District," *International Journal of American Linguistics*, **XXIII**, pt. 2, 1957.
Pelzel, J. C., "Japanese Kinship: a Comparison," in M. Freedman, ed., *Family and Kinship in Chinese Society*. Stanford: Stanford Univ. Press, 1970.
Pennington, Lady Sarah, *Letters on Different Subjects*, 4 vol. London, 1767.
Penton, Stephen, *The Guardian's Instruction*. London, 1688.
Perkin, Harold, *The Origins of Modern English Society, 1780–1880*. London: Routledge & Kegan Paul, 1969.
Piozzi, H. L., *Observations and Reflections, 1789*. Edited by H. Barrows. Ann Arbor: Univ. of Michigan Press, 1967.
Plumb, J. H., "The New World of Children in Eighteenth Century England," *Past and Present*, No. 67, 1975, 64–95.
Plumb, J. H., ed., *Studies in Social History*. London: Longmans, Green, 1955.
Pottle, F. A., ed., *Boswell in Holland 1763–64*. London: McGraw-Hill, 1962.
A Present for Servants. London, 1787.
The Present State of Matrimony ... by Philogamous. London, 1739.
Price, Cecil, *Cold Caleb*. London: Andrew Melrose, 1956.
Pugh, Benjamin, *A Treatise of Midwifery*. London, 1754.

Quick, John, *A Serious Inquiry . . . Whether a Man May Lawfully Marry His Deceased Wife's Sister.* London, 1703.
Quinton, John, *Treatise of Warm Bath Water*, 2 vol. Oxford, 1733.
[Ramesey William], *The Gentleman's Companion*, London, 1672.
Rand, Benjamin, *Life . . . of Shaftesbury.* London: Swan Sonnenschein, 1900.
Rapp, Dean, "Social Mobility in the Eighteenth Century: The Whitbreads of Bedfordshire, 1720–1815," *Economic History Review*, XXVII, 1974, 380–394.
Ravenel, H. H., *Eliza Pinckney.* New York: Scribner's, 1896.
Razzell, P. E., "Population Change in Eighteenth-Century England: A Reappraisal," *Economic History Review*, XVIII, 1965, 312–332.
Reflections on Celibacy and Marriage. London, 1771.
Rich, G. W., "Changing Icelandic Kinship," *Ethnology*, XV, 1976, 1–19.
Richardson, Samuel, *Pamela.* New York: Norton.
Roberts, K., and Roberts, A. M., eds. and trans., *Moreau de St Méry's American Journey.* Garden City, New York: Doubleday, 1947.
Roberts, P., ed., *The Diary of Sir David Hamilton, 1709–1714.* Oxford: Clarendon Press, 1975.
[Robinson, Robert], *A Discourse Concerning the Laws of Inheritance in Fee.* London, 1736.
Rochester, Earl of, *Complete Poems.* Edited by D. M. Veith. New Haven: Yale Univ. Press, 1968.
Rosaldo, M. Z., and Lamphere, Louise, eds., *Woman, Culture and Society.* Stanford: Stanford Univ. Press, 1974.
Rosenberg, C. E., ed., *The Family in History.* Philadelphia: Univ. of Pennsylvania Press, 1975.
Rothblatt, Sheldon, "The Student Sub-Culture and the Examination System in Early 19th Century Oxbridge," in Lawrence Stone, ed., *The University in Society*, 2 vol. Princeton: Princeton Univ. Press, 1974.
Rouse, W. H. D., *A History of Rugby School.* London: Duckworth, 1898.
Rousseau, J. J., *Emile.* Translated by B. Foxley. London: Dent, 1914.
Russell, J. C., "Aspects Demographiques des Débuts de la Féodalité," *Annales: E.S.C.*, XX, 1965, 118–127.
Russell Barker, G. E., and Stenning, A. H., *The Record of Old Westminsters*, 2 vol. London: Westminster School, 1928.
Ryerson, Alice, "Medical Advice on Childrearing, 1550–1900," *Harvard Educational Review*, XXXI, 1961, 302–323.
Ryland, Frederick, ed., *Swift's Journal to Stella.* London: George Bell, 1897.
St. James Evening Post. London, 1715–1755.
Salmon, Thomas, *A Critical Essay Concerning Marriage.* London, 1724.
Sansom, G. B., *Japan: A Short Cultural History.* New York: Appleton-Century-Crofts, 1962.
Sargeaunt, John, *Annals of Westminster School.* London: Methuen, 1898.
Schlatter, R. B., *The Social Ideas of Religious Leaders 1660–1688.* London: Oxford Univ. Press, 1940.
Schochet, G. J., *Patriarchalism in Political Thought.* New York: Basic Books, 1975.
Schochet, G. J., "Patriarchalism, Politics and Mass Attitudes in Stuart England," *Historical Journal*, XII, 1969, 413–441.
Schücking, Levin L., *The Puritan Family.* London: Routledge & Kegan Paul, 1969.
Seaborne, Malcolm, *The English School.* Toronto: Univ. of Toronto Press, 1971.

Seaton, Thomas, *The Conduct of Servants in Great Families*. London, 1720.
Sedgwick, Romney, *The House of Commons 1715–1754*, 2 vol. New York: Oxford Univ. Press, 1970.
[Seymour, A. C. H.], *The Life and Times of Selina Countess of Huntingdon*, 2 vol. London, 1839.
Shaftesbury, Lord, *Inquiry Concerning Virtue*. London, 1699.
Shaw, W. A., *Calendar of Treasury Books*. XXI, pt. 1; XVII, pt.1.
Shebbeare, John, *The Marriage Act*, 2 vol. London, 1754.
Sherson, Errol, *The Lively Lady Townshend*. London: William Heinemann, 1926.
Shorter, Edward, "Illegitimacy, Sexual Revolution and Social Change in Modern Europe," *Journal of Interdisciplinary History*, II, 1971, 237–272.
Shorter, Edward, *The Making of the Modern Family*. New York: Basic Books, 1975.
Simpson, A. W. B., *An Introduction to the History of the Land Law*. London: Oxford Univ. Press, 1961.
Smellie, William, *A Treatise on the Theory and Practice of Midwifery*, 2 vol. London, 1764.
Smith, Hugh, *Letters to Married Women*. London, 1774.
Smith, R. J., "Stability in Japanese Kinship Terminology: The Historical Evidence," in R. J. Smith and R. K. Beardsley, eds., *Japanese Culture*. New York: Wenner–Gren Foundation, 1962.
Smith, R. J., and Beardsley, R. K., eds., *Japanese Culture*. New York: Wenner–Gren Foundation, 1962.
Smith, Thomas C., *The Agrarian Origins of Modern Japan*. Stanford: Stanford Univ. Press, 1959.
Smith, W. J., *The Grenville Papers*, 4 vol. London, 1852–1853.
Smith-Rosenberg, Carroll, "The Hysterical Woman: Sex Roles and Role Conflict in 19th Century America," *Social Research*, XXXIX, 1972, 652–678.
Smyth, Charles, *Simeon and Church Order*. Cambridge: University Press, 1940.
Solly, G. A., *Rugby School Registers: 1 April 1675–October 1857*. Rugby: George Over, 1933.
Spargo, John, *The Bitter Cry of the Children*. New York: Johnson, 1966.
Spring, David, "English Landownership in the Nineteenth Century: a Critical Note," *Economic History Review*, IX, 1957, 472–484.
Spring, Eileen, "The Settlement of Land in Nineteenth-Century England," *American Journal of Legal History*, VII, 1964, 209–223.
Spufford, Margaret, *Contrasting Communities*. London: Cambridge Univ. Press, 1974.
Stanhope, George, *A Sermon Concerning Temptations*. London, 1703.
Stebbing, Henry, *A Dissertation on the Power of States to Deny Civil Protection to the Marriages of Minors*. London, 1755.
Stebbing, Henry, *An Enquiry into the Force and Operation of the Annulling Clauses in a Late Act*. London, 1754.
Steele, Richard, *The Tatler*. London, 1709–1711.
Steele, Richard, *The Tender Husband*. London, 1778.
Stenton, D. M., *The English Woman in History*. London: Allen & Unwin, 1957.
Stephan, Dom John, "Notes on Household Management in the 18th Century," *Notes & Queries*, CCIV, 1959, 97–99, 144–147, 168–172.
Stephens, J. E., ed., *Aubrey on Education*. London: Routledge, 1972.
Stone, Lawrence, *The Crisis of the Aristocracy, 1558–1641*. Oxford: Clarendon Press, 1965.

Stone, Lawrence, *The Family, Sex and Marriage in England 1500–1800*. New York: Harper & Row, 1977.
Stone, Lawrence, "The Rise of the Nuclear Family in Early Modern England," in C. E. Rosenberg, ed., *The Family in History*. Philadelphia: Univ. of Pennsylvania Press, 1975.
Strickon, Arnold, "Class and Kinship in Argentina," *Ethnology*, I, 1962, 500–515.
Tanner, L. E., *Westminster School*. London: Country Life, 1934.
Tanner, Nancy, "Matrifocality," in M. Z. Rosaldo and Louise Lamphere, eds., *Woman, Culture and Society*. Stanford: Stanford Univ. Press, 1974.
Taylor, Jeremy, *Ductor Dubitantium*. London, 1660.
Thale, Mary, ed., *The Autobiography of Francis Place (1771–1854)*. Cambridge: University Press, 1971.
Theobald, John, *The Young Wife's Guide*, London, 1764.
[Thicknesse, Philip], *Man-midwifery Analysed*. London, 1764.
Thirsk, Joan, "Younger Sons in the Seventeenth Century," *History*, LIV, 1960, 358–377.
Thirsk, Joan, ed., *The Agrarian History of England and Wales, 1500–1640*. Cambridge: University Press, 1967.
Thomas, D. N., "Marriage Patterns in the British Peerage in the Eighteenth and Nineteenth Centuries," M. Phil. Thesis, University of London, 1969.
Thomas, Keith, "The Double Standard," *Journal of the History of Ideas*, XX, 1959, 195–216.
Thompson, E. P., "Patrician Society, Plebeian Culture," *Journal of Social History*, VII, 1974, 382–405.
Thompson, E. P., "'Rough Music': le Charivari Anglais," *Annales: E.S.C.*, XXVII, 1972, 285–312.
Thompson, Roger, *Women in Stuart England and America*. London: Routledge & Kegan Paul, 1974.
Thomson, G. S., ed., *Letters of a Grandmother 1732–1735*. London: Jonathan Cape, 1943.
Thomson, G. S., *The Russells in Bloomsbury 1669–1771*. London: Jonathan Cape, 1940.
Thornton, P. M., *Harrow School and Its Surroundings*. London: W. H. Allen, 1885.
Tiger, Lionel, and Fox, Robin, *The Imperial Animal*. New York: Holt, Rinehart and Winston, 1971.
Tillotson, John, *Works*, 3 vol. London, 1728.
The Times. London.
Tissot, S. A., *Three Essays . . . Third on Onanism*. Dublin, 1772.
A Treatise Concerning Adultery and Divorce. London, 1700.
The Trial Between . . . Norfolk, Plaintiff and John Jermaine, Defendant, in Action of Trepass . . . . . London, n.d.
Trials for Adultery, 7 vol. London, 1779–1780.
Trumbach, Randolph, "London's Sodomites: Homosexual Behavior and Western Culture in the Eighteenth Century," *Journal of Social History*, XI, 1977, 1–33.
Turner, Daniel, *The Force of the Mother's Imagination*. London, 1729.
Tyrer, Frank, and Bagley, J. J., eds., *The Great Diurnal of Nicholas Blundell*, 3 vol. Lancashire and Cheshire Record Society, 1968–1972.
Underwood, Michael, *A Treatise of the Disorders of Childhood*. London, 1797.
Utter, R. P., and Needham, G. B., *Pamela's Daughters*. New York: Macmillan, 1936.
Vanbrugh, Sir John, *The Provoked Wife*, 1697. Edited by C. A. Zimansky. Lincoln, Nebraska: Univ. of Nebraska Press, 1966.
Vanbrugh, Sir John, *The Relapse*, 1696. Edited by C. A. Zimansky. Lincoln, Nebraska: Univ. of Nebraska Press, 1970.

Vaughan, Edward, ed., *The Reports and Arguments of . . . Sir John Vaughan*. London, 1706.
Veith, Ilza, *Hysteria: The History of a Disease*. Chicago: Univ. of Chicago Press, 1965.
[Venette, N.], *The Pleasure of Conjugal Love Explained*. London, 1740.
Verney, Lady, ed., *Verney Letters of the Eighteenth Century*, 2 vol. London: Ernest Benn, 1930.
Wake, Joan, *The Brudenells of Deene*. London: Cassell, 1953.
Wake, Joan and Webster, D. C., eds., *The Letters of Daniel Eaton*. Northamptonshire Record Society, 1971.
Walcott, Robert, *English Politics in the Early Eighteenth Century*. Oxford: Clarendon Press, 1956.
[Walsh, William], *A Dialogue Concerning Women*. London, 1691.
Walzer, Michael, *The Revolution of the Saints*. Cambridge, Mass.: Harvard Univ. Press, 1965.
[Warrington, Lord, George,] *Considerations upon the Institution of Marriage*. London, 1739.
Warrington, Lord, Henry, *Works*. [Edited by J. Delaheuze]. London, 1694.
Weinberg, Ian, *The English Public Schools*. New York: Atherton, 1967.
Wenner, N. K., "Dependency Patterns in Pregnancy," in J. H. Masserman, ed., *Sexuality of Women*. New York: Grune & Stratton, 1966.
West, M. J., ed., *Reports of Cases . . . in Chancery*. London, 1827.
Wheatley, H. B., ed., *The Diary of Samuel Pepys*, 3 vol. London: George Bell, 1924.
White, Charles, *A Treatise on the Management of Pregnant and Lying-in Women*. London, 1772.
Whiting, J. M. W. and Child, I. L., *Child Training and Personality: A Cross-Cultural Approach*. New Haven: Yale Univ. Press, 1953.
The Widow's Catechism. London, 1709.
Wingfield-Stratford, Esme, *The Lords of Cobham Hall*. London: Cassell, 1959.
Wolf, E. R., "Kinship, Friendship and Patron–Client Relations in Complex Societies," in Michael Banton, ed., *The Social Anthropology of Complex Societies*, London: Tavistock, 1966.
Woods, Charles B., "Notes on Three of Fielding's Plays," *Publications of the Modern Language Association*, LII, 1937, 359–373.
Wrigley, E. A., "Family Limitation in Pre-Industrial England," *Economic History Review*, XIX, 1966, 82–109.
Wroe, Richard, *A Sermon at the Funeral of the . . . Earl of Warrington*. London, 1694.
Wyndham, Maud, *Chronicles of the Eighteenth Century*, 2 vol. London: Hodder & Stoughton, 1924.
Yale, D. E. C., ed., *Lord Nottingham's Chancery Cases*. 2 vol. Selden Society, 1951–1961.
Yalman, Nur, *Under the Bo Tree*. Berkeley: Univ. of California Press, 1971.
Yorke, P. C., *The Life of Hardwicke*, 3 vol. Cambridge: University Press, 1913.
Young, Arthur, *Travels in France*. Edited by Constantia Maxwell. Cambridge: University Press, 1950.

Index

A

Abergavenny, Lady, 156
Abergavenny, Lord, 156
Abortion, 171–172
Addison, Joseph, 132, 263
Alleyne, John, 27
Althorp, Lord, 84, 219, 242
Ancaster, first duke of, 52, 102
Ancaster, second duke of, 102
Ancaster, third duke of, 79, 85
Anne, Princess, 180
Argyll, duchess of, 98, 159
Ariès, Philippe, 5
Arnold, Thomas, 256, 264
Artificial foods for children, 205–207
Ashburnham, Lady, 40
Ashburnham, Lord, 136, 139, 146

Astell, Mary, 100, 152, 250
Aston, Catherine, 92
Aston, Lady, 92–93
Aston, Lord, 168
Astruc, Jean, 204
Athenry, Lord, 56
Austen, Jane, 96, 175–176
Aylesford, Lord, 243

B

Bagot, Lady Barbara, 183–184, 201
Bagot, Louisa, 183–184, 201
Barrington, Bishop Shute, 157
Bastards, 66, 161–163
Bateman, Lord, 284
Baxter, William, 146
Beauchamp, Lord, 195

315

Beauclerk, Lord Sidney, 93
Beauclerk, Topham, 158
Beaufort, dukes of, 80
Beaufort, fourth duke of, 167–168
Beckford, William, 284
Bedford, fourth duke of, 169
Bedford, third duke of, 77
Befu, Harumi, 8
Bellamont, Lady, 216
Bellfield, Lady, 31
Bellfield, Lord, 31
Benedict, Ruth, 15
Bentham, Jeremy, 269
Berkeley, Lord, 194
Berkner, L. K., 5
Bertie, Lord Albemarle, 162
Bertie, Peregrine, 94
Bertie family (dukes of Ancaster), 42, 58–61, 62
Bessborough, Caroline countess of, 189
Bessborough, Henrietta countess of, 218
Blackstone, William, 42
Blandford, Lady, 54
Blundell, Nicholas, 178
Bolingbroke, Diana viscountess, 158
Bolingbroke, first viscount, 22, 63, 160
Bolingbroke, second viscount, 157–158
Bolton, duke of, 58
Boscawen, Mrs., 25, 184–185, 195, 196, 222–223, 244–246, 249
Bossy, John, 121
Boswell, James, 124, 135, 175 n.29
Bowater, John, 109–111
Bowlby, John, 10
Boyer, Abel, 40
Breeching, 251–252
Bridgewater, Lord, 241
Bristol, Elizabeth countess of, 99–100, 133, 136, 137, 138–139, 173–175, 181, 246
Bristol, first earl of, 83, 91–93, 125, 133, 136, 173–175, 188, 225, 253, 267
Brook, Lord, 267
Brooke, Henry, 204
Brooke, Lady, 205
Brownlow, Jane, 81
Brudenell, James, 252
Buccleugh, duchess of, 169–170, 185
Buchan, William, 201–202, 216
Buckinghamshire, duke of, 205–206
Buckinghamshire, Lady, 243

Bunbury, Lady Sarah, see Lady Sarah Lennox
Bunbury, Louisa, 248–249
Burke, Edmund, 35
Burnet, Bishop Gilbert, 124, 141, 168
Bute, Lady, 171–172

C

Cadogan, William, 189–190, 207, 225, 226, 240
Cannon, Thomas, 284
Cardigan, Lord, 255
Carlisle, Lady, 151
Carteret, Lady, 169
Carteret, Lord, 56
Caudle, 185
Cavendish, Harriet, 163
Cavendish, Lord John, 220
Cavendish, Lord Richard, 261–262, 267
Chamberlain family, 180–181
Chamberlain, Hugh, 180
Chandos, duke of, 124, 135
Charles II, King, 168
Charlotte, Queen, 176
Chesterfield, Lord, 58, 64, 69, 94, 151, 152, 163, 237, 253, 262, 265, 267, 282
Cheyne, George, 232
Childbirth, 180–185
Children, see also Education; Infant mortality; Nursing mothers
  adult reactions to, 224–228
  discipline of, 243–250
  health in, 188–230, 259, 263, 266–267, 271–272, 274, 277
  mourning for parents, 35
  as property, 52–53, 160–163
  sexual innocence of, 22, 257, 259–262, 279–280
Churchill, Lady Henrietta, 126
Clare, fourth earl of, 47
Clare, Margaret Lady, 47
Clarendon, Lord, 170, 262
Class differences in family patterns, 16, 19, 21, 32, 288–289
Clavering, Ann, 244
Cleland, John, 284
Clermont, Lady, 171
Coke, Lady Mary, 40, 55, 106, 115, 185
Cold bathing, 191–192

Index

Collins, Mrs., 200–201
Connections
  in politics, 61–63
  in religion, 63–64
Connolly, Lady Louisa, 247
Contraception, 170–176
Cousin marriage, 19–21
Cowper, Dame Sarah, 23, 25, 30, 141, 175 n.29
Cowper, first earl, 134, 246
Cowper, Georgiana countess, 38, 241
Cowper, Henrietta countess, 233–234
Cowper, Lady Sarah, 128
Cowper, Mary countess, 39, 244
Cowper, second earl, 79, 233–234, 248, 267
Cowper, Spencer, 93–94, 109
Cowper, third earl, 284
Cowper, William, 260–261, 276
Cowslade, John, 256
Criminal conversation, 155–156
Crying, 224–225

D

Dalkeith, Lady, 169–170, 250
Darnley, Lord, 270–273
Dartmouth, first earl of, 43–44, 53, 80, 243
Dartmouth, second earl of, 63, 143, 253, 263, 275–280
Deceased wife's sister, 26–32
Deerhurst, Lord, 84
Defoe, Daniel, 139, 177–178
Delany, Mrs. Mary
  on childbearing, 184–185
  on childcare, 192, 241, 246, 248–249
  on cousin marriage, 21
  on inheritance, 96
  on kindred obligations, 65
  on marriage to a brother's widow, 30
  on mourning, 35–39
  on remarriage, 28, 51, 54, 57
  on romantic marriages, 105, 108
  on treatment of sisters, 128
de la Place family, 266
deMause, Lloyd, 9 n.5
Derby, Elizabeth countess of, 159–160
Derby, ninth earl of, 44, 96, 125, 135, 142
Derby, twelfth earl of, 159
Devonshire, dukes of, history of settlement, 89–91

Devonshire, first duke of, 163
Devonshire, fifth duke of, 144
Devonshire, Georgiann duchess of, 84–85, 144, 159, 169, 171, 218–222, 225, 267
Divorce, 155–160
Domesticity
  and childbearing, 165–166
  and childcare, 208-229
  and equality of women, 150–153
  facilitated by nuclear households, 127–128
  and larger society, 287–288
  and male avoidance of women, 243–252, 281–284
  and marriage of servants, 148–150
  and remarriage, 27–29, 56–57
  and romantic marriage, 75–76
  and schools, 265–281
  servants as threat to, 129–131
Double standard of sexual behavior
  for men, 283–284
  for women, 154–160
Dorchester, Lord, 75–76, 241–242
Dorset, sixth earl of, 137, 241
Dorset, third duke of, 160
Douglas, Lady Lucy, 152
Duby, Georges, 4
Dugard, Samuel, 19–20, 171
Duncannon, Lord, 111–112
Duncombe, Frances, 109–111
Dupplin, Lady, 193
Dysart, Lord, 105, 163

E

Eaton, Daniel, 133
Education
  aim of, 252–254, 275
  boarding house system in great schools, 268–273
  class heterogeneity in schools, 264–265
  health at school, 259, 263–264, 274, 277
  isolation, violence and rebellion, 257–259
  parental surrogates in private schools, 265–267, 273–280
  private versus public, 254–256
  religious instruction, 249–250, 262–263
  sexual behavior at school, 257, 260–262, 279–280

Egalitarianism, 3, 119–124, 150–153, 165–166, *see also* Domesticity; Patriarchy
Egerton, Lady Caroline, 29
Egerton, Lady Louisa, 28
Eland, Lord, 178
Elstrob, Mrs., 129
Erikson, Erik, 9–10
Erskine, Thomas, 158
Ethiopia, 14, 17, 33, 64–65, 117
Eton college, 254, 258–259, 261, 262–263, 264, 270–273, 278
European family
  changes in its history, 1–3
  class differences in, 16
  cousin marriage, 33
  historiography, 4–6
Euston, Lord, 30
Evelyn, John, 142, 177
Evelyn, Lady Jane, 98
Evelyn, Sir John, 43
Exeter, Lady, 55
Eyre, Justice, 161

F

Family law, *see also* Inheritance
  bastardy, 160–163
  common law courts versus spiritual courts, 18–19
  forbidden degrees of marriage, 18–33
  Marriage Act, 107–109
  rights of women, 54, 81–83
Family prayers, 141–145
Family settlements
  continuity of names and titles, 46–50
  and daughters, 97–113
  and eldest son, 77–81
  mediate between kindred and patrilineage, 66, 70–71
  and remarriage, 58–61
  and rights of women, 43–45, 81–83
  and romantic marriage, 71, 83–87, 97–113
  settlement process defined, 72–76
  and younger sons, 87–97
Farber, Bernard, 31
Favors, 113–114
Female role, *see* Women
Fermor, Lady Sophia, 83

Fertility, ideas of, 166–169
Fielding, Charles, 284
Fielding, Henry, 108, 156–157
Finch, Edward, 61
Finch, Heneage, 102–103
Finch, Henry, 77, 94
Finch, Lady Isabella, 51, 77, 162
Finley, J. H., 9
Fitzroy, Lady Georgiana, 111
Fitzwalter, Lady Caroline, 106
Fitzwalter, Lord, 181
Fitzwilliam, Lord, 114, 262–263
Fleetwood, Bishop William, 100, 129, 140, 146, 152, 245, 247
Fleming, Caleb, 168
Foley, Andrew, 21
Foley family, 62
Footmen, 138–139
Fordwicke, Lord, 259
Forster, Richard, 138
Fox, Henry, 242, 261
Fox, Lady Caroline, 169, 172, 195, 209–217, 247, 259, 261, 267
Fox, Robin, 8
Frazier, Sir Alexander, 180
French schools, 256, 266
Friendship and kinship, 61–67
Freud, Sigmund, 9

G

Gagnon, J. H., 10
Gainsborough, Lady, 161
Generational differences, 289–292
Germain, Lord George, 283
Genoa, class differences in kinship, 16
Gilpin, William, 276, 279–280
Glass, Rev. Samuel, 277–278
Godolphin, Lord, 54
Godolphin, Sidney, 126
Goldsmith, Oliver, 282
Goodenough, Samuel, 273–275
Gower, first earl, 27–28
Gower, first Lord, 102
Gower, Mary Lady, 25, 29, 40
Gower, second earl, 28, 47
Gower, Susanna countess, 252, 254
Grafton, third duke of, 111, 157–158, 242, 266
Grantham, Lady, 39, 185, 192, 252

Grantham, Lord, 127
Granville, Grace, 114
Grenville, George, 258–259
Grey, Lady, see Lady Royston
Grey, Lady Henrietta, 206, 252
Grey of Werke, Lord, 30
Guardianship of children, 52–54, 161
Guilford, first earl of, 53, 55
Guilford, Lady, see Anne countess of Rockingham

H

Halifax, Lord, 98–99, 131, 132, 134, 177, 239, 244, 281
Hamilton, duchess of, 40
Hamilton, Sir David, 181, 205
Hanway, Jonas, 147, 202
Harcourt, Lady, 38
Harcourt, Lord, 248
Hardwicke, Lady, 132
Hardwicke, Lord, 43, 58, 87, 95, 107, 108, 125, 195–196
Harley family, 62
Harris, Walter, 190, 193, 203
Harrow school, 260, 275, 277–279
Hawkins, Caesar, 176
Heasel, Anthony, 250
Herbert, Lord, 115, 127
Herlihy, David, 4
Hertford, Algernon Lord, 47, 114, 143, 205, 255–256
Hertford, Frances countess of, 93, 105–106, 137, 194–195
Hertford, Lord, 74, 95, 103 n.109
Hervey, Augustus, 131
Hervey, George, 266
Hervey, Henry, 92–93
Hervey, John Lord, 106, 194, 232, 261, 283
Hervey, Thomas, 92
Hervey, William, 92
Hill, Christopher, 5, 9
Hill, John, 52, 203
Hoben, Allan, 8
Holland, Caroline Lady, see Lady Caroline Fox
Hollingsworth, T. H., 7
Homosexual behavior, 260–261, 283–284
Hotham, Lady, 37
Hough, Bishop, 54, 99

Household size and composition, 124–129
Howe, Anne, 105
Hughes, Diane, 4
Hunt, David, 9 n.5
Hunter, William, 176–177, 183, 207, 216
Huntingdon, Selina countess of, 63–64, 182
Hysteria and childhood experience, 230–231, 233–234

I

The Illegal Lovers, 27
Infant mortality
  and attachment to mothers, 208–229
  attitudes toward, 188–191
  and disease, 191–197
  and feeding, 197–208
  incidence, 187–188
Inheritance
  by daughters and wives, 43–45
  by eldest sons, 77–80
  law of, 41–42
  by parents, 43
  tying land to titles, 46–50
  by younger sons, 87–91, 96–97

J

Japan, 15, 17, 32–33
Jersey, Lord, 80
Johnson, Samuel, 124, 135, 230
Jointures, 82
Josselin, Ralph, 288–289

K

Kaye, Lady, 54
Kaye, Sir Arthur, 43–44
Keate, Thomas, 259
Kent, duke of, 57, 194
Kent, F. W., 4
Kildare, Emily Lady, see Emily duchess of Leinster
Kindred
  comparisons with Ethiopia 14–15, with Japan, 15
  conflicts with patrilineage in remarriage, 50–61
  definition of, 13–14

Kindred *(continued)*
  exemplified in mourning, 33–41
  exemplified in prohibited degrees of marriage, 18–33
  family settlement mediates between kindred and patrilineage, 66, 70–71
  need of friends and patrons, 61–67
Kingston, Lord, *see* Lord Dorchester
Kinship, *see* Family settlements; Inheritance; Kindred; Marriage; Mourning; Patrilineage; Remarriage
Kinship ceremonies
  at birth, 184–185
  at death, 33–41
  at marriage, 113–117
Kinship terminology, 25, 64–66, 293–296
Knox, Vicesimus, 257

L

Lancaster, Lorraine, 4
Lansdowne, Lord, 99
Laslett, Peter, 5, 9
Leeds, Mary duchess of, 226
Leicester, earl of, 163
Leigh, second Lord, 96–97
Leinster, Emily duchess of, 35, 52, 195, 209–217, 246
Lennox family, 208–217
Lennox, Lady Sarah, 65, 78, 120, 157, 159–160, 162, 209–217, 220, 249 n. 37, 264
Lennox, Lord George, 128
Leveson Gower family, remarriages in, 27–29
Leviticus, 18, 23, 25–26, 177
Lewisham, Lady, 53
Lincoln, earls of, 49
Lincoln, Lady, 200–201, 251–252
Lincoln, Lord, 83
Lindsey, Lord, 57
Lisburne, Lord, 64
Locke, John, 43, 191–192, 224, 227–228, 245, 248, 250–251
Lovett, Mary, 227
Lucan, Lord, 84
Luxborough, Lady, 63
Lyttleton, Thomas, 266

M

Macclesfield, first earl of, 87, 156
Macclesfield, Lady, 156
Macpherson, C. B., 5, 9
Male role, *see also* Physicians
  avoidance of women, 243–252, 281–284
  in childbearing, 165–166, 180–183
  in childcare, 204–206, 237–242, 270–281
  and homosexuality, 283–284
  as patriarch, 119, 141, 150–163
  and violence, 235, 252, 257–259, 272, 284–285
Malpas, Lord, 84
Malton, Lord, *see* Rockingham, second marquess of
Manchester, duchess of, 130
Mandeville, Bernard, 231
Manley, Mrs., 100
Manners, Lady Frances, 157
Mansfield Park, 96
March, Lord, 261, 263
Markham, William, 261, 269–270
Marlborough family, 54
Marlborough, first duke of, 46, 57
Marlborough, Sarah duchess of, 25, 57, 101, 241
Marlborough, second duchess of, 39
Marlborough, third duke of, 72, 162
Marriage
  forbidden degrees, 18–33
  remarriage, 26–30, 50–61
  romantic marriage, 29, 83–87, 97–113
  of servants, 146–150
Marriage Act of 1753, 107–109
Marriage brocage, 100–102
Masturbation, 260–261
Mauriceau, François, 176, 179, 182
Mead, Richard, 233
Melancholia and childhood experience, 230–231, 234
Middlesex, Lord, 114
Middleton family, 45
Middleton, Lord, 142
Moles (false conceptions), 179–180
Molesworth, Lord, 31
Montagu, duke of, 35, 39

Index

Montagu, Lady Mary Wortley, 21, 75–76, 99, 171, 192, 193, 194, 196, 241
Mourning
  for aunts and uncles, 36–37
  changes in, 37–38
  for cousins, 37–38
  defined, 34
  as expression of personal feeling, 39–40
  for parents, 35–36
  and patriarchy, 38–39
  for royal family, 38–39
  for spouses, 34–35
Moss, Bishop, 109–111

N

Nakane, Chie, 8
Napier, Lady Sarah, see Lady Sarah Lennox
Nelson, James, 202–203, 207, 228
Newcastle, dukes of, 47–50
Newcastle, Henry Cavendish duke of, 47
Newcastle, second duke of, 282
Newcastle, Thomas Pelham duke of, 47–50, 62, 83
Newcome family, 266
Newport, Lady, 102
Norbury, Rev. John, 270–273
Norfolk, fifth duke of, 72
Norfolk, sixth duke of, 155
North, Francis Lord, see first earl of Guilford
North, Frederick Lord, 62
Northumberland, duchess of, 196
Northumberland, Elizabeth duchess of, 227, 264
Nottingham, Lady, 37
Nottingham, second earl of, 46, 62, 99, 125, 142, 145
Nursing mothers, 203–204, 207–208, 212, 215, 216, 218, 220–223

O

Onania, 170–171
Orford, Lord, 61, 162
Orrery, Lord, 77, 129, 240–241
Osborn, Lady Sarah, 171
Osborne family (dukes of Leeds), 103–105
Osborne, Lady Bridget, 103–105

Ossory, Lord, 157–158
Overeating, 231–232
Oxford, Lady, 47–49, 96

P

Paget, Lord, 137
Pamela or Virtue Rewarded, 148–150
Parr, Samuel, 275, 279–280
Patriarchy
  children as property, 52–53
  and control of marriage, 75–76, 107–109
  declines over servants, 38, 141–150
  definition of, 119–124
  maintained over wives and children, 150–163
  and male role in childcare, 237–242
  and mourning, 38–39
  rejection of dependence on women, 61, 243–252
  and remarriage, 52, 54
Patrilineage
  conflicts with kindred in remarriage, 50–61
  exemplified in inheritance, 41–50
  family settlement mediates between kindred and, 66, 70–71
  insufficient beyond family concerns, 61–67
  ownership of children, 53
Pelham, Frances, 200–201
Pelham, Henry, 50
Pelham, Lady Katherine, 200–201
Pembroke, Elizabeth countess of, 37–38, 158
Pembroke, Mary countess of, 98
Pembroke, tenth earl of, 127
Pennington, Lady Sarah, 197–198, 228
Percival, Lord, 127
Percy family, 47
Percy, Lord, 157
Petre, Lady, 125–126
Petre, Lord, 127
Physicians
  role in childbirth, 180–183
  role in childcare, 190–197, 202–207, 225–229
Pierrepoint, Lady Evelyn, 27–28
Pin money, 83

Pinckney, Mrs., 207–208, 247
Piozzi, Mrs. Hester, 132
Place, Francis, 289
Polworth, Lord, 128
Portland, Dorothy duchess of, 85, 220, 227, 243–244, 246–247, 251
Portland, Elizabeth duchess of, 194
Portland, Margaret duchess of, 108, 129, 143, 253, 268–270
Portland, second duke of, 129, 143, 268–270
Portland, third duke of, 62, 69, 79, 85, 147, 158, 268–270, 273–275
Pregnancy, 176–180
Private schools, 265–267
Pugh, Benjamin, 179

Q

Quick, John, 29

R

Radnor, Lord, 277–278
Ramesey, William, 65
Razzell, P. E., 196
Remarriage
  arranged for in settlements, 58–61
  conflict of kindred and patrilineage, 50–51
  incidence, 26, 51
  by men, 55–56
  to sisters-in-law, 26–32
  by women, 51–55
Richardson, Samuel, 148–150, 247, 289
Richmond, Sarah duchess of, 209
Richmond, second duke of, 106–107, 208–209
Richmond, third duke of, 53, 80, 247
Rickets, 191–192
Ridge, Thomas, 92
Rochefoucauld, François de la, 112–113, 126, 132
Rochester, John Wilmot Lord, 20, 177, 260
Rockford, Lord, 163
Rockingham, Anne countess of, 35, 55, 56, 63, 81, 183–184, 201
Rockingham, first earl of, 74
Rockingham, Mary marchioness of, 264–265

Rockingham, Mary marchioness of, 28, 37, 145, 262–263
Rockingham, second marquess of, 78, 261
Romantic marriage
  and divorce, 157–160
  and family settlement, 71, 83–87, 97–113
  and living arrangements, 127–128
  and marriage ceremonies, 113–117
  and remarriage, 29
Roos, Lord, 155
Rousseau, J. J., 214–215, 219, 226, 237
Royston, Lady, 36, 185
Rugby school, 258, 264, 280
Ruglen, Lord, 266
Ryerson, Alice, 223–224, 223n. 93

S

St. Albans, duchess of, 81
St. Albans, first duke of, 93
St. John, John, 266
St. John, Lady, 56, 63
St. John, Lord, 56, 70
St. John of Bletsoe, Lords, 84
Salmon, Thomas, 22
Savile, Henry, 177–178
Scarsdale, Lord, 163
Seaton, Thomas, 140
Second sons, 96–97
Servants
  and decline of patriarchy, 141–150
  management of, 132–141
  mourning by, 38
  numbers of, 124–126
Sexual behavior
  abstinence, 173–176
  in adolescence, 260–262
  adultery in women, 51–52, 154–160
  in adult males, 281–284
  contraception, 170–176
  forbidden partners, 18–33
  forbidden times, 177–178
  homosexuality, 260–261, 283–284
  of servants, 146–150
Sexual roles, see Male role; Women
Shaftesbury, fourth earl of, 255
Shaftesbury, third earl of, 77, 161, 204
Shebbeare, John, 107
Shorter, Edward, 5, 120
Sibling solidarity, 31–32, 61

Index

Sicily, 65
Simon, W. S., 10
Sloane, Sir Hans, 181
Smallpox inoculation, 193–197
Smellie, William, 179–180, 182, 226
Smithson, Sir Hugh, 105–106
Smithson, Lady Betty, see Northumberland, Elizabeth duchess of
Smyth, Charles, 142
Somerset, Lady Harriet, 249
Somerset, seventh duke of, see Hertford, Algernon Lord
Somerset, sixth duke of, 99, 124
The Spectator, 235
Spencer family, 84
Spencer, Georgiana countess, 65–66, 111–112, 144, 217–222
Spencer, John, 106
Spencer, John, see Althorp, Lord
Spencer, Lady Harriet, 111–112
Stafford, marquess of, see Gower, second earl
Stamford, Lady, see Grey, Lady Henrietta
Stanhope, Lady, 137, 143
Stanhope, Lord, 46
Stebbing, Henry, 107–108
Stone, Lawrence, 5–6, 120–122
Strafford, Lady, 243
Strafford, Lord, 194
Sumner, Robert, 277
Sunderland, Lady, 255
Sunderland, Lord, 57, 132
Sutherland, Lord, 263
Sutton family, 195
Swaddling, 226
Swift, Jonathan, 40

T

Tankerville, first earl of, 99, 101
Tankerville, second earl of, 138–139
Tavistock, Lady, 169
Taylor, Jeremy, 19, 177
Temple, Lord, 130–131
Teynham, Lord, 30
Thanet, Lady, 47
Thicknesse, Philip, 182–183
Thomas, D. N., 7
Thomas, Keith, 154
Thurlow, Lord, 254
Tillotson, Archbishop John, 203–204

Titchfield, Lord, see Portland, third duke of
Toilet training, 227–228
Torrington, Arthur earl of, 49
Torrington, fourth viscount, 79
Townshend, Charles, 91, 102, 284
Townshend, Lady, 261
Townshend, second viscount, 194
Townshend, third viscount, 91, 150
Tufton, Lady Bell, 105
Twysden, Lady, 196

U

Underwood, Michael, 202, 228

V

Vanbrugh, Sir John, 93, 101
Vane, Lady Anne, 157
Vane, Lord, 49
Vaughan, Sir John, 19–20, 26
Verney, John, 85–86
Villiers, Lord, 267

W

Waldegrave, second earl, 194
Walpole, Horace, 31, 35, 40, 47, 52, 91, 106, 114, 142, 145, 159, 167–168, 169, 189, 217
Walpole, Sir Robert, 114, 205–206
Warrington, first earl of, 61, 99, 125, 134, 144–145, 239, 244
Warrington, second earl of, 157
Weaning, 227
Wentworth, Lady, 128
Wentworth, Lady Harriet, 131
Westminster school, 195, 254, 257–258, 260–261, 263, 264–265, 268–270, 275, 278
Wet nurses, 197–204
Weymouth, Lord, 62
Wharton, Lord, 101
Wharton, Mary, 102
Whipping, 245–246
Williams, Rev. William, 103–105
Wightwich, John, 86
Willoughby de Broke, George Lord, 80
Willoughby de Broke, John Lord, 109–111

Willoughby de Broke, Louisa Lady, 184
Willoughby de Broke, Richard Lord, 85–87
Wilkes, John, 130
Winchester school, 258, 270
Winchilsea, Lord, 77
Women, *see also* Nursing mothers
  as equals of men, 150–153
  household managers, 132–134
  preference for male children, 243–244
  pregnancy as disease or natural process, 176–185
  property rights of women, 43–45, 54, 81–83, 97–113
  as sexual property, 51–52, 155–160
Wortley, Edward, 75–76
Wynne, Dame Grace, 60

Y

Yorke, Charles, 95
Yorke family, 77, 95
Yorke, Joseph, 95
Younger sons, 87–97, 102

STUDIES IN SOCIAL DISCONTINUITY

Under the Consulting Editorship of:

CHARLES TILLY
University of Michigan

EDWARD SHORTER
University of Toronto

William A. Christian, Jr. Person and God in a Spanish Valley

Joel Samaha. Law and Order in Historical Perspective: The Case of Elizabethan Essex

John W. Cole and Eric R. Wolf. The Hidden Frontier: Ecology and Ethnicity in an Alpine Valley

Immanuel Wallerstein. The Modern World-System: Capitalist Agriculture and the Origins of the European World-Economy in the Sixteenth Century

John R. Gillis. Youth and History: Tradition and Change in European Age Relations 1770 – Present

D. E. H. Russell. Rebellion, Revolution, and Armed Force: A Comparative Study of Fifteen Countries with Special Emphasis on Cuba and South Africa

Kristian Hvidt. Flight to America: The Social Background of 300,000 Danish Emigrants

James Lang. Conquest and Commerce: Spain and England in the Americas

Stanley H. Brandes. Migration, Kinship, and Community: Tradition and Transition in a Spanish Village

Daniel Chirot. Social Change in a Peripheral Society: The Creation of a Balkan Colony

Jane Schneider and Peter Schneider. Culture and Political Economy in Western Sicily

Michael Schwartz. Radical Protest and Social Structure: The Southern Farmers' Alliance and Cotton Tenancy, 1880-1890

Ronald Demos Lee (Ed.). Population Patterns in the Past

David Levine. Family Formations in an Age of Nascent Capitalism

Dirk Hoerder. Crowd Action in Revolutionary Massachusetts, 1765-1780

Charles P. Cell. Revolution at Work: Mobilization Campaigns in China

Frederic L. Pryor. The Origins of the Economy: A Comparative Study of Distribution in Primitive and Peasant Economies

Harry W. Pearson. The Livelihood of Man by Karl Polanyi

Richard Maxwell Brown and Don E. Fehrenbacher (Eds.). Tradition, Conflict, and Modernization: Perspectives on the American Revolution

Juan G. Espinosa and Andrew S. Zimbalist. Economic Democracy: Workers' Participation in Chilean Industry 1970-1973

Arthur L. Stinchcombe. Theoretical Methods in Social History

Randolph Trumbach. The Rise of the Egalitarian Family: Aristocratic Kinship and Domestic Relations in Eighteenth-Century England

In preparation

H. A. Gemery and J. S. Hogendorn (Eds.). The Uncommon Market: Essays in the Economic History of the Atlantic Slave Trade

Tamara K. Hareven (Ed.). Transitions: The Family and the Life Course in Historical Perspective